A Concise Lexicon of Late Biblical Hebrew

Supplements
to
Vetus Testamentum

VOLUME 160

The titles published in this series are listed at *brill.com/vts*

A Concise Lexicon of
Late Biblical Hebrew

*Linguistic Innovations in the Writings of the
Second Temple Period*

By

Avi Hurvitz

In collaboration with

Leeor Gottlieb, Aaron Hornkohl and Emmanuel Mastéy

BRILL

LEIDEN | BOSTON

Library of Congress Cataloging-in-Publication Data

Hurvitz, Avi.
   A concise lexicon of late biblical Hebrew : linguistic innovations in the writings of the Second Temple period / by Avi Hurvitz ; in collaboration with Leeor Gottlieb, Aaron Hornkohl and Emmanuel Mastey.
      pages cm. — (Supplements to Vetus Testamentum, ISSN 0083-5889 ; v. 160)
   Includes bibliographical references.
   ISBN 978-90-04-26611-7 (hardback : alk. paper) — ISBN 978-90-04-26643-8 (e-book : alk. paper) 1. Hebrew language—Grammar, Comparative. 2. Hebrew language, Post-Biblical—Grammar, Comparative. 3. Hebrew language, Talmudic—Grammar, Comparative. 4. Aramaic language—Grammar, Comparative. 5. Bible. Old Testament—Language, style. 6. Rabbinical literature—History and criticism. I. Title.
   PJ4564.H87 2014
   492.4'7—dc23

                                                                                    2014005274

This publication has been typeset in the multilingual 'Brill' typeface. With over 5,100 characters covering Latin, IPA, Greek, and Cyrillic, this typeface is especially suitable for use in the humanities. For more information, please see brill.com/brill-typeface.

ISSN 0083-5889
ISBN 978 90 04 26611 7 (hardback)
ISBN 978 90 04 26643 8 (e-book)

This book is printed on acid-free paper.

PRINTED BY DRUKKERIJ WILCO B.V. - AMERSFOORT, THE NETHERLANDS

This volume is dedicated with gratitude to Mark and Becky Lanier and the Lanier Theological Library for their long and faithful support in the production of this dictionary.

Contents

Bibliography: Works Cited in the *Lexicon*   244

Preface

Although numerous dictionaries of Biblical Hebrew (BH) are available to us, no attempt has yet been made to publish a lexicon devoted specifically to Late Biblical Hebrew (LBH), i.e., to that linguistic stratum of Hebrew that begins to appear on the Biblical scene no earlier than the Second Temple period (fifth century BCE), after the fall of the Judaean monarchy. LBH thus constitutes a link between the Bible and post-Biblical Talmudic literature; hence, it has immense importance for the whole spectrum of Jewish literature at this period of time. The significance of the *Lexicon* for Jewish studies is prominent in five disciplines: Hebrew linguistics, Biblical philology, Qumran studies, Talmudic literature, and Rabbinic liturgy—all of which rely heavily on the lexical analysis of terminology and phraseology.

The proposal for this project was approved in 2003 by the Israel Science Foundation, which is administered by the Israel Academy of Sciences and Humanities. I am indebted to the Academy for its generous support in realizing this project. The actual composition of the *Lexicon* and all the concomitant administrative work was conducted at the Hebrew University of Jerusalem, to which I also express my sincere gratitude. In subsequent years, the project received encouragement and financial support from Dr. Albert D. Friedberg of Toronto, to whom I owe much thanks for his generosity. I am also grateful to Mr. W. Mark Lanier of Houston, Texas, who showed great interest in promoting the work on the *Lexicon* and whose financial assistance enabled us to complete the manuscript. It was also Mr. Lanier's initiative to include our *Lexicon* in a monograph series to be published by Brill. Moreover, I would like to extend my abundant gratitude to Dr. Weston Fields, a dear friend and colleague, for his indispensable support and perseverance in the final years of our project.

This volume is the result of the joint efforts of my dedicated research team. Each member made an invaluable contribution to the project according to his specific field of expertise: Dr. Leeor Gottlieb, who participated in the project from its inception, amassed much of the Biblical, Qumranic, and Rabbinic textual material and meticulously organized the initial basic outline of the work; Dr. Aaron Hornkohl masterfully treated the extra-Biblical non-Rabbinic material (the Documents from the Judaean Desert, epigraphical inscriptions, Imperial Aramaic papyri, and more) and was also in charge of compiling the modern scholarly literature; Mr. Emmanuel Mastéy, erudite in Rabbinic literature, was responsible for the Rabbinic quotations as well as for arranging the Biblical and Rabbinic references for publication. All the members of the team made significant contributions to the "Comments" section, which concludes the analysis and evaluation of the linguistic sources and the relevant scholarly literature. The final manuscript of the *Lexicon* was skillfully edited by Ḥani Davis, who enhanced the formulation of the text, double-checked the scholarly literature and much of the source material, and organized it graphically for publication.

Last, but not least, I extend my heartfelt gratitude to my wife Gila, who stood by my side for the duration of this project. Her encouragement, sage advice, and endless patience have allowed me to complete this work.

I thank all involved for their painstaking efforts in producing this important volume.

Avi Hurvitz
Jerusalem, August 2013

Prolegomenon

I   Introductory Remarks

1   *Continuity and Change in Biblical Hebrew (= BH)*

The history of the Hebrew language is commonly divided into the Biblical, Mishnaic (or Rabbinic), Medieval, and Modern periods. BH may thus be described as a self-contained entity having its own distinct linguistic profile. Yet, despite its seemingly uniform façade, beneath the surface BH exhibits a remarkable diversity of styles and plurality of linguistic traditions extending over some one thousand years. Furthermore, we are often confronted with tangible diachronic developments that may serve as chronological milestones in tracing the linguistic history of BH. The commonly used division in this connection distinguishes between three historical periods (see below, §II.2. Strata in BH): Archaic, Classical (or Standard), and Late (or post-Classical). Most significant are the differences observable between Classical BH (= CBH [SBH]), which reflects pre-Exilic times, and Late BH (= LBH), which displays numerous post-Classical neologisms unattested in the earlier sources. Our lexicon, concerned with the third of these linguistic layers, sets out to compile a selected repertoire of LBH elements that encompass primarily lexical innovations coined in post-Exilic times.

2   *BH in the Second Temple Period*

The fifth century BCE was a critical turning point in the history of the Hebrew language; texts written from this point on reveal unique linguistic features that are entirely absent in the earlier sources. Many of these innovations are first attested in texts dating to the Persian period and are widely ascribed to the influence of contemporary Imperial Aramaic (= IA). Thus, for instance, אִגֶּרֶת *letter*, a term prevalent in the Aramaic correspondence of the Persian imperial administration, is confined in BH (10×) to the distinctively late compositions of Esther, Nehemiah, and Chronicles (in CBH, סֵפֶר functions as the standard term for *letter* [alongside its common meaning of *book, literary composition*]; see Hurvitz 2000a: 150–151). Talmudic literature also sheds light on the post-Classical repertoire of LBH. Thus, for example, the characteristic Rabbinic term מִדְרָשׁ is rooted specifically in Chronicles (the noun מִדְרָשׁ, documented in Chronicles [2×], is completely absent in Classical Biblical literature; the verb דָּרַשׁ in CBH means *seeking out* God and not searching in the [written] Law and commandments of God). It is clear, therefore, that מִדְרָשׁ, denoting the study and interpretation of a text, is a product of the Late Biblical period and should be classified

© KONINKLIJKE BRILL NV, LEIDEN, 2014 | DOI 10.1163/9789004266438_002 linguistically as a late lexical term (see Hurvitz 1972: 131–134; 1995a). מִדְרָשׁ and אִגֶּרֶת are, therefore, two linguistic elements that belong to the vocabulary of Second Temple period Hebrew.

3   *The State of the Research and Methodological Principles*

Distinguishing between First and Second Temple BH was undoubtedly one of the greatest achievements of nineteenth-century Biblical philological scholarship (Bergsträsser, S. R. Driver, Ewald, Gesenius, König, Nöldeke, and many others), and its validity has been fully confirmed by more recent research in the twentieth century and beyond—in no small measure due to the discovery of Qumranic Hebrew (= QH), which reflects the transition from BH to Rabbinic Hebrew (= RH). Much credit in this respect is due to E. Y. Kutscher, whose monumental *The Language and Linguistic Background of the Isaiah Scroll (1QIsaᵃ)* (1959 [Hebrew]; 1974 [English]), along with the publications of the aforementioned nineteenth-century and other twentieth-century scholars, have laid a firm foundation for the diachronic study of LBH and the linguistic milieu in which it developed. All these enable us to identify with confidence usages belonging to the post-Classical era.

II   The Linguistic and Historical Setting of LBH*

1   *Introduction*

As noted above, the fifth century BCE marks a watershed in the history of BH, resulting directly from two pivotal historical events: the Babylonian Captivity and the Restoration. The displacement of a significant proportion of the Hebrew-speaking population, and its subsequent return to Judah after 70 years (i.e., some two generations) of minority status within a distinctive Aramaic-speaking majority, inevitably caused a disruption in the gradual development of the Hebrew language. Moreover, with the Restoration, IA became the *lingua franca* "from India to Ethiopia" (Esth. 1:1), including the Land of Israel, and influenced the development of languages throughout the entire region, inter alia Hebrew (Kautzsch 1902; Wagner 1966 [cf. the review of Nöldeke [1903] on Kautzsch; as well as Hurvitz 1968; Kutscher 1970: 358–360 [= 1977: 101–103]; and the review of Morag [1972] on Wagner; see also Naveh and Greenfield 1984 (= Greenfield 2001: I 232–246)]), Akkadian (von Soden 1966, 1968, 1977; Kutscher 1970: 356–358 [= 1977: 99–101]), Arabic (Fraenkel 1886; Jeffery 1938), Ethiopic/Geʿez (Nöldeke 1910–11; Polotsky 1964), and possibly even Persian

---

*   This is a somewhat modified version of my entry, "Hebrew Language, Late" (Hurvitz 2013).

(Kutscher 1970: 391–393 [= 1977: 134–136]). Not surprisingly, then, many lexical, grammatical, and syntactical innovations that first appear in Restoration-period Hebrew derive from Aramaic's far-reaching influence and demonstrate that the history of Hebrew is inextricably intertwined with that of Aramaic. Furthermore, despite early instances of contact between the two (e.g., יְגַר שָׂהֲדוּתָא *mound of testimony* [Gen. 31:47]), only fifth-century BCE Aramaic can be said to have had a decisive influence on Hebrew due to the intimate ties established between speakers and writers of the two languages after the Persian conquest of Palestine.

2   *Strata in BH*

Biblical literature was composed by different writers over an extended period of time. It is thus only natural that the works comprising the Hebrew Bible differ from one another literarily (e.g., prose vs. poetry), historically (First Temple vs. Second Temple periods), and geographically (the Land of Judah vs. the region of the northern tribes). Indeed, BH is not a homogeneous language; while tracing its history and development, it is possible to discern striking linguistic differences among the extant Biblical books.

As noted above (§I), BH may be divided chronologically and historically into three principal periods (Rabin 1971: 65–70; Kutscher 1982: §§17, 111–125; Sáenz-Badillos 1993: 56–62, 68–75, 112–129; Hadas-Lebel 1995: 70–114; Hornkohl 2013): (1) Archaic Biblical Hebrew (= ABH) found mainly in the poems preserved in the 'Pentateuch' and 'Former Prophets'; (2) Classical (or Standard) Biblical Hebrew (= CBH or SBH) used in the prose of the 'Pentateuch', 'Former Prophets', and Classical prophecies of the 'Latter Prophets'; and (3) Late Biblical Hebrew (= LBH) known primarily from the later compositions in the 'Writings'. This broad division is somewhat schematic, as linguistic change is usually gradual. Moreover, characteristically late features may appear at random and sporadically in texts commonly regarded as early (e.g., נְכָסִים *possessions* [Josh. 22:8]). In addition, transition-period compositions often exhibit intermediate stages of linguistic development, in which the 'old' and 'new' coexist (e.g., the language of Ezekiel; see Hurvitz 1982; Rooker 1990). Nevertheless, the tripartite division is generally valid as adequately reflecting BH's typological and chronological phases.

Since the narrow scope of the Hebrew Bible prevents an exhaustive description of BH's linguistic strata, the use of extra-Biblical material becomes indispensable. The material from Ugarit and El-Amarna (second half of the second millennium BCE) is particularly illuminating for the language of ABH; the Hebrew inscriptions of the First Temple period complement CBH/SBH prose; and post-Biblical Hebrew and Aramaic material (e.g., the Dead Sea Scrolls

[= DSS], Rabbinic literature [both Hebrew and Aramaic], and IA) shed invaluable light on LBH.

Viewing CBH as the standard language of the Hebrew Bible and using it as a reference point, ABH is characterized by elements inherited from earlier times while LBH, from the post-Exilic period, is recognizable by linguistic innovations that deviate from Classical norms. Such deviations result from the growth and development observable in any language, but from the perspective of Classical usage they constitute a departure from traditional conventions and are sometimes perceived as the result of 'collapse' and 'deterioration'. Hence, Persian-period Hebrew may be subjectively classified as the 'Silver Age', much as CBH, which was normative in the First Temple period (Gesenius 1815; Ginsberg 1970: 112), may be classified as its 'Golden Age'.

3   *The Literary Sources and Linguistic Complexion of LBH*
         Literary Texts

Since there are no extant extra-Biblical Hebrew literary texts that may be securely dated to the Persian period, and contemporaneous Hebrew epigraphic finds are scant, reliable comparative data regarding Persian-period Hebrew can only be gleaned from post-Exilic Biblical sources. Despite this paucity of evidence, however, the distinctive linguistic profile of Persian-period Biblical literature unambiguously typifies its language as LBH, and not CBH (Rabin 1970: 316–320).

Methodologically, Late Biblical literature may be divided into two groups: (1) books datable on the basis of explicit references to historical episodes and/or individual figures: in the 'Writings'—Esther (King Ahasuerus [1:1, and *passim*]); Daniel (King Cyrus of Persia [1:21, 10:1]); Ezra ([King Cyrus of Persia [1:1 and *passim*]); Nehemiah (King Artaxerxes [2:1, 5:14, 13:6]), Chronicles (Shealtiel…Zerubbabel [= Zerubbabel son of Shealtiel (Hag. 1:1); 1 Chron. 3:17–19]; King Cyrus of Persia [2 Chron. 36:22]); in the 'Latter Prophets'— 'Second Isaiah' (Cyrus [44:28; 45:1], Haggai (King Darius [1:1, 15; 2:10]); and Zechariah (Darius [1:1, 7; 7:1]; with the possible exception of chapters 9–14); (2) books assigned to post-Exilic times (on the basis of non-linguistic arguments) by almost unanimous consensus in the scholarly literature: in the 'Writings'—Qohelet; in the 'Latter Prophets'—Malachi.

The linguistic character of LBH is thus established first and foremost on the basis of features documented exclusively, or predominantly, in compositions from the first group. Data derived from books in the second category must be treated with caution.

Linguistic Affinities

The distinctive linguistic characteristics of LBH fall into four main categories: (1) Persian loanwords; (2) cases of late Aramaic interference; (3) RH elements; and (4) independent inner-BH developments. The distinction between these categories is not always sharp or clear-cut. One may occasionally question whether the appearance of a late linguistic feature employed in Late Biblical literature (and attested in late extra-Biblical sources) should be attributed to external influence or internal development. Furthermore, in cases of acknowledged external influence, it is not always clear whether it was Aramaic or Rabbinic Hebrew that gave rise to a phenomenon suspected of being late. By the same token, one could argue that Persian loanwords in the Bible, listed above as an independent category, are in fact just a subcategory of 'cases of late Aramaic interference' since, according to the evidence at our disposal, these words penetrated BH via Aramaic and not by direct contact between Hebrew and Persian. Consensus has yet to be reached regarding similar questions; however it should be emphasized that all these conflicting opinions are peripheral, as they relate only to matters of classification and interpretation. A Biblical Hebrew element proven to be post-Classical is a neologism even if its exact origin or categorization is disputed. Thus, for example, regardless of whether אִגֶּרֶת *letter* is an Aramaic loanword in Akkadian or vice versa (see Kaufman 1974: 48), it penetrated into BH in post-Exilic times and consequently—whatever its origin—is to be classified as a characteristic LBH feature.

(1) Persian Loanwords

It is widely acknowledged in the scholarly literature that the penetration of Persian loanwords into Hebrew via IA did not precede the Persian conquest; this is confirmed linguistically by the Biblical distribution of words of undeniable Persian origin, which are limited almost exclusively to unequivocally late compositions in Hebrew and Aramaic. The appearance of Persian loanwords in Biblical texts thus constitutes a sort of 'Archimedean point' on which one can confidently rely for chronological observations (Seow 1996: 647; Eskhult 2003: 12–14).

The Persian loanwords that took root in the Bible in large measure represent the realms of governance and administration (in contrast to words borrowed from Akkadian, which reflect various aspects of the material culture) (Kutscher 1961: 22), e.g., אֲדַרְכֹּן, *Daric* (Ezra 8:27; 1 Chron. 29:7); גִּזְבָּר, *treasurer* (Ezra 1:8); גְּנָזִים, *treasuries* (e.g., Esth. 3:9); גִּנְזַךְ, *treasury* (1 Chron. 28:11); דָּת, *command, decree* (e.g., Esth. 1:13); פִּתְגָם, *edict, sentence* (Qoh. 8:11; Esth. 1:20). Despite this clear-cut historical and linguistic evidence, it has been argued in recent years that Persian loanwords could have reached the writers of Biblical literature much earlier than the fifth century BCE, when we witness for the first time unambiguous documentary evidence of intimate linguistic contact (albeit via Aramaic mediation, as noted) between Persian and Hebrew. However, as this claim is incompatible with the concrete linguistic testimony at our disposal and devoid of any tangible textual basis, it is no more than mere conjecture (see the entry גֶּנֶז, comment b).

(2)   *Cases of Late Aramaic Interference*

In terms of extent and degree of influence, Aramaic was the most decisive factor shaping LBH. Indeed, sporadic 'Aramaisms' that perhaps ought to be regarded as 'archaisms' appear already in the earliest Biblical books, especially in poetic parallelism (e.g., בוֹא || אָתָא [אָתָה], *come* [Deut. 33:2]; דֶּרֶךְ || אֹרַח, *way* [Gen. 49:17]) (G. R. Driver 1953), and Aramaic affinities are quite common in Wisdom Literature (which flourished already in ancient times in Aramaic-speaking regions east of Canaan/Israel; see, e.g., Torczyner [Tur-Sinai] 1965). However, the fact that an overwhelming Aramaic influence is undiscernible in CBH is corroborated by both the lack of Aramaisms in pre-Exilic epigraphic material from Judah and the Bible's own inadvertent testimony in the Judaean officials' request to Rabshakeh (during Sennacherib's siege of Jerusalem): "Please speak to your servants in Aramaic, for we understand it; do not speak to us in Judean within the hearing of the people on the wall" (2 Kgs. 18:26). The episode clearly demonstrates that the commoners in Judah—in contrast to noblemen—did not understand Aramaic ca. 700 BCE.

This situation changed drastically in post-Exilic times (Kutscher 1961: 52; Hurvitz 1968; 2003a; Naveh and Greenfield 1984: 118–119 [= Greenfield 2001: I 235–236]). Biblical sources from this period exhibit a massive wave of linguistic elements whose penetration into Hebrew, or whose intensified use, is directly attributable to the heavy influence of IA. Indeed, IA served as the language of culture and administration used by the Persian Empire's upper classes, including the Jewish writers of the Restoration period. This development finds clear expression in the language of prose, but its mark is also felt in the language of poetry and prophecy. Examples of this phenomenon include: אִגֶּרֶת, *letter* (e.g., Esth. 9:29; like BA אִגַּרְתָּא [e.g., Ezra 4:11] vs. סֵפֶר [e.g., 1 Kgs. 21:8–9]); אִם טוֹב...עַל, *if it pleases* ... (e.g., Neh. 2:5; like BA הֵן עַל...טָב [Ezra 5:17] vs. אִם טוֹב ...בְּעֵינֵי, *if it be good in the eyes of* ... [e.g., 1 Kgs. 21:2]); אַרְגְּוָן, *purple* (2 Chron. 2:6; like BA אַרְגְּוָנָא [e.g., Dan. 5:7] vs. אַרְגָּמָן [e.g., Exod. 28:5–8]); מַאֲמַר הַמֶּלֶךְ, *royal command* (Esth. 1:15; like BA כְּמֵאמַר כָּהֲנַיָּא [Ezra 6:9] vs. דְּבַר הַמֶּלֶךְ [e.g., 2 Sam. 24:4]; מִצְוַת הַמֶּלֶךְ [e.g., 2 Kgs. 18:36]).

The prolonged struggle between the two languages came to an end in the Rabbinic period, when Aramaic almost completely supplanted Hebrew as both a written and spoken language.

(3)　　*Rabbinic Hebrew Elements*

Though RH was BH's chronological successor, typologically it is difficult to explain certain RH elements as genetic developments emerging from BH. This is the case with regard to lexical items whose absence from the Bible is merely accidental (e.g., שֶׁכֶב, *lower millstone*; only its counterpart, רֶכֶב, *upper millstone* [Judg. 9:53], is mentioned) and with regard to certain grammatical features that look earlier than their BH counterparts (e.g., RH's morphologically simpler, and probably more ancient, feminine demonstrative pronoun זוֹ, *this*, in contrast to Biblical זֹאת). Some prototype(s) of RH evidently existed already in pre-Exilic times alongside CBH, perhaps only as a spoken register and/or in certain parts of Israel (Segal 1927: 11; Bendavid 1967–71: I 13ff.; Rabin 1970: 313–314, 317–318; Rendsburg 1990b). Nevertheless, even those who maintain that RH (or some prototype thereof) did exist somewhere in pre-Exilic times admit that its manifest penetration into the literary compositions of the Hebrew Bible is a late phenomenon (Bendavid 1967–71: I 74–80; Rendsburg 1990a: 165–166). LBH links CBH and RH in that it reflects both the decline of the former and the rise of the latter.

Features characteristic of RH are discernible in the chronologically problematic Song of Songs, e.g., -שֶׁ *that, which* (vs. אֲשֶׁר [which appears only in the book's title]), but they find especially clear expression in Qohelet (widely assigned to the latest phases of the Hebrew Bible; see above, §II.3: Literary Sources), e.g., חוּץ מִמֶּנִּי, *apart from me* (Qoh. 2:25 vs. זוּלָתִי [e.g., Hos. 13:4]; מִבַּלְעָדַי [e.g., Isa. 43:11]) and in the distinctive LBH corpus, e.g., בַּקָּשָׁה, *request* (e.g., Esth. 5:8 vs. שְׁאֵלָה [e.g., 1 Kgs. 2:16]; מִשְׁאָלָה [e.g., Ps. 20:6]).

Of particular significance in this category are technical terms and expressions that reflect the distinctive conceptual world of the Talmudic sages, e.g., מִדְרָשׁ, *(a written version of a) story, commentary.* In CBH √דרש = *look for, explore, seek* (*God, persons, objects*), but in LBH √דרש = *explore, interpret, expound* ([*sacred*] *texts*)' (noted above, §I.2; for a similar semantic shift, cf. *search > research* in English). Other specifically Rabbinic technical terminology includes, for instance, הַתָּמִיד *the perpetual* (*sacrifice*) (Dan. 11:31 vs. עוֹלַת הַתָּמִיד [Num. 28:10]); תַּעֲנִית *fast* (Ezra 9:5 vs. צוֹם [2 Sam. 12:16]).

(4)　　*Independent Internal Developments*

IA and RH features in LBH demonstrate the latter's vulnerability to external influences, but LBH may also have known independent internal developments

(Rabin 1971: 70) that merit a separate category. Yet, if 'independent developments' denote linguistic phenomena not paralleled in extra-Biblical sources, this category becomes difficult to fill with concrete examples. Since it is precisely the testimony of extra-Biblical material that can decisively corroborate a given Biblical feature's lateness, this category, by its very definition, is problematic. Some features may be idiosyncratic, not characteristic of LBH in general; others may eventually be confirmed as characteristic of LBH by the discovery of new texts, but may then require recategorization (cf. above, [2] *Cases of Late Aramaic Interference*; [3] *Rabbinic Hebrew Elements*). Consider, for example, the expression לַעֲשׂוֹת סְפָרִים *making* (= *writing, compiling*) *books*, which appears in the Bible only in Qoh. 12:12. There are three possible explanations for this expression's exceptional usage in the Hebrew Bible: (1) it is Classical, and only by chance does not occur in early Biblical compositions; (2) it is post-Classical, and only by chance occurs very infrequently in Late Biblical literature; (3) it is an 'idiosyncratic' linguistic innovation of the author of Qohelet that is not necessarily characteristic of contemporary Hebrew in general. Only by enlisting as evidence the expression עבד√ *to make* + ספר *book*—which was discovered in the Aramaic papyri of Elephantine—can we conclude that the testimony from Elephantine completely excludes the third theory, substantially weakens the first, and greatly strengthens the second (Ginsberg 1961: 135).

The aforementioned features are attested in all Persian-period Biblical works, but not in the same way or to the same extent. Most late writers were inspired by—or, if you wish, imitated—the Classical style, however their levels of success varied. Furthermore, all late works exhibit an accumulation of LBH features, and therefore it becomes clear that no late writer could entirely divorce himself from his immediate linguistic milieu. For example, the writer of Esther had a good command of the Classical style but frequently resorted to Persian loanwords ("Despite the pressure of the Aramaic and Mishnaic expressions whose imprints are discernible throughout the scroll, the writer succeeded in overcoming them and in connecting the majority of its clauses with remarkably good biblical syntax" [Bendavid 1967–71: I 61]; see also S. R. Driver 1913: 484; Polzin 1976: 3, 74; cf. Rabin 1958a: 152–153; in general, see Bergey 1983: 168–186), whereas varying levels of inelegance and/or awkwardness, constituting more obvious linguistic signs of lateness, are characteristic of Ezra ("his style proves that the expert in Torah does not necessarily have a command of its style" [Bendavid 1967–71: I 65]; see also S. R. Driver 1913: 505–506, 553), Nehemiah ("He was a royal official and a man of action but did not have a polished style.... [H]e saw it as his duty to write in the literary language, but he did not have complete mastery of it" [Bendavid 1967–71: I 65]; see also S. R. Driver 1913: 505–506, 553), Chronicles ("the Chronicler... has many pecu-

liarities of his own, and may be said to show the greatest uncouthness of style"
[ibid., 505]; "either . . . the language itself is in decadence, or . . . the author has
an imperfect command of it" [ibid., 535]; and Daniel ("much of the Silver Age
material [the Hebrew of Daniel] sounds . . . generally poor" [Ginsberg 1970:
114]; see also S. R. Driver 1913: 505–506). Qohelet does not seem to imitate CBH
but is widely regarded as a linguistic forerunner of later RH ("The language
of the book . . . does not reflect the standard literary Hebrew of the postexilic
period . . . [but] the literary deposit of the vernacular" [Seow 1996: 666]; see
also S. R. Driver 1913: 473–474, 505; Bendavid 1967–71: I 77–79; Schoors 1992–
2004). However, while exhibiting indisputable signs of lateness, the Hebrew
of other Second Temple compositions does not represent a marked departure
from CBH, e.g., Haggai, Zechariah, and Malachi ("the language of Hag-Zec-Mal
is indeed part and parcel of LBH; yet, diachronically it must be located in an
early stage of the LBH development" [Shin 2007: 160]; see also S. R. Driver 1913:
156, 505–506; Hill 1981 [on Malachi]; 1982 [on Zechariah]), and 'Second Isaiah'
("the latest great author of the Golden Age is Deutero-Isaiah" [Ginsberg 1970:
112]). The reason for this is twofold: first, prophetic literature's semi-poetic language tends to adhere to Classical norms and to avoid neologisms that deviate
from traditional conventions; second, these prophets were active at the beginning of the Persian period, when CBH may have been better preserved than
it was later on. Moreover, despite a marked tendency to archaize, especially
in the domain of the lexicon (but also in grammar and syntax), Hellenistic–
Roman-era Hebrew, like that of Ben-Sira and the DSS (some also consider
Daniel, Qohelet, and Chronicles to be of Hellenistic provenance), belongs to
the same linguistic milieu as that of Persian-period Hebrew (see Naveh and
Greenfield 1984: 122 [= Greenfield 2001: I 239]).

4   Criteria for Identifying Distinctive LBH Features

Not every deviation from CBH should be explained diachronically; divergences
may reflect poetic language, personal style, dialectal and register differences,
or simply pure chance—even if they occur exclusively in Late Biblical writings. A linguistic feature considered indicative of LBH must therefore stand
the test of satisfying three complementary criteria (Hurvitz 1972: 67–69; 2000a:
148–150).

(1)   Late Biblical Distribution

The Biblical distribution of an LBH feature must be limited exclusively, or
predominantly, to acknowledged late compositions (Esther, Daniel, Ezra,
Nehemiah, Chronicles), which would justify doubts regarding a feature's antiquity within the linguistic history of BH.

(2)   Linguistic Contrast with Classical Equivalents

Early Biblical literature demonstrates that it is possible to use linguistic alternatives in comparable contexts, thereby removing any suspicion that a feature's absence from CBH stems from accidental distribution or from the limited scope of the Hebrew Bible. In other words, the *argumentum* of absence from CBH cannot be faulted for being *ex silentia*.

(3)   Extra-Biblical Corroboration

The linguistic element under examination must be commonly attested in extra-Biblical sources contemporary with or following LBH (the DSS, Ben-Sira, RH, IA, etc.). Such a wide-ranging correlation with Late Biblical evidence shows that the neologism in question cannot be dismissed as an insignificant single occurrence of BH, since it is characteristic of the late linguistic milieu as a whole, far beyond the confines of BH. The extra-Biblical material thus serves as a 'control group' for inner-BH analysis.

While none of these criteria is decisive in and of itself, their combined evidence provides a reliable measure for creating an inventory of distinctive LBH linguistic features from Biblical compositions of acknowledged lateness. By adhering to the three methodological guidelines presented above, it would be possible to glean post-Classical linguistic features from compositions recognized to have been written in Late Biblical times (e.g., the book of Esther). However, in order to date chronologically problematic texts merely on the basis of their late linguistic profile we must consider yet another criterion—accumulation.

(4)   Accumulation

A text suspected of being of post-Classical provenance can be so classified only if it contains an abundance of late linguistic features. The sporadic appearance of such characteristic elements in texts of unknown date is not sufficient to prove lateness, since early authors could at times employ rare or foreign words whose intensified usage became typical only in the Second Temple period. Therefore, an accumulation of linguistic innovations in a given chronologically disputed text is of considerable significance for determining its linguistic lateness.

Aside from the two major groups of Late Biblical compositions listed above (§II.3. *The Literary Sources and Linguistic Complexion of LBH*), one should mention here additional works that exhibit a discernible accumulation of neologisms: (1) certain psalms found, for the most part, in the final third of the Psalter (103, 117, 119, 124, 125, 133, 144, 145), along with three (41:14, 72:18–20,

106:47–48) of the book's four concluding doxologies (Hurvitz 1972); and (2) the narrative framework of Job (1–2; 42:7–17; Hurvitz 1974b). The language of several other biblical compositions may also include potential post-Classical imprints (for instance, Joel, Jonah, Proverbs, the poetic speeches of Job, Song of Songs, Ruth), yet for various reasons they are inconclusive for dating purposes.

Finally, it should also be noted that the Biblical material in the Pentateuch known as 'P', widely considered to be of late provenance by adherents of the Graf-Wellhausian documentary hypothesis, is characterized by a thoroughly Classical linguistic profile that is best explained, we believe, as a genuine marker of CBH (Hurvitz 1974a).

5 Concluding Remarks

"The reader of Late Biblical books"—to employ the colorful language of Bendavid—"discerns therein three scents: (1) that of Biblical Hebrew style struggling to survive, (2) that of Aramaic penetrating from without, and (3) that of popular ('Rabbinic') Hebrew sprouting and growing from within" (Bendavid 1967–71: I 60). The three dominant components characterizing LBH thus reflect the trilingual nature of Jewish society in the Persian period: Biblical Hebrew, which was singled out almost exclusively for the writing of literary compositions; Aramaic, which was used extensively for outside communication; and Rabbinic Hebrew, or some ancestor thereof, which was commonly used as an internal spoken language (Rabin 1958a: 152). These linguistic elements appear in all the books belonging to the late layers of Biblical literature, although, as noted above, not with the same frequency or in the same manner throughout the various Biblical compositions.

In other words, it is impossible to view Persian-period BH as a monolithic stylistic stratum or a unified linguistic entity. Rather, LBH is a 'repertoire' of linguistic innovations that in many cases have close ties to IA and/or RH. However, despite these stylistic variations, we can by no means ignore the distinctive post-Classical affinities that characterize the Second Temple linguistic milieu in both Biblical and extra-Biblical sources. As Gesenius, the 'father of biblical lexicography', astutely observed long ago: "Even in the language of the Old Testament, notwithstanding its general uniformity, there is noticeable a certain progress from an earlier to a later stage. Two periods, though with some reservations, may be distinguished: the *first*, down to the end of the Babylonian exile; and the *second*, after the exile" (GKC: 12, §2l).

III   The Conceptual Plan of *The Concise Lexicon of Late Biblical Hebrew*

Unlike the standard dictionaries, whose scope and extent are dictated by the
contents of the Biblical concordance, this lexicon includes only 80 lexical
entries, selected specifically for a diachronic investigation of LBH. In line with
our 'tripartite model' suggested above (§II.4. *Criteria for Identifying Distinctive
LBH Features*; see also Hurvitz 2000a: 148–150), the relevant primary sources
adduced in each entry are divided into two categories—CBH materials that
regularly appear in the earlier Biblical writings; and, linguistic usages that
are documented in both Biblical and extra-Biblical post-Exilic sources. The
late external texts provide us with comparable material from contemporaneous non-Biblical texts, which, as already noted, serve as a 'control group' for
inner-BH analysis. Whenever applicable, BA's related lexemes are also cited in
each individual LBH lemma. The cardinal significance of BA for our purposes
lies in the fact that this form of Aramaic, preserved in the OT, is part and parcel
of IA, which played a major role in shaping the historical development of LBH.
Each entry concludes with a discussion, evaluation, and selected bibliographical references (as well as direct quotations from the scholarly literature) under
the heading 'Comments'. The references are culled from the realms of both
Biblical philology and Hebrew linguistics. This section of the entry thus provides us with methodological justification for our diachronic enterprise.

    In view of the fact that our attention is devoted primarily to the 'watershed'
separating Classical from post-Classical BH, a great emphasis is placed in our
Lexicon on the issue of 'linguistic contrast', which is illuminated by means of
a varied selection of examples contrasting CBH with LBH, BH with RH, and
Hebrew with Aramaic (particularly Targumic Aramaic). It is these contrasts
specifically that are indispensable for understanding the background of the
emergence and development of LBH neologisms. Consequently, no attempt
is made either to compile a comprehensive inventory of all the available
Aramaic, Rabbinic, or epigraphic sources that have relevance to the entries in
question, or to provide an all-inclusive bibliography relating to the various linguistic aspects presented here; such topics are treated at length in the standard
dictionaries and grammars, and therefore are unnecessary to cite here.

IV   The Non-Diachronic Approach to BH

Despite the repeated and sweeping claims against the diachronic approach
to BH voiced recently in certain scholarly circles, the dominant view among
leading Biblical philologists, Hebrew linguists, and Semitists is that LBH is a

viable linguistic phase in the historical development of BH. As noted, LBH is the latest linguistic stratum in the Hebrew Bible. It is best represented in works from the Second Temple period, during the years of the Persian regime, and constitutes a link between the literary products of the Biblical and post-Biblical Hebrew sources (the DSS, Ben-Sira, and Rabbinic literature). It also exhibits conspicuous affinities to the various Aramaic dialects of the post-Exilic period (IA, Nabatean, etc.). In other words, our *Lexicon* is, by definition, diachronic in nature and thus constitutes part and parcel of the discipline of Historical Linguistics. Since its basic methodological principles and philological guidelines are largely rejected by the non-diachronic school of BH, as openly revealed in their publications (see especially Young, Rezetko, and Ehrensvärd 2008), the gulf between the two opposing parties is hardly bridgeable. Indeed, no common ground for a potentially meaningful dialogue in this connection seems to be in sight at the moment. Thus, our policy all along was to refrain from futile polemics. (Nevertheless, there are two entries in which we introduced, for purposes of illustration, critical comments relating to the nondiachronic line of argumentation: דִּרְמֶשֶׂק [comment **d**] and אֵין + infinitive [comment **b**].) Rather, our goal was to draw attention to, and focus on the actual diachronic analysis of the Biblical data in compliance with the guidelines described above—guidelines that dominate the scholarly work of the leading experts on the linguistic history of BH. Detailed discussions of our general approach or of specific positions regarding individual cases may be found in the scholarly literature (see extensive treatment in Zevit and Miller-Naudé 2012) and do not warrant lengthy and often repetitive arguments and counter-arguments that would have taken us well beyond the desired framework of this volume.

Structure of the Entries

In comparison to standard dictionaries of BH, this lexicon is neither a guide to the general semantic range of the Hebrew word discussed nor an exhaustive record of its etymological relationship to corresponding words in the extra-Biblical sources. Its main goal is to present linguistic and textual data (including the definitions of each entry) that, when considered as a whole, provide every indication that the word or phrase at the head of the entry ought to be classified as LBH. To this end, each entry is designed to display information that may be helpful in determining the diachronic status of the linguistic item included in the *Lexicon*. Each entry contains the following sections:

Lemma—The entry opens with a form of a Biblical word: verbs are listed as unvocalized root forms (e.g., √יחש), while all other words appear as vocalized ground forms (e.g., יַחַשׂ). A ground form that is not documented as such in the Bible appears within brackets (e.g., [צֹרֶךְ]).

The lemma is followed by standard linguistic definitions, e.g., adj. (= adjective), adv. (= adverb), f. (= feminine), Hiph (= Hiphʿil), Hitp (= Hitpaʿel), m. (= masculine), n. (= noun), Niph (= Niphʿal), Pi (= Piʿel), pl. (= plural), pr. (= proper), ptc. (= participle), Pu (= Puʿal), Qal, sg. (= singular), vb. (= verb). The meaning of the word follows, in italics.

Only those occurrences of a word's late meaning or form are listed. Thus, for example, the entry √כעס includes only *Qal* forms since other conjugations of the root are not exclusively late. Note also that some forms or meanings are deemed late only in certain contexts, e.g., √דרש in the specific context of God's (written) Law and commandments. Selected Biblical quotations follow to illustrate the usage of each word.

Below is an example of the **Lemma** section (this and subsequent sections are drawn from the entry אִגֶּרֶת):

אִגֶּרֶת, pl. אִגְּרוֹת n. f. *letter, missive, epistle; royal letter, edict*: Neh. 2:7 אִם עַל 17, 19, וְאִגֶּרֶת פְּתוּחָה בְּיָדוֹ 6:5 ;9 ,8, הַמֶּלֶךְ טוֹב אִגְּרוֹת יִתְּנוּ לִי עַל פַּחֲווֹת עֵבֶר הַנָּהָר וְגַם 2 Chron. 30:1 ;לְקַיֵּם אֵת אִגֶּרֶת הַפֻּרִים 29 ,Esth. 9:26; אִגְּרוֹת שָׁלַח טוֹבִיָּה לְיָרְאֵנִי וַיֵּלְכוּ הָרָצִים בָּאִגְּרוֹת מִיַּד הַמֶּלֶךְ וְשָׂרָיו 6, אִגְּרוֹת כָּתַב עַל אֶפְרַיִם וּמְנַשֶּׁה

Entries containing proper nouns and geographical names—see דרמשק, דויד, and ירושלים—are accompanied by Biblical textual witnesses of non-Masoretic texts from the Judaean Desert.

Biblical Aramaic (BA)—One of the main features of LBH words is the overwhelming influence of IA on contemporary Hebrew. Therefore, cognate forms in BA are highly significant for dating purposes, some of which are listed and some also quoted:

> אִגְּרָה BA Ezra 4:8 חֲדָה אִגְּרָה כְּתַבוּ ,11; 5:6 עֲבַר פַּחַת תַּתְּנַי שְׁלַח דִּי אִגַּרְתָּא פַּרְשֶׁגֶן
> נְהָרָה

Classical Biblical Hebrew (CBH) Alternatives—In many cases, LBH neologisms supplant earlier CBH (or Standard Biblical Hebrew = SBH) expressions. Wherever possible, concrete examples of these earlier phrases are juxtaposed with their later counterparts ("linguistic contrast"):

ספר (of royal/official letters), e.g.

2 Sam. 11:14	בְּיַד אוּרִיָּה	סֵפֶר אֶל יוֹאָב וַיִּשְׁלַח	וַיִּכְתֹּב דָּוִד
1 Kgs. 21:8	אֶל הַזְּקֵנִים ...וַתִּשְׁלַח	...סְפָרִים	וַתִּכְתֹּב [אִיזֶבֶל]
2 Kgs. 10:1	אֶל שָׂרֵי יִזְרְעֶאל ...וַיִּשְׁלַח	סְפָרִים	וַיִּכְתֹּב יֵהוּא
[~ 2 Chron. 30:1	עַל אֶפְרַיִם וּמְנַשֶּׁה	כָּתַב	וְגַם אִגְּרוֹת...וַיִּשְׁלַח יְחִזְקִיָּהוּ]

External Post-Classical Source—After presenting the relevant Biblical data, each entry shifts its focus to the distribution and usage of the discussed word within the extra-Biblical written sources from the beginning of the Second Temple period until roughly the end of the Talmudic era. These sources reflect post-CBH usage and serve as a distinctive "control group" for the intra-Biblical analysis. The sources are divided into two groups of texts: The first falls under the rubric of **Renderings/Paraphrases/Glosses**, which includes, by and large, attestations of the entry word in the corpus of Aramaic Targumim of the Pentateuch and the Prophets (particularly Onqelos, Neophyti 1, Pseudo-Jonathan, and Jonathan).

The number of occurrences of the word in each of the aforementioned Targums is listed and one or more examples are cited while aligning the text with the corresponding Hebrew MT in brackets. In several cases, further evidence is cited from additional Targumic and other works—under the title Other Sources—but we have not enumerated the occurrences of the word throughout these textual sources. These sources may include the Fragmentary

Targum, various Hagiographa Targumim, the Peshiṭta, as well as selected instances from Qumranic material (e.g., Genesis Apocryphon).

Renderings/Paraphrases/Glosses

TN 3x, e.g.

Deut. 24:3 וישני יתה גברא אחרייה ויכתוב לה **אגרא** דשיבוקין וישווי בידה

[~ [וּשְׂנֵאָהּ הָאִישׁ הָאַחֲרוֹן וְכָתַב לָהּ **סֵפֶר** כְּרִיתֻת וְנָתַן בְּיָדָהּ

TJ 23x, e.g.

2 Sam. 11:14 והוה בצפרא וכתב דויד **אגרתא** לות יואב ושדר ביד אוריה

[~ [וַיְהִי בַבֹּקֶר וַיִּכְתֹּב דָּוִד **סֵפֶר** אֶל יוֹאָב וַיִּשְׁלַח בְּיַד אוּרִיָּה

Other Sources

FTV Num. 22:7 ואזלו חכימי מואב׳... **ואגרן חתימין** בידיהון ואתין לות בלעם

[~ [וַיֵּלְכוּ זִקְנֵי מוֹאָב... **וּקְסָמִים** בְּיָדָם וַיָּבֹאוּ אֶל בִּלְעָם

BT Meg. 19a **מגלה** נקראת **ספר** ונקראת **אגרת**. נקראת **ספר** שאם תפרה בפשתן פסולה, ונקראת **אגרת** שאם הטיל בה שלשה חכי גידים כשרה

The second group of External Post-Classical Sources, i.e., those that seem to be independent of a direct Biblical influence, appears in the section called **Independent Use**. These texts document the usage of the entry word in contexts, genres, or dialects that indicate the word's vitality in the contemporary sources. They are grouped by language (mainly Hebrew and Aramaic) with an internal division based on their approximate chronological order:

Independent Use

Heb.

M MoʿedQ 3:3 ואילו כותבים במועד: קידושי נשים, גיטים ושוברין, דייתקי, מתנה ופרוזבולים, **איגרות** שום **ואיגרות** מזון, שטרי חליצה ומאונים ושטרי בירורין וגזירות בית דין **ואיגרות** שלרשות

M Ohal. 17:5 מעשה שהיו **איגרות** באות ממדינת הים לבני כהנים גדולים

MekhRI Yithro 1 "ויאמר אל משה: אני חותנך יתרו בא אליך ואשתך ושני בניה עמה"
(pp. 192–193) (שמ׳ יח 6) – ר׳ יהושע אומר: כתב לו **באיגרת**. ר׳ אלעזר המודעי אומר: שלח לו ביד שליח

Aram.

TAD I 4.8 (= Cowley 31):28	...**אגרה** חדה בשמן שלחן על דליה ושלמיה...
TAD IV 7.56:8–9	...ישלחון **אגרה** על אפלניס זֹי על **אגרת**[א]
NH 53:1–2 (Yardeni I p. 170)	**אגרת** שמעון בר כוסבה שלם ליהונתן ב[ר] בעיה
PAT 0259 II:103–104 (= Cooke 147 iiC:4–5)	גרמנקוס קיסר **באגרתא** די כתב לסטטילס פשק די...

M Giṭ. 9:3			ר' יודה אומ': ודן די יהוֹיי ליך מיני
	תירוכין	ספר	
(marg.:	גרושין ו	(וגט	
	שיבוקין	**אגרת**	

BT Ber. 55a	ואמ' רב חסדא: חילמא דלא מיפשר **כאגרתא** דלא מקרין

Comments—Unlike conventional Biblical lexica that generally define every single word attested in the Old Testament, this work sifts through the vast body of Biblical Hebrew and focuses on only a small fraction of the ancient vocabulary, which, based on the linguistic criteria presented in the Prolegomenon, lead us to classify the entry word as Late Biblical Hebrew. The sources meeting these criteria appear in the sections mentioned above; the specific linguistic phenomena they exhibit are often elaborated on in short comments and observations. This section often includes direct quotations from the scholarly literature that relate to various linguistic aspects of the discussed lemma.

Bibliography—Each entry closes with bibliographical references relevant to the specific lemma. Listed in abbreviated form, these references appear in alphabetical order by author's name. The full bibliographical reference appears in the comprehensive Bibliography at the end of the volume. It should be noted that the bibliography in each entry is selective and in no way exhaustive, nor does it refer generally to the contentions of the so-called "Minimalists" or "Challengers" who, by and large, tend to reject the premise upon which conventional diachronic linguistic research of Biblical Hebrew is founded (see Proleg. §IV).

List of Abbreviations and Sigla

2 Tg. Esth.	Second Targum of Esther
adj.	adjective
adv. phr.	adverbial phrase
adv.	adverb
AHw	*Akkadisches Handwörterbuch*
Akkad.	Akkadian
Ant.	*Antiquities of the Jews*
Aram.	Aramaic
ARN	ʾAvot de-Rabbi Natan
AZ	ʿAvodah Zarah
BA	Biblical Aramaic
BB	Bava Batra
BCE	Before the Common Era
BDB	Brown, Driver and Briggs
Bekh.	Bekhorot
Ber.	Berakhot
BH	Biblical Hebrew
BHS	*Biblia Hebraica Stuttgartensia*
Bik.	Bikkurim
BM	Bava Metziʿa
BMM	Baraita de-Melekhet ha-Mishkan
BQ	Bava Qama
BS	Ben Sira
BT	Babylonian Talmud
CAD	*Chicago Assyrian Dictionary*
CBH	Classical Biblical Hebrew
CD	Damascus Covenant
CDA	*Concise Dictionary of Akkadian*
CE	Common Era
cf.	confer, compare
comp.	compound
cstr.	construct
DJD	*Discoveries in the Judaean Desert*
DJPA	*Dictionary of Jewish Palestinian Aramaic*
DSS	Dead Sea Scrolls
EA	El Amarna
EBH	Early Biblical Hebrew

Edu.	ʿEduyot
Eruv.	ʿEruvin
EN	Ephal-Naveh
Exod. Rab.	Exodus Rabbah
f.	feminine
frg.	fragment
FTP	Fragment Targum, ms. 110 of Bibliothèque Nationale de France, Paris
FTV	Fragment Targum, ms Vatican 440
g.n.	geographical name
GB	Gesenius-Buhl
Gen.	Genesis
Gen. Rab.	Genesis Rabbah
Giṭ.	Giṭṭin
GKC	Gesenius-Kautzsch-Cowley
Ḥag.	Ḥagigah
HALOT	*Hebrew and Aramaic Lexicon of the Old Testament*
HB	Hebrew Bible
Heb.	Hebrew
Hiph	Hiphʿil
Hitp	Hitpaʿel
Hor.	Horayot
Ḥul.	Ḥullin
IA	Imperial Aramaic
idiom.	idiomatic (phrase)
Idum.	Idumaean
Impf.	imperfect
Inf.	Infinitive
JA	Jewish Aramaic
JM	Joüon-Muraoka
KAI	*Kanaanäische und Aramäische Inschriften*
KB	Köhler-Baumgartner
Kel.	Kelim
Ker.	Keritut
Ket.	Ketubot
Kh.	Khirbet
Kil.	Kilʾaim
Kip.	Kippurim
KJV	King James Version
Krael.	Kraeling
Lam. Rab.	Lamentations Rabbah

LB	Late Babylonian
LBH	Late Biblical Hebrew
Lev. Rab.	Leviticus Rabbah
liturg. phr.	liturgical phrase
loc.	location
lw.	loanword
LXX	Septuagint
M	Mishnah
m.	masculine
Ma'asS	Ma'aser Sheni
Macc.	Maccabees
Mak.	Makkot
marg.	reading in margin
Matt.	Matthew
Me'il.	Me'ilah
Meg. Ta'an.	Megillat Ta'anit
Meg.	Megillah
MekhRI	Mekhilta of R. Ishmael
MekhRS	Mekhilta of R. Shimon b. Yoḥai
Men.	Menaḥot
MH	Mishnaic Hebrew
Mid.	Middot
MMT	*Miqṣat Ma'aśe Ha-Torah*
mng.	meaning
Mo'edQ	Mo'ed Qatan
MPAT	*Manual of Palestinian Aramaic Texts*
Ms.	manuscript
MT	Masoretic Text
Mur.	Muraba'at
n.	noun
NA	New Akkadian
Nab.	Nabatean
Nash.	Nashim
Naz.	Nazir
NB	New Babylonian
ND	Naḥal David
Ned.	Nedarim
Nez.	Neziqin
NḤ	Naḥal Ḥever

Nid.	Niddah
Niph	Niph'al
NJPS	New Jewish Publication Society Translation
NRSV	New Revised Standard Version
NṢ	Naḥal Ṣe'elim
NWS	North Western Semitic
Ohal.	Ohalot
OSA	Old South Arabian
OT	Old Testament
p., pp.	page, pages
PA	Palestinian Aramaic
Palm.	Palmyrene
Pap.	Papyrus
Par.	Parah
pass.	passive
PAT	*Palmyrene Aramaic Texts*
Pers.	Persian
Pes.	Pesaḥim
Pesh.	Peshiṭta
PesiqRK	Pesiqta de-Rav Kahana
Pet.	Petiḥta
Phoen.	Phoenician
phr.	phrase
pl.	plural
pr.	proper
prep.	preposition
Proleg.	Prolegomenon
PT	Palestinian Talmud (Talmud Yerushalmi)
ptc.	participle
Pu	Pu'al
QA	Qumranic Aramaic
QH	Qumranic Hebrew
Qid.	Qiddushin
Qoh. Rab.	Qohelet Rabbah
Qoh.	Qohelet (Ecclesiastes)
RA	Rabbinic Aramaic
RH	Rabbinic Hebrew
RoshH	Rosh Hashanah
RSV	Revised Standard Version

Ruth Rab.	Ruth Rabbah
s.o.	someone
San.	Sanhedrin
SBH	Standard Biblical Hebrew
Semaḥ.	Semahot
sg.	singular
Shab.	Shabbat
Sheq.	Sheqalim
Shev.	Shevi'it
Song	Song of Songs
Soṭ.	Soṭah
Suk.	Sukkah
Syr.	Syriac
T	Tosefta
Ta'an.	Ta'anit
TAD	*Textbook of Aramaic Documents from Ancient Egypt*
Tam.	Tamid
Tem.	Temurah
Ter.	Terumot
Tg.	Targum
TJ	Targum Jonathan
TM	Tibat Markeh
TN	Targum Neofiti
TO	Targum Onqelos
Teh.	Teharot
TPJ	Targum Pseudo-Jonathan
Ug.	Ugaritic
v.	verse
vb.	verb
Yad.	Yadayim
Yev.	Yevamot
Zav.	Zavim
Zev.	Zevaḥim
(ק')	קרי, *qere* form
(כת')	כתיב, *ketiv* form

Sigla

~	corresponding Masoretic text
⟨ ⟩, ℵ	added or reconstructed by the editor
{ }	erased
[ ]	possible completion of a text
/	alternate reading in Qumranic texts
ȯ, ō (depending on edition)	damaged letter whose reading seems almost certain
å	damaged letter whose reading is uncertain
ọ	extremely damaged letter
ọ̇	erased by the scribe
o	unidentifiable letter (in *DJD* texts)

אִגֶּרֶת, pl. **אִגְּרוֹת** n. f. *letter, missive, epistle; royal letter, edict*: Neh. 2:7 אִם עַל הַמֶּלֶךְ
אִגְּרוֹת שָׁלַח 17, 19, וְאִגֶּרֶת פְּתוּחָה בְּיָדוֹ 6:5; 8, 9, טוֹב אִגְּרוֹת יִתְּנוּ לִי עַל פַּחֲווֹת עֵבֶר הַנָּהָר
וְגַם אִגְּרוֹת כָּתַב עַל Chron. 30:1 2; לְקַיֵּם אֶת אִגֶּרֶת הַפֻּרִים 29 ,9:26 .Esth; טוֹבִיָּה לְיָרְאֵנִי
וַיֵּלְכוּ הָרָצִים בָּאִגְּרוֹת מִיַּד הַמֶּלֶךְ וְשָׂרָיו 6, אֶפְרַיִם וּמְנַשֶּׁה

פַּרְשֶׁגֶן אִגַּרְתָּא דִּי שְׁלַח תַּתְּנַי פַּחַת עֲבַר נַהֲרָה 5:6; 11, כְּתָבוּ אִגְּרָה חֲדָה Ezra 4:8 אִגְּרָה BA

CBH Alternatives

ספר (of royal/official letters), e.g.

וַיִּכְתֹּב דָּוִד	**סֵפֶר** אֶל יוֹאָב וַיִּשְׁלַח	בְּיַד אוּרִיָּה	2 Sam. 11:14
וַתִּכְתֹּב [אִיזֶבֶל]	**סְפָרִים** ... וַתִּשְׁלַח ...	אֶל הַזְּקֵנִים	1 Kgs. 21:8
וַיִּכְתֹּב יֵהוּא	**סְפָרִים** ... וַיִּשְׁלַח ...	אֶל שָׂרֵי יִזְרְעֶאל	2 Kgs. 10:1
[וַיִּשְׁלַח יְחִזְקִיָּהוּ ... וְגַם **אִגְּרוֹת**	כָּתַב	עַל אֶפְרַיִם וּמְנַשֶּׁה	2 Chron. 30:1 ~]

External Post-Classical Sources
Renderings/Paraphrases/Glosses

TN 3x, e.g.

וישני יתה	גברא אחרייה	ויכתוב לה **אגרא** דשיבוקין	וישווי בידה	Deut. 24:3
[וּשְׂנֵאָהּ	הָאִישׁ הָאַחֲרוֹן	וְכָתַב לָהּ **סֵפֶר** כְּרִיתֻת	וְנָתַן בְּיָדָהּ	~]

TJ 23x, e.g.

יהוה בצפרא וכתב דויד **אגרתא** לות יואב	ושדר	ביד אוריה		2 Sam. 11:14
[וַיְהִי בַבֹּקֶר וַיִּכְתֹּב דָּוִד **סֵפֶר** אֶל	יוֹאָב וַיִּשְׁלַח	בְּיַד אוּרִיָּה		~]

Other Sources

ואזלו חכימי מואב' ... **ואגרן חתימין** בידיהון	ואתין לות	בלעם		FTV Num. 22:7
[וַיֵּלְכוּ זִקְנֵי מוֹאָב ... **וּקְסָמִים**	בְּיָדָם	וַיָּבֹאוּ אֶל	בִּלְעָם	~]

BT Meg. 19a	**מגלה** נקראת **ספר** ונקראת **אגרת**. נקראת **ספר** שאם תפרה בפשתן פסולה, ונקראת **אגרת** שאם הטיל בה שלשה חבכי גידים כשרה

Independent Use
Heb.

M MoʻedQ 3:3	ואילו כותבים במועד: קידושי נשים, גיטים ושוברין, דייתקי, מתנה ופרוזבולים, **איגרות** שום **ואיגרות** מזון, שטרי חליצה ומאונים ושטרי בירורין וגזירות בית דין **ואיגרות** שלרשות
M Ohal. 17:5	מעשה שהיו **איגרות** באות ממדינת הים לבני כהנים גדולים

© KONINKLIJKE BRILL NV, LEIDEN, 2014 | DOI 10.1163/9789004266438_005

"וַיֹּאמֶר אֶל מֹשֶׁה: אֲנִי חֹתֶנְךָ יִתְרוֹ בָּא אֵלֶיךָ וְאִשְׁתְּךָ וּשְׁנֵי בָנֶיהָ עִמָּהּ"   MekhRI Yithro 1
(שמ' יח 6) – ר' יהושע אומר: כתב לו **באיגרת**. ר' אלעזר המודעי   (pp. 192–193)
אומר: שלח לו ביד שליח

Aram.

...**אגרה** חדה בשמן שלחן על דליה ושלמיה...   TAD I 4.8 (= Cowley 31):28
...ישלחון **אגרה** על אפלניס זֹי על **אגרת**[א]   TAD IV 7.56:8–9
אגרת שמעון בר כוסבה שלם ליהונתן ב[ר] בעיה   NḤ 53:1–2 (Yardeni I p. 170)
גרמנקוס קיסר **באגרתא** די כתב לסטטילס פשק די...   PAT 0259 II:103–104
     (= Cooke 147 iiC:4–5)

ר' יודה אומ': ודן די יהויי ליך מיני   ספר   תירוכין   M Giṭ. 9:3
(וגט   גרושין ו :.marg)
אגרת   שיבוקין
ואמ' רב חסדא: חילמא דלא מיפשר **כאגרתא** דלא מקרין   BT Ber. 55a

COMMENTS

a. אגרת is unattested not only in CBH, but also in pre-Exilic Hebrew epigraphy (Lachish letters) and Ugaritic—all three of which make consistent use of the general old NWS term ספר.

b. The exact provenance of the lexeme is not certain but, whatever its origin (most probably Akkadian or Aramaic), אגרת is widely believed to have reached Hebrew via the IA scribal formulary during the Achaemenid period. In this Aramaic corpus, "[t]he lexeme 'grh/t prevails in most texts, in official letters as well as in more private letters. The lexeme spr only occurs in some private letters, both on papyrus and ostraca" (Folmer 1995: 630). Even though within Aramaic itself אגרת is already attested in the Assur ostracon (KAI 233:4 אגרת מלך בבל), dated to the 7th century BCE, its penetration into BH is not documented prior to the Persian period.

c. Evidently, אגרת did not instantly and fully eliminate its Classical counterpart ספר. The coexistence of the two in LBH is particularly conspicuous in the book of Esther, where they occasionally appear side by side without a clear-cut distinction between the different possible meanings (in RH there is an unmistakable distinction between the two: ספר invariably denotes a *book*, a *literary composition* [e.g., ספר התורה], whereas אגרת signifies a *letter* or *legal document* [e.g., אגרת ביקורת, a *document fixing the value of property*; אגרת מזון, a *document relating to alimony*; cf. also RA, אגרת שיבוקין, a *writ of divorce*, e.g., M Giṭ. 9:3 above]. This semantic differentiation is also found in Tg. Aram., which regularly renders ספר *letter* by אגרתא, but ספר *literary composition* by ספרא).

d. In much the same way as in Hebrew, note that *egi/ertu* is a latecomer in the linguistic history of Akkadian; it is classified as Neo-Assyrian, Neo-Late Babylonian (*AHw* I 190a; *CAD* IV [E] 45b–46b).

e. "In conclusion, אגרת penetrated the literary Hebrew lexical stock at some point in the post-exilic period where it shared, together with the already commonly used ספר, the semantic sphere 'letter' " (Bergey 1983: 149).

BIBLIOGRAPHY

AHw I 190a • BDB 8b, 1078a • *CAD* IV [E] 45b–46b • Kaddari 9b

Bendavid 1967–71: I 64 • Bergey 1983: 148–149 • Eskhult 2003: 13, 22 • Folmer 1995: 629–632, 687–689, 712 • Hurvitz 1972: 21–22; 2000a: 150–151 • Joosten 1999: 148 • Kaufman 1974: 48 • Kühlwein 1997: 808–809 • Kutscher 1970: 357, 363, 386 (= 1977: 100, 106, 129); 1972: 128 • Loewenstamm 1962: 966–967 • Mankowski 2000: 22–25, 155, 164 • Muffs 1969: 187 note 4 • Polak 2006b: 120 • Polzin 1976: 126 • Sáenz-Badillos 1993: 117 • von Soden 1966: 8; 1977: 185 • Wagner 1966: 19 no. 3a

אֲדָר pr. n. name of 12th month, derived from Akkad. *addaru*: Esth. 3:7 לְחֹדֶשׁ שְׁנֵים
עָשָׂר הוּא חֹדֶשׁ אֲדָר ,13 ;8:12; 9:1, 15, 17 בְּיוֹם שְׁלוֹשָׁה עָשָׂר לְחֹדֶשׁ אֲדָר; 19, 21

BA אֲדָר Ezra 6:15 יוֹם תְּלָתָה לִירַח אֲדָר

CBH ALTERNATIVES

Months are generally named by their numerical order, e.g., 1 Kgs. 12:32 בַּחֹדֶשׁ
הַשְּׁמִינִי בְּיֶרַח; in a few cases they follow the Canaanite pattern, e.g., 1 Kgs. 8:2
הָאֵתָנִים . Only in the LBH corpus do we find both (the older) numerical system
and (the more recent) Mesopotamian names side by side in one and the same
verse, e.g., Esth. 3:7 לְחֹדֶשׁ שְׁנֵים עָשָׂר הוּא חֹדֶשׁ אֲדָר.

EXTERNAL POST-CLASSICAL SOURCES
Renderings/Paraphrases/Glosses

TPJ 4x, e.g.

למימר	בכרן יומא הדין	בשבעה בירחא **דאדר**	ומליל ה׳ עם משה
[~	לֵאמֹר	בְּעֶצֶם הַיּוֹם הַזֶּה	[וַיְדַבֵּר ה׳ אֶל מֹשֶׁה

Deut. 32:48

Other Sources

דמן נטופה	חלדי	**דאדר**	ירחא	לתריסר	תריסראה
[~	הַנְּטוֹפָתִי	חֶלְדַּי	הַחֹדֶשׁ	עָשָׂר	לִשְׁנֵים	הַשְּׁנֵים עָשָׂר

Tg. 1 Chron. 27:15

Independent Use
Heb.

M Meg. 1:4	קראו את המגילה **באדר** הראשון, נתעברה השנה, קורים אותה **באדר** השיני. אין בין **אדר** הראשון **לאדר** השיני אלא קריאת מגילה ומתנות לאביונים
MekhRI Pisḥa 2 (p. 8)	"שמור את חדש האביב ועשית פסח" (דב׳ טז 1 –) שמור את הפסח לאביב ואביב לפסח, שיבא אביב בזמנו. הא כיצד? עבר את **אדר**
Sifre Num. 44 (p. 49)	נמצינו למדים שבעשרים ושלשה **באדר** התחילו אהרן ובניו המשכן וכל הכלים לימשח. בראש חודש הוקם המשכן. בשני נשרפה פרה...
T Taʿan. 1:7 (Moʿed p. 325)	חצי תשרי מרחשון וחצי כסליו – זרע. חצי כסליו טבת וחצי שבט – חורף. חצי שבט **אדר** וחצי ניסן – קור. חצי ניסן אייר וחצי סיון – קציר. חצי סיון תמוז וחצי אב – קיץ. חצי אב אלול וחצי תשרי – חום
ʿEin Gedi (Naveh 1978: no. 70): 5–7	ניסן אייר סיון תמוז אב אילול תשרי מרחשון כסליו טבית שבט **ואדר**

Aram.

TAD II 3.11 (= Krael. 10):1   ב 20 **לאדר**, הו יום 8 לכיחך, שנת 3 ארתחששש
         מלכא...

EN 96:1   ב 2 **לאדר** שנת 3 פלפס מלכא

EN 11:1–2   ב 25 **לאדר** אחרי [= אדר שני] שנת 2

4Q318 8:1   **אדר**: ב 1 וב 2 דכרא, ב 3 וב 4 תורא

PAT 0923:2–9   ...רבא בר עתעקב בר ידיעבל בר עתעקב עקבי חיא
         שנין...מית יום 4 **באדר** שנת...

Nṣ 8:1 (Yardeni I p. 67)   [...] **לאדר** שנת תלת לחרות ישראל על ימי שמעון בן
         כוסבה נשי ישר[אל בכפ]ר ברו...

1 Tg. Esth. 3:7   בכן שרי שמשי (ס)פרא לצבעא פייסא דעדבין קדם המן...
         ושרי בירחיא. בניסן ולא על מן בגלל זכותא דפיסחא באייר ולא
         על מן בגלל דביה נחת מונא...כד מטא לסוף תריסר ירחי שתא
         דאיהוא ירחא **דאדר**...

Greek

Ant. 11:107   τοῦ δ' ἐνάτου τῆς Δαρείου βασιλείας ἔτους εἰκάδι καὶ τρίτη
         μηνὸς δωδεκάτου ὃς καλεῖται παρὰ μὲν ἡμῖν Ἄδαρ παρὰ δὲ
         Μακεδόσιν Δύστρος

COMMENTS

a. Akkadian month-name forms throughout our entries (אֲדָר, אֱלוּל, טֵבֵת, כִּסְלֵו, שְׁבָט, סִיוָן, נִיסָן) follow Kaufman 1974: 114–115.

b. "The names of the months found in MH...are of Sumerian-Akkadian origin...A few of these names already turn up in LBH, e.g., אֱלוּל, נִיסָן, etc. In SBH the names are still in Canaanite-Hebrew, e.g. חֹדֶשׁ הָאָבִיב (Ex 13,4) for the later נִיסָן and זִו (I Kings 6,1) for the later אִיָּר" (Kutscher 1982: 49 §72).

c. "[T]he numeral month names were in use in Hebrew throughout the first millennium B.C.E. They persist also in the late biblical books.... Only toward the end of the Second Temple period did the Babylonian names replace the numeral system" (D. Talshir and Z. Talshir 2004: 554). "The Hebrew Bible, then, exhibits at least traces of three methods for naming months: with names, some of which are attested in Canaanite sources; by ordinal numbers; and by Babylonian month names. But in no case does one learn the lengths of all the months, nor is intercalary procedure ever described" (Vanderkam 1992: 816).

d. It was noted that "[t]he Imperial Aramaic names are clearly derived from the NB/LB calendar" (Kaufman 1974: 114). The (late) Babylonian provenance of the month-names was acknowledged in Talmudic literature as well; cf. PT RoshH 1:1 (p. 664) (2 ח א״מל) "שמות חדשים עלו בידם מבבל. בראשונה "בירח האיתנים
...בראשונה "בירח בול" (מל״א ו 38)...בראשונה "בירח זיו" (מל״א ו 37)...מיכן והילך

"ויהי בחודש ניסן שנת עשרים" (נחמ׳ ב 1) "ויהי בחודש כסליו שנת עשרים" (נחמ׳ א 1)
"בחודש העשירי הוא חודש טבת" (אסתר ב 16)

e. In sharp contrast to its linguistic environment, Qumran literature does not make regular use of the Babylonian month-names, most probably reflecting "what obstinate resistance there was in some religious circles. In spite of it, however, the Babylonian month-names were in the end accepted by orthodox Judaism" (de Vaux 1965: I 185).

BIBLIOGRAPHY

BDB 12b; 294b • *HALOT* I 16b • Kaddari 13a

Friedberg 2000: 561–565 • Kaufman 1974: 114–115 • Kutscher 1974: 114; 1982: 49 §72 • Morgenstern 1924 • Naveh 1978: 153 • Schrader 1885–88: I 68–70 • D. Talshir and Z. Talshir 2004: 549–555 • Vanderkam 1992: 816 • de Vaux 1965: I 185–186 • Wagner 1966: 20–21 no. 4

[אֲדַרְכֹּן] n. m. *drachma* (δραχμή): Ezra 8:27 וּכְפֹרֵי זָהָב עֶשְׂרִים לַאֲדַרְכֹנִים אָלֶף וּכְלֵי
וַיִּתְּנוּ לַעֲבוֹדַת בֵּית הָאֱלֹהִים זָהָב…וַאֲדַרְכֹנִים…1 Chron. 29:7; נְחֹשֶׁת מֶצְהָב טוֹבָה שְׁנַיִם
וְכֶסֶף…
Cf. דַּרְכְּמוֹן

CBH ALTERNATIVES
Cf. comment c below.

EXTERNAL POST-CLASSICAL SOURCES
Renderings/Paraphrases/Glosses
LXX Gen. 24:22   ἐνώτια χρυσᾶ ἀνὰ **δραχμὴν**   ὁλκῆς
[~   [נֶזֶם זָהָב **בֶּקַע** מִשְׁקָלוֹ

LXX Exod. 38:26 (39:3)   **δραχμὴ**   μία τῇ κεφαλῇ
[~   **בֶּקַע** לַגֻּלְגֹּלֶת]

Independent Use
Heb.
M Sheq. 2:4   שכשעלו ישראל מן הגולה היו שקלים **דרכונות**
M BB 10:2   כתוב בו: …**דרכונות** דיאינן ונימחקו – אין פחות משנים
T Sheq. 2:4 (Moʻed p. 206)   זו היתה עשירה מכולם שהיו בה איסטראות של זהב
ודריאכונות של זהב
T BB 11:2 (Nez. p. 167)   הנושא ונותן עם חבירו בשוק ואמ' לו: דהב דאת חייב לי –
אין פחות מדינר של זהב. **דריאבון**[!] – נותן לו כל מה
סדריאבון[!] שוה

Aram.
Vööbus 52:18–22 (Syr.)   אן נוזף גברא לגברא **דריכונא** [ומשכנא] לא סים לה
וכרטיסא לא עבד לה…לא שליט למוזפנא דנסב משכנא
מן קנינה דהו חיבא או מן נכסוהי

Phoen.
KAI 60:1–6 (1st cent. BCE)   …לעטר אית שמעבעל בן מגן…עטרת חרץ
בדרכנם 20 למחת…ישאן בכסף אלם בעל צדן
דרכמנם 20 למחת…

Greek (LXX)
Tob. 5:15   ἀλλ᾿ εἰπόν μοι τίνα σοι ἔσομαι μισθὸν διδόναι **δραχμὴν**
τῆς ἡμέρας καὶ τὰ δέοντά σοι ὡς καὶ τῷ υἱῷ μου

Comments

a. "In the Old Testament, there are two similar words that appear to refer to coins in texts of the Persian period: *ᵃdarkōnîm* . . . and *darkᵉmōnîm*. . . . [C]ertainly on the surface the most attractive suggestion [is] . . . seeing Drachmas in *darkᵉmōnîm* and Darics in *ᵃdarkaōnîm*, the *mem* of *darkᵉmōnîm* being the distinguishing factor. In both cases, the *-ōn* ending would reflect the Greek genitive plural. Both types of coins were, of course, current in the Persian period" (Williamson 1977b: 125). Or, in a different formulation, "[t]he word אדרכון—in terms of its form—is none other than the דריכוס, which is the Persian *sheqel* of gold; whereas the דרכמון is the Greek δραχμή" (Avi-Yonah and Liver 1962: 823). It is noteworthy that the spellings דרכנם (= אדרכונים?) and דרכמנם (= דרכמונים) were used interchangeably in the Phoenician inscription from Piraeus quoted above (*KAI* 60:1–6), which may imply that the two Biblical terms were synonymous. There are, however, alternative explanations for the Phoenician evidence (cf., e.g., Cooke 1903: 96). Be that as it may, regardless of the precise meaning and function of אדרכון and דרכמון—whether they are simply two variant forms of a single lexeme or two distinct currencies; whether one of them is borrowed from Persian and the other from Greek, or both are loans from one and the same language—their very appearance in the Bible (Ezra, Nehemiah, and Chronicles) must be assigned to post-Exilic times and reflects—historically—the Second Temple vocabulary of BH.

b. It is interesting to observe that "[i]n 1 Chron. 29:7, the text lists the total contributions donated to the . . . Temple in the days of David in *ᵃdarkōnîm* of gold, and this is certainly an anachronism. . . . The writer availed himself of the language that was current in his day" (Avi-Yonah and Liver 1962: 823). In a somewhat different formulation, it has been noted that "[t]he appearance of darics in the time of David and Solomon—four centuries before their actual use—is a clear anachronism" (Klein 2006: 536). And similarly, "the Chronicler employs . . . new words even in cases where they are out of place as being entirely anachronistic . . . [I]n 1 Chron. 29, 7 אדרכן is used about David's raising money for the building of the Temple" (Eskhult 2003: 13). For further cases of the Chronicler's introduction of linguistic and historical anachronisms into texts describing pre-Exilic events and episodes, see the entries עֲזָרָה, גִּנְזַךְ, בִּירָה.

c. Minted coinage was apparently unknown before the Persian period, as indicated by the fact that the standard reference literature dealing with Ancient Near Eastern numismatics begins its coverage only in this period (see, e.g., Meshorer 1982; Japhet 1993: 508). Thus, the historical and linguistic evidence adduced above is firmly corroborated by the archaeological-numismatic data.

d. On the linguistic lateness of Persian loanwords in general in BH, see Proleg. §II.3 Linguistic Affinities, *Persian Loanwords*; the entry גֶּנֶז, comment **b.**

e. Note the tradition cited in M Sheq. 2:4, quoted above, which clearly states that after the return from exile the older measure of weight, *sheqalim*, was replaced by *darkonot*.

BIBLIOGRAPHY

BDB 12b, 204a • *HALOT* I 17a • Ben-Iehuda I 77a note 4

Avi-Yonah and Liver 1962: 823 • Cooke 1903: 96–97 • Curtis and Madsen 1910: 29 no. 22 • S. R. Driver 1913: 539–540 • Eskhult 2003: 12–13 • Japhet 1993: 508 • Klein 2006: 536 • Meshorer 1982 • Mussies 1992: 195 • Seow 1996: 647 • Williamson 1977b: 125

אַחֲרֵי (כָּל) זֹאת / אַחַר זֶה adv. phr. *after that, following this*: וַיְחִי אִיּוֹב אַחֲרֵי Job 42:16 וְעַתָּה מַה נֹּאמַר אֱלֹהֵינוּ (cf. Hurvitz 1974b: 24–25); Ezra 9:10 זֹאת מֵאָה וְאַרְבָּעִים שָׁנָה אַחַר זֶה שָׁלַח סַנְחֵרִיב מֶלֶךְ 2 Chron. 21:18 וְאַחֲרֵי כָּל זֹאת נְגָפוֹ ה' בְּמֵעָיו 32:9; אַחֲרֵי זֹאת אַחֲרֵי כָל זֹאת...עָלָה נְכוֹ...לְהִלָּחֵם בְּכַרְכְּמִישׁ 35:20; אַשּׁוּר עֲבָדָיו יְרוּשָׁלְָיְמָה

בָּאתַר דְּנָה חֲזֵה 7:6, 7; אֱלָהּ רַב הוֹדַע לְמַלְכָּא מָה דִּי לֶהֱוֵא **אַחֲרֵי דְנָה** BA Dan. 2:29, 45 הֲוֵית בְּחֶזְוֵי לֵילְיָא

CBH ALTERNATIVES

כן (אחר(י) (ויהי), e.g.

וַיְהִי אַחֲרֵי **כֵן**	וַיַּךְ דָּוִ(י)ד אֶת פְּלִשְׁתִּים וַיַּכְנִיעֵם (2 Sam. 8:1 (‖ 1 Chron. 18:1			
וְאַחֲרֵי] **כָּל זֹאת** נְגָפוֹ ה' [~ 2 Chron. 21:18				

וַיְהִי אַחֲרֵי כֵן וַיִּקְבֹּץ בֶּן הֲדַד מֶלֶךְ אֲרָם אֶת כָּל מַחֲנֵהוּ... עַל שֹׁמְרוֹן 2 Kgs. 6:24				
אַחַר זֶה] שָׁלַח סַנְחֵרִיב מֶלֶךְ אַשּׁוּר עֲבָדָיו יְרוּשָׁלַיְמָה [~ 2 Chron. 32:9				

בְּיָמָיו	עָלָה... מֶלֶךְ מִצְרַיִם עַל מֶלֶךְ אַשּׁוּר עַל נְהַר פְּרָת 2 Kgs. 23:29					
אַחֲרֵי כָל זֹאת...] עָלָה... מֶלֶךְ מִצְרַיִם לְהִלָּחֵם... עַל פְּרָת [~ 2 Chron. 35:20						

(cf. comment **b** below)

EXTERNAL POST-CLASSICAL SOURCES
Renderings/Paraphrases/Glosses

TN 35x, e.g.

ובתר כדן תיעול לוותה ותזדמן לוותה ותיסב יתה לך לאתה Deut. 21:13					
וְאַחַר כֵּן] תָּבוֹא אֵלֶיהָ וּבְעַלְתָּהּ וְהָיְתָה לְךָ לְאִשָּׁה [~					

TPJ 47x, e.g.

ובתר כדין נפק אחוי וידיה אחידא בעקיבא דעשו Gen. 25:26							
וְאַחֲרֵי כֵן] יָצָא אָחִיו וְיָדוֹ אֹחֶזֶת בַּעֲקֵב עֵשָׂו [~							

Independent Use
Aram.

[...] **באתר דנה** ...[4Q551 f3:3

וכדי אהך לבית עלמי תהון רשיה ושליטה אתרי מתנתא דא או במה NH 7:15–17 די א[שבוק מנהון וד]י לא אשתרהן] ולא אתזבן לפרנוס נפשי מן (Yardeni I p. 96) **באתר דנה**...למקנא ולמזבנו ולמנחל ולמורתו...

וכן אמ' [שמואל הקטן] בשעת מיתתו: שמעו' וישמע' לחרבא ושאר כל העם   Semaḥ. 8:7
לביזא ועקן סגיאין יהון **אחרי דנה**. ובל שוון[!] ארמית אמרן

COMMENTS

a. "Adverbials of time are expressed in several ways in Biblical Hebrew. In Late Biblical Hebrew there arose the expression אחר זה . . . perhaps under the influence of אחרי דנה or באתר דנה in Imperial Aramaic, as well as אחרי זאת . . . [and] "אחרי כל זאת" (D. Talshir 1987a: 167). Note that the number of 'function words', like אחר(י), אחר(י), הדברים האלה, כן אחר, is usually rather "limited and their formation unchanging within a single linguistic phase. The many changes that took place between one phase and the next are evidently instructive not only regarding the function words themselves, but also regarding the essential nature of the linguistic framework in general, that is to say the creativity and productivity of the intermediate period (Late Biblical Hebrew)" (ibid., 166).

b. Commenting on 2 Chron. 35:20 אַחֲרֵי כָל זֹאת . . . עָלָה נְכוֹ מֶלֶךְ מִצְרַיִם לְהִלָּחֵם בְּכַרְכְּמִישׁ, Z. Talshir (1996: 222 note 30) remarks: "[t]his formulation is undoubtedly the Chronicler's contribution. He similarly designs other links; cf. 'And after all this [ve'ḥry kl z't] the Lord smote him . . .' (2 Ch. xxi 18, not in Kings). In Classical Biblical Hebrew phrases such as 'ḥry hdbrym h'lh, 'ḥry kn would be expected. Late Biblical Hebrew uses 'ḥry z't on other occasions (Ezra ix 10; Job xlii 16), though not as an introductory formula."

c. The omission of CBH וַיְהִי from the idiom וַיְהִי אַחַר/אַחֲרֵי is just one example of a continual, wide-ranging process in which this particle fell into disuse and gradually disappeared from the later strata of ancient Hebrew. To be sure, וַיְהִי was still common in BH as a whole—including the book of Esther, which belongs to the distinctive LBH corpus—"to mark the modifier that opens a new action sequence (Esth. 1.1; 2.8; 3.4; 5.1, 2), as found in CBH. . . . On the other hand, in many sentences he [the author] brings the infinitive clause without ויהי (1.2, 4, 5, 10; 2.1, 8, 12, 15, 19; 9.25), as found often in Chronicles and Ezra-Nehemiah. These phenomena indicate the retreat of the classical style and syntax, and thus the influence of the colloquial" (Polak 2003: 96).

BIBLIOGRAPHY

BDB 29b

Hurvitz 1974b: 24–25 • Polak 2003: 96 • D. Talshir 1987a: 166–167 • Z. Talshir 1996: 222 note 30

אֵין + inf. *may not + inf., it is not permitted to, it is not possible to, there is no need to*: Qoh. 3:14; Esth. 4:2; 8:8 אֵין לְהָשִׁיב...נִכְתָּב בְּשֵׁם הַמֶּלֶךְ כִּי כְתָב אֲשֶׁר; Ezra 9:15 וְגַם לַלְוִיִּם אֵין לָשֵׂאת 1 Chron. 23:26; הִנְנוּ לְפָנֶיךָ בְּאַשְׁמָתֵינוּ כִּי אֵין לַעֲמוֹד לְפָנֶיךָ עַל זֹאת הֲלֹא 20:6; כָּל הַכֹּהֲנִים הַנִּמְצָאִים הִתְקַדָּשׁוּ אֵין לִשְׁמוֹר לְמַחְלְקוֹת 2 Chron. 5:11; אֶת הַמִּשְׁכָּן וְהַשֹּׁעֲרִים לְשַׁעַר וָשַׁעַר אֵין לָהֶם לָסוּר 35:15; אַתָּה הוּא אֱלֹהִים בַּשָּׁמַיִם...וְאֵין עִמְּךָ לְהִתְיַצֵּב מֵעַל עֲבֹדָתָם

CBH ALTERNATIVES

לֹא + impf., e.g.

Deut. 4:2	**וְלֹא תִגְרְעוּ** מִמֶּנּוּ	עַל הַדָּבָר אֲשֶׁר אָנֹכִי מְצַוֶּה אֶתְכֶם	**לֹא תֹסִפוּ**
Deut. 13:1	**וְלֹא תִגְרַע** מִמֶּנּוּ	עָלָיו	**לֹא תֹסֵף**
[~ Qoh. 3:14	**אֵין לִגְרֹעַ**	וּמִמֶּנּוּ	עָלָיו] **אֵין לְהוֹסִיף**

Deut. 7:24	**יִתְיַצֵּב** אִישׁ בְּפָנֶיךָ עַד הִשְׁמִדְךָ אֹתָם	**לֹא**
Ps. 5:6	**יִתְיַצְּבוּ** הוֹלְלִים לְנֶגֶד עֵינֶיךָ	**לֹא**
[~ 2 Chron. 20:6	וּבְיָדְךָ כֹּחַ וּגְבוּרָה] וְאֵין עִמְּךָ **לְהִתְיַצֵּב**	

Deut. 24:10	אֶל בֵּיתוֹ לַעֲבֹט עֲבֹטוֹ	**לֹא תָבֹא**
[~ Esth. 4:2	אֶל שַׁעַר הַמֶּלֶךְ בִּלְבוּשׁ שָׂק	כִּי] **אֵין לָבוֹא**

POST-CLASSICAL EXTERNAL SOURCES

Independent Use

Heb.

CD 4:10–12	וּבִשְׁלוֹם הַקֵּץ לְמִסְפַּר הַשָּׁנִים הָאֵלֶּה **אֵין** עוֹד **לְהִשְׁתַּפֵּחַ** לְבֵית יְהוּדָה כִּי אִם לַעֲמוֹד אִישׁ עַל מְצוּדוֹ
1QS 3:16	וּבִהְיוֹתָם לִתְעוּדוֹתָם כְּמַחֲשֶׁבֶת כְּבוֹדוֹ יְמַלְאוּ פְּעֻלָּתָם **וְאֵין לְהִשְׁנוֹת**
1QHa 16:35	וְרַגְלִי נִלְכָּדָה בְּכֶבֶל וַיֵּלְכוּ כְּמַיִם בִּרְכַּי **וְאֵין לִשְׁלוֹחַ** פַּעַם וְלֹא מִצְעָד לְקוֹל רַגְלִי
1QHa 20:33–34	[...] לְסַפֵּר כֹּל כְּבוֹדְכָה וְלֹהִתְיַצֵּב לִפְנֵי אַפְּכָה **וְאֵין לְהָשִׁיב** דָּבָר עַל תּוֹכַחְתְּכָה
1Q34bis f3ii:2	[...] **וְאֵין לַעֲבוֹר** חֻקֵּיהֶם
4Q396 f1–2iii:11	[...] **אֵין לְהַאֲכִילָם** מֵהַקֳּ[דָ]שִׁים
BS (B) 10:23	**אֵין לִבְזֹת** דַּל מַשְׂכִּיל **וְאֵין לְכַבֵּד** כָּל אִישׁ חָמָס
BS (B) 39:21	**אֵין לֵאמֹר** זֶה רַע מִזֶּה כִּי הַכֹּל בְּעִתּוֹ יִגְבַּר
MekhRI Vayehi 6 (p. 112)	"וְהוּא בְאֶחָד וּמִי יְשִׁיבֶנּוּ וְנַפְשׁוֹ אִוְּתָה וַיָּעַשׂ" (אִיּוֹב כג 13) – דָּן יְחִידִי לְכָל בָּאֵי הָעוֹלָם **וְאֵין לְהָשִׁיב** עַל דְּבָרָיו...וּמָה אַתָּה מְקַיֵּם "וְהוּא בְאֶחָד וּמִי יְשִׁיבֶנּוּ"?...**אֵין לְהָשִׁיב** עַל דִּבְרֵי מִי שֶׁאָמַר וְהָיָה הָעוֹלָם

Sifre Deut. 307 (p. 344)   "תמים פעלו" (דב' לב 4) – פעולתו שלימה עם כל באי
                             העולם **ואין להרהר** אחר מעשיו אפילו עילה של כלום

COMMENTS

a. "The combination *ʾêyn* + *liqtōl*—that is, *ʾêyn* negating the infinitive construct
with *l-*—is a syntactical construction not very frequently attested in Biblical
Hebrew.... Meaning, basically, 'it is not possible to ...', 'there is no need to ...',
it occurs some ten times in the OT—almost always in the distinctively late
books of Esther, Ezra and Chronicles. *ʾêyn* + *liqtōl* is common in the DSS as
well carrying, semantically, the sense of a prohibition" (Hurvitz 1990: 145–146).
"The modal use of the infinitive with ־ל (לקטל) is typical of LBH, of QH, and
of Aramaic, but is only rarely found in MH" (Qimron and Strugnell 1994: 80).
In addition, "[f]ive times in Ben Sira we find the syntagm אין לקטל without an
intervening element.... Thus we find אין לאמר 'one should not say' ..., אין לבזות
'it is not proper to despise ...', and ... ואין לבקש 'there is no need to seek' ..." (van
Peursen 1999: 227). In sum, "[f]or the expression of a negative command both
לא תקטל and אין לקטל are used.... The difference between the two expressions
is primarily diachronic: אין לקטל is characteristic of later Hebrew" (van Peursen
1999: 238; see also Kutscher 1971: 1588a).

b. In contrast to the prevailing view presented above, it has been claimed that
the supporters of a late date for אֵין + inf. *may not/need not* "list numerous LBH
references... However, the EBH [= CBH] instance in 1 Sm 9:7 אֵין־לְהָבִיא 'not
able to bring' is missing from their lists. Consequently, there is no chronological value to this comparison. Equally EBH and LBH" (Fredericks 1988: 132–133).
This statement is erroneous (cf. Proleg. §IV): (1) Statistically, the LBH corpus
comprises but a small fraction of the entire Hebrew Bible. Consequently, if
eight out of nine occurrences of אֵין + inf. *may not/cannot/need not* are documented in this limited corpus, one is more than justified in regarding the phenomenon under examination here as a feature typically characteristic of LBH;
(2) Regardless of statistics, 1 Sam. 9:7 וּתְשׁוּרָה אֵין לְהָבִיא לְאִישׁ הָאֱלֹהִים cannot
be considered, either semantically or syntactically, as a case of the characteristically late אֵין + inf. structure discussed in this entry. Its meaning in no
way bears the notion of *prohibition, impossibility*, or *needlessness*, but rather
predicates the nonexistence of something (cf. the standard translations, e.g.,
KJV—"and there is not a present to bring to the man of God"; JPS—"and there
is nothing we can bring to the man of God as a present"). This is because the
structure of 1 Sam. 9:7, i.e., the negative particle אֵין preceding the infinitive
לְהָבִיא, at first glance resembles the characteristically late syntagm under discussion, but, as a matter of fact, it largely differs syntactically from the latter. Unquestionably, the syntactic element negated by אֵין in 1 Sam. 9:7 is not
the infinitive, but a noun (תְּשׁוּרָה), and this becomes clear when it is realized

that the order of the words could just as easily have been וְאֵין תְּשׁוּרָה לְהָבִיא לְאִישׁ הָאֱלֹהִים. Syntactically, then, this verse is no different from verses such as Gen. 19:31 וְאִישׁ אֵין בָּאָרֶץ לָבוֹא עָלֵינוּ כְּדֶרֶךְ כָּל הָאָרֶץ, which means וְאֵין אִישׁ בָּאָרֶץ לָבוֹא עָלֵינוּ כְּדֶרֶךְ כָּל הָאָרֶץ 'there is no man in the land to come...'; and Num. 20:5 וּמַיִם אַיִן לִשְׁתּוֹת, which means וְאֵין מַיִם לִשְׁתּוֹת 'there is no water to drink'. Conversely, in the LBH examples adduced above, אֵין negates the infinitive, not the noun, and the word order cannot be reversed. Thus, despite its apparent similarity to the late syntagm in question, 1 Sam. 9:7 is irrelevant to our discussion. It "has nothing to do with prohibition; it means 'there is nothing to bring to the man of God'. . . . The use of the אין לקטול construction in the prohibitive sense is found only in Late Biblical Hebrew" (Seow 1996: 663–664).

c. 2 Chron. 14:10 אֵין עִמְּךָ לַעְזוֹר בֵּין רַב לְאֵין כֹּחַ does not carry the semantic nuance of the 'prohibitive sense' (cf. NJPS, KJV, NRSV) and therefore is not included in this discussion (note, however, that this verse, too, seems to bear the linguistic style of the Second Temple period).

d. It is noteworthy that the diachronic development 'לֹא + imperfect' → 'אֵין + infinitive', attested in the linguistic history of BH (cf. above), is in perfect harmony with the corresponding shift of 'אַל + imperfect' → 'לֹא + infinitive' observable in NWS epigraphy (Canaanite-Hebrew-Aramaic-Punic):

Tabnit (Phoen. [*KAI* 13: 3–4])	**תפתח** עלתי	**אל**	אל	אדם ...	כל	את	מי
Eshmunʿazar (Phoen. [*KAI* 14: 4])	ז **יפתח** אית משכב	**אל**		אדם ...	כל	את	קנמי
Silwan (Heb. [*KAI* 191: B 2])	**זאת**	**יפתח** את	אשר	האדֹם			ארור
versus							
King Uzziah (Aram. [*MPAT* 70: 1–4])	**למפתח**[!]	**ולא**		עוזיה ...[!]	לכה התית טסי[ן]
Qidron epitaph (Aram. [*MPAT* 71: 1–3])	**למפתח** לעל[ם]	**ולא**		אבהתנ[ה]
Zybqit (Punic [*KAI* 70: 4])	**לפתח**	**אבל**					

e. All in all, the lateness of the prohibitive syntactical construction 'אֵין + infinitive' may be established definitively on the basis of a rich variety of sources dated to the Second Temple period—Biblical and extra-Biblical, Hebrew and Aramaic, literary and epigraphic alike. "The writers of the sectarian scrolls tried to imitate SBH, but... [s]ome characteristics indicate that their language should be in some respect considered as an offshoot of LBH, especially Chronicles.... A case in point is the employment of the infinitive construct plus לא for the prohibitive, e.g., ולוא לצעוד 'they must not walk' (1QS 1:13). This construction, which is practically absent from SBH [= CBH], is all the more interesting since it crops up in the languages spoken in Jerusalem at the time, as we see from Aramaic and Greek inscriptions of Jerusalem (and also in Punic, i.e. late Canaanite of North Africa)" (Kutscher 1982: 99 §161).

BIBLIOGRAPHY

BDB 34b • JM 570–571, §160 *j*

Bergey 1983: 75–77 • Carmignac 1974 • Davila 1991: 821 • S. R. Driver 1892: 274 §202; 1913b: 538 note 40 • Fassberg 2000: 55 • Fensham 1982: 23 • Fredericks 1988: 132–133 • Hurvitz 1990: 145–147 • Kutscher 1971: 1588a; 1982: 99 §161 • Paton 1908: 62–63 • Qimron 1986: 78–79 §400.12 • Qimron and Strugnell 1994: 80 • Rooker 2003: 45–47 • Schoors 1992–2004: I 183 • Segal 1911–12: 139 • Seow 1996: 663–664 • Williamson 1977a: 50 • van Peursen 1999: 227–238

אֱלוּל pr. n. name of 6th month, derived from Akkad. *e/ilūlu*: Neh. 6:15 וַתִּשְׁלַם
הַחוֹמָה בְּעֶשְׂרִים וַחֲמִשָּׁה לֶאֱלוּל

CBH ALTERNATIVES

Months are generally named by their numerical order, e.g., 1 Kgs. 12:32 בַּחֹדֶשׁ
הַשְּׁמִינִי; in a few cases they follow the Canaanite pattern, e.g., 1 Kgs. 8:2 בְּיֶרַח
הָאֵתָנִים. Only in the LBH corpus do we find both (the older) numerical system
and (the more recent) Mesopotamian names side by side in one and the same
verse; e.g., Esth. 3:7 לְחֹדֶשׁ שְׁנֵים עָשָׂר הוּא חֹדֶשׁ אֲדָר.

EXTERNAL POST-CLASSICAL SOURCES
Renderings/Paraphrases/Glosses
TPJ IX

Num. 14:37	במותנא **באלול** יומן בשבעא	...גובריא ומיתו
[~	בְּמַגֵּפָה	וַיָּמֻתוּ] הָאֲנָשִׁים מוֹצִאֵי דִבַּת הָאָרֶץ רָעָה

Other Sources

Tg. 1 Chron. 27:9	דמן תקוע	עקש	בר	עירא	**דאלול** **לירחא** אשתאה
[~	הַתְּקוֹעִי	עִקֵּשׁ	בֶּן	עִירָא	הַשִּׁשִּׁי] **לַחֹדֶשׁ** **הַשִּׁשִּׁי**

Independent Use
Heb.

Mur. 29:1 (Yardeni I p. 48)	...ב 14 **לאלול** שֹנֹת 2 לגאלת ישראל
M Bekh. 9:5	ר' מאיר או': באחד **באלול** ראש שנה למעשר בהמה.
	בן עזיי אומ': **האלוליין** מתעשרין בפני עצמן
T RoshH 1:10 (Mo'ed p. 307)	המודר הנאה מחבירו לשנה נדר הימנו שנים עשר
	חדש מיום ליום. אם אמ' לשנה זו, אפי" לא נדר
	הימנו אלא מאחד **באלול** אין לו אלא עד אחד בתשרי
T Ta'an. 1:7 (Mo'ed p. 325)	חצי תשרי מרחשון וחצי כסליו – זרע. חצי כסליו
	טבת וחצי שבט – חורף. חצי שבט אדר וחצי ניסן – קור.
	חצי ניסן אייר וחצי סיון – קציר. חצי סיון תמוז וחצי
	אב – קיץ. חצי אב **אלול** וחצי תשרי – חום
'Ein Gedi (Naveh 1978:	ניסן אייר סיון תמוז אב **אילול** תשרי מרחשון
no. 70): 5–7	כסליו טבית שבט ואדר
Aram.	
EN 6:1–2	...ב 4 **לאלול** שנת 1 חלפת נשיף
EN 58:1–2	...ב 7 **לאלול** שנת 6 עבדאדה לחנאל
Cooke 78:3–4 (Nab.)	...בירח **אלול** שנת 1 לחרתת מלך נבטו
4Q345 f1R:1	...ב **באלול** שֹ]נת
NḤ 1:1 (Yardeni I p. 271)	בתמונה **באלול** שנת עשרין ותלת לרבאל מלכא מלך נבטו

NṢ 11:1 (Yardeni I p. 124)	...**לאלול** שנת תמנה...
1 Tg. Esth. 3:7	בכן שרי שמשי (ס)פרא לצבעא פייסא דעדבין קדם המן...
	ושרי בירחיא. בניסן ולא על מן בגלל זכותא דפיסחא...
	באלול לא על מן בגלל דביה סליק משה בטורא דסיני
	למסב לוחין אוחרניתא...כד מטא לסוף תריסר ירחי
	שתא דאיהוא ירחא דאדר...

Greek (LXX)

| 1 Macc. 14:27 | Ὀκτωκαιδεκάτῃ Ελουλ ἔτους δευτέρου καὶ ἑβδομηκοστοῦ καὶ ἑκατοστοῦ—καὶ τοῦτο τρίτον ἔτος ἐπὶ Σιμωνος ἀρχιερέως μεγάλου |

COMMENTS

a. See the entry אֲדָר for general comments on month-names and the bibliography there. See also BDB 47a.

אֶרֶץ יִשְׂרָאֵל comp. g. n. *the Land of Israel*: [1 Sam. 13:19; 2 Kgs. 5:2, 4; 6:23—see comment **a** below] Ezek. 27:17; 40:2; 47:18; 1 Chron. 22:2; 2 Chron. 2:16; 30:25 וַיִּשְׂמְחוּ כָּל קְהַל יְהוּדָה וְהַכֹּהֲנִים וְהַלְוִיִּם וְכָל הַקָּהָל הַבָּאִים מִיִּשְׂרָאֵל וְהַגֵּרִים הַבָּאִים מֵאֶרֶץ יִשְׂרָאֵל וְהַיּוֹשְׁבִים בִּיהוּדָה; 34:7; (1 Chron. 13:2 אַחֵינוּ הַנִּשְׁאָרִים בְּכֹל אַרְצוֹת יִשְׂרָאֵל; see comment **d** below).

CBH Alternatives
ארץ כנען, ישראל, הארץ

External Post-Classical Sources
Renderings/Paraphrases/Glosses
TN 1x

וחמא מן שירויא ארום טב הוה וית **ארעא דישראל** ארום שמינין פריה							Gen. 49:15
[וַיַּרְא מְנֻחָה כִּי טוֹב וְאֶת הָאָרֶץ כִּי נָעֵמָה							~]

TPJ 16x, e.g.

ואיתן שלמא **בארעא דישראל** ... ואיבטיל רשות חיות ברא מן **ארעא דישראל**		Lev. 26:6
[וְנָתַתִּי שָׁלוֹם בָּאָרֶץ ... וְהִשְׁבַּתִּי חַיָּה רָעָה מִן הָאָרֶץ		~]

TJ 76x, e.g.

ושדוכת **ארעא דישראל** ארבעין שנין		Judg. 5:31
[וַתִּשְׁקֹט הָאָרֶץ אַרְבָּעִים שָׁנָה		~]

ואתברו פלשתאי ולא אוסיפו עוד למיעל בתחום **ארעא דישראל**		1 Sam. 7:13
[וַיִּכָּנְעוּ הַפְּלִשְׁתִּים וְלֹא יָסְפוּ עוֹד לָבוֹא בִּגְבוּל יִשְׂרָאֵל		~]

Other Sources
Tg. Ps. 76:9

ארעא דעמי דחילת			
ארעא דישראל שדוכת			
[אֶרֶץ יָרְאָה וְשָׁקָטָה			~]

MekhRI Amalek 2 (pp. 182–183)   "את **הארץ** הטובה" (דב׳ ג 25)—זו **ארץ ישר׳**

Independent Use
Heb.

הנטע **בארץ ישראל** כראשית הוא לכוהנים ומעשר הבקר והצון לכוהנים הוא	4Q396 f1–2iii:2–4
ואם עם רב בא **לארץ ישראל** ושלחו עמו חמישית אנשי המלחמה	11QT 58:6–7

M Orlah 3:9	ספק העורלה. **בארץ ישרא׳** אסור ובסורייה מותר, ובחוצה לארץ
	יורד ולוקח ובלבד שלא יראנו לוקט
M Yev. 16:7	שמעתי שאין משיאין את האשה **בארץ ישר׳** על פי עד אחד...
T Ber. 3:15	העומדים בחוצה לארץ מכוונין את לבם כנגד **ארץ ישראל**, שנ׳
(Zer. pp. 15–16)	"ויתפללו[!] דרך ארצם" (דה״ב ו 38)
MekhRI Pisḥa 1 (p. 2)	ועד שלא נבחרה **ארץ ישר׳** היו כל הארצות כשרות לדברות.
	משנבחרה **ארץ ישראל** יצאו כל הארצות

Aram.

4Q198 f1:7	יתבין **בארע ישראל** כלהֹוֹ[ן]
PT Shev. 4:9 (p. 192)	ר׳ יוסי בן חנינה מנשק לכיפתא דעכו ואמ׳: עד כה היא
	ארעא דיש׳
Gen. Rab. 33:6 (p. 311)	דלא טפת **ארעא דיש׳** במבולה
Gen. Rab. 96:5 (p. 1240)	ר׳ מאיר דמך באסייה. אמ׳ לבני **ארעא דישראל:** הא
	משיחכון דידכון אפילו כן צווה ואמר תנו ארוני בים שהוא
	ארץ ישראל

COMMENTS

a. "The expression ארץ ישראל is rare in BH but very common in MH. In BH it is found more in the later books than in the earlier ones, and on the few occasions where it is found in the early books it does not denote a country as a complete geographical unit, but as either the area of Israelite settlement (Jos 11:22 [ארץ בני ישראל], 1 Sam 13:19), or the area of the kingdom of the ten tribes (2 Kgs 5:2, 6:23). ... It is ... clear that in MMT (as in 11QT[a] 58:6) the term denotes the whole of the land of Israel as a geographical entity, or rather as an entity constituted by its purity and by the purity of its inhabitants. ... It appears that for halakhic purposes ארץ ישראל was preferred, while in other types of literature the historical name for the southern kingdom and the Persian province (Aramaic יהוד), יהודה (ארץ) = 'Judaea', continued to be used" (Qimron and Strugnell 1994: 88).

b. "It is an open question whether ארץ ישראל in the later writings (e.g. Ezek 40:3, 1 Chr 22:2, 2 Chr 2:16) refers to a geographical unit comprising the whole country" (Qimron and Strugnell 1994: 88). In all events, in the latter passages quoted from Chronicles, as well as in 2 Chron. 30:25, ארץ ישראל is mentioned in contexts from the days of David and Solomon, yet this term was never used in descriptions relating to these two kings in the historiographical books of Samuel and Kings. Whatever the precise meaning of ארץ ישראל in these three verses, its very appearance in Chronicles in connection with the United Monarchy may be regarded as an anachronism.

c. As in the case of certain other distinctive LBH features, use of the idiom אֶרֶץ יִשְׂרָאֵל is not limited solely to late material; the phrase also occurs, albeit sporadically, in Biblical material generally thought to be early (in this case, the books of Samuel and Kings). Whatever its exact nuance there—whether referring to the entire territory populated by the Israelite tribes or to a portion thereof—the idiom's status as a marker of linguistic lateness is manifested not in exclusively late attestations, but rather in markedly intensified late usage. Indeed, the anomalous use of several distinctive LBH features is known in CBH, where such usage "may be admissible ... but ... isolated, rare, and unproductive" (Bendavid 1967–71: I 127; cf. also I 151); their usage becomes prevalent and characteristic only in late material. In slightly different formulations, "[a]nother feature often observable in Hebrew of the same age [as that of Chronicles, Esther, and Ecclesiastes] is the *frequent* occurrence in it of a word or construction which occurs only *exceptionally* in the earlier Hebrew" (Driver 1913: 505 note ‡) and "it is the *intensified application and expansion* ... that marks a turning point ... in the history of the Hebrew language" (Hurvitz 1995b: 183 note 70). The criterion of 'intensification' thus enables us to identify usages acceptable in (but not characteristic of) CBH—usages whose increased late frequency marks them as especially characteristic of LBH.

d. The plural form ארצות, which appears in 1 Chron. 13:2 אַחֵינוּ הַנִּשְׁאָרִים בְּכֹל אַרְצוֹת יִשְׂרָאֵל, refers to all the regions of Israelite settlement within the borders specified in v. 5 מִן שִׁיחוֹר מִצְרַיִם וְעַד לְבוֹא חֲמָת.

BIBLIOGRAPHY

Bendavid 1967–71: I 127, 151 • S. R. Driver 1913: 505 note ‡ • Hurvitz 1995b: 183 note 70 • Qimron 1986: 88 §500.1 • Qimron and Strugnell 1994: 88

√ **בהל** vb. **Niph** *be in haste; do hastily*: Qoh. 8:3; **Pi** *hasten, make haste, act hastily*: Qoh. 5:1; 7:9; Esth. 2:9; 2 Chron. 35:21; **Pu** ptc. *hastened*: Esth. 8:14 הָרָצִים...יָצְאוּ; Prov. 20:21 ([כת'] מבחלת [ק'] מְבֹהֶלֶת); **Hiph** *hasten, hurry*: Esth. 6:14; 2 Chron. 26:20 (see comments **b, c** below)

BA בְּהִתְבְּהָלָה Dan. 2:25 הַנְעֵל לְדָנִיֵּאל קֳדָם מַלְכָּא; 3:24; 6:20; cf. n. Ezra 4:23 אֲזַלוּ בִּבְהִילוּ (see comment **e** below)

CBH ALTERNATIVES

√רוץ, √מהר (when transitive; see BDB 555a)

Gen. 41:14	וַיְשַׁלַּח פַּרְעֹה וַיִּקְרָא אֶת יוֹסֵף **וַיְרִיצֻהוּ** מִן הַבּוֹר
[~ 2 Chron. 26:20	וְהִנֵּה הוּא מְצֹרָע בְּמִצְחוֹ **וַיַּבְהִלוּהוּ** מִשָּׁם וְגַם הוּא נִדְחַף לָצֵאת]

Gen. 18:6	שְׁלֹשׁ סְאִים קֶמַח סֹלֶת לוּשִׁי וַעֲשִׂי עֻגוֹת **מַהֲרִי**
[~ Esth. 2:9	תַּמְרוּקֶיהָ וְאֶת מָנוֹתֶהָ לָתֵת לָהּ אֵת **וַיְבַהֵל**]

EXTERNAL POST-CLASSICAL SOURCES
Renderings/Paraphrases/Glosses

TO 2x, e.g.

Exod. 12:11	הוא קדם ה'	פסחא	**בבהילו**	יתיה	ותיכלון
[~	הוא לה'	פֶּסַח	**בְּחִפָּזוֹן**	אֹתוֹ	וַאֲכַלְתֶּם]

Other Sources

MekhRS 12:11	"וככה תאכלו אתו [מתניכם חגרים...ואכלתם אֹתו **בְּחִפָּזוֹן**]"
(p. 14)	(שמ' יב 11) וג'–אוכלים אותו בחפזון. **בבהילות** יוצאי דרכים

Independent Use
Heb.

4Q215 f1–3:4–5	ותקרא חנה את שמה בלהה כי כאשר נולדהֹ [...] **מתבהלת** לינוק ותואמר מה **מתבהלת** היאה בתי ותקרא עוד בלהה
4Q385 f4:2–3	**ויתבהלו** הימים מהר עד אשר יאמרו האדם הלא ממהרים הימים
M Avot 5:7	החכם אינו מדבר לפני מי שהוא גדול ממנו...ואינו **נבהל** להשיב...
MekhRS 6:2 (p. 4)	אמ' לו הקב"ה למשה: אני הוא שאמרתי והיה העולם...אני הוא שאמרתי לאברהם בין הבתרים "ידוע תדע ⟨כי גר יהיה זרעך⟩" (בר' טו 13) ועכשיו הרי שבועה **מבוהלת** ⟨ובאת⟩ לפני להוציא את בני ישראל ממצרים, ואני מבקש להוציאם ואתה אומר לי "שלח נא ביד תשלח" (שמ' ד 13)

Gen. Rab. 2:4 (p. 17) כבר היה שמעון בן זומא עומד ותוהא. עבר ר׳ יהושע שאל

[noun; cf. above בשלומו פעם ופעמיים ולא השיבו. בשלישית השיבו **בבהילות**

Ezra 4:23]

Aram.

1QApGen 2:3 באדין אנה למך **אתבהלת** ועלת על בתאנוש אנ[תי...

PT Ket. 1:1 (p. 954) "ותהום כל העיר עליהם" (רות א 19)–ואיפשר כן, כל קרתא

מתבהלה בגין נעמי על עליבתא?

COMMENTS

a. "The [standard] meaning of the root בהל in the Bible is the same as in modern Hebrew [*be frightened*]. However, in Late Biblical literature the Pi'el and Hiph'il also mean *hasten* .... Semantically this should come as no surprise, for both meanings are often interrelated. Yet, the fact that the second meaning [*hasten*] emerges only in distinctly late writings calls for an explanation. It may be considered that the Aramaic root רהב caused [this semantic development]; in Syriac this root means both *fear* and *haste*" (Kutscher 1963–64: 122–123 [= 1977: 398–399]).

This basic concept regarding the lateness of בְּהֵל *hasten* may be found in the following statements: (1) "In a few Hebrew verbs we find a combination of a sememe belonging to the [semantic] field of *fear*, on the one hand, and a sememe belonging to the field of *haste*, on the other. The ordinary use of this verb is in the domain of *fear*, but in several texts it is employed in the realm of *movement* and displays the sememe of *haste*. These texts are all late" (Morag 1978: 146a [= 1995: 171]); (2) "The root *bhl* has two meanings in both Hebrew and Aramaic: 'to hasten' and 'to be terrified' ... In Hebrew the meaning 'to hasten' clearly came to be attached to the root *bhl* at a late period under Aramaic influence" (Otzen 1975: 3–4).

b. The Biblical occurrences of √בהל presented in the above lemma reflect only the later meaning, *to hasten*. In two places in Psalms (48:6; 83:16), √בהל appears in contexts that can be construed as having both meanings of the verb. However, as noted, it is only in the late books that the meaning *to hasten* is not merely possible, but indeed unquestionable.

c. By the same token, the expression נִבְהָל לַהוֹן (Prov. 28:22) can be explained according to either meaning of the root, i.e., *rush in pursuit of wealth* or *be excited / pressed / worried about wealth*. A similar expression is found in RH, בהול על ממונו (also בהול על מתו) and in Tg. 1 Chron. 26:24, מתבהיל על ממונא, and it, too, can sustain both meanings.

d. The new semantic connotation of *haste* did not eliminate altogether the older meaning *alarmed, frightened, terrified.* They coexist both in LBH and RH.

e. Aram. הִתְפְּעַל = Heb. Niph. הִתְבְּהֵל is used in BA, and it may well be that in the QH examples cited above, the הִתְפַּעֵל conjugation was employed under the influence of Aram הִתְבְּהֵל. Similarly, the noun (ת)בהילו, employed in BA (בְּהִילוּ), in Aramaic Targums and in RH, is quoted above, even though this noun is unattested in the vocabulary of BH.

BIBLIOGRAPHY

BDB 96 • GB 85 • Ben-Iehuda I 470b

Bergey 1983: 111–112 • Crenshaw 1988: 116 • Delitzch 1877: 190–196 • S. R. Driver 1913: 475 no. 2 • Gordis 1968: 248 • Kutscher 1963–64: 122–123 [= 1977: 398–399] • Magnanini 1968: 368 • Morag 1978: 146a (= 1995: 171) • Otzen 1975: 3–5 • Paton 1908: 62, 177 • Polzin 1976: 129 • Robinson 1895: 52 • Schoors 1992–2004: II 250 • Wagner 1966: 33 no. 36 • Whitley 1979: 48 • R. M. Wright 2003: 144–146; 2005: 82–84

בּוּץ, בַּץ n. m. *byssus, fine cloth, fine linen*: Ezek. 27:16; Esth. 1:6 חוּר כַּרְפַּס; וְדָוִיד מְכֻרְבָּל בִּמְעִיל בּוּץ 2 15:27; 8:15; 1 Chron. 4:21; וּתְכֵלֶת אָחוּז בְּחַבְלֵי בוּץ וְאַרְגָּמָן Chron. 2:13; 3:14; 5:12

CBH ALTERNATIVES

שֵׁש, e.g.

Exod. 36:35   וַיַּעַשׂ אֶת הַפָּרֹכֶת תְּכֵלֶת וְאַרְגָּמָן וְתוֹלַעַת שָׁנִי **וְשֵׁשׁ** מָשְׁזָר

[~ 2 Chron. 3:14   וַיַּעַשׂ אֶת הַפָּרֹכֶת תְּכֵלֶת וְאַרְגָּמָן וְכַרְמִיל **וּבוּץ**]

Gen. 41:42   וַיַּלְבֵּשׁ אֹתוֹ בִּגְדֵי **שֵׁשׁ** וַיָּשֶׂם רְבִד הַזָּהָב עַל צַוָּארוֹ

[~ Esth. 8:15   בִּלְבוּשׁ מַלְכוּת... וַעֲטֶרֶת זָהָב... וְתַכְרִיךְ **בּוּץ**...]

בַּד, e.g.

Lev. 6:3   וְלָבַשׁ הַכֹּהֵן מִדּוֹ **בַד** וּמִכְנְסֵי **בַד** יִלְבַּשׁ עַל בְּשָׂרוֹ

[~ 1 Chron.   וְדָוִיד]   מְכֻרְבָּל   בִּמְעִיל **בּוּץ**

15:27

[~ 2 Chron.   וְהַלְוִיִּם הַמְשֹׁרְרִים... מְלֻבָּשִׁים   **בּוּץ**]

5:12

EXTERNAL POST-CLASSICAL SOURCES
Renderings/Paraphrases/Glosses

TO 44x, e.g.

Gen. 41:42[a]   ואעדי פרעה ית עזקתיה... ויהב יתה על ידא דיוסף

[~   וַיָּסַר פַּרְעֹה אֶת טַבַּעְתּוֹ... וַיִּתֵּן אֹתָהּ עַל יַד יוֹסֵף]

Gen. 41:42[b]   ואלביש יתיה לבושין **דבוץ**

[~   וַיַּלְבֵּשׁ אֹתוֹ בִּגְדֵי **שֵׁשׁ**]

Exod. 28:42   ועיביד להון מכנסין **דבוץ**... מחרצין ועד ירכן יהון

[~   וַעֲשֵׂה לָהֶם מִכְנְסֵי **בָד**... מִמָּתְנַיִם וְעַד יְרֵכַיִם יִהְיוּ]

TN 87x, e.g.

Exod. 27:16   תכלא וארגוון וצבע דזהורי טבא **ובוץ** שזיר עובד צייר

[~   תְּכֵלֶת וְאַרְגָּמָן וְתוֹלַעַת שָׁנִי **וְשֵׁשׁ** מָשְׁזָר מַעֲשֵׂה רֹקֵם]

Lev. 16:32   ויכפר כהנא די רבי יתיה... וילבוש ית לבושי **בוצה**

[~   וְכִפֶּר הַכֹּהֵן אֲשֶׁר יִמְשַׁח אֹתוֹ... וְלָבַשׁ אֶת בִּגְדֵי **הַבָּד**]

TPJ 45x, e.g.

Exod. 39:27	ולבנוי	לאהרן	גרדי	עובד	**דבוץ**	כיתונין	ית	ועבדו
[~	וּלְבָנָיו	לְאַהֲרֹן	אָרֶג	מַעֲשֵׂה	**שֵׁש**	הַכָּתְנֹת	אֶת	וַיַּעֲשׂוּ

Lev. 16:23	**בוּעָא דמילת**	לבושי	וישלח	זימנא	למשכן	ובנוי	אהרן	ויעול
[~	**הַבָּד**	בִּגְדֵי	אֶת	וּפָשַׁט	מוֹעֵד	אֹהֶל	אֶל	אַהֲרֹן	וּבָא

TJ 16x, e.g.

1 Sam. 2:18	**דבוץ**	כרדוט	אסיר	עולימא	ה'	קדם	משמיש	ושמואל
[~	**בָּד**	אֵפוֹד	חָגוּר	נַעַר	ה'	פְּנֵי	אֶת	מְשָׁרֵת	וּשְׁמוּאֵל

Other Sources

Pesh. Exod. 28:39	**דבוּעָא**	מצנפתא	ועבד	**דבוּעָא**	כותינא	ועבד
[~	**שֵׁש**	מִצְנֶפֶת	וְעָשִׂיתָ	שֵׁש	הַכְּתֹנֶת	וְשִׁבַּצְתָּ

Pesh. Lev. 16:23	**דבוּעָא**	לבֿושא	ונשלח
[~	**הַבָּד**	בִּגְדֵי	אֶת	וּפָשַׁט

Sifra Tzav 1:2   "ולבש הכהן מדיו][!]" (וי' ו 3)—כמידתו. "בד"—שיהוא שלבוץ

Independent Use
Heb.

M Yoma 3:4   פרסו סדין **שלבוץ** בינו לבין העם

M Yoma 7:1   בא לו כהן גדול לקרות. אם רוצה בבגדי **בוץ** קורא, ואם לאו באסטלת לבן משלו

PT Yoma 7:5 (p. 594)   לא נחלקו ר' ור' אלעזר ביר' שמעון על אבניטו שלכהן גדול ביום הכיפורים שהוא **שלבוץ** ועל שאר ימות השנה שיש בו כלאים

Aram.

1QApGen 20:31   ויהב לה מלכא [כסף וד]הב [ש]גיא ולבוש שגי די **בוץ** וארגואן

TN Gen. 50:1   ומחזקא באבנא בועה **בוצה** וארגוונא

Comments

a. "Linen cloth—*bād*—is mentioned [in the Bible] more than twenty times. *Bûṣ*, another term for a linen-fabric, occurs seven times, all of them in late biblical writings (Ez. 27:16; Esth. 1:7, 8:15; 1 Chr. 15:27; 2 Chr. 2:13, 3:14, 5:12), where it replaces the earlier *šēš*. It is probable that these terms pertain to varieties of fine linen which in Israel were used almost exclusively by royalty and cultic personnel.... *Pištîm*, on the other hand, in biblical language seems to refer to a cheaper kind of linen, more commonly used (Lev. 13:47, 49; Deut. 22:11;

Jer. 13:1), although Ezekiel employs the terms with reference to priestly garments (Ez. 44:17, 18)" (Talmon 1963: 179).

b. The wording of the two Biblical accounts describing the fabrication of the veil—in the Jerusalem Temple (2 Chron. 3:14) and the Tabernacle (Exod. 36:35)—are almost identical (see CBH Alternatives, above). However, it is only in the late book of Chronicles that we find the late term בּוּץ in this connection. Exodus employs here שֵׁשׁ, a lexeme that over time went out of circulation from the Hebrew vocabulary (in RH it appears only in quotations of or allusions to the Pentateuch). Likewise, the Egyptian Pharaoh clothes his viceroy in "garments of fine linen" (בגדי שש; Gen. 41:42), whereas in a similar situation the Persian King Ahasuerus bestows upon Mordechai a "mantle of fine linen" (תכריך בוץ; Esth. 8:15). The terminological shift from שש to בוץ was clearly made in the realms of both the holy (cultic domain) and profane (royal court).

c. Brenner notes with regard to MH that "The late biblical tendency to employ *bûṣ* instead of *šēš* continues, to the point that now *bûṣ* seems to be the normative usage, the better known term of the two. When the writer of the archaizing War Scroll from Qumran uses *šēš* rather than *bûṣ*, as is dictated by his biblical source material [in the Pentateuch], he adds the word *lābān* as an explanatory gloss to *šēš* (12:9). However, the more frequent designations for 'white/hueless textiles' in MH are simply *bəgādîm ləbānîm*, and *bigdê* or *kəlê lābān* 'white garments'" (1980: 42).

d. The distribution pattern of *buṣu* within Akkadian (NB, NA) indicates that the lexeme—in much the same way as in Hebrew—is a newcomer on the Akkadian linguistic scene as well. Although its ultimate origin has not yet been definitively established, its geographical diffusion (Aramaic, Akkadian, Canaanite) points to a "northern" milieu. This linguistic evidence fully accords with the literary tradition underlying Ezek. 27:16, where בוץ is associated with Aramaic (while its counterpart שֵׁשׁ is said to have come from a "southern" region—Egypt [Ezek. 27:7]). Note that both שש and בוץ are discussed in Lambdin 1953: 147–148, 155. Yet, at the very outset of his study, he openly admits that "several words have been included…whose Egyptian origin is very doubtful"—בוץ being one of them (p. 145).

e. As noted, each of the two discussed terms is associated, both linguistically and geographically, with a different cultural milieu: "southern" (Egypt [שֵׁשׁ]), on the one hand, and "northern" (Mesopotamia [בוּץ]), on the other. It is therefore reasonable to conclude that we are confronted here materially with two distinct commodities rather than two synonymous words pertaining to one identical commercial item. Still, שש and בוץ serve terminologically as functional equivalents ("fine/expensive linen") whose usage in the Hebrew Bible stands the test of "linguistic contrast" (see Proleg. §II[4]; cf. אִגֶּרֶת, comment c; עֲזָרָה, comment c) and is therefore valid for dating purposes.

f. The appearance of בץ in a Canaanite inscription dated to the 9th century BCE (Kilamu [*KAI* 24:12–13 בֵץ.כסי.ובימי.למנערי.כתן.חז.בל.ומי] and once in Punic [*KAI* 76A:6 ...בבוץ ומכסא תח...]) is not necessarily indicative of its linguistic history within Hebrew. In and of itself, the existence of a lexeme in an early phase of one language does not rule out *a priori* the possibility that it reached another language in later times (cf. the entry אִגֶּרֶת, comment b).

g. Note that Aram. בוצינא and Akkad. *buṣinnu* = *lamp wick* is a compound of the noun *buṣu* and the morpheme *-innu* (Kaufman 1974: 45).

BIBLIOGRAPHY

BDB 101a • Ben-Iehuda I 489b note 1 • GB 96 • *HALOT* I 116a

Bendavid 1967–71: I 68, 90, 339 • Bergey 1983: 94–95 • Brenner 1980 • Curtis and Madsen 1910: 28 no. 9 • Gesenius 1815: 38 • Grintz 1975a: 13–15; 1975b 178–180 • Hurvitz 1967a: 117–121 • Japhet 1993: 306–307, 545 • Kaufman 1974: 45 • Keil 1872: 311 • Kogut 1997: 141–147 • Lambdin 1953: 147–148, 155 • Paton 1908: 62 • Polzin 1976: 130 • Talmon 1963: 179 • Williamson 1977a: 41

בִּזָּה n. f. *booty, plunder, spoils*: Esth. 9:10, 15, 16; Dan. 11:24, וּבַבִּזָּה לֹא שָׁלְחוּ אֶת יָדָם; וּתְנֵם לְבִזָּה בְּאֶרֶץ שִׁבְיָה 3:36 Neh. ;9:7 Ezra; וְנִכְשְׁלוּ בְחֶרֶב וּבְלֶהָבָה בְּשְׁבִי וּבְבִזָּה 33 וַיַּעֲזֹב הֶחָלוּץ אֶת הַשִּׁבְיָה וְאֵת הַבִּזָּה 28:14; וַיָּבֹזּוּ בִזָּה רַבָּה 25:13; 2 Chron. 14:13

CBH Alternatives

שלל, מלקוח, בז, e.g.

Num. 14:3	**לָבַז**		נָשֵׁינוּ וְטַפֵּנוּ יִהְיוּ
Jer. 30:16	**לָבַז**		וְהָיוּ שֹׁאסַיִךְ לִמְשִׁסָּה וְכָל בֹּזְזַיִךְ אֶתֵּן
[~ Neh. 3:36	**לְבִזָּה**		וְהָשֵׁב חֶרְפָּתָם אֶל רֹאשָׁם וּתְנֵם

Num. 31:12	**הַשָּׁלָל**	וְאֶת	**הַמַּלְקוֹחַ**	וְאֶת	**הַשְּׁבִי**	וַיָּבִאוּ אֶל מֹשֶׁה...אֶת
[~ Dan. 11:33	**וּבְבִזָּה**				**בְּשְׁבִי**	וְנִכְשְׁלוּ בְחֶרֶב וּבְלֶהָבָה
[~ 2 Chron. 28:14	**הַבִּזָּה**	וְאֵת			**הַשִּׁבְיָה**	וַיַּעֲזֹב הֶחָלוּץ אֶת

2 Sam. 3:22		עִמָּם הֵבִיאוּ	רָב	**וְשָׁלָל**
[~ 2 Chron. 14:13		הָיְתָה בָהֶם	רַבָּה	**בִזָּה** כִּי]

1 Sam. 14:32		**הַשָּׁלָל** (ק׳)	אֶל	הָעָם	וַיַּעַט (ק׳)
1 Sam. 15:21		**מֵהַשָּׁלָל**		הָעָם	וַיִּקַּח
[~ Esth. 9:15	לֹא שָׁלְחוּ אֶת יָדָם	**וּבַבִּזָּה** ...	הַיְּהוּדִים (ק׳)		וַיִּקָּהֲלוּ]

External Post-Classical Sources

Renderings/Paraphrases/Glosses

TO 10x, e.g.

Exod. 15:9	**בִּיזְתָא**	אֲפַלֵּיג	אַדְבֵּיק	אַרְדּוֹף	סַנְאָה	אֲמַר	דַהֲוָה
[~	**שָׁלָל**	אֲחַלֵּק	אַשִּׂיג	אֶרְדֹּף	אוֹיֵב	אָמַר	]

TN 9x, e.g.

Deut. 20:14	בְּעִלֵי דבביכון	יַת **בִּיזַת**	וְתֵיכְלוּן	לְכוֹן	תְבַזּוֹן ...	וּבְעִירַהּ	נְשַׁיָּיה וְטַפְלַיָּיה
[~	אֹיְבֶיךָ	אֶת **שְׁלַל**	וְאָכַלְתָּ	לָךְ	תָּבֹז ... וְהַבְּהֵמָה		הַנָּשִׁים וְהַטַּף]

TPJ 9x, e.g.

Num. 31:32	לְחֵילָא	דַּנְפִקוּ עַמָּא	שַׁיּוּר **בִּיזְתָא** דְּבַזוּ	דִּבְרָתָא	סְכוּם	וַהֲוָת
[~	הַצָּבָא	עִם אֲשֶׁר בָּזְזוּ **הַבָּז**	יֶתֶר הַמַּלְקוֹחַ			וַיְהִי]

Num.	אַלְפִין	וַחֲמִשָּׁא	וְשׁוּבְעִין	מְאָה	שִׁית עֲנָא	מִנְיַן	
[~	אֲלָפִים	וַחֲמֵשֶׁת	אֶלֶף וְשִׁבְעִים	מֵאוֹת	צֹאן שֵׁשׁ	]	

TJ 58x, e.g.

ושדר **מבזתא**...למימר הא לכון מתנא **מבזת** סנאי עמא דה׳ 1 Sam. 30:26

[~ ה׳ **מְשְׁלַל** אֹיְבֵי בְּרָכָה לָכֶם הִנֵּה לֵאמֹר...**מֵהַשָּׁלָל** [וַיִּשְׁלַח

Other Sources

אפליג **ביזתא** עם יתבי שכם ועם יתבי סכות אמשח מישר אמשה תחומא Tg. Ps. 108:8

[~ אֲמַדֵּד סֻכּוֹת וְעֵמֶק שְׁכֶם [אֲחַלְּקָה

בלחוד בעירֹא בזן לן **ובזתא** דקורֹיא דכבשן Pesh. Deut. 2:35

[~ לָכַדְנוּ אֲשֶׁר הֶעָרִים **וּשְׁלַל** לָנוּ בָּזַזְנוּ הַבְּהֵמָה [רַק

כיון שראה פרעה כך אמר: כולנו שוין **בביזה**, שנאמר ״אחלק MekhRI Shira 7
שלל״ (שמות טו 9) (p. 139)

Independent Use
Heb.

[יו]שְׁבִי פלשת ומצרים **לבזה** וחורבה 4Q462 f1:14

ומנין **שביזת** הים גדולה **מביזת** מצרים? שנא׳ ״ותרבי ותגדלי MekhRI Pisḥa 13
ותבאי בעדי עדיים״ (יח׳ טז 7). ״בעדי״ – זו **ביזת** מצרים. (p. 47)
״עדיים״ – זו **ביזת** הים. ואומר ״כנפי יונה נחפה בכסף״
(תה׳ סח 14) – זו **ביזת** מצרים. ״ואברותיה בירקרק חרוץ״
(שם) – זו **ביזת** הים. ״תורי זהב נעשה לך״ (שה״ש א 11) – זו
ביזת הים. ״עם נקדות הכסף״ (שם) – זו **ביזת** מצרים

משנתמלאו ישראל **בביזה**, התחילו מבזבזין את **הביזה**. מקרעים Sifre Num. 131
כסות ומשליכים, (מעקרין) בהמה ומשליכים, לפי שלא היו (p. 170)
מבקשים אלא כלי כסף וכלי זהב

״ויקח משה את עצמות יוסף״ וגו׳ (שמ׳ יג 19) – מלמד שכל העם T Soṭ. 4:7
היו עסוקין **בביזה** והוא עוסק במצוה (Nash. p. 171)

רבון העולמים, פדה והצל את עמך ישר׳ מן הדבר ומן החרב ומן BT Ket. 8b
הביזה ומן השדפון

Aram.

ושמע מלך סודם די אתיב אברם כול שביתא וכול **בזתא** 1QApGen 22:12–13

לבתר יומין מת קיסר הרשע ואימני ליה מלכא תחותיה. גזר על Qoh. Rab. 11:1(1)
ההיא מדינתא כל גברין לקטלא וכל נשיא **לביזה**

Comments

a. "The lexeme בזה 'spoil, booty' occurs 10 times in the Hebrew Bible, always in clearly late books.... This expression does not occur anywhere in exilic or pre-exilic texts. Instead, the terms (a) שלל and (b) בז are employed to express the same meaning of 'spoil, booty'.... Note however that שָׁלָל continued to appear in exilic and post-exilic books.... Whereas SBH בַז occurs in exilic but not in post-exilic texts.... The ... evidence suggests בִזָה 'spoil, booty' is a form that developed within the Hebrew language during the post-exilic period and replaced the earlier expression בַז (but not שָׁלָל)" (R. M. Wright 2005: 133–134).

b. The shift from Classical masculine בַז to post-Classical feminine בִזָה is one of the few examples of the phenomenon in ancient Hebrew; cf. גַן > [גִנָה] 'garden' (the latter, limited to Esth. and Song in the Bible, is also attested in Rabbinic literature). Whether such forms took hold under the influence of the determined form in Aramaic, e.g., גנא, בזא (see S. R. Driver 1913: 448–449), or due to the more general tendency to expand short forms to simulate triliterality is unclear.

c.

Num. 31:12	הַמַּלְקוֹחַ וְאֵת הַשָּׁלָל	וְאֵת	הַשְּׁבִי	אֵת	וַיָּבִאוּ אֶל מֹשֶׁה ...
[~ Dan. 11:33	וּבְבִזָּה		בִּשְׁבִי		[וְנִכְשְׁלוּ בְחֶרֶב
[~ 2 Chron. 28:14	הַבִּזָּה	וְאֵת	הַשִּׁבְיָה	אֵת	[וַיַּעֲזֹב הֶחָלוּץ

Note that Dan. 11:33 and 2 Chron. 28:14 pair together שבי(ה) and בזה. Interestingly, TN on Num. 31:12 uses these same two words in contrast to the three in Hebrew: **ית שביתה וית בזתא**. (The Palestinian Targum tradition pairs these two words in Exod. 15:9 **אשבי מנהון שבי רבה ואבוז מנהון בזה רבה** [TN; cf. also TPJ]). See also 1QApGen 22:12–13 **כול שביתא וכול בזתא** (quoted above). This may point to an Aramaic idiom that pairs the two as an expression.

d. Due to the fact that Aram. בזא may denote both the determined m. sg. and the absolute f. sg., no statistical figures for this form are presented here for the Aramaic Targums.

BIBLIOGRAPHY

BDB 103a • Kaddari 93b

Bergey 1983: 39 • Curtis and Madsen 1910: 28 no. 10 • S. R. Driver 1913: 484, 507 no. 23 • Keil 1872: 27; 1877: 44 note 2 • Paton 1908: 62–63 • Polzin 1976: 130 • Qimron 1986: 88 • Williamson 1977a: 43 • R. M. Wright 2005: 133–135

בִּירָה בִּירָנִית [בִּירָנִית; see comment g below], pl. בִּירָנִיּוֹת n. f. *fortress, (royal) citadel;
the Temple: Esth. 1:2, 5; 2:3, 5 בְּשׁוּשַׁן הַבִּירָה הָיָה יְהוּדִי אִישׁ, 8; 3:15; 8:14; 9:6, 11, 12;
Dan. 8:2 הַמְּדִינָה בְּעֵילָם אֲשֶׁר הַבִּירָה בְּשׁוּשַׁן וַאֲנִי; Neh. 1:1; 2:8 שַׁעֲרֵי אֶת לִקְרוֹת עֵצִים
כִּי לֹא לְאָדָם הַבִּירָה כִּי לַה' אֱלֹהִים 1 Chron. 29:1; חֲנַנְיָה שַׂר הַבִּירָה 7:2; הַבִּירָה אֲשֶׁר לַבָּיִת
19 הַכִינוֹתִי אֲשֶׁר הַבִּירָה וְלִבְנוֹת 2 Chron. 17:12 מִסְכְּנוֹת וְעָרֵי בִּירָנִיּוֹת בִּיהוּדָה וַיִּבֶן; 27:4

BA Ezra 6:2 בְּבִירְתָא בְּאַחְמְתָא

CBH Alternatives

הבית, ארמון (= the Temple)

1 Kgs. 5:32	**הַבָּיִת**	לִבְנוֹת	וַיָּכִינוּ הָעֵצִים וְהָאֲבָנִים...
[~ 1 Chron. 29:19	**הַבִּירָה** אֲשֶׁר הֲכִינוֹתִי	וְלִבְנוֹת	וְלַעֲשׂוֹת הַכֹּל...]

External Post-Classical Sources

Renderings/Paraphrases/Glosses

TPJ 1x

Lev. 25:29	**שׁוּר** דְּמַפְּקָן **בְּבִירָנִין**	מוֹתְבָא	בֵּית	יְזַבּוֹן	אֲרוּם	וּגְבַר
[~	**חוֹמָה**...	עִיר	בֵּית מוֹשַׁב	יִמְכֹּר	כִּי	וְאִישׁ]

TJ 36x, e.g.

Jer. 6:5	**בִּירְנִיתְהָא**	וּנְחַבֵּיל	בְּלֵילְיָא	וְנִיסַק	קוּמוּ
[~	**אַרְמְנוֹתֶיהָ**	וְנַשְׁחִיתָה	בַּלָּיְלָה	וְנַעֲלֶה	קוּמוּ]

Other Sources

PT Pes. 7:8 (p. 541) אמ' ר' יוחנן: מגדל היה עומד בהר הבית והיה קרוי **בירה**. ר'
שמעון בן לקיש אמ': כל הר הבית קרוי **בירה** – "לעשות הכל
ולבנות **הבירה** אשר הכינותי" (דה"א כט 19)

Independent Use

Heb.

M BQ 6:5 ומודים חכמ' לר' יהודה במדליק את **הבירה** שהוא משלם כל
מה שבתוכה, שכן דרך בני אדם להניח בבתים

Sifra Tzav 4:4 ר' יוסי הגלילי או': אין כל העניין הזה מדבר אילא בפרים
הנשרפין ושעירין הנישרפין, ליתן עליהם בלא תעשה על
אכילתן וללמד שפסוליהן נישרפין לפני בית **הבירה**

Gen. Rab. 39:1 (p. 365) אמר ר' יצחק: לאחד שהיה עובר ממקום למקום וראה **בירה**
אחת דולקת. אמר: תאמר **שהבירה** היתה בלא מנהיג? הציץ
בעל **הבירה**, אמר לו: אני הוא בעל **הבירה**

BT Pes. 118b   שלש מאות ששים וחמשה שוקים יש בכרך גדול שלרומי וכל
אחד ואחד ⟨י⟩ש בו שלש מאות ששים וחמש **בורות**[!] וכל
בירה ובירה יש בה שלש מאות ששים וחמש מעלות

Aram.

TAD II 2.2 (= Cowley 6):4	ימאת לי ביהו אלהא ביב **בירתא**
TAD II 2.4 (= Cowley 9):16	כתב עתרשורי בר נבוזראבן ספרא זנה בסון **בירתא**
TAD III 2.3:12 (Bisitun)	אחר עבדו קרבא בֹּתֹגר שמה **ברתא** באררט
Drijvers As55 (D1):2	אנא זרבין...שליטא ד**בירתא**...
PT Ber. 2:3 (p. 18)	אמ' ליה: מה שמיה? מנחם. אמ' ליה: ומה שמיה
	דאבוי? אמ' ליה: חזקיה. אמ' ליה: מן הן הוא? אמ'
	ליה: מן **בירת** מלכא דבית לחם יהודה

COMMENTS

a. "This word is definitely LBH appearing in Est. 1.2–9.12 ten times, in Dan 8.2, Neh 1.1, 2.8, 7.2 with the meaning 'citadel, acropolis' (the plural form with this meaning is in II Chr 17.12, 27.4). This word also appears in 1 Chr 29.1.19 with the meaning 'temple'. Mhe[1] [Mishnaic Hebrew of the Tannaim] (both the Mishna and Tosefta) attests this word often. The form of the plural is *bîrāniyyôt*. This form is related to the Akkadian plural *birānātu*. Our entry is also attested in Imperial Aramaic 'fortresses' and Nabatean 'temple'. Earlier synonyms in Hebrew are *hêkāl* 'temple', *'armôn* 'citadel', *bêt YHWH* 'temple' or *habbayit* 'the temple' " (Polzin 1976: 130).

b. Note that in 12 out of 16 occurrences of the sg. בירה (all appearances in Esth. as well as Dan. 8:2, Neh 1:1), the noun is part of the idiom שושן הבירה. Other expressions attested in LBH are שר הבירה (Neh. 7:2) and שערי הבירה (Neh. 2:8).

c. הבירה in 1 Chron. 29:1, 19 = the [Jerusalem] Temple. "The usage of the word בירה in 1 Ch 29:1, 19 as a term designating the Temple is definitely an anachronism" (Avi-Yonah 1954: 51).

d. דמפקן in TPJ (Lev. 25:29) is most probably a scribal error for דמקפן (= *encircled*) (cf. TO and TN ad loc.; TPJ v. 31).

e. The appearances of בירה in the Qumran fragments of Jubilees (4Q221; 4Q223–224, DJD XIII) are reconstructed and therefore not recorded here.

f. Bergey refrained from fixing a precise date for the loanword בירה due to its wide semantic range, which does not allow us to determine the exact nuances of the term within BH (cf. above PT Pes. 7:8). Note, however, that the decisive fact here for purposes of dating is that בירה—which clearly denotes some kind of fortification, whatever the particular rendering one prefers to adopt in any individual Biblical verse—is attested in the HB exclusively in distinctly late writings.

g. "The singular form... is בירה, and it is this form that appears in all the sources: in the Bible, in Tannaitic literature, and in the Palestinian and [Babylonian] Talmuds.... Only in printed editions [of the Talmud] do we find the singular form בירנית, which appears neither in the language of the Tannaim, in foreign languages, nor in Talmudic manuscripts, and it is certainly not original. It was created as a back-formation of the pl. בירניות alongside which it appears; however, this occurred only as part of the later process of textual transmission" (Breuer 2002: 243).

BIBLIOGRAPHY

BDB 108a • *HALOT* I 123b • Kaddari 98a

Avi-Yonah 1954: 51 • Bergey 1983: 190 note 1 • Breuer 2002: 242–243 • Eskhult 2003: 13, 22 • Keil 1872: 297 • Hurvitz 1972: 18–20, 22 • Kaufman 1974: 44 • Lemaire and Lozachmeur 1987: 262 • C. A. Moore 1971: 5 • Paton 1908: 62–63, 134 • Polzin 1976: 130 • Sáenz-Badillos 1993: 117 • Wagner 1966: 34 no. 40 • Williamson 1977a: 43–44

בֵּית (הָ)אוֹצָר comp. n. *storehouse* (*treasury*): Mal. 3:10 הָבִיאוּ אֶת כָּל הַמַּעֲשֵׂר אֶל בֵּית הָאוֹצָר וְהַלְוִיִּם יַעֲלוּ אֶת מַעֲשַׂר Neh. 10:39; וְאֶת הַכֵּלִים הֵבִיא בֵית אוֹצַר אֱלֹהָיו Dan. 1:2; הַמַּעֲשֵׂר...אֶל הַלְּשָׁכוֹת לְבֵית הָאוֹצָר

CBH Alternatives

אוֹצר, e.g.

1 Kgs. 7:51	בֵּית ה'	**בְּאֹצְרוֹת**		נָתַן	הַכֵּלִים	וְאֶת
[~ Dan. 1:2	אֱלֹהָיו	**אוֹצַר** בֵּית		הֵבִיא	הַכֵּלִים	[וְאֶת

Josh. 6:19	**אוֹצַר** ה' יָבוֹא		לַה'	קֹדֶשׁ הוּא...וְזָהָב	וְכֹל כֶּסֶף
[~ Neh. 10:39	**לְבֵית הָאוֹצָר**	לְבֵית אֱלֹהֵינוּ...	הַמַּעֲשֵׂר	מַעֲשַׂר	[יַעֲלוּ אֶת

External Post-Classical Sources
Renderings/Paraphrases/Glosses

TO 1x

Exod. 1:11	רעמסס	וית	פיתום	ית	לפרעה	**בית אוצרי**	קרוי	ובנו
[~	רַעַמְסֵס	וְאֶת	פִּתֹם	אֶת	לְפַרְעֹה	**מִסְכְּנוֹת**	עָרֵי	[וַיִּבֶן

TPJ 1x

Exod. 1:11	פילוסין	וית	טאנוס	ית	דפרעה	**בית אוצרוי**	לשום	קוריין...	ובניין
[~	רַעַמְסֵס	וְאֶת	פִּתֹם	אֶת	לְפַרְעֹה	**מִסְכְּנוֹת**	עָרֵי	[וַיִּבֶן	

TJ 1x

1 Kgs. 9:19	לשלמה	דהואה	**אוצריא**	**בית**	קרוי	כל	וית
[~	לִשְׁלֹמֹה	אֲשֶׁר הָיוּ	**הַמִּסְכְּנוֹת**		עָרֵי	כָּל	[וְאֵת

Other Sources

BT Pes. 118b   "וְהָיָה סַחְרָהּ וְאֶתְנַנָּהּ קֹדֶשׁ לַה' לֹא יֵאָצֵר וְלֹא יֵחָסֵן" (יש' כג 18). תנו רב יוסף "ולא יאצר"—**בבית אוצרו**, "ולא יחסן"—בבית גנזיו

Independent Use

Heb.

3Q15 8:1–2   (?)...[בא]מא שבדרך מזרח **בית אוצר**

M Eruv. 8:4   הנותן את עירובו...**בבית האוצרות** – הרי זה עירוב

M Soṭ. 8:2   אחד הבונה בית התבן, בית הבקר, בית העצים, **בית האוצרות**

Sifre Deut. 36 (p. 67)   "ובשעריך" (דב' ו 9) – שומע אני שערי בתים והלולים והרפת...**ובית האוצרות** ובית העצים ואוצרות יין ואוצרות תבואה ואוצרות שמן במשמע

Aram.

See comment **b** below (בֵּית גִּנְזִין).

COMMENTS

a. "Both אוֹצָר and בֵּית אוֹצָר have the same meaning, the first is typical Biblical Hebrew, while the second is Late Biblical and Mishnaic Hebrew, as well as Aramaic.... Moreover, the Targum of עָרֵי מִסְכְּנוֹת 'store cities' is בֵּית אוֹצָרַיָּא [*sic*; Sperber: בֵּית אוֹצָרֵי] (TO) and בֵּית אוֹצָרוֹי (PsJ), 'storehouses,' i.e., בֵּית אוֹצָרוֹת (Exod. 1:11)" (Lefkovits 2000: 247).

b. The additional בית in בֵּית אוֹצָר may well be regarded as a later calque influenced by the corresponding Aram. בֵּית גִּנְזִין (note also BA: Ezra 5:17 בְּבֵית גִּנְזַיָּא; 7:20 בֵּית גִּנְזֵי מַלְכָּא; גִּנְזַיָּא דִי מַלְכָּא). Furthermore, the pattern בֵּית-χ is generally very common in the Aramaic dialects and RH, often replacing CBH expressions that do not contain the *nomen regens* בית (see Abramson 1985: 219–220; Hurvitz 1993: 81, 82 note 15; 1995b: 181–183; Z. Talshir 1996: 229; Elwolde 2002: 111, 113). In many cases, בית may be rendered *place of* ... (cf. the entries בֵּית הַכַּפֹּרֶת, בֵּית מִקְדָּשׁ, בֵּית קְבָרוֹת, בֵּית קֹדֶשׁ הַקֳּדָשִׁים). The phenomenon in question does not apply, however, to geographical names (e.g., בֵּית שֶׁמֶשׁ, בֵּית לֶחֶם, בֵּית אֵל), which form a separate linguistic category.

c. The reading of אוצר in the Copper Scroll quoted above is disputed (אחצר?, אווצר?); see Lefkovits 2000: 247.

BIBLIOGRAPHY

Abramson 1985: 219–220 • Bendavid 1967–71: II 444 • Ehrensevärd 2003: 182 • Elwolde 2002: 111, 113 • Hurvitz 1993: 78–82; 1995b: 181–183 • Lefkovits 2000: 245–247 • Shin 2007: 59–63 • Z. Talshir 1996: 229 • Young, Rezetko, and Ehrensevärd 2008: II 68

בֵּית הַכַּפֹּרֶת comp. n. *the place of the Ark cover; the Holy of Holies* (?):
1 Chron. 28:11 וַיִּתֵּן דָּוִיד לִשְׁלֹמֹה בְנוֹ אֶת תַּבְנִית הָאוּלָם...וּבֵית הַכַּפֹּרֶת
Cf. בֵּית קֹדֶשׁ הַקֳּדָשִׁים

CBH ALTERNATIVES

כפרת(?), קדש הקדשים(?), דביר; see TO, TPJ, comment **c** below.

EXTERNAL POST-CLASSICAL SOURCES
Renderings/Paraphrases/Glosses

TO 1x

Lev. 16:2 ולא יהי עליל... לקודשא... ארי בעננא אנא מתגלי על **בית כפורי**
[~ וְאַל... אֶל הַקֹּדֶשׁ... כִּי בֶּעָנָן אֵרָאֶה עַל **הַכַּפֹּרֶת**]

TPJ 1x

Lev. 16:2 ארום בעננני איקרי שכינתיה מתגליא על **בית כפורי**
[~ כִּי בֶּעָנָן אֵרָאֶה עַל **הַכַּפֹּרֶת**]

TJ 14x, e.g.

1 Kgs. 6:19 **ובית כפורי** בגו ביתא... למתן תמן ית ארון קימא דה'
[~ וּדְבִיר בְּתוֹךְ הַבַּיִת... לְתִתֵּן שָׁם אֶת אֲרוֹן בְּרִית ה']

2 Kgs. 11:11 מעיבר ביתא מימינא עד עיבר ביתא מסמלא למדבחא **ולבית כפורי**
[~ מִכֶּתֶף הַבַּיִת הַיְמָנִית עַד כֶּתֶף הַבַּיִת הַשְּׂמָאלִית לַמִּזְבֵּחַ וְלַבָּיִת]

Ezek. 41:23 ותרתין דשין להיכלא **ולבית כפורי**
[~ וּשְׁתַּיִם דְּלָתוֹת לַהֵיכָל וְלַקֹּדֶשׁ]

Independent Use
Heb.

M Mid. 5:1 ואחת עשרה אמה לאחורי **בית הכפרת**

T Tem. 4:8 (p. 556) אין עושין אותן ריקועין אפילו אחורי **בית הכפרת**

Sifre Num. 116 "ולמבית לפרוכת" (במ' יח 7)—מיכן אמרו: מקום היה אחורי
(p. 133) **בית הכפרת** ששם בודקים יחוסי כהונה
(בית לפרוכת the printed edition reads)

BT Yoma 21a אף על פי שנכפפין אחת עשרה אמה אחורי **בית הכפרת**,
עומדין צפופין ומשתחוין רוחין. וזה אחד מעשרה ניסים שנעשו
במקדש

BT Zev. 55b לול קטן היה אחורי **בית הכפרת**, היה גבהו שמונה אמות

COMMENTS

a. The pattern בֵּית-χ is generally very common in the Aramaic dialects and RH, often replacing CBH expressions that do not contain the *nomen regens* בית (Abramson 1985: 219–220; Hurvitz 1995b: 181–183; Z. Talshir 1996: 229; Elwolde 2002: 111, 113). In many cases, בית may be rendered *place of ...* (see the entries בֵּית קֹדֶשׁ הַקֳּדָשִׁים, בֵּית קְבָרוֹת, בֵּית מִקְדָּשׁ, בֵּית אוֹצָר). The phenomenon in question does not apply to geographical names (e.g., בֵּית שֶׁמֶשׁ, בֵּית לֶחֶם, בֵּית אֵל), which form a separate linguistic category.

b. Note the graphic similarity between בית הכפרת and בית הפרכת in Ben Sira 50:5 (B: מה נהדר בהשגיחו מאהל ובצאתו מבית הפרכת) and in Rabbinic literature (e.g., Sifre Num. 116, above).

c. The correspondence between LBH בֵּית הַכַּפֹּרֶת and Targumic בית כפורי (see the examples above) does not necessarily imply that the two phrases are identical in meaning. For our purposes, it is enough to indicate that the expression was coined in the late Biblical period, when the use of the grammatical pattern בֵּית-χ greatly increased. In any event, it is striking that the Targumists identified early sacral terms, such as דְּבִיר, with the Aramaic linguistic counterparts of LBH בֵּית הַכַּפֹּרֶת.

BIBLIOGRAPHY

Abramson 1985: 219–220 • Elwolde 2002: 111, 113 • Hurvitz 1982: 138–141; 1995b: 172–174, 181–183 • Tal 1975: 169 • Z. Talshir 1996: 229

[**בֵּית מִקְדָּשׁ**] comp. n. (*the place of*) *the Temple*: 2 Chron. 36:17 וַיַּהֲרֹג בַּחוּרֵיהֶם בַּחֶרֶב
בְּבֵית מִקְדָּשָׁם

CBH Alternatives

בֵּית (ה' / אֱלֹהִים), e.g.

2 Kgs. 11:15   וְהַבָּא אַחֲרֶיהָ הָמֵת בֶּחָרֶב כִּי אָמַר הַכֹּהֵן אַל תּוּמַת **בֵּית ה'**
[~ 2 Chron. 36:17   **בְּבֵית מִקְדָּשָׁם**   בַּחֶרֶב   וַיַּהֲרֹג בַּחוּרֵיהֶם

מִקְדַּשׁ (ה'), e.g.

Lam. 2:20   **בְּמִקְדַּשׁ** אֲדֹנָי כֹּהֵן וְנָבִיא   אִם יֵהָרֵג
[~ 2 Chron. 36:17   **בַּחוּרֵיהֶם בַּחֶרֶב בְּבֵית מִקְדָּשָׁם**   וַיַּהֲרֹג   ]
(see comment **f** below)

External Post-Classical Sources
Renderings/Paraphrases/Glosses

TO 7x, e.g.

Lev. 19:30   ית יומי שביא דילי תיטרון **ולבית מקדשי** תהון דחלין אנא ה'
[~   אֶת שַׁבְּתֹתַי תִּשְׁמֹרוּ **וּמִקְדָּשִׁי** תִּירָאוּ אֲנִי ה'

TN 29x, e.g.

Lev. 15:31   דלא יסאבון ית **בית מקדשי** דאיקר שכינתיה שריה ביניהון
[~   בְּטַמְּאָם אֶת **מִשְׁכָּנִי** אֲשֶׁר בְּתוֹכָם

TPJ 24x, e.g.

Gen. 28:22   ואבנא הדא דשויתי קמא תהי מסדרא **בבי מוקדשא דה'**
[~   וְהָאֶבֶן הַזֹּאת אֲשֶׁר שַׂמְתִּי מַצֵּבָה יִהְיֶה **בֵּית אֱלֹהִים**

TJ 38x, e.g.

1 Sam. 3:15   ושכיב שמואל עד צפרא ופתח ית דשי **בית מקדשא דה'**
[~   וַיִּשְׁכַּב שְׁמוּאֵל עַד הַבֹּקֶר וַיִּפְתַּח אֶת דַּלְתוֹת **בֵּית ה'**

Isa. 10:32   מוביל... בידיה על טור **בית מקדשא** דבציון ועל עזרתא דבירושלם
[~   יְנֹפֵף יָדוֹ הַר **בַּת** (ק') צִיּוֹן גִּבְעַת יְרוּשָׁלִָם

Other Sources

Pesh. 1 Kgs. 6:21   **בית מקדשא** קדם
[~   **הַדְּבִיר** לִפְנֵי

T Ber. 3:16 (Zer. p. 16)	העומדים בירושלם מכוונין את לבם כנגד **בית המקדש** שנ'
	"והתפללו אל **הבית הזה**" (דה"ב ו 32)
Sifra Qedoshim 4:3	יכול יהא בינן **בית המקדש** דוחה את השבת, תל' לו' "את
	שבתתי תשמרו **ומקדשי** תיראו" (וי' יט 30)
BT Meg. 11b	אמר [בלשאצר]: מדלא איפרוק השתא תולא מיפרקי. אפיק מני
	דבי מקדשא ואשתמש בהו. והינו דקא אמ' ליה דניאל: "ועל מרי
	שמיא התרוממתה ולמניא די **ביתיה** היתיו קדמך" וג' (דנ' ה 23),
	וכת' "ביה בליליא קטיל בלשצר מלכא" (שם, ה 30)

Independent Use
Heb.

M Ma'aserS 5:2	אמתיי שיבנה **בית המקדש** יחזור הדבר לכמות שהיה
Gen. Rab. 71:3	שמותיהן כעורין ומעשיהם נאין אילו בני הגולה "בני בקבוק בני
(p. 825)	חקופה בני חרחור" (עז' ב 51) וזכו ועלו ובנו **בית המקדש**
Sifre Deut. 152	"וקמת ועלית" (דב' יז 8) – מגיד שארץ ישראל גבוהה מכל
(p. 206)	הארצות **ובית המקדש** גבוה מכל ארץ ישראל

Aram.

Ghôr eṣ-Ṣâfieh Tombstone I	תתניח נפשה דשאול בר [...].[לת דמית בריש ירח
(*MPAT* A50, p. 270) 1–8	מרחשון משתה קדמיתה דשמטתה, שנת תלת
	מא ושתין ורבע שנין לחרבן **בית מקדשה**, שלם
PT Ta'an. 3:8 (p. 722)	הדין חוני המעגל בר בריה דחוני המעגל הוה סמיך
	לחרבן **בית מוקדשא**
Gen. Rab. 13:2 (p. 114)	מרי תבני **בית מקדשך**

COMMENTS

a. The pattern בֵּית-χ is generally very common in the Aramaic dialects and
RH, often replacing CBH expressions that do not contain the *nomen regens* בית
(Abramson 1985: 219–220; Hurvitz 1995b: 181–183; Z. Talshir 1996: 229; Elwolde
2002: 111, 113). In many cases, בית may be rendered *place of . . .* (see the entries
בֵּית אוֹצָר, בֵּית הַכַּפֹּרֶת, בֵּית קְבָרוֹת, בֵּית הַקֳּדָשִׁים, בֵּית קֹדֶשׁ). The phenomenon in question does not apply to geographical names (e.g., בֵּית שֶׁמֶשׁ, בֵּית לֶחֶם, בֵּית אֵל),
which form a separate linguistic category.

b. Both בית and מקדש, which serve as standard terms designating the Jerusalem
Temple, never appear as one unified construct compound in CBH. The combination בית (ה)מקדש is recorded only once in the entire Hebrew Bible, in
2 Chron. 36:17. However, it is precisely this *hapax* that gains ground in the
post-Biblical period; indeed in Rabbinic literature it becomes predominant in
both Tannaitic and Amoraic sources, in halakhic and aggadic texts, in Hebrew

(בית המקדש) and Aramaic (בי[ת] מ[ו]קדשא) alike. The formation underlying בית־(ה)מקדש—i.e., χ-בית—is quite often indicative of post-Classical Hebrew writings (see comment **a** above), demonstrating that the appearance of בית (ה)מקדש in the Bible, specifically in the late book of Chronicles, heralds the emergence of a new linguistic term that became standard only in post-Biblical times.

c. The term in 2 Chronicles is used with a pronominal suffix, unlike the fixed compound בית (ה)מקדש, which is the standard idiom in RH, may indicate that the latter expression had not yet crystallized as a *terminus technicus* in LBH.

d. The antiquity of the CBH idiom בית ה'—in contrast to the lateness of its post-Classical counterpart, בית מקדש—is corroborated by a pre-Exilic epigraphic inscription from Arad (18:9–10): בית יהוה הא ישב *He dwells in the House of Yahweh* (see Aharoni 1966: 6; the context is not entirely clear). In much the same way, Ugaritic and Canaanite denote the deity's temple or residence בת (= בית) and מקדש; the composite term בית (ה)מקדש is not found in the vocabulary of both these dialects.

e. בית (ה)מקדש is not found in QH; its absence is particularly felt in the Temple Scroll!

f. The book of Lamentations is chronologically a product of the post-Classical period. However, the CBH alternative presented above (Lam. 2:20) clearly draws on, or conforms to, the older, pre-Exilic, linguistic convention of מקדש ה', as in Josh. 24:26.

BIBLIOGRAPHY

Abramson 1985: 219–220 • Aharoni 1966: 5–7 • Bendavid 1967–71: I 182, II 444 • Elwolde 2002: 111, 113 • Hurvitz 1972: 134 note 176; 1995b: 166–168, 181–183 • Z. Talshir 1996: 229

[בֵּית קְבָרוֹת] comp. n. *burial site*: Neh. 2:3 בֵּית קְבָרוֹת אֲבֹתַי

CBH ALTERNATIVES

קבר

Judg. 8:32	אָבִיו בְּעָפְרָה	**בְּקֶבֶר**	וַיִּקָּבֵר	וַיָּמָת...
2 Sam. 17:23	אָבִיו	**בְּקֶבֶר**	וַיִּקָּבֵר	וַיֵּלֶךְ אֶל בֵּיתוֹ אֶל עִירוֹ... וַיָּמָת
2 Sam. 19:38	אָבִי וְאִמִּי	**קֶבֶר**	עִם	בְּעִירִי	אֻמַת
[~ Neh. 2:3	אֲבֹתַי	**קְבָרוֹת**	**בֵּית**	הָעִיר	]

EXTERNAL POST-CLASSICAL SOURCES
Renderings/Paraphrases/Glosses

TN 2X

Gen. 23:6	מתך	ית	קבר	**קבָרִינָן**	שפר	**בבית**	
[~	מֵתֶךָ	אֶת	קבֹר	**קְבָרֵינוּ**	בְּמִבְחַר	]	

Deut. 33:21 ארום אתר מזומן הוא **לבית קבורה** ליה תמן... סופריהון דישראל קבור

[~ סְפוּן מְחֹקֵק חֶלְקַת שָׁם כִּי]

TPJ 12X, e.g.

Gen. 35:20 ואקים יעקב קמתא על **בית קבורתא** היא קמת **בית קבורתא** דרחל

[~ רָחֵל **קְבֻרַת** מַצֶּבֶת הוּא **קְבֻרָתָהּ** עַל מַצֵּבָה יַעֲקֹב וַיַּצֵּב]

Gen. 37:35 ואמר ארום איחות לות ברי כד אבילנא **לבי קבורתא**

[~ **שְׁאֹלָה** אָבֵל בְּנִי אֶל אֵרֵד כִּי וַיֹּאמֶר]

TJ 1X

Ezek. 39:11 בעדנא ההוא אתין לגוג אתר כשר **לבית קבורא** בישראל

[~ בְּיִשְׂרָאֵל קֶבֶר שָׁם מְקוֹם לְגוֹג אֶתֵּן הַהוּא בַּיּוֹם]

Other Sources

Tg. Ps. 143:7 לא תסלק שכינתך מיני ואמתלית עם נחותי גוב **בית קבורתא**

[~ בוֹר יֹרְדֵי עִם וְנִמְשַׁלְתִּי מִמֶּנִּי פָּנֶיךָ תַּסְתֵּר אַל]

Tg. 2 Chron. 16:14 וקברו יתיה **בבית קבורתיה** די תקין ליה

[~ לוֹ כָּרָה אֲשֶׁר **בְּקִבְרֹתָיו** וַיִּקְבְּרֻהוּ]

Independent Use

Heb.

M Yad. 4:7

קובלין אנו עליכם צדוקים שאתם מטהרין את אמת
המים הבאה **מבית הקברות**

T Ter. 1:3 (Zer. p. 107)

איזה הוא שוטה? היוצא יחידי בלילה והלן **בבית הקברות**

T Shab. 6:12 (Moʻed p. 24)

הזורק ברזל **לבית הקברות** ואמ׳ חדא – הרי זה מדרכי
האמורי

Sifre Deut. 222 (p. 256)

"והתעלמת מהם" (דב׳ כב 1) – פעמים שאתה מתעלם
ופעמים שאין אתה מתעלם. כיצד? היה כהן והיא **בבית
הקברות**, או שהיה זקן ואינה לפי כבודו, או שהיתה שלו
מרובה משל חבירו – פטור

PT Ber. 2:2 (p. 16)

לא יכנס אדם **לבית הקברות** ויעשה צרכיו שם

Aram.

Cooke 94:1 (Nab.)

קברא דנה...וצריחא זעירא די גוא מנה די בה **בתי
מקברין**...

PAT 0518 (CIS II 4166):1–2

מערתא דה די **בת קבורא** עבד מעיתו

PAT 0522 (CIS II 4170):1

בת מקברתא דה בנא זבידא בר מקימו

Drijvers As16 (D31):2–4

אנא סלוך בר מקימו עבדת לי **בית קבורא** הנא

COMMENTS

a. The pattern בֵּית-χ is generally very common in the Aramaic dialects and RH, often replacing CBH expressions that do not contain the *nomen regens* בית (see Abramson 1985: 219–220; Hurvitz 1995b: 181–183; Z. Talshir 1996: 229; Elwolde 2002: 111, 113). In many cases, בית may be rendered *place of*... (see the entries בֵּית קֹדֶשׁ הַקֳּדָשִׁים, בֵּית מִקְדָּשׁ, בֵּית הַכַּפֹּרֶת, בֵּית אוֹצָר). The phenomenon in question does not apply to geographical names (e.g., בֵּית שֶׁמֶשׁ, בֵּית לֶחֶם, בֵּית אֵל), which form a separate linguistic category.

b. According to the prevailing view among Talmudic scholars, "[i]n contrast to בית הקברות in the printed editions, the regular idiom in tannaitic literature is בין הקברות. This is probably the original Palestinian expression and is dominant in the Mss of the Mishnah.... It seems, however, that the original idiom in the Bavli is בית הקברות since this is the version in all the manuscripts" (Breuer 2002: 252–253). Regardless of the historical and linguistic contexts in which each of these two forms was coined, the very appearance of the Biblical *hapax* בֵּית הַקְּבָרוֹת specifically in the late book of Nehemiah—coupled by the employment of corresponding expressions in other contemporary Aramaic dialects (see above)—point to its post-Classical nature and justifies its classification as LBH. The CBH equivalents of this term are regularly קֶבֶר and קְבֻרָה (see Aram. Tg. above).

c. Although we are dealing here with a compound phrase cast in a fixed syntactical formation (בֵּית-χ), the textual data from the extra-Biblical sources (see
above) exhibit certain variations in the *nomen rectum*. Always derived from
קבר√, its grammatical-morphological pattern (מקברתא, קבורתא, קבורה, קבורא,
מקברין) and precise semantic meaning (burial ground, tomb-grave, sepulcher,
cemetery) are not uniform (Hurvitz 1992: 63 note 12).

BIBLIOGRAPHY

Abramson 1985: 219–220 • Bar-Asher 1984: 210 (= 2009: 100) • Bendavid 1967–71: I 199
• Breuer 2002: 252–253 • Elwolde 2002: 111, 113 • Hurvitz 1992: 59–68; 1995b: 181–183 •
Lieberman 1935–36: 55–56; 1955–92: VIII 109 • Z. Talshir 1996: 229

וַיַּעַשׂ אֶת **בֵּית קֹדֶשׁ הַקֳּדָשִׁים** comp. n. (*the place of*) *the Holy of Holies*: 2 Chron. 3:8
בֵּית קֹדֶשׁ הַקֳּדָשִׁים, 10 וַיַּעַשׂ בְּבֵית קֹדֶשׁ הַקֳּדָשִׁים כְּרוּבִים שְׁנַיִם

CBH ALTERNATIVES

דביר, קדש הקדשים, e.g.

1 Kgs. 6:20	וַיְצַפֵּהוּ זָהָב	... עֶשְׂרִים אַמָּה אָרֶךְ	**הַדְּבִיר**	וְלִפְנֵי
[~ 2 Chron. 3:8	וַיְחַפֵּהוּ זָהָב	...אַמּוֹת עֶשְׂרִים	אָרְכּוֹ...**בֵּית קֹדֶשׁ הַקֳּדָשִׁים** אֶת וַיַּעַשׂ

1 Kgs. 6:23	שְׁנֵי כְרוּבִים	**בַדְּבִיר**	וַיַּעַשׂ
[~ 2 Chron. 3:10	כְּרוּבִים שְׁנַיִם	**בְּבֵית קֹדֶשׁ הַקֳּדָשִׁים**	וַיַּעַשׂ]

EXTERNAL POST-CLASSICAL SOURCES
Renderings/Paraphrases/Glosses

TN 5x, e.g.

Lev. 16:33	יכפר	מדבחה	וית	...**קדשיה**	**קדש**	**בית**	ית	ויכפר
[~	יְכַפֵּר	הַמִּזְבֵּחַ	וְאֶת	...**הַקֹּדֶשׁ**	**מִקְדַּשׁ**		אֶת	וְכִפֶּר]

TPJ 1X

Num. 4:19	ולא ימותון באישא מצלהבא ויזוחון עיניהון מן **בית קודש קודשיא**
[~	וְלֹא יָמֻתוּ בְּגִשְׁתָּם אֶת **קֹדֶשׁ הַקֳּדָשִׁים**]

TJ 2x, e.g.

Ezek. 41:4	ומשח ית אורכיה...ופותיא...ואמר לי דין **בית קודש קודשיא**
[~	וַיָּמָד אֶת אָרְכּוֹ...וְרֹחַב...וַיֹּאמֶר אֵלַי זֶה **קֹדֶשׁ הַקֳּדָשִׁים**]

Independent Use
Heb.

M Mid. 4:5	...ובלולים היו פתוחים בעלייה לבין קודש הקדשים שבהן משלשין את האומנים בתיבות כדי שלא יזונו את עיניהן **מבית קודש הקדשים**
M Sheq. 4:4	מותר התרומה – מה היו עושין בה? רקועי זהב ציפוי **לבית קודש הקדשים**
T Sot. 13:6 (Nash. p. 232)	שמעון הצדיק שמע דבר **מבית קדש הקדשים**: בטילת עבידתא די אמר סנאה לאיתאה להיכלא ונהרג גס קלגס ובטלו גזרותיו, ובלשון ארמי שמע
T Kel. BQ 1:7 (p. 569)	אבא שאול אומר: עליית **בית קדשי** קדשים חמורה **מבית קדשי הקדשים**
Sifre Deut. 43 (p. 95)	שוב פעם אחת היו עולים לירושלם. הגיעו לצופים קרעו בגדיהם. הגיעו להר הבית וראו שועל יוצא **מבית קודש הקדשים**. התחילו הם בוכים ורבי עקיבה מצחק

Gen. Rab. 61:7 (pp. 668–669)	ביקש [אלכסנדר מוקדון] לעלות לירושלם. אמרו לו כותאי: היזהר שאין מניחין אותך להיכנס **לבית קודש הקדשים** שלהם...כיון שהגיע **לבית קודש הקדשים** אמר לו: עד כאן יש לנו רשות להיכנס, מיכן ואילך אין לנו רשות להכנס
BT Yoma 77b	נחל היוצא **מבית קדשי הקדשים** כתחלה דומה לקרני חגבים. כיון שמגיע לפתח היכל נעשה כחוט של שתי

COMMENTS

a. The pattern בֵּית-χ is generally very common in the Aramaic dialects and RH, often replacing CBH expressions that do not contain the *nomen regens* בית (Abramson 1985: 219–220; Hurvitz 1995b: 181–183; Z. Talshir 1996: 229; Elwolde 2002: 111, 113). In many cases, בית may be rendered *place of* . . . (see the entries בֵּית קְבָרוֹת, בֵּית מִקְדָּשׁ, בֵּית הַכַּפֹּרֶת, בֵּית אוֹצָר). The phenomenon in question does not apply to geographical names (e.g., בֵּית שֶׁמֶשׁ, בֵּית לֶחֶם, בֵּית אֵל), which form a separate linguistic category.

b. The term בֵּית קֹדֶשׁ הַקֳּדָשִׁים is composed of the two CBH components בית and קדש הקדשים, which even appear in close proximity in 1 Kgs. 8:6 וַיָּבִאוּ הַכֹּהֲנִים אֶת אֲרוֹן בְּרִית ה' אֶל מְקוֹמוֹ אֶל דְּבִיר הַבַּיִת אֶל קֹדֶשׁ הַקֳּדָשִׁים. Yet, the fusion of the two into a single compound term, attested in the book of Chronicles, is not found in the parallel CBH texts of the 'synoptic chapters' in Kings. This seems to indicate that the term בית קדש הקדשים had not yet been coined in the Classical era.

BIBLIOGRAPHY

Abramson 1985: 219–220 • Elwolde 2002 111, 113 • Hurvitz 1982: 138–141; 1995b: 171–172, 181–183 • Z. Talshir 1996: 229

וְהַבִּנְיָן...רֹחַב 41:12; וַיָּמָד אֶת רֹחַב הַבִּנְיָן 40:5 .Ezek: **בִּנְיָן** *n. m. structure, building*
10, 5, 42:1; 15, שִׁבְעִים אַמָּה וְקִיר הַבִּנְיָן חָמֵשׁ אַמּוֹת רֹחַב סָבִיב סָבִיב וְאָרְכּוֹ תִּשְׁעִים אַמָּה
וְאֶל פְּנֵי הַבִּנְיָן לְשָׁכוֹת

מַן אִנּוּן שְׁמָהָת גֻּבְרַיָּא דִּי דְנָה בִנְיָנָא בָּנַן 5:4 Ezra BA

CBH Alternatives
בית, e.g.

1 Kgs. 6:3	וְהָאוּלָם...עֶשְׂרִים אַמָּה אָרְכּוֹ עַל פְּנֵי רֹחַב **הַבָּיִת**
[~ Ezek. 40:5	וַיָּמָד אֶת רֹחַב **הַבִּנְיָן**]

External Post-Classical Sources
Renderings/Paraphrases/Glosses
TJ 20x, e.g.

2 Sam. 5:11	ושלח חירם...אזגדין לות דויד...וארדיכלין דאומנין **בבנין** כותליא
[~	וַיִּשְׁלַח חִירָם...מַלְאָכִים אֶל דָּוִד... וְחָרָשֵׁי אֶבֶן קִיר]

Jer. 51:53	ארי תבני בבל **בנינין** דרמן עד ציit שמיא
[~	כִּי תַעֲלֶה בָבֶל הַשָּׁמַיִם]

Other Sources

Tg. Qoh. 3:3	עידן בחיר לסתרא **בנינא** ועידן בחיר למבני חורבנא
[~	עֵת לִפְרוֹץ וְעֵת לִבְנוֹת]

Pesh. Ps 118 (117):22	כאפא דאסליו בֹּניא הי הות **לרישה** **דבנינא**
[~	אֶבֶן מָאֲסוּ הַבּוֹנִים הָיְתָה לְראשׁ **פִּנָּה**]

Independent Use
Heb.

11QT 33:9	רחוֹק קירוֹ מקירוֹ שבע אמות °°וֹל **בנינו** ומקרוותיו כבֵית הכיוֹר
M Ta'an. 4:8	"וביום שמחת לבו" (שה"ש ג 11) – זה **ביניין** בית המקדש, יהי רצון שיבנה במהרה בימינו
T Meg. 1:17 (Mo'ed p. 347)	אין בין שילו לירושלם אלא שבשילו **בנין** אבנים מלמטה ויריעות מלמעלה, וירושלם **בנין** אבנים מלמטה ותקרה מלמעלה
MekhRS 3:7 (p. 1)	מאחר שהיו משקיעין את בניהן במים היו חוזרי' וכובשים אותם **בבנין**
BMM 7 (p. 185)	בית קדש הקדשים שעשה שלמה, היה לו כותל פתח ודלתות ...אבל **בבנין** האחרון לא היה שם כותל אלא שני פסין
BT Suk. 51b	מי שלא ראה **בנין** בית המקדש לא ראה **בנין** מפואר מעולם. איזה הוא זה? אמ' אביי ואיתימ' רב חסדא: זה **בנין** הרודוס

Aram.

TAD II 3.4	ננתן לך בית לדמות ביתך…ננתן לך כספך…**ובנינא** זי תבנה בה
(= Krael. 3):21–23	
11Q18 f9:2–5	…עמודין שבעה…ובנא **בנין** עלוי עמ[…]…וכול **בנינא** דן…
TPJ Gen. 1:29	וית כל אילני סרקא לצרוך **בייניא** ולאסקותא
[~	[וְאֵת כָּל הָעֵץ
PT Meg. 3:6 (p. 767)	עשרת בני המן ומלכי כנען נכתבין אריח על גבי אריח ולבינה
	על גבי לבינה דכל **בינין** דכן לא קאים
TM 5:182–184 (p. 317)	**בנינא** אזהרו דלם תסטון מן תחומיכון דקבעת לוכון, יסתר כל
	וישרי רגזה

COMMENTS

a. The noun בִּנְיָן, which appears only in Ezekiel, is terminologically a later counterpart of CBH בַּיִת. The newcomer בִּנְיָן did not entirely supplant the older בַּיִת, and both may be found simultaneously (see Ezek. 40:5 וְהִנֵּה חוֹמָה מִחוּץ **לַבַּיִת**…וַיָּמָד אֶת רֹחַב הַבִּנְיָן), possibly with a certain semantic differentiation that may have developed—בַּיִת as a general term for *house* and בִּנְיָן in the sense of *structure, compound*. However, the detailed descriptions of Solomon's Temple recorded in the late book of Chronicles faithfully refer to the CBH בַּיִת, which is the term exclusively attested in this context in the book of Kings. RH, in contrast, often refers to the Jerusalem Temple as בנין (see above, BT Suk. 51b).

b. The post-Classical term בִּנְיָן is also used in BA (Ezra 5:4 גֻּבְרַיָּא דִּי דְנָה בִנְיָנָא בָּנַיִן) alongside בַּיִת (v. 9 בַּיְתָא דְנָה לְמִבְנְיָה), which is certainly the prevailing term in the Aramaic chapters of Daniel and Ezra.

c. The morphological pattern of בִּנְיָן becomes common in the ל"י/ה"ל roots in Aramaic and RH (עִנְיָן, מִנְיָן, בִּנְיָן), which suggests that the infiltration of בִּנְיָן into Ezekiel and עִנְיָן into Qohelet might be ascribed to the extensive influence of Aramaic on LBH (see JM: "anomalous Hebrew form…[Aramaism]"). This is not to say, however, that the pattern was entirely unknown in CBH; cf. קִנְיָן, which is attested in the Pentateuch and Joshua.

d. It is interesting to note that the form בִּנְיָה *structure, building*—like the etymologically and morphologically related בִּנְיָן—appears also in BH only in Ezekiel (41:13).

BIBLIOGRAPHY

BDB 125b • *HALOT* I 140b • JM 241 §88M, *c*

Elwolde 2002: 110 • Hurvitz 1982: 132–135 • Kautzsch 1902: 23 • Qimron 1980: 242; 1986: 89 • Rabin 1960: 108; 1962: 1075 • Wagner 1966: 36 no. 44

√בעת vb. Niph *to be frightened, terrified*: Esth. 7:6 וְהָמָן נִבְעַת מִלִּפְנֵי הַמֶּלֶךְ וְהַמַּלְכָּה;
Dan. 8:17 נִבְעַתִּי וָאֶפְּלָה עַל פָּנָי; 1 Chron. 21:30 כִּי נִבְעַת מִפְּנֵי חֶרֶב מַלְאַךְ ה'

CBH ALTERNATIVES

פחד, חרד

Isa. 19:16		ה'		תְּנוּפַת יַד	מִפְּנֵי	וְחָרַד וּפָחַד...
[~1 Chron. 21:30		ה'	מַלְאַךְ	חֶרֶב	מִפְּנֵי	כִּי **נִבְעַת**...]
[~ Esth. 7:6			הַמֶּלֶךְ וְהַמַּלְכָּה		מִלִּפְנֵי	וְהָמָן **נִבְעַת**]

EXTERNAL POST-CLASSICAL SOURCES
Renderings/Paraphrases/Glosses

TO 1x

Deut. 20:3		מן קדמיהון	תיתברון	ולא	**תתבעתון**	ולא	תדחלון	לא
[~		מִפְּנֵיהֶם	תַּעַרְצוּ	וְאַל	**תַּחְפְּזוּ**	וְאַל	תִּירְאוּ	אַל]

TJ 10x, e.g.

1 Sam. 21:2	דויד	לקדמות	אחימלך	**ואתבעית**	כהנא	אחימלך לות ...דויד ואתא
[~	דָוִד	לִקְרַאת	אֲחִימֶלֶךְ	**וַיֶּחֱרַד**	הַכֹּהֵן	אֲחִימֶלֶךְ אֶל ...דָוִד וַיָּבֹא]

1 Sam. 23:26	דויד	על	כמנין	וגברוהי	ושאול ...למיזל	**מתבעית**	דוד והוה
[~	דָוִד	אֶל	עֹטְרִים	וַאֲנָשָׁיו	וְשָׁאוּל ...לָלֶכֶת	**נֶחְפָּז**	דָוִד וַיְהִי]

Other Sources

BT Meg. 3a "וראיתי אני דניאל לבדי את המראה והאנשים אשר היו עמי לא ראו
את המראה אבל **חרדה** גדולה נפלה עליהם ויברחו בהחבא" (דנ' י 7)
...וכי מאחר דלא חזו מאי טעמא **איבעית**?

Independent Use
Heb.

| 1QHᵃ 9:23–25 | ואני יצר החמר ומגבל המים...ונעוה בלא בינה **ונבעתה**
במשפטי צדק |
|---|---|
| 1QHᵃ 11:14–15 | ויושבי עפר כיורדי ימים **נבעתים** מהמון מים |
| Sifra Qedoshim 1:3 | היה קוצר, קצר מלוא ידו, תלש מלוא קומצו, הכהו קוץ,
עקצתו עקרב, **ניבעת**, נפל מידו על הארץ, הרי הוא
שלבעל הבית |
| Sifre Deut. 192 (p. 233) | וכולם היו צריכים להביא עדותם חוץ מן הירא ורך הלבב
שעדיו עמו: שמע קול הגפת תריסים **ונבעת**, קול צהלת סוסים
ומרתת, קול ליעוז קרנים ונבהל |
| T RoshH 1:15
(Moʻed p. 309) | עולה הייתי במעלה אדומים וראיתיו רבוץ בין שני סלעים,
ראשו דומה לעגל, אזניו דומות לגדי, קרניו דומות לצבי וזנבו
מונחת לו בין יריכותיו. ראיתיו. **נבעתתי** ונפלתי לאחורי |

Aram.

PT Shab. 16:1 (p. 438)   ...אפילו כן אנא מתבעית בליליא

PT AZ 5:4 (p. 1408)   זמנין דו חמי סייגין כובין והוא סבור דינון בני נש והוא **מתבעת**

COMMENTS

a. "The Niphal of בעת 'be terrified (of someone or something)' occurs only in late books of the Hebrew Bible.... The term נבעת does not occur in early books, which instead use (a) פחד or (b) ירא in similar contexts.... Although the terms פחד and ירא do continue in postexilic texts, the ... evidence suggests that the Niphal of בעת began to be used instead of פחד and ירא in the post-exilic period. The Niphal of בעת continued to be employed in postbiblical Hebrew, thus confirming its late character. It occurs ... in the literature of the DSS.... It also appears sporadically in Tannaitic literature.... The early terms פחד and ירא continue to appear in post-biblical texts, but the distribution of the Niphal of בעת in postexilic and postbiblical literature and its contrast with earlier פחד and ירא clearly show that the Niphal of בעת 'be terrified' is a feature of LBH" (R. M. Wright 2005: 85–86).

BIBLIOGRAPHY

BDB 130a

Bergey 1983: 137–138 • S. R. Driver 1913b: 507 no. 15 • Polzin 1976: 145–146 • R. M. Wright 2005: 85–87

בַּקָּשָׁה n. f. *petition, request, desire*: Esth. 5:3, 6 וּמַה בַּקָּשָׁתֵךְ... מַה שְׁאֵלָתֵךְ ;7–8 ;7:2– 3; 9:12; Ezra 7:6 כֹּל בַּקָּשָׁתוֹ ... וַיִּתֶּן לוֹ הַמֶּלֶךְ

CBH Alternatives
משאלה, שאלה

1 Sam. 1:27	וַיִּתֵּן	ה'	לִי	אֶת **שְׁאֵלָתִי**
Ps. 20:6	יְמַלֵּא	ה'		כָּל **מִשְׁאֲלוֹתֶיךָ**
Ps. 37:4	וְיִתֵּן		לְךָ	**מִשְׁאֲלֹת לִבֶּךָ**
[~ Ezra 7:6	[וַיִּתֶּן]	לוֹ הַמֶּלֶךְ ...	כֹּל	**בַּקָּשָׁתוֹ**

External Post-Classical Sources
Renderings/Paraphrases/Glosses

MekhRI Amalek 2 (p. 182)   "אעברה נא ואראה" (דב' ג 25) – ואין "**נא**" אלא לשון **בקשה**

T Ber. 3:6 (Zer. p. 13)   "לשמוע אל הרנה ואל התפלה" וג' (מל"א ח 28) "הרנה" – זו רנה..."תפלה" – זו **בקשה**

Independent Use
Heb.

4Q251 f13:2   [כי **הבקשה** ה]

11QPsa 24:4–5   הט אוזנכה ותן לי את שאלתי **ובקשתי** אל תמנע ממני

M Ned. 11:12   האומרת...שמים ביני לבינך – יעשו דרך **בקשה**

T Kip. 3:18 (Mo'ed p. 247)   שמנה ברכות מברך עליהן באותו היום...ושאר תפלה תחנה **ובקשה** שעמך ישראל צריכין ליושע מלפניך

MekhRS 17:14 (p. 125)   מנין שכל **בקשות** שביקש משה מלפני הק' נתן לו?

Sifre Num. 136 (p. 183)   ראו איזו עבירה עברתי וכמה **בקשות** ביקשתי ולא נסלח לי

Sifre Deut. 26 (p. 36)   משל למלך שגזר ואמר: כל מי שאוכל פגי שביעית יהיו מחזירים אותו בקנפון. הלכה אשה אחת בת טובים, לקטה ואכלה פגי שביעית והיו מחזירים אותה בקנפון. אמרה לו: **בבקשה** ממך אדוני המלך, הודיע סרחוני שלא יהו בני המדינה אומרים: דומה שנמצא בה דבר נאוף או שנמצא בה דבר כשפים

BT Ber. 57a   הרואה ביצה בחלום – **בקשתו** תלויה. נשברת – נעשתה **בקשתו**

Comments
a. "[B]*aqqashah*, which appears seven times in Esther and once in Ezra... is formally an (Aram.) pael infinitive with very strong noun characteristics... Several

times *she'elah* stands in parallelism to *baqqashah*, which means 'petition,' 'wish,' 'desire,' 'longing,' 'request.' In Esther, *she'elah* is always used in the same expressions as *baqqashah* both in content and in form. The expressions in which it is found are so stereotyped that one would be justified in concluding that it is part of a fixed form in the ceremonial of the court, which also was the setting for *baqqashah*.... At all events, in the OT this word is found exclusively in literary contexts that have their setting in the Persian period. The textual form of Ezra and Esther is late" (Wagner 1985: 241).

b. "[T]he form קַטָּלָה ... is identical with the Aramaic infinitive *Pa'el*, but is used in MH. rather more as a true abstract than as a *nomen actionis*. Examples: כַּפָּרָה 'atonement'; כַּוָּנָה 'devotion' (direction of the mind); סַכָּנָה 'danger'; קַבָּלָה 'receipt'.... The BH. instances are comparatively late: בקרה (Ezek. xxxiv. 12), בקשה (Esther v. 7; Ezra vii. 6), נאצה (Neh. ix. 18, 26; cf. Ezek. xxxv. 12), and נחמה (Job vi. 10; Ps cxix. 50)" (Segal 1908: 706–707). In other words, although numerous forms of the verb בקש are widely documented throughout Biblical literature, the noun בקשה – cast in the Aramaic nominal pattern *qaṭṭālāh*— represents a linguistic innovation whose appearance in BH reflects the Second Temple linguistic milieu.

c. The BH particle נָא, equivalent to RH בַּקָּשָׁה (see MekhRI above), may be rendered in Targumic Aramaic by בְּבָעוּ (Aram. בּבעו = Heb. בְּבקשה); see Fassberg 1994: 51–56; 70–73:

| Num. 12:13 | לָהּ | נָא | רְפָא | נָא | אֵל |
| TO | יתה | כען | אסי | בבעו | אלהא |

| Judg. 9:38 | בּוֹ | עַתָּה וְהִלָּחֶם | | נָא | צֵא |
| TJ | ביה | כען ואגיח קרבא | | בבעו | פוק |

It has also been observed that in several cases the synoptic chapters of Chronicles do not make use of the archaic נא employed in the parallel texts of Sam.-Kgs., and, similarly, that MT נא is missing in some Biblical passages from Qumran. Hence the suggestion that this particle was no longer part of "the living linguistic usage underlying the Hebrew of the late books. ... In RH נא was not current and the sages found it necessary to interpret it" (Qimron 1971: 114).

Bibliography

HALOT I 152b–153a • GKC §84[b] e • Kaddari 122b

Bergey 1983: 133–134 • S. R. Driver 1913: 484 • Hadas-Lebel 1995: 111 • Fassberg 1994: 36–73, 51–56, 70–73 • Hurvitz 1965: 226–227; 1972: 59–60, 150 • Naveh and Greenfield 1984: 120 (= Greenfield 2001: I 237) • Paton 1908: 62–63 • Qimron 1971: 113–114 • Segal 1908: 706–707 • Wagner 1966: 133; 1985: 241

בָּרוּךְ אַתָּה ה' liturg. phr. *Blessed are You YHWH*: Ps. 119 (cf. *Proleg.* §II.4 *Criteria for Identifying Distinctive LBH Features*):12 בָּרוּךְ אַתָּה ה' לַמְּדֵנִי חֻקֶּיךָ; בָּרוּךְ אַתָּה ה' אֱלֹהֵי יִשְׂרָאֵל אָבִינוּ מֵעוֹלָם וְעַד עוֹלָם 1 Chron. 29:10

CBH Alternatives

ברוך ה', e.g.

Exod. 18:10	הִצִּיל אֶתְכֶם מִיַּד מִצְרַיִם	אֲשֶׁר		ה'	**בָּרוּךְ**
1 Sam. 25:32	שְׁלָחֵךְ הַיּוֹם הַזֶּה לִקְרָאתִי	אֲשֶׁר	יִשְׂרָאֵל	אֱלֹהֵי ה'	**בָּרוּךְ**
1 Kgs. 8:15	דִּבֶּר בְּפִיו אֵת דָּוִד אָבִי	אֲשֶׁר	יִשְׂרָאֵל	אֱלֹהֵי ה'	**בָּרוּךְ**
[~ 1 Chron. 29:10	מֵעוֹלָם וְעַד עוֹלָם	יִשְׂרָאֵל...	אֱלֹהֵי ה'	**אַתָּה**	**בָּרוּךְ**]

External Post-Classical Sources

Independent Use

Heb.

1QH[a] 8:26	**ברוך אתה אדוני** גדול העצה ורב העליליליה
1QH[a] 13:22	**ברוך אתה**
	אֽוֹדְכָֽה **אֲדוֹנִי** כי לא עזבתה יתום ולא בזיתה רש
[~ Gen. 24:27	**בָּרוּךְ**] ה' אֱלֹהֵי אֲדֹנִי אַבְרָהָם אֲשֶׁר לֹא עָזַב חַסְדּוֹ וַאֲמִתּוֹ

M Ber. 4:4	הושע ה' את עמך את ישרא'...**ברוך אתה ה'** שומע תפילה
M Ta'an. 2:4	מי שענה את אברהם בהר המוריה הוא יענה אתכם וישמע בקול צעקתכם היום הזה בָּ' א' ה' גָּאַל יִשְׂרָאֵל...בָּ' א' ה' שומע תפילה

Aram.

1QApGen 20:12–13	בליליא דן צלית...**בריך אנתה אל עליון** מרי לכול עלמים
FTV Gen. 16:13	**בריך את הוא אלהא** קיים כל עלמ'יא די חמית בצערי

Comments

a. The formula ברוך אתה ה' is one of the most common key phrases in the vocabulary of Second Temple/post-Biblical Jewish liturgy (as attested in the DSS and throughout RH texts and traditional prayer formulae). In the Hebrew Bible it appears only twice: once in Chronicles, which belongs to the distinctive LBH corpus, and again in Psalms 119, which is widely assigned to the Second Temple period (on both linguistic and non-linguistic grounds). The phrase is unattested in CBH, which often makes use of the expressions בָּרוּךְ ה׳ (blessed is the Lord) and אוֹדְךָ ה׳ (I thank you, Lord).

b. "The liturgical use of framing benedictions, particularly as closings, and the second person address to God as 'You' in blessing formulae, are innovations vis-à-vis the classic biblical blessing, which opens a spontaneous personal expression of praise about God. These innovations also have some, albeit limited and generally late, biblical roots; however, they are essentially Second Temple period developments that serve as forerunners of the rabbinic liturgical benediction" (Chazon 2012: 379–380).

c. Note that the Qumranic sectarian texts "demonstrate that the Qumran community followed accepted liturgical conventions in writing its own prayers" (ibid., 378 note 13). This is visible, inter alia, in a text in which "the original third person formula was corrected to a second person address by placing cancellation dots around the Tetragrammaton and adding אתה אדני supralinearly" (ibid., 378 note 14). Cf. the example from 1QH^a 13:33 quoted above.

d. In summary, "we may safely conclude that ברוך אתה יהוה represents a development in late Hebrew, even though the earlier expression ברוך יהוה continues to appear in post-exilic and post-biblical texts" (R. M. Wright 2005: 60).

BIBLIOGRAPHY

Chazon 2012: 379–380 • Hurvitz 1972: 50, 144–145 • R. M. Wright 2005: 59–60

גִּזְבָּר n. m. *treasurer*: Ezra 1:8 וַיּוֹצִיאֵם כּוֹרֶשׁ מֶלֶךְ פָּרַס עַל יַד מִתְרְדָת הַגִּזְבָּר

Cf. [גְּנַז], [גִּנְזַךְ]

BA Ezra 7:21 שְׁלַח לְמִכְנַשׁ; cf. גדבריא in Dan 3:2 שִׂים טְעֵם לְכֹל גִּזַּבְרַיָּא דִּי בַּעֲבַר נַהֲרָה לַאֲחַשְׁדַּרְפְּנַיָּא...גְדָבְרַיָּא...וְכֹל שִׁלְטֹנֵי מְדִינָתָא, 3—perhaps a "by-form" (*HALOT* V 842a)

External Post-Classical Sources
Renderings/Paraphrases/Glosses

Sifre Num. 123 (p. 151) — "ויקחו" (וי׳ כד 2) – מתרומת הלשכה. "אליך" (שם)
– שתהא **גיזבר** לדבר. וכשם שהיה משה **גיזבר** לדבר,
כך היה אהרן **גיזבר** לדבר

Independent Use
Heb.

M Bik. 3:3 — הפחות והסגנים **והגיזברים** יוצאין לקראתם

M Sheq. 5:2 — אין פוחתים משלשה **גיזברים** ומשבעה מרכולים
ואין עושין שררה על הציבור בממון פחות משנים

T Sheq. 2:15 (Mo'ed p. 211) — שלשה **גזברין** מה הן עושין? בהן היו פודין את
הערכין ואת החרמין ואת ההקדשות ואת מעשר
שני וכל מלאכת הקדש בהן היתה נעשית

PT Pes. 4:8 (p. 521) — **הגזבר** היה מחלפן ביד אחר

BT Shab. 31a–b — כל אדם שיש בו תורה ואין בו יראת שמים דומה
לגזבר שמסרו לו מפתחות הפנימיות ומפתחות
החיצונות לא מסרו

Aram.

Aggoula 22:1–8 — ביום 26 בשבט דכיר אסרדין בר אסרתרץ ואסרחיל
ואסרדין אחוהי ואבדא בר עבר/דמ[רתן] **גזברא**...

Dura-Europos (Naveh 1978: no. 88 [= Frey 828]: 1–7) — הדין ביתʰ אתבני בשנת חמש מאה חמשין
ושית...ודקמו על עיביתהּ הֹדֹי אברם **גיזברהּ** ושמואל
[בר ס]פרה

Comments

a. "[A] loanword from Old Persian *ganzabara* (→ *גְּנַז*)" (*HALOT* V 1843b–1844a). In Akkadian, the lexeme is attested only in late sources (*CAD* G 43a; *CDA* 90a). "The Persian word *ganzabara* (in גזבר the *nun* assimilated with the *zayin*) means = 'the person bearing the treasure'. The element בר is identical with

the German word *Bahre* and the English *bear*, whose root means = 'carry', etc."
(Kutscher 1961: 24). On Persian loanwords in general, see [גְּנַז], comment **b**.

b. "An original t sound in a Persian loan word (גִּזְבְּרַיָּא 'treasurers' E[zra] 7:21)
was wrongly spelled with ד in D[an] 3:2f (גְּדָבְרַיָּא)" (F. Rosenthal 1961: 15 §17).
"The correct vocalization is probably גִּזְבְּרַיָּא ... and the geminated t indicates
the assimilation of the נ" (Plesner 1954: 463). גדבריא may be a "by-form" of
גזבריא (see above).

c. The term גזבר, which in the Hebrew Bible unequivocally denotes the function of *treasurer*, is not found in lists and accounts related to pre-Exilic times
and therefore we cannot determine with certainty whether any of the royal
officials mentioned in these sources was specifically in charge of the treasury,
as was the case of the גזבר in the Second Temple period.

BIBLIOGRAPHY

BDB 159a, 1086a • *HALOT* I 186a, V 1843b • *CAD* G, 43a • *CDA* 90a • Ben-Iehuda II 733a
note 1 • Kaddari 151a

Kutscher 1961: 24 • Plesner 1954: 463 • F. Rosenthal 1961: 15 §17, 58 §189 • Seow 1996: 647

[גְּנַז] n. m. *treasury*: only pl. cstr. Esth. 3:9 לְהָבִיא אֶל גִּנְזֵי הַמֶּלֶךְ ;4:7

Cf. גֹּבֶר, גִּנְזַךְ

BA Ezra 5:17 וּבַקָּרוּ בְּבֵית סִפְרַיָּא דִּי גִנְזַיָּא מְהַחֲתִין תַּמָּה בְּבָבֶל; 6:1 בְּבֵית גִּנְזַיָּא דִּי מַלְכָּא ;
בֵּית גִּנְזֵי מַלְכָּא 7:20

CBH ALTERNATIVES
אוצר, e.g.

1 Kgs. 14:26	**אוֹצְרוֹת**	בֵּית	הַמֶּלֶךְ	וַיִּקַּח אֶת אֹצְרוֹת בֵּית ה' וְאֶת
[~ Esth. 3:9	**גִּנְזֵי**		הַמֶּלֶךְ	וַעֲשֶׂרֶת אֲלָפִים כִּכַּר כֶּסֶף...לְהָבִיא אֶל]

EXTERNAL POST-CLASSICAL SOURCES
Renderings/Paraphrases/Glosses
TJ 27x, e.g.

1 Sam. 25:29 ותהי נפשא דרבוני גניזא **בגנז** חיי עלמא קדם ה' אלהך
[~ וְהָיְתָה נֶפֶשׁ אֲדֹנִי צְרוּרָה **בִּצְרוֹר** הַחַיִּים אֶת ה' אֱלֹהֶיךָ]

2 Kgs. 20:13 ואחזינון ית כל בית **גנזוהי**... וית כל דאשתכח **בגנזוהי**
[~ וַיַּרְאֵם אֶת כָּל בֵּית **נְכֹתֹה**... וְאֶת כָּל אֲשֶׁר נִמְצָא **בְּאוֹצְרֹתָיו**]

Other Sources
BT Pes. 118b "ולא יאצר" (יש' כג 18) – בבית אוצרו, "ולא יחסן" (שם) – בבית גנזיו

Independent Use
Heb.
MekhRS 3:8 (p. 2) מה עשה המלך? תפס את העבד בידו והכניסו לבית
גנזיו והראהו כלי כסף וכלי זהב אבני' טובות ומרגליות
וכל מה שיש לו בבית גנזיו
Sifre Deut. 343 (p. 398) מראה הוא את גנזיו ואת כל אשר לו
ARN B 7 (p. 22) לאכול מגנזיו של מלך
BT San. 110a משאוי שלש מאות פרדות לבנות היו טעונות מפתחות
בית גנזיו שלקרח

Aram.
TAD I A6.2 (= Cowley 26):4 **וישתלח על המר/דכריא זי גנזא**
TAD I A6.13 (= Driver 10):5 ...יהנפק ויהיתה ויאתה עם **גנזא** זי מני שים
להיתיה בבאל
BT Meʿil. 17b ועול לבי **גזא** שקול כל מה דאית לכן

COMMENTS

a. "The [Persian] loanwords that [Hebrew] acquired [during the Persian period] are all related to government and administration.... Obviously, the eyes of the Persian rulers, like those of all rulers, were fixed upon profit—the taxes they could impose on the conquered lands. It is thus understandable that the Persian noun for *'treasure/treasury'* penetrated Hebrew and Aramaic in the form of גנז.... The basic notion of √גנז is *to store for safekeeping*.... From this developed the meaning *to conceal*.... The word also passed into Arabic, where it denotes also *concealment of corpses*, i.e., *burial*" (Kutscher 1961: 22–23). Two other Persian loanwords in BH are derived from the root גנז–גִּנְזַךְ and גְּזְבָּר.

b. Persian Loanwords: The striking correlation between the historical age reflected in books like Esther, Daniel, Ezra-Nehemiah, Chronicles, and certain unmistakable linguistic ties of these compositions with the Persian lexicon (e.g., פתשגן, נשתון, פרתמים, פתבג, פתגם, דת, גנז), cannot be ignored or dismissed. The prevailing view in the scholarly literature is that the identifiable Persian loanwords in the Hebrew Bible may well serve as chronological markers of the Second Temple linguistic milieu. With slight differences in formulation, this widely held opinion may be illustrated by the following three statements:

1. "There is no doubt regarding the Persian words, that they all were borrowed in the early Second Temple period, apparently via Imperial Aramaic" (Rabin 1962: 1079; see also Seow 1996: 646–650);

2. "The fact that in the latter part of the Second Temple period Judaism was undergoing far-reaching changes... has long attracted the attention of students of Judaism. The most obvious of these changes was in the use of language—the structure, syntax, morphology and lexicon of the later writings in Hebrew display differences which put them apart from the earlier books, and a new language was added to the range of sacred expression, which figures already in some of the later biblical books.... [B]oth Hebrew and Aramaic absorbed a great number of Persian words and coined certain expressions under the influence of Persian, as they also did subsequently under that of Greek" (Shaked 1984: 308);

3. "Persian words are in most cases readily recognized and the direct influence of this language is, in all probability, limited to the Achaemenid era" (Eskhult 2003: 11).

c. The (more recent) √גנז did not completely replace its (earlier) Classical equivalent √אצר; both are attested in similar contexts in LBH (cf. Esth. 3:9 גִּנְזֵי הַמֶּלֶךְ versus 1 Chron. 27:25 אֹצְרוֹת הַמֶּלֶךְ).

d. √גנז is attested in LBH only as a noun, whereas in RH and in the post-Biblical Aramaic dialects it is widely employed in verbal forms as well, e.g.:

M Shab. 16:1	כל כתבי הקדש...אף על פי כתובין בכל לשון טעונים **גניזה**
M Sheq. 6:1	שכן מסורת בידם מאבותיהם ששם הארון **גנוז**
M Mid. 1:6	ארבע לשכות היו בבית המוקד...ומה היו משמשות?
	...מזרחית צפונית בה **גנזו** בני חשמוניי את אבני המזבח
	ששיקצום מלכי יון
T Pe'ah 4:18 (Zer. p. 60)	אבותי **גנזו** אוצרו' למטה ואני **גנזתי** למעלה
T Sot. 13:1	**משנגנז** ארון נגנז עמו צנצנת המן
(Nashim p. 229)	
BT Shab. 30b	בקשו חכמים **לגנוז** ספר קהלת מפני שדבריו סותרין זה את זה

TO Gen. 41:36	ויהי	עיבורא	**גניז**	לעמא	דארעא	לשבע	שני	כפנא
[~	[וְהָיָה	הָאֹכֶל	**לְפִקָּדוֹן**	לָאָרֶץ	לְשֶׁבַע	שְׁנֵי	הָרָעָב

TO Deut. 32:34	הלא	כל	עובדיהון	גלן	קדמי	**גניזין**	ליום דינא	באוצרי
[~	[הֲלֹא	הוּא	כָּמֻס	עִמָּדִי	**חָתֻם**	בְּאוֹצְרֹתָי

TJ 2 Kgs. 20:17	ויתנטיל	כל	דבביתך	**ודגנזו**	אבהתך...	לבבל
[~	[וְנִשָּׂא	כָּל	אֲשֶׁר בְּבֵיתֶךָ	וַאֲשֶׁר אָצְרוּ	אֲבֹתֶיךָ...	בָּבֶלָה

TJ Hos. 13:12	**גניזין**	חובי בית	אפרים	נטירין	לאתפרעא כל	חטאיהון
[~	[**צְרוּר**	עֲוֹן	אֶפְרָיִם	צְפוּנָה	חַטָּאתוֹ

e. וּבְגִנְזֵי בְּרֹמִים in Ezek. 27:24 does not seem to belong to this entry; see Commentaries and Lexicons.

BIBLIOGRAPHY

BDB 170b • *HALOT* I 199a • Kaddari 162b

Eskhult 2003: 11–14 • Hurvitz 2006: 193 note 6 • Kutscher 1961: 21–24 • Rabin 1962: 1079 • Seow 1996: 646–650; 1997: 12–13 • Shaked 1984: 308, 513–514

[גִּנְזַךְ] n. m. *storeroom, treasury*: 1 Chron. 28:11 וַיִּתֵּן דָּוִיד לִשְׁלֹמֹה בְנוֹ אֶת תַּבְנִית הָאוּלָם וְאֶת בָּתָּיו וְגַנְזַכָּיו וַעֲלִיֹּתָיו וַחֲדָרָיו הַפְּנִימִים וּבֵית הַכַּפֹּרֶת

Cf. [גְּנֵז], גִּזְבָּר

CBH ALTERNATIVES

אוצר? (see comment **b** below).

EXTERNAL POST-CLASSICAL SOURCES
Independent Use
Heb.

Gen. Rab. 61:4 (p. 661)   תאמר שנחשד עליה בריה? תלמוד לומר "ושמה קטורה" (בר' כה 1) – כזה שהוא חותם **גנזכה** ומוציאה בחותמה

COMMENTS

a. "[T]he word גנזך = *treasury*, which occurs once (1Ch 28:11), is related to this root [= the Persian גנז], with the addition of the Persian suffix "-ךְ" (Kutscher 1961: 24). Thus, although the term is rare in the extra-Biblical Jewish sources, there can be little doubt that it reflects the linguistic milieu of the Persian/ Second Temple period. On Persian loanwords in general, cf. entry [גְּנֵז], comment **b**.

b. "[T]he Chronicler employs . . . new words even in cases where they are out of place, as being entirely anachronistic. . . . [T]hese new words replace obvious synonyms that are found in similar situations in the texts from which he otherwise draws much of his material. There are several such instances. . . . [For example,] 1 Chronicles 28.11 employs גנזך . . . and not אוצר, in the account of how David provides Solomon with a design for the temple" (Eskhult 2003: 13).

c. According to the account in 1 Chron. 28, the Temple plan that David entrusted to Solomon used certain terms that are not attested either in CBH in general or in the corresponding 'synoptic' chapters in Kings in particular. Thus, for example, "[t]he term used here [1 Chron. 28:11] for 'treasuries' is *ganzak*, a Persian loanword. . . . Altogether it would seem . . . that this collection of infrequent terms reflects the late usage of the Chronicler's time" (Japhet 1993: 495).

d. Another possible usage of the word גנזך in Rabbinic literature is found in PT Ber. 2:5 (p. 20) בנימן גנזכייה נפק ומור משמיה דרב: מותר, where the Aramaic suffix -יי(ה) may indicate that the said Benjamin was *in charge of the* גנזך. Conversely, D. Rosenthal (1991) has suggested that the word should be interpreted as a geographical epithet (gentilic).

Bibliography

BDB 170b • *HALOT* I 199a

Curtis and Madsen 1910: 29 no. 19, 300 • S. R. Driver 1913: 539 • Eskhult 2003: 13 • Hurvitz 1972: 16 • Japhet 1993: 495 • Kutscher 1961: 23–24 • Polzin 1976: 132 • Rabin 1962: 1079 • D. Rosenthal 1991 • Seow 1996: 647 • Wagner 1966: 42 no. 60 • Williamson 1977a: 42 • R. M. Wright 2005: 113

√**דוח** vb. *to rinse* (*a sacrifice*; cf. comment a): **Hiph** Ezek. 40:38 שָׁם יָדִיחוּ אֶת
אֶת מַעֲשֵׂה הָעוֹלָה יָדִיחוּ בָם 2 Chron. 4:6; הָעֹלָה

CBH Alternatives

√רחץ, e.g.

Exod. 29:17–18	לה'	עֹלָה הוּא	וְרָחַצְתָּ...	וְאֶת הָאַיִל תְּנַתֵּחַ לִנְתָחָיו
Lev. 1:13	לה'	עֹלָה הוּא...	יִרְחַץ בַּמָּיִם...	וְהַקֶּרֶב וְהַכְּרָעַיִם
[~ Ezek. 40:38		הָעֹלָה	יָדִיחוּ אֶת	שָׁם	[וְלִשְׁכָּה...

External Post-Classical Sources
Independent Use
Heb.

M Pes. 6:1	אלו דברים בפסח דוחין את השבת: שחיטתו וזריקת דמו ומיחוי קרביו והקטר חלביו. אבל צלייתו והדחת קרביו אינן דוחים
M Mid. 5:3	שש לשכות היו בעזרה...שבצפון לשכת המלח, לישכת הפרווה, לישכת המדיחין...לשכת המדיחין קרבי קדשים
M Tam. 4:2	הכרס מדיחין אתה בבית מדיחין כל צרכה. הקרביים מדיחין אתן...על שולחנות שלשייש שבין העמודים
T Zev. 9:9 (p. 494)	עולה הרי מפשיט ומנתיח ומוריד את הדם וזורקה למטה. מוריד את הקרבים ומדיחן במים

Comments
a. √דוח in *hiph'il* (הֵדִיחַ) appears only four times in the Hebrew Bible: in Isa. 4:4 (in a non-sacrificial setting, parallel to its common CBH counterpart רחץ); in Jer. 51:34 (within a context that is not quite clear [some scholars suggest emending the vocalization of the form from הֱדִיחָנִי (Q) to הִדִּיחָנִי, thus deriving it from נדח, and not from דוח; cf. *HALOT* I 216a]); and in Ezek. 40:38 and 2 Chron. 4:6, where it is used as a technical term associated with the *rinsing/ cleansing* of a sacrificial offering (עֹלָה). Both הֵדִיחַ and רָחַץ, having the basic meaning of *wash*, continue to function in RH, but in contrast to BH its usage is greatly intensified (in cultic and non-cultic contexts). The increased frequency of הֵדִיחַ in RH finds clear expression in the fact that the *rinsing/cleansing* of sacrifices, invariably referred to in the Pentateuch by רָחַץ, is denoted in Rabbinic literature by הֵדִיחַ (see the above examples, which were deliberately selected to reflect cultic contexts only). It is this linguistic development that best accounts for the late distribution pattern of הֵדִיחַ in a sacrificial context in BH.

b. The lateness of הֵדִיחַ is further demonstrated by the textual modification evident in the following 'synoptic passages':

1 Kgs. 7:38–39	וְחָמֵשׁ...	מִיָּמִין	חָמֵשׁ...	וַיִּתֵּן...	וַיַּעַשׂ עֲשָׂרָה כִיּרוֹת
2 Chron. 4:6	וַחֲמִשָּׁה	מִיָּמִין	חֲמִשָּׁה	וַיִּתֵּן	וַיַּעַשׂ כִּיּוֹרִים עֲשָׂרָה

1 Kgs.	וְאֵת הַיָּם...		מִשְּׂמֹאלוֹ
2 Chron.	וְהַיָּם...		מִשְּׂמֹאול לְרָחְצָה בָהֶם אֶת מַעֲשֵׂה הָעוֹלָה יָדִיחוּ בָם

"Two salient observations concerning the 'added' material in the above parallel texts are worthy of comment. First of all, it is to be noted that the Chronicler has additional material concerning cleansing practices which does not occur in the earlier text from Kings. In describing the cleansing of the offering he uses the root דוח. The addition of this term supports the argument that this was the common term used to refer to the cleansing of the sacrifice in his day, in the Second Temple period. It is also striking that in the additional material in the Chronicler's account, the earlier term for cleaning the sacrifice, רחץ, occurs two times. However, the Chronicler employs רחץ to refer to the cleaning of non-sacrificial material, i.e. the laver and the priests. This suggests that the use of רחץ in referring to 'cleansing of sacrifices' was no longer part of the living language at the time of the Chronicler's writing and had been in fact replaced by the later Hiphil דוח" (Rooker 1990: 165). Whether the Chronicler's use of two forms for cleansing suggests a semantic and/or functional distinction or is simply for purposes of lexical variety, the fact remains that a semantic narrowing of the root דוח to denote a sacrificial context did eventually take place; cf. BT Ber. 51a: מבחוץ – "שטיפה", מבפנים – "הדחה". In any event, the very appearance of √דוח on the Biblical scene as part of the cultic terminology associated with sacrifices is a linguistic innovation unattested in the Pentateuch.
c. 2Q26 f1:1–3 [...] הֻדִּיחוּ לוחא לממֹּ[...]סלקו מיא עלא מן [...] וֹנֹטֹלוֹ לוחא מן מיא...[...]
is highly questionable and does not refer to a sacrificial ritual. Furthermore, we find no evidence for the vitality of √דוח in Aramaic (Tg. 2 Chron. 4:6 מדיחין is only an echo of the Hebrew Vorlage ידיחו).

BIBLIOGRAPHY

Hurvitz 1974a: 35–36; 1982: 63–65 • Rooker 1990: 164–166 • Zimmerli 1979–83: II 367

דָּוִיד (*plene spelling*) pr. n. *David*: 1 Kgs. 3:14; 11:4, 36; Ezek. 34:23; Amos 6:5; 9:11;
Zech. 12:7–8, 10, 12; 13:1; Ps. 122:5; Song 4:4; Ezra 3:10; 8:2, 20; Neh. 3:15–16; 12:24,
36–37, 45–46; 1 Chron. 2:15; 3:1, 9; 4:31; 6:16; 7:2; 9:22; 10:14; 11:1, 3–7, 9–11, 13, 15–18,
25; 12:1, 9, 17–20, 22–24, 32, 39–40; 13:1–2, 5–6, 8, 11–13; 14:1–3, 8, 10–12, 14, 16–17;
15:1–4, 11, 16, 25, 27, 29; 16:1–2, 7, 43; 17:1–2, 4, 7, 15–16, 18, 24; 18:1–11, 13–14, 17;
19:2–6, 8, 17–19; 20:1–3, 7–8; 21:1–2, 5, 8–11, 13, 16–19, 21–26, 28, 30; 22:1–5, 7, 17;
23:1, 6, 25, 27; 24:3, 31; 25:1; 26:26, 31–32; 27:18, 23–24, 31–32; 28:1–2, 11, 20; 29:1,
9–10, 20, 22–24, 26, 29; 2 Chron. 1:1, 4, 8–9; 2:2, 6, 11, 13, 16; 3:1; 5:1–2; 6:4, 6–8, 10,
15–17, 42; 7:6, 10, 17–18; 8:11, 14; 9:31; 10:16, 19; 11:17–18; 12:16; 13:5–6, 8, 23; 16:14; 17:3;
21:1, 7, 12, 20; 23:3, 9, 18; 24:16, 25; 27:9; 28:1; 29:2, 25–27, 30; 30:26; 32:5, 30, 33; 33:7,
14; 34:2–3; 35:3–4, 15

4QSamᵃ f61i+62:5			דויד	מעם	יואב	ויצא	
[~ 2 Sam. 3:26			דָוִד	מֵעִם	יוֹאָב	וַיֵּצֵא]	

1QIsaᵃ 6:13–14	אפרים	על	ארם	נחה	לאמור	דויד	לבית	ויגד	
[~ Isa. 7:2	אֶפְרָיִם	עַל	אֲרָם	נָחָה	לֵאמֹר	דָוִד	לְבֵית	וַיֻּגַּד]	

11QPsᵃ 23:7–8	נעים	ומה	...נעים	טוב	מה	הנה	לדויד	ה מעלות[!]	שיר
[~ Ps. 133:1	נָעִים	וּמַה	...נָעִים	טוֹב	מַה	הִנֵּה	לְדָוִד	הַמַּעֲלוֹת	שִׁיר]

CBH Alternatives

דוד (*defective spelling*), e.g.

2 Sam. 5:12	יִשְׂרָאֵל	עַל	לְמֶלֶךְ	ה'	הֱכִינוֹ	כִּי	דָוִד	וַיֵּדַע	
[~ 1 Chron. 14:2	יִשְׂרָאֵל	עַל	לְמֶלֶךְ	ה'	הֱכִינוֹ	כִּי	דָוִיד	וַיֵּדַע]	

2 Sam. 8:5	אִישׁ	אֶלֶף	וּשְׁנַיִם	עֶשְׂרִים	בַּאֲרָם	דָוִד	וַיַּךְ		
[~ 1 Chron. 18:5	אִישׁ	אֶלֶף	וּשְׁנַיִם	עֶשְׂרִים	בַּאֲרָם	דָוִיד	וַיַּךְ]		

External Post-Classical Sources
Independent Use
Heb.

BS (B) 47:2	כי כחלב מורם מקדש כן דויד מישראל
BS (B) 49:4	לבד מדויד יחזקיהו ויאשיהו כלם השחיתו
CD 5:5	ויעלו מעשי דויד מלבד דם אוריה
1QM 11:1–2	ואת גולית הגתי איש גבור חיל הסגרתה ביד דויד עבדכה
4Q174 f1–2i:11	הואה צמח דויד העומד עם דורש התורה
4Q252 5:3–4	עד בוא משיח הצדק צמח דויד
11Q13 2:9–10	כאשר כתוב עליו בשירי דויד
Frey 621:1–4	פה ינוח אשת לאון בן דויד מן מילו

COMMENTS

a. The distribution in MT of דוד and דויד is highly illuminating (see detailed statistics in the BH tables below). "Just as we know that the defective three-letter spelling is the original alphabetic spelling of the name David, and that it preceded the four-letter fuller spelling in time, so we also know that the books of Samuel and Kings are older than the Chronicler's work; and in a general way the data correspond to this elementary observation about the spelling of the name David in the books of the Bible. With certain equally obvious exceptions, it is clear that the older books (not just in content but in composition, compilation, and publication) have the earlier spelling and the later books have the more developed spelling...the occurrence of the three-letter name in a book would point to an earlier date of composition in its present form, while the presence of the four-letter spelling of the name would point to a later date" (Freedman 1983: 93).

b. Kutscher (1974: 5) notes that "the Masoretic Text [of Isaiah] clearly reflects the normal orthography of the First Commonwealth, and the Scroll that of the Second Commonwealth. The evolution of the orthography of the proper noun דויד points to the same conclusion. In the Scroll it is always written דויד (with a *yod*)," as demonstrated in the QH table below.

c. Note the following in the tables below:

1. The numbers recorded are the output of our computerized search of the MT (per BHS) and the DSS. Some earlier studies portray slightly different statistics for the distribution of the two spellings in the books of the MT (Freedman 1983: 89 note 1; cf. p. 244 § A.1 below). Nevertheless, this does not change the general picture emerging from the tables below.

2. The division between Biblical and non-Biblical scrolls in QH is intended for purposes of comparison to MT books but does not necessarily reflect the canonical status of these texts in the eyes of the Qumran community.

3. The group of books categorized as "Transitional and/or Uncertain" shows a preference for the traditional form with the defective spelling.

4. The number of occurrences in Psalms does not distinguish between the titles of the psalms (in which we find the vast majority of the name's appearance) and the psalms themselves.

5. In some cases, the physical condition of the DSS limits the degree of certainty of our readings. Therefore, the numbers of occurrences listed in the QH table may not be entirely precise but reliably reflect the general picture in this corpus.

6. Since 11Q5 (The Psalms Scroll) includes both canonical and non-canonical psalms, it appears in both the Biblical and the non-Biblical sections of the QH table.

d. We have made no attempt to describe the spelling of the name David in Rabbinic literature (see above, Independent Use). The complex process of textual transmission revealed in the manuscripts of this literature has blurred the diachronic development of the orthography of this name that is readily discernable in the DSS.

BH		
CBH		
MT	דוד	דויד
1 Sam.	291	–
2 Sam.	285	–
1 Kgs.	75	3
2 Kgs.	18	–
Isa.	10	–
Hosea	1	–
Amos	–	2
Total:	680	5

Transitional and/or Uncertain

MT	דוד	דויד
Jer.	15	–
Ezek.	3	1
Ps.	87	1
Prov.	1	–
Song	–	1
Ruth	2	–
Total:	108	3

LBH		
MT	דוד	דויד
Zech.	–	6
Qoh.	1	–
Ezra	–	3
Neh.	–	8
1 Chron.	–	187
2 Chron.	–	74
Total:	1	278

QH			
Biblical			
	Scroll no.	דוד	דויד
Sam.	1Q7	–	2
	4Q51	1	47
	4Q52	8	–
Kgs.	5Q2	1	–
Isa.	1QIsa	–	11
	1Q8	1	1
	4Q64	1	–
Jer.	4Q70	–	1
Zech.	4Q80	–	1
Ps.	5/6Hev1b	3	–
	4Q83	–	2
	4Q85	1	1
	4Q98	–	1
	11Q5	–	12
	11Q6	–	1
	11Q8	–	1
	Total:	16	81

Non-Biblical			
	Scroll no.	דוד	דויד
	CD	1	2
	1QM	–	1
	4Q161	–	1
	4Q174	–	4
	4Q177	–	2
	4Q245	–	1
	4Q252	–	2
	4Q285	–	1
	4Q398	–	1
	4Q457	–	1
	4Q479	–	2
	4Q504	–	1
	4Q522	–	1
	6Q9	–	1
	11Q5	–	2
	11Q11	–	1
	11Q13	–	1
	11Q14	–	1
	Total:	1	26

BIBLIOGRAPHY

JM 9 §3 *a* note 5

Andersen and Forbes 1986: 6–9 • Freedman 1983 • Gesenius 1815: 30 • Naveh and Greenfield 1984: 120–121 (= Greenfield 2001: I 237–238) • Kutscher 1974: 5, 99–100 • Qimron 1978: 146; 1986: 91 • Rooker 1990: 68–71

[דַּרְכְּמוֹן] n. m. *drachma* (δραχμή): Ezra 2:69 וָאֶלֶף שֵׁשׁ רִבֹּאות דַּרְכְּמֹנִים זָהָב; Neh. 7:69 וּמֵרָאשֵׁי הָאָבֹות נָתְנוּ לְאֹוצַר הַמְּלָאכָה זָהָב דַּרְכְּמֹנִים אֶלֶף 70 הַתִּרְשָׁתָא נָתַן לָאֹוצָר, 71 זָהָב דַּרְכְּמֹנִים שְׁתֵּי רִבֹּות וְכֶסֶף מָנִים אַלְפַּיִם וּמָאתָיִם

Cf. אֲדַרְכֹּון

CBH ALTERNATIVES
See comment **b** below.

EXTERNAL POST-CLASSICAL SOURCES
Renderings/Paraphrases/Glosses
TPJ 3X
Gen. 24:22   ונסיב גברא קדשא דדהבא **דרכמונא** מתקליה קבל **דרכמונא** לגולגלתא
[~   מִשְׁקָלֹו   בֶּקַע   זָהָב   נֶזֶם   הָאִישׁ   וַיִּקַּח]

Exod. 38:26   קודשא   בסילעי   סילעא   פלגות   לגלגלתא   **דרכמונא**
[~   הַקֹּדֶשׁ   בְּשֶׁקֶל   הַשֶּׁקֶל   מַחֲצִית   לַגֻּלְגֹּלֶת   בֶּקַע]

Other Sources
LXX Gen. 24:22   ἐνώτια χρυσᾶ ἀνὰ **δραχμὴν**   ὁλκῆς
[~   מִשְׁקָלֹו   בֶּקַע   זָהָב   נֶזֶם]

LXX Exod. 38:26   **δραχμὴ**   μία τῇ κεφαλῇ
[~ Exod. 39:3   לַגֻּלְגֹּלֶת   בֶּקַע]

Independent Use
Phoen.
KAI 60:1–6   ... לעטר אית שמעבעל בן מגן...עטרת חרץ **בדרכנם**
(1st cent. BCE)   ...למחת 20 **דרכמנם** צדן בעל אלם בכסף ישאן...למחת 20

Aram.
Lam. Rab. 3:6   לבתר יומין אתא ר׳ יהושע בן לוי לטבריה ואיתקבל גבי ר׳ חייא
רבא ויהב לתלמידוויי דר׳ יהושע **דרכמונין** ואמ׳ להון: זילו עבידו
לרבכון כמנהגיה

Greek (LXX)
Tob. 5:15   ἀλλ᾽ εἰπόν μοι τίνα σοι ἔσομαι μισθὸν διδόναι **δραχμὴν** τῆς
ἡμέρας καὶ τὰ δέοντά σοι ὡς καὶ τῷ υἱῷ μου

COMMENTS

a. "In the Old Testament, there are two similar words that appear to refer to coins in texts of the Persian period: *ᵃdarkōnîm* ... and *darkᵉmōnîm*. ... [C]ertainly on the surface the most attractive suggestion [is] ... seeing Drachmas in *darkᵉmōnîm* and Darics in *ᵃdarkaōnîm*, the *mem* of *darkᵉmōnîm* being the distinguishing factor. In both cases, the *-ōn* ending would reflect the Greek genitive plural. Both types of coins were, of course, current in the Persian period" (Williamson 1977b: 125). Or, in a different formulation, "[t]he word אדרכון—in terms of its form—is none other than the דריכוס, which is the Persian *sheqel* of gold; whereas the דרכמון is the Greek δραχμή" (Avi-Yonah and Liver 1962: 823). It is noteworthy that the spellings דרכנס (= אדרכונים?) and דרכמנס (= דרכמונים) were used interchangeably in the Phoenician inscription from Piraeus quoted above (*KAI* 60:1–6), which may imply that the two Biblical terms were synonymous. There are, however, alternative explanations for the Phoenician evidence (cf., e.g., Cooke 1903: 96–97). Be that as it may, regardless of the precise meaning and function of אדרכון and דרכמון—whether they are simply two variant forms of a single lexeme or two distinct currencies; whether one of them is borrowed from Persian and the other from Greek, or both are loans from one and the same language—their very appearance in the Bible (Ezra, Nehemiah, and Chronicles) must be assigned to post-Exilic times and reflects—historically—the Second-Temple vocabulary of BH.

b. Minted coinage was apparently unknown before the Persian period, as indicated by the fact that the standard reference literature dealing with Ancient Near Eastern numismatics begins its coverage only in this period (see, e.g., Meshorer 1982; Japhet 1993: 508). Thus, the historical and linguistic evidence adduced above is firmly corroborated by the archaeological-numismatic data.

c. On the linguistic lateness of Persian loanwords in general in BH, see Proleg. §II.3 Linguistic Affinities, *Persian Loanwords*; the entry גֶּנֶז, comment **b**.

BIBLIOGRAPHY

BDB 204a • *HALOT* I 232b • Kaddari 196b

Avi-Yonah and Liver 1962: 823 • Cooke 1903 • S. R. Driver 1913: 539 • Eskhult 2003: 12 • Meshorer 1982 • Mussies 1992: 195 • Williamson 1977b: 125

דַּרְמֶשֶׂק g.n. *Damascus*: 1 Chron. 18:5, 6; 2 Chron. 16:2; 24:23; 28:5, 23 וַיִּזְבַּח לֵאלֹהֵי
דַרְמֶשֶׂק

1QIsaᵃ 6:8; 7:23; 9:23; 14:3, 5; e.g.

1QIsaᵃ 14:3	מפלה	מעי	והיית	מעיר	מוסר **דרמשק**	הנה **דרמשק** משא
[~ Isa. 17:1	מַפָּלָה	מְעִי	וְהָיְתָה	מֵעִיר	מוּסָר **דַּמֶּשֶׂק**	הִנֵּה **דַּמֶּשֶׂק** מַשָּׂא]

CBH ALTERNATIVES

דמשק, e.g.

2 Sam. 8:5	בַּאֲרָם	דָּוִד	וַיַּךְ	צוֹבָה	מֶלֶךְ	לַהֲדַדְעֶזֶר	לַעְזֹר	**דַּמֶּשֶׂק** אֲרָם וַתָּבֹא
[~ 1 Chron. 18:5	בַּאֲרָם	דָּוִיד	וַיַּךְ	צוֹבָה	מֶלֶךְ	לַהֲדַדְעֶזֶר	לַעְזוֹר	**דַּרְמֶשֶׂק** אֲרָם וַיָּבֹא]

1 Kgs. 15:18	לֵאמֹר **בְּדַמֶּשֶׂק**	הַיֹּשֵׁב	אֲרָם	מֶלֶךְ	... הֲדַד בֶּן	אֶל ...	וַיִּשְׁלַחֵם
[~ 2 Chron. 16:2	לֵאמֹר **בְּדַרְמֶשֶׂק**	הַיּוֹשֵׁב	אֲרָם	מֶלֶךְ	הֲדַד בֶּן	אֶל	וַיִּשְׁלַח]

EXTERNAL POST-CLASSICAL SOURCES
Renderings/Paraphrases/Glosses

TN 4x, e.g.

Gen. 14:15	**לדרמשק**	צפון מן	די	חובה	עד	יתהון ורדף
[~	**לְדַמֶּשֶׂק**	מִשְּׂמֹאל	אֲשֶׁר	חוֹבָה	עַד	וַיִּרְדְּפֵם]

TPJ 3x, e.g.

Gen. 15:2	**בדרמשק**		ביתי פרנסת	...	בר ואליעזר
[~	אֱלִיעֶזֶר	דַּמֶּשֶׂק	הוּא	בֵיתִי	מֶשֶׁק	וּבֶן]

Other Sources

FTV Gen. 14:15	**דרמסק**	דמיצפון	עינותה	עד	ורדפינון
[~	**לְדַמֶּשֶׂק**	מִשְּׂמֹאל אֲשֶׁר	חוֹבָה	עַד	וַיִּרְדְּפֵם]

1QApGen 22:9–10	**דרמשק** שמאל על ... לחלבון דבקו עד ... להון רדף והוא
[~ Gen. 14:15	**לְדַמֶּשֶׂק** מִשְּׂמֹאל ... חוֹבָה עַד וַיִּרְדְּפֵם]

Pesh. 1 Kgs. 20:34	**בדרמסוק**	לך	אעבד	וְשׁוּקָא...
[~	**בְּדַמֶּשֶׂק**	לְךָ	תָּשִׂים	וְחוּצוֹת...]

Independent Use

Heb.

M Yad. 4:3	וכשבא ר' יוסי בן **דורמסקית** אצל ר' אליעזר ללוד אמ' לו: מה
	חידוש היה לכם בבית ה מדרש[!] היום
T Ter. 7:13	מים שהדיח בהן עובטין **ודרמסקניות** לחולה אין בהן משום גלוי
(Zer. p. 146)	
T BM 7:4 (Nez. p. 99)	השוכר את הפועל להביא ענבים ותפוחים **ודרמסקנות** לחולה
	והלך ומצאו שמת או שהבריא לא יאמר לו טול מה שהבאת
	בשכרך אלא נותן לו שכרו משלם
Sifre Deut. 1 (p. 7)	"משא דבר ה' בארץ חדרך ודמשק..." (זכ' ט 1) – אמר לו
	רבי יוסי בן **דור**/[**מסקית**]: יהודה ברבי, למה אתה מעוית עלינו
	את הכתובים? מעיד אני עלי שמים וארץ שאני **מדמשק** ויש
	שם מקום ששמו חדרך
PT Qid. 1:9 (p. 1159)	"את הקיני ואת הקניזי ואת הקדמוני" (בר' טו 19) – ר' יודה
	אמ': שלמאה שכייה נבטייה. ר' שמעון אמ': אסיא ואסטטיה
	ודרמשק
Gen. Rab. 44:23	"את הקיני ואת הקניזי ואת הקדמוני" (בר' טו 19) – ר' א':
(pp. 445–446)	ערווייה שלמייה נוטייה. ר' שמעון בן יוחי א': **דרמסקוס** ואסיא
	ואספמיא

Aram.

PT Shab. 1:6 (p. 374)	חד תלמיד מן סימאי אזל לאנטוייריס וייתון ליה **דרמסקינא**
	ואכל. חד תלמיד מן דר' יהושע בן לוי אזל לתמן ואייתי ליה
	דרמסקינא ולא אכל

COMMENTS

a. "Almost all the books of the Bible use the form דמשק exclusively.... The form דרמשק is found in one book only—Chronicles, and this is one of the latest of the Biblical works and dates from the period of the Second Commonwealth" (Kutscher 1974: 3–4).

b. "The Massoretic text of Isaiah reads דַּמֶּשֶׂק, whereas the Scroll [=1QIsᵃ] has דרמשק seven times. The early sources of this name, viz. the Egyptian, Akkadian, and [Old] Aramaic inscriptions, show only a form without /r/ that parallels the Massoretic form.... [T]he form of דרמשק...appears in MH and Syriac" (Kutscher 1982: 94 §153).

c. The form דרמשק, recorded in the Genesis Apocryphon, is "the spelling found in the late books of the OT.... [I]n earlier OT books it is *Dammeśeq*.... The Aramaic form with *reš* represents the resolution of a doubling with a liq-uid (compare *korsê, manda'*). Once the form developed, it persisted in the

Aramaic-speaking area" (Fitzmyer 2004: 242). In a slightly different formulation, the emergence of the late form דרמשק may be described as follows: "All the evidence of *reš* in the name is relatively late, the earliest being the book of Chronicles. This is clearly, therefore, a secondary form, due to dissimilation of the doubled *mem*. . . . In Official Aramaic a doubled consonant is frequently replaced by /n/ + simple consonant (e.g., חִנְטִין, לְהַנְסָקָה). It is rare to find /r/ in this role, though it is documented in Ancient and Official Aramaic, as well as Late Aramaic. The דרמשק of Chronicles fits this pattern well" (Elitzur 2004: 196–197).

d. In spite of the overwhelming evidence for the linguistic lateness of דַּרְמֶשֶׂק, an objection has recently been voiced on methodological grounds. In this connection, two arguments deserve comment. (1) דַּרְמֶשֶׂק never completely supplants the Classical form דַּמֶשֶׂק in late works; and (2) there is no certainty that the Chronicles' use of the form דַּרְמֶשֶׂק actually reflects the Chronicler's own language and not that of some later copyist (Rezetko 2010). Neither of these arguments, however, is valid. First, the continued late usage of the Classical דַּמֶשֶׂק in no way impugns the exclusively late linguistic status of דַּרְמֶשֶׂק. The decisive issue is not when a given Classical element ceased to be employed, but when a linguistic innovation became available as a substitute for its Classical counterpart. As demonstrated above, דַּרְמֶשֶׂק occurs only in late material. Second, the claim that textual 'fluidity' may be responsible for the presence of late linguistic features in Biblical texts cannot account for such an accumulation of late linguistic features precisely in those compositions unanimously dated to the post-Exilic period. Were דַּרְמֶשֶׂק merely a result of the vagaries of scribal transmission, rather than a feature characteristic of LBH itself, we should expect to find it scattered here and there throughout Biblical literature, and not confined to a late work such as Chronicles (cf. Proleg. §IV).

e. "We are thus forced to conclude that the form דרמשק was not yet used (in literature at any rate), in Isaiah's time, i.e. the eighth century BCE. Now, since the Masoretic Text of the book of Isaiah contains the form דמשק but not דרמשק, it could—at least as far as this is concerned—date back to the days of Isaiah, whereas the Isaiah Scroll (= 1QIsaᵃ), since it uses the form דרמשק, obviously cannot" (Kutscher 1974: 4).

f. Note that some of the quotations adduced above from RH and RA do not name the city itself, but rather persons or commodities related to Damascus. The decisive significance of these forms for our discussion lies in the fact that their geographical component includes the secondary, i.e., later, *reš*: דורמסקית (and not דמסקית*); דרמסק[י]ן (and not דמסק[י]ן*), or the like.

BIBLIOGRAPHY

HALOT I 232b • Kaddari 196b–197a

Elitzur 2004: 193–200, 308, 360, 363 • Fitzmyer 2004: 242 • Gesenius 1815 (1973): 29 • Hurvitz 1972: 17–18; 2006: 196–200 • Kutscher 1974: 3–4; 1982: 94 §153 • Rezetko 2010 • F. Rosenthal 1939: 16–18 • Schattner-Rieser 1994: 195

דרש√ + God's [written] Law and commandments (תּוֹרָה, מִצְוֹת, פִּקּוּדִים, חֻקִּים)
vb. collocation *to enquire, investigate, study God's word*: **Qal** Isa. 34:16 (see comment b below); Ps. 119:45, 94 (see comment a below) כִּי פִקּוּדֶיךָ דָרָשְׁתִּי, 155 כִּי
שָׁמְרוּ 1 Chron. 28:8; עֶזְרָא הֵכִין לְבָבוֹ לִדְרוֹשׁ אֶת תּוֹרַת ה' Ezra 7:10; חֻקֶּיךָ לֹא דָרָשׁוּ
וְדִרְשׁוּ כָּל מִצְוֹת ה' אֱלֹהֵיכֶם

Cf. מִדְרָשׁ

CBH ALTERNATIVES
הגה√ (cf. Josh. 1:8 and Ps. 1:2 below)

שָׁמוֹר תִּשְׁמְרוּן אֶת מִצְוֹת ה'... וִירַשְׁתָּ אֶת הָאָרֶץ		Deut. 6:17–18
[שָׁמְרוּ וְדִרְשׁוּ כָּל מִצְוֹת ה'... לְמַעַן תִּירְשׁוּ אֶת הָאָרֶץ		~ 1 Chron. 28:8]

EXTERNAL POST-CLASSICAL SOURCES
Renderings/Paraphrases/Glosses

וְאַל יָמֵשׁ ... **אִישׁ דּוֹרֵשׁ** בַּתּוֹרָה יוֹמָם וָלַיְלָה		1QS 6:6
[לֹא יָמוּשׁ סֵפֶר הַתּוֹרָה הַזֶּה מִפִּיךָ **וְהָגִיתָ** בּוֹ יוֹמָם וָלַיְלָה		~ Josh. 1:8]
] וּבְתוֹרָתוֹ **יֶהְגֶּה** יוֹמָם וָלָיְלָה		~ Ps. 1:2]

Independent Use
Heb.

1QS 6:7–8	והרבים ישקודו ביחד את שלישית כול לילות השנה לקרוא בספר **ולדרוש** משפט ולברך ביחד
CD 6:3–9	"בְּאֵר חֲפָ[רֻ]הָ שָׂרִים כָּרוֻהָ נְדִיבֵי[ן] הָעָם [במחוקק" (במ' כא 18) – הבאר הי[א]ה התור[ה]... והמחוקק הוא **דּוֹרֵשׁ הַתּוֹרָה** אשר אמר ישעיה מוציא כלי למעשיהו
M Sheq. 1:4	אלא שהכהנים **דורשים** מקרא זה לעצמן: "וכל מינחת כהן כליל תהיה לא תאכל" (וי' ו 16)
T BQ 9:7 (Nez. p. 44)	ועוד זו **דָּרַשׁ** ר' נחמיה: "אם יקום והתהלך בחוץ על משענתו ונקה המכה" (שמ' כא 19) – וכי עלת על לב שיהא זה מהלך בשוק וזה נהרג על ידיו? אלא אפי' מת מחמת מכה ראשונה פטור

Aram.
TJ ix

Judg. 5:9	אנא שליחא לשבחא לספרי ישראל דכד הות עקתא ההיא לא פסקו **מלמדרש** באוריתא
[~	לִבִּי לְחוֹקְקֵי יִשְׂרָאֵל]

PT Hor. 3:8 (p. 1430)	ר' אבא בר כהנא אזל לחד אתר. אשכח ר' לוי יתיב **דָּרַשׁ**: "איש אשר יתן לו האלהים עושר ונכסים וכבוד..." (קה' ו 21)

COMMENTS

a. The noun מִדְרָשׁ, associated semantically with *study/interpretation/exposition/commentary*, is recorded in the Hebrew Bible in the late book of Chronicles alone (cf. מִדְרָשׁ). The verb דרש is to be found in CBH, but its meaning in earlier literature is consistently *seek/search/look for/inquire after* (particularly of God or a person). Only in the later writings (Ezra, Chronicles, Ps. 119 [on the linguistic profile of this psalm, see Proleg. §II.4]) does the verb begin to refer specifically to God's written law (תּוֹרָה) and commandments (חֻקִּים, פִּקּוּדִים, מִצְוֹת)—these serving as syntactical accusatives—thus heralding the extensively widespread usage of √דרש in post-Biblical Jewish sources (QH, RH, RA). Contrast, for instance, the following verses:

Gen. 25:22	ה'		אֶת	לִדְרֹשׁ	וַתֵּלֶךְ
[~ Ezra 7:10	ה'	תּוֹרַת	אֶת	לִדְרוֹשׁ	הֵכִין לְבָבוֹ [עֶזְרָא

Isa. 9:12	דָרָשׁוּ	לֹא	צְבָאוֹת	ה' וְאֶת	הַמַּכֵּהוּ	וְהָעָם לֹא שָׁב עַד
Isa. 31:1	דָרָשׁוּ	לֹא		ה' וְאֶת	לְעֶזְרָה...	הוֹי הַיֹּרְדִים מִצְרַיִם
[~ Ps. 119:155	דָרָשׁוּ	לֹא	חֻקֶּיךָ	כִּי	יְשׁוּעָה	[רָחוֹק מֵרְשָׁעִים

This linguistic development is clearly discernible with the emergence of the later phrase *searching in God's written word* at the expense of the earlier *seeking out God*. "Instead of priest and prophet came rabbi and scholar, and instead of prophecy and 'the word of God' [דבר ה'] came interpretation and 'the word of Torah' [דבר תורה]" (Gertner 1962: 3 and note 4). From a slightly different perspective, it has been observed that "whereas the expression 'to inquire (לדרש) of YHWH' occurs in a mantic context of prophetic inquiry in 1 Kgs. 22:8, for example, and the expression 'to inquire of Elohim' occurs in a mantic context of legal inquiry in Exod. 18:15, the expression used in Ezra 7:10 is significantly 'to inquire (לדרש) of *the Torah of* YHWH'. Here the text of divine words serves, as it were, as an *oraculum* for rational-exegetical inquiry" (Fishbane 1985: 245). Fishbane correctly describes this development—in linguistic terms—as a "semantic shift" (ibid.). While the Biblical examples cited above may not strictly reflect the Rabbinic concept of interpretation typically associated with דרש in post-Biblical times, the very fact that the action is performed on a written text—a usage not attested in CBH—clearly indicates that LBH דרש is a forerunner of the later Rabbinic meaning.

b. The exact nuance of √דרש in Isa. 34:16 דִּרְשׁוּ מֵעַל סֵפֶר ה' וּקְרָאוּ is uncertain. On the one hand √דרש relates to a written text associated with God (סֵפֶר + ה'), but on the other, it is accompanied here by the preposition מֵעַל, in contrast to the regular linguistic usage in LBH and RH.

c. The root דרש is employed twice in the above quote from the Damascus Covenant (CD 6:3–9), but only the second occurrence makes use of the late meaning (i.e., *study a text/extrapolate*). The first occurrence, אשר קרא אל את כולם שרים כי דרשוהו ולא הושבה פארתם בפי אחד, does not differ in meaning from the earlier *seek*, as in Ps. 34:5 דָּרַשְׁתִּי אֶת ה' וְעָנָנִי.

d. Note that Arabic دَرَسَ (*darasa*) 'to study earnestly' is probably borrowed from Jewish-Christian circles ("Always used in the Qur'an of studying deeply into or searching the Scriptures and the reference is always directly or indirectly to the Jews and Christians" [Jeffery 1938: 128]).

e. Finally, it is interesting to note that—typologically—an analogous case of the modification attested in the meaning of BH √דרש may be observed in the corresponding linguistic development underlying the English semantic shift "search" > "research" (of written texts).

BIBLIOGRAPHY

Fishbane 1985: 245 • Gertner 1962: 3, 4–8 • Hayneman 1946: 185 • Hurvitz 1972: 131–134; 1995a: 1–10 • Jeffery 1938: 128–129 • Milgrom 1991–2001: III 2111 • R. M. Wright 2005: 64–67

דָּת n. f. *law, decree*: Esth. 1:8, 13 וְיִכָּתֵב בְּדָתֵי פָרַס וּמָדַי וְלֹא יַעֲבוֹר 15, 19, כָּל יֹדְעֵי דָת וָדִין; 2:12; 3:8 וְהַדָּת נִתְּנָה בְּשׁוּשַׁן הַבִּירָה 15, 14, וְאֶת דָּתֵי הַמֶּלֶךְ אֵינָם עֹשִׂים 4:3, 8, 11, 16; 8:13, 14, 17; 9:1, 13, 14; Ezra 8:36 וַיִּתְּנוּ אֶת דָּתֵי הַמֶּלֶךְ לַאֲחַשְׁדַּרְפְּנֵי הַמֶּלֶךְ

BA דָּתָא, דָּת 14, 21, לְעֶזְרָא כָהֲנָא סָפַר דָּתָא Dan. 2:13, 15; 6:6, 9, 13, 16; 7:25; Ezra 7:12 דָּתָא 26; דָּתֵי Dan. 2:9; דָּתֵי Ezra 7:25. Cf. also Dan. 3:2, 3 דְּתָבְרַיָּא = *the judges*

CBH ALTERNATIVES

חקה, משפט

וְלֹא תֵלְכוּ **בְּחֻקֹּת**	הַגּוֹי	אֲשֶׁר אֲנִי מְשַׁלֵּחַ מִפְּנֵיכֶם			Lev. 20:23
וַיֵּלְכוּ **בְּחֻקּוֹת**	הַגּוֹיִם	אֲשֶׁר הוֹרִישׁ ה׳	מִפְּנֵי	בְּנֵי יִשְׂרָאֵל	2 Kgs. 17:8
הָיוּ עֹבְדִים **כְּמִשְׁפַּט**	הַגּוֹיִם...				2 Kgs. 17:33
וּכְמִשְׁפְּטֵי	הַגּוֹיִם...	לֹא	עֲשִׂיתֶם		Ezek. 5:7
וְדָתֵיהֶם שֹׁנוֹת מִכָּל עָם וְאֶת דָּתֵי הַמֶּלֶךְ אֵינָם עֹשִׂים	]				[~ Esth. 3:8

| כִּי עָשִׂיתָ | **מִשְׁפָּטִי** | וְדִינִי | Ps. 9:5 |
| [כִּי כֵן דְּבַר הַמֶּלֶךְ לִפְנֵי כָּל יֹדְעֵי | **דָּת** | וָדִין | [~ Esth. 1:13 |

EXTERNAL POST-CLASSICAL SOURCES
Independent Use
Heb.

M Ket. 7:6   ואלו יוצאות שלא בכתובה: העוברת על **דת משה ויהודים.**
אי זו היא **דת משה**? מאכילתו שאינו מעושר ומשמשתו נידה
ולא קוצה לה חלה ונודרת ואינה מקיימת. ואי זו היא **דת**
יהודים? יוצא וראשה פרוע וטווה בשוק ומדברת עם כל אדם

T Ket. 7:6 (Nash. p. 80)   יוציא ויתן כתובה מפני שלא נהג עמה **כדת משה וישראל**

T Ket. 7:7 (Nash. p. 80)   כל אילו נשים שעברו על **הדת** צריכות התראה ויוצאות שלא
בכתובה

Aram.

Xanthos 1 (Dupont-Sommer 1979): 1–27   בירח סיון שנת חד ארתחשסש מלכא...אתעשתו
בעלי אורן כרפא למעבד לכנדוך אלהא כבידשי
וכנותה ועבדו כמרא לסימין בר כדורס...זי יהבו
לכדוך אלהא...שנה בשנה תור ודמא זנה שביק זי לה
דתה דך כתב זי מהחסן אף הן איש מתום יהנצל מן
כנדוך אלהא...יבעון מנה

1QApGen 6:8   בא[ד]ין לבני נשין נסבת מן בנת אחי ובנתי לבני אחי
יהבת **כדת** חוק עלמא

COMMENTS

a. "דת 'decree, law' occurs in LBH prose, twenty times in Esther and once in Ezra. Whereas this lexeme does not appear in EBH, the semantic spheres of תורה, חק/ה, and משפט include the referent 'decree, law' throughout BH.... דת occurs in contexts where תורה, חק/ה, and משפט, semantically speaking, could have appeared.... [L]inguistic contrast and distribution show that דת became part of the Hebrew vocabulary sometime during the post-exilic period" (Bergey 1983: 116–118). In a slightly different manner: "Although the terms חקה/חק, תורה, משפט occur in late books, the distribution of דת indicates that it entered Biblical Hebrew from Persian (perhaps via Aramaic influence) during the post-exilic period, and began to replace חקה/חק, תורה, משפט in similar contexts" (R. M. Wright 2005: 116).

b. "Whereas דת in Esther and Ezra is used to refer to Persian customs and law (but note the references [in Aramaic] to דתא די־אלה in Ezra 7.12 and כדת אלהך in Ezra 7.14)... in rabbinic literature the term had taken on a broader application. Compare דת משה in M. Ketuvot 7.6 and T. Ketuvot 7.6 to תורת משה in Josh. 8.31 et passim" (R. M. Wright 2005: 116).

c. In Deut. 33:2 (אשדת K, אֵשׁ דָּת Q), the meaning *edict/law* is hardly applicable—either textually or linguistically; cf. BDB 206b; GB 171; S. R. Driver 1902: 393; Tigay 1996: 320.

BIBLIOGRAPHY

BDB 77b; 206b • *HALOT* I 234b • GB 170b–171a • Ben-Iehuda II 1011b note 2 • Kaddari 198b Bergey 1983: 116–118 • S. R. Driver 1902: 393; 1913: 484–485, 501 • Eskhult 2003: 12, 22 • Naveh and Greenfield 1984: 121 (= Greenfield 2001: I 238) • Margulis 1969: 206 • Paton 1908: 65, 146 • Rabin 1962: 1079 • Sáenz-Badillos 1993: 127 • Seow 1996: 647 note 23 • Tigay 1996: 320 • Torczyner 1938: 7 • R. M. Wright 2005: 113, 115–117

[זָוִית], pl. זָוִיֹּת n. f. *corner*: Zech. 9:15 וְשָׁתוּ הָמוּ כְּמוֹ יָיִן וּמָלְאוּ כַּמִּזְרָק כְּזָוִיֹּת מִזְבֵּחַ; Ps. 144:12 בְּנוֹתֵינוּ כְזָוִית מְחֻטָּבוֹת

CBH Alternatives

פנה (קצה, פאה, מקצוע), e.g.

Exod. 27:1–2	הַמִּזְבֵּחַ ...	וְעָשִׂיתָ אֶת
1 Kgs. 7:34	וְעָשִׂיתָ קַרְנֹתָיו עַל אַרְבַּע **פִּנֹּתָיו** ...	
	וְאַרְבַּע כְּתֵפֹת אֶל אַרְבַּע **פְּנוֹת** הַמְּכֹנָה הָאֶחָת	
[~ Zech. 9:15	**כְּזָוִיֹּת** מִזְבֵּחַ	הָמוּ כְּמוֹ יָיִן וּמָלְאוּ כַּמִּזְרָק]

External Post-Classical Sources

Renderings/Paraphrases/Glosses

TO 13x, e.g.

Exod. 25:26	רגלוהי	זויתא דלארבע	ארבע	על	עזקתא	ית	ותתין
[~	רַגְלָיו	הַפֵּאֹת אֲשֶׁר לְאַרְבַּע	אַרְבַּע	עַל	הַטַּבָּעֹת	אֶת	וְנָתַתָּ]

Exod. 38:5	לאריחיא	אתרא	דנחשא	לסרדא	זויתא	בארבע	עזקתא	ארבע	ואתיך
[~	לַבַּדִּים	בָּתִּים	הַנְּחֹשֶׁת	לְמִכְבַּר	הַקְּצָוֹת	בְּאַרְבַּע	טַבָּעֹת	אַרְבַּע	וַיִּצֹק]

TN 13x, e.g.

Exod. 38:1–2	זוייתה	ארבעתי	על	קרנתיה	ועבד	דעלתה...	מדבחה	ית	ועבד
[~	**פִּנֹּתָיו**	אַרְבַּע	עַל	קַרְנֹתָיו	וַיַּעַשׂ	הָעֹלָה...	מִזְבַּח	אֶת	וַיַּעַשׂ]

TPJ 11x, e.g.

Exod. 36:29	זיוויין	לתרתין	לתריהון	עבד	היכדין	מלרע...	מזווגין	והוון
[~	**הַמִּקְצֹעֹת**	לִשְׁנֵי	לִשְׁנֵיהֶם	עָשָׂה	כֵּן	מִלְמַטָּה...	תוֹאֲמִם	וְהָיוּ]

TJ 16x, e.g.

1 Kgs. 7:30	להון	כתפין	זויתיה	וארבע	חדא...	לבסיסא	נחשא	גלגלי	וארבעה
[~	לָהֶם	כְּתֵפֹת	**פַּעֲמֹתָיו**	וְאַרְבָּעָה	הָאֶחָת...	לַמְּכוֹנָה	נְחֹשֶׁת	אוֹפַנֵּי	וְאַרְבָּעָה]

Other Sources

Pesh. Exod. 36:28	דמשכנא	**לזויתא**	עבדו	דפין	תרין	ותרֵין
[~	הַמִּשְׁכָּן	**לִמְקֻצְעֹת**	עָשָׂה	קְרָשִׁים	וּשְׁנֵי]

Pesh. Job 38:6	**בזוֹיתה**	כּאֹפא	שׁדא	מנו	עברֹיה או	קמו	מנא	על
[~	**פִּנָּתָהּ**	אֶבֶן	יָרָה	מִי	הָטְבָּעוּ אוֹ	אֲדָנֶיהָ	מָה	עַל]

Independent Use

Heb.

M MaʿaserS 4:12	האומר לבנו מעשר שני **בזווית** זו ומצאו **בזווית** אחרת הרי אלו חולין
T Ber. 3:5 (Zer. p. 12)	אמ׳ ר׳ יהודה: כשהיה ר׳ עקיבא מתפלל עם הצבור היה מקצר בפני כולם וכשהוא מתפלל בינו לבין עצמו אדם מניחו **בזוית** זו ומוצאו **בזוית** אחרת מפני הכרעות והשתחואות
BMM 13 (pp. 212–213)	נמצא בארבעת **זויות** המשכן ארבע מחנות, שמשמשין לכל הצדדין, שנ׳ "איש על דגלו" וגו׳ (במ׳ ב 2)
PT Eruv. 1:6 (p. 457)	**קרן זוית** יוצא מיכן **וקרן זוית** יוצא מיכן נידון כלחיים
PT Suk. 1:1 (p. 637)	נעץ ארבע קנים בארבע **זויות** של כרם וקשר גמי מלמעלן מציל משם פיאה

Aram.

TAD 2.2.1	אנה אתית עליך ויהבת לי תרע ביתא זילך למבנה אגר 1 תמה
(= Cowley 5): 3–5	אגרא זך זילך הי זי דבקה לביתא זילי **לזוֹיתה** זי לעליה אגרא זך
	תדבק לשׁטר ביתי מן ארעא ועד עלא ומן **זוית** ביתי זי לעליה ועד בית זכריה
	(interlinear)
4Q554 f1ii:9	ומש[ח מן תר]עֹא דן עד **זוית(א)** די מדנחא רסין 25

COMMENTS

a. זָיִת, whose basic meaning is 'corner', appears twice in the Hebrew Bible—once in the chronologically disputable book of Psalms (144:12) and again in the late book of Zechariah (9:15), which is historically related to the Persian period. However, in CBH we find an assortment of terms covering the various semantic nuances of זָיִת (*corner, angle, joint*, etc.)—קָצֶה, פֵּאָה, פִּנָּה, מִקְצוֹעַ—which may well be regarded as its Classical equivalents, and hence the widely held view that זָיִת is to be classified as a late Aramaic loanword in BH (see, e.g., BDB 265a). Formulated slightly differently: "The lexeme זוית, used extensively in MH and Aramaic, is not attested in SBH.... The distribution pattern of זוית in BH ... is best explained, therefore, as a neologism of LBH" (Shin 2007: 51). Shin also correctly notes that CBH words such as פִּנָּה and מִקְצוֹעַ are regularly rendered זוית in the Targums and the Peshiṭta and that זוית also occurs in the Elephantine Papyri, the DSS, and Rabbinic sources.

b. "The Masoretes always knew well how to preserve the ancient Aramaic *qamaṣ* within Hebrew (i.e., in loanwords borrowed from Aramaic). Cf. זָיִת, כְּתָב, etc." (Kutscher 1937: 142 [= 1977: 373]).

c. "In the Midrashim זוית also means 'a place', as in PA: זוי" (Lieberman 1967–96: I 29).

d. The compound Rabbinic expression קרן זוית *corner* is a redundant phrase consisting of BH קרן and RH זוית, each of which means 'corner'.

e. Arabic زاوية is also regarded as a loan from Aramaic זָוִיתָא (Fraenkel 1886: 11).

BIBLIOGRAPHY

BDB 265a • *HALOT* I 266b

Fraenkel 1886: 11, 168 • Kutscher 1937: 142 (= 1977: 373) • Hurvitz 1972: 164–165; 1982: 81 note 84 • Lieberman 1967–96: I 29 • Rabin 1962: 1075 • Robinson 1895: 52 • Shin 2007: 48–51 • Wagner 1966: 48 no. 76

זכר√ + (ל)טוב(ה) (idiomatic phrase) *remember s.o. for good, with favor, in kind-ness:* Neh. 5:19 זָכְרָה לִּי אֱלֹהַי לְטוֹבָה כֹּל אֲשֶׁר עָשִׂיתִי; 13:31

CBH Alternatives

זכר√ (without modification)

2 Kgs. 20:3		אֲשֶׁר..	אֵת		נָא	**זְכָר**
[~ Neh. 5:19	עָשִׂיתִי	אֲשֶׁר	כֹּל	**לְטוֹבָה**	לִי אֱלֹהַי	זָכְרָה]

External Post-Classical Sources
Renderings/Paraphrases/Glosses

TO 1x

Num. 10:9   ותיבבון בחצוצרתא וייעול **דוכרנכון לטבא** קדם ה׳ אלהכון

[~   וַהֲרֵעֹתֶם בַּחֲצֹצְרֹת **וְנִזְכַּרְתֶּם** לִפְנֵי ה׳ אֱלֹהֵיכֶם]

TN 14x, e.g.

Gen. 41:36   ויהוי מזונא **לדכרן טב** לארעא לשבעתי שני כפנא...

[~   וְהָיָה הָאֹכֶל **לְפִקָּדוֹן** לָאָרֶץ לְשֶׁבַע שְׁנֵי הָרָעָב...]

Exod. 17:14   כתב דא **דוכרן טב** בספרא ... ארום ... אשיציא ית דכרניה דעמלק

[~   כְּתֹב זֹאת **זִכָּרוֹן** בַּסֵּפֶר ... כִּי ... אֶמְחֶה אֶת זֵכֶר עֲמָלֵק]

TPJ 6x, e.g.

Exod. 30:16   ותיסב ית כספא דכיפוריא... ויהי לבני ישראל **לדוכרן טב** קדם ה׳

[~   וְלָקַחְתָּ אֶת כֶּסֶף הַכִּפֻּרִים... וְהָיָה לִבְנֵי יִשְׂרָאֵל **לְזִכָּרוֹן** לִפְנֵי ה׳]

TJ 2x

Isa. 38:10   אנא אמרית... בתרעי שאול **על דוכרני לטב** איתוסף על שני

[~   אֲנִי אָמַרְתִּי... בְּשַׁעֲרֵי שְׁאוֹל **פֻּקַּדְתִּי** יֶתֶר שְׁנוֹתָי]

Zeph. 2:7   ארי **ייעול דוכרנהון לטבא** קדם ה׳ אלההון ויתיב גלותהון

[~   כִּי **יִפְקְדֵם** ה׳ אֱלֹהֵיהֶם וְשָׁב שְׁבִיתָם (ק׳)]

Other Sources

Tg. Ps. 111:4   **דוכרן טב** עבד לפרישוותיה

[~   **זֵכֶר** עָשָׂה לְנִפְלְאֹתָיו]

| Tg. Ps. 115:12 | יבריך | לטב | יתן | דכר | דה' | מימרא |
| [~ | יְבָרֶךְ | | | זְכָרָנוּ | [ה' | |

Independent Use

Heb.

BS (B) 45:1	משה זכרו לטובה
M San. 2:2	המלך...לא חולץ ולא חולצין לאשתו ולא מיבם ולא
	מייבמים את אשתו. ר' יהודה או': אם רצה לחלוץ וליבם
	זכור לטוב
T RoshH 1:12 (Mo'ed p. 308)	אמרו לפניו מלכיות זכרונות ושופרות...זכרונות – כדי שיבא זכרונכם לטובה לפניו
BT Shab. 13b	ברם זכור אותו האיש לטוב וחנניה בן חזקיה שמו, שאילמלא הוא נגנז ספר יחזקאל
Kh. Susiya (Naveh 1978: no. 75): 1–3	זכור לטובה קדושת מרי רבי איסי הכהן המכובד בירבי שעשה הפסיפוס הזה
Beit al-Ashwal (Naveh 1978: no. 105): 1–4	כתב יהודה זכור לטוב אמן שלום אמן
Dalton (Naveh 1978: no. 107): 8, 11	זכור לטוב...זכור לטוב

Aram.

Cooke 106: 1–4 (Nab.)	דכיר בטב ושלם שעדו בר גרמאלבעלי עד עלם
PAT 0333: 1	דכרן טב לבעלשמן עבד עגילו בר מלכו
KAI 242: 1–5 (Hatra)	צלמא דעבדסמיא...אקים לנפשה על חייהי דדה ודאחיהי...דכיר לטב
KAI 245: 2 (Hatra)	בל דכיר שמעני לטב אנא עבדי כתבית
KAI 257: 1–2 (Hatra)	דכרנא טבא למלכין בר שמישו...
Mount Gerizim (Magen et al. no. 147)	די הקרב דליה בר שמעון עלוהי ועל בנוהי אבנא [דה ל]דכרן טב קדם אלהא באתרא דנה
Korazin (Naveh 1978: no. 17): 1–3	דכיר לטב יודן בר ישמעל דעבד הדן סטוה ודרגוה
Na'aran (Naveh 1978: no. 58): 1–2; (idem, no. 59): 1–3	דכיר לטב פינחס כהנא בר יוסטה דיהב טימי פסיפסה...דכירה לטב רבקה אתתה ד(פינחס
Jericho (Naveh 1978: no. 69): 1–4	דכירין לטב יהוי דכרנהון לטב כל קהלה ק[די]שה ...דסייע יתהון מלכיה דעלמה ואתחזקון ועבדון פסיפסה

COMMENTS

a. The late character of the various phrases exemplified above is particularly evident in the Targumim, where 'remember + for good' is used to render the single word 'remember' in the Biblical Vorlage.

b. In Hebrew and Aramaic epigraphic sources, זכר√ + טוב and דכר√ + טָב, respectively, are fixed blessing formulae for the living and the dead. In RH, the phrase זכור לטוב is frequently added upon the mention of Elijah.

BIBLIOGRAPHY

Healey 1996: 177–186 • Hurvitz 1972: 54–56 • Stadel 2012

√זמן vb. **Pu** ptc. *be fixed, appointed* (of time): Ezra 10:14 יָבֹא לְעִתִּים מְזֻמָּנִים; Neh.
13:31 בְּעִתִּים מְזֻמָּנוֹת, לְעִתִּים מְזֻמָּנִים 10:35

Cf. [זְמַן]

BA Dan. 2:9 וּמִלָּה כִדְבָה וּשְׁחִיתָה הַזְדְּמִנְתּוּן (ק׳) לְמֵאמַר קָדָמַי

CBH Alternatives
See comment **a** below.

1 Sam. 1:3	מִיָּמִים יָמִימָה		... וְעָלָה הָאִישׁ הַהוּא
1 Sam. 7:16	שָׁנָה בְּשָׁנָה	מִדֵּי	וְהָלַךְ
[~ Neh. 10:35	בְּשָׁנָה שָׁנָה **מְזֻמָּנִים**	לְעִתִּים	[לְהָבִיא לְבֵית אֱלֹהֵינוּ ...

Gen. 18:14	אָשׁוּב אֵלֶיךָ כָּעֵת חַיָּה	לַמּוֹעֵד	
2 Sam. 24:15		עֵת מוֹעֵד	מֵהַבֹּקֶר וְעַד
[~ Ezra 10:13–14	**לְעִתִּים מְזֻמָּנִים**	יָבֹא	[וְכֹל אֲשֶׁר בְּעָרֵינוּ ...

External Post-Classical Sources
Renderings/Paraphrases/Glosses
TO 24x, e.g.

Exod. 19:11	ויהון **זמינין**... ארי ביומא תליתאה מתגלי ה׳ לעיני כל עמא	
[~	[וְהָיוּ **נְכֹנִים**... כִּי בַּיּוֹם הַשְּׁלִישִׁי יֵרֵד ה׳ לְעֵינֵי כָל הָעָם	

TN 50x, e.g.

Num. 26:9	כנשתה **מזמני** ואבירם דתן הוא	
[~	הָעֵדָה (ק׳) **קְרִיאֵי** וַאֲבִירָם דָּתָן [הוּא	

TPJ 60x, e.g.

Deut. 22:6	אי **איזדמן** שרכפא דציפר דכי קדמך ... לא תיסב אימא מעל בניא	
[~	[כִּי **יִקָּרֵא** קַן צִפּוֹר לְפָנֶיךָ ... לֹא תִקַּח הָאֵם עַל הַבָּנִים	

TJ 61x, e.g.

Jer. 22:7	**ואזמין** עלך מתכלין גבר וזיניה	
[~	[וְקִדַּשְׁתִּי עָלֶיךָ מַשְׁחִתִים אִישׁ וְכֵלָיו	

Other Sources

FTV Gen. 19:31	וגבר לית בארעא **למזדמנ(א)** לוותן כנימוס כל ארעא	
[~	[וְאִישׁ אֵין בָּאָרֶץ **לָבוֹא** עָלֵינוּ כְּדֶרֶךְ כָּל הָאָרֶץ	

Pesh. 1 Kgs. 1:49   ודחלו כולהון גבר̈א **דמזמנין** הוו ... ואזלו גבר לאורחה
[~   [וַיֶּחֶרְדוּ ... כָּל **הַקְּרֻאִים** ... וַיֵּלְכוּ אִישׁ לְדַרְכּוֹ

1QApGen 21:25   כול אלן **אזדמנו** כחדא לקרב לעמקא די סד̈יא
[~MT Gen. 14:3   [כָּל אֵלֶּה **חָבְרוּ** אֶל עֵמֶק הַשִּׂדִּים

Sifre Deut. 227 (p. 259)   "כי יִקָּרֵא" (דב׳ כב 6) – פרט **למזומן**
Sifre Deut. 396 (p. 314)   "אשר קרך" (דב׳ כה 18) – אין "קרך" אלא **שנזדמן** לך
Sifra Aḥare 4:1   "ושלח ביד איש...**עיתי**" (וי׳ טז 21) – שיהא **מזומן**

Independent Use
Heb.
M Ber. 7:3   כיצד **מזמנין**? בשלשה אומ׳: נברך, בשלשה והוא או׳: ברכו

T BM 7:8 (Nez. p. 100)   השוכר את הפועל **ונזדמן** לו אנגריא לא יאמר לו: הרי זה
לפניך אלא נותן לו שכרו במה שעשה

ARN A 2 (p. 10)   אמר לי הקב״ה: "לך אל העם וקדשתם היום ומחר" (שמ׳ יט 10)
ואני שאני **מזומן** לכך בכל יום ויום ובכל שעה ‹ושעה› ואיני
יודע אימתי מדבר עמי או ביום או בלילה, על אחת כמה וכמה
שאפרוש מן האשה; והסכימה דעתו לדעת המקום

BT Yoma 39b   אותה שנה שמת בה שמעון הצדיק אמר להן: בשנה זו הוא
[= אני] מת. אמרו לו: מנין אתה יודע? אמ׳ להן: בכל יום
הכפורים היה **מזדמן** לי זקן אחד לבוש לבנים ועטוף לבנים,
נכנס עמי ויוצא עמי, והיום **נזדמן** לי זקן אחד לבוש שחורין
ועטוף שחורין, נכנס עמי ולא יצא עמי

Aram.
PT Mo'edQ 3:7 (p. 821)   ר׳ שמעון בן לקיש הוה מהלך באיסרטא. **איזדמן** ליה
חד כותיי והוה מגדף והוה קרע, מגדף והוה קרע

BT RoshH 31b   ההיא איתתא **דאזמנוה** לדינא קמי אמימר לנהרדע

COMMENTS
a. We do not presume that there is a concrete case in which one specific CBH word neatly fills the same function as the later זמן√. However, the CBH alternatives (above) provide a similar literary context, in which one may expect to find זמן√, yet it is never documented in the earlier writings.

b. In the *Pi'el*, *Pu'al* and *Hiph'il* forms of RH, and in the *Qal*, *Pa'el* and *Aphel* forms of Aramaic, זמן means *to summon*, *to invite*, whereas in *Hitpa'el* and *Etpa'al/Etpe'el* it may mean *to chance upon* (see above examples). However, both meanings stem from the common basic notion of time, and therefore we have adduced the above various verbal forms of √זמן that are not limited to the *Pu'al* conjugation used in LBH.

c. The word מזומן in Sifre Deut. 227 (see above) is an antonym of יקרא (= יִקָּרֶה).

BIBLIOGRAPHY

BDB 273b • *HALOT* I 273b

Barton 1908: 103 • S. R. Driver 1913: 475 no. 5 • Fredericks 1988: 197–198 • Seow 1996: 652; 1997: 13

זְמֵן [זְמַן] (pausal form) n. m. *appointed/specific time, time*: Neh. 2:6 וַיֹּאמֶר לִי
הַמֶּלֶךְ...עַד מָתַי יִהְיֶה מַהֲלָכְךָ...וָאֶתְּנָה לוֹ זְמָן ;Qoh. 3:1 לְכֹל זְמָן וְעֵת לְכָל חֵפֶץ תַּחַת
הַשָּׁמָיִם (see comment **b** below); Esth. 9:27 כִּכְתָבָם וְכִזְמַנָּם, 31 לְקַיֵּם אֶת יְמֵי הַפֻּרִים
הָאֵלֶּה בִּזְמַנֵּיהֶם

Cf. √זמן

BA זְמָן Dan. 2:16; 7:12; זִמְנָא Dan. 3:7 בֵּהּ זִמְנָא, 8; 4:33; 7:22; Ezra 5:3; זִמְנִין Dan. 6:11,
7:25; זִמְנַיָּא Dan 2:21 וְהוּא מְהַשְׁנֵא עִדָּנַיָּא וְזִמְנַיָּא ;וְזִמְנִין תְּלָתָה בְּיוֹמָא בָּעֵא בָּעוּתֵהּ 14

CBH Alternatives

מועד, e.g.

| Num. 9:2 | | | | **בְּמוֹעֲדוֹ** | אֶת הַפָּסַח ...| וַיַּעֲשׂוּ |
| [~ Esth. 9:31 | | **בִּזְמַנֵּיהֶם** | הָאֵלֶּה | הַפֻּרִים | אֶת יְמֵי | לְקַיֵּם |

Exod. 9:5   וַיָּשֶׂם   ה'   **מוֹעֵד**   לֵאמֹר   מָחָר יַעֲשֶׂה ה' הַדָּבָר הַזֶּה
[~ Neh. 2:6   וָאֶתְּנָה לוֹ   **זְמָן**   ...עַד מָתַי יִהְיֶה מַהֲלָכְךָ]

Exod. 13:10   וְשָׁמַרְתָּ   אֶת הַחֻקָּה   הַזֹּאת   **לְמוֹעֲדָהּ** מִיָּמִים יָמִימָה
[~ Esth. 9:27   לִהְיוֹת עֹשִׂים אֵת שְׁנֵי הַיָּמִים הָאֵלֶּה   כִּכְתָבָם **וְכִזְמַנָּם**   בְּכָל שָׁנָה וְשָׁנָה]

External Post-Classical Sources
Renderings/Paraphrases/Glosses

TO 205x, e.g.

Num. 9:2   **בְּזִמְנֵיהּ**   פִּסְחָא   יַת   יִשְׂרָאֵל   בְּנֵי   וְיַעְבְּדוּן
[~   **בְּמוֹעֲדוֹ**   הַפָּסַח   אֶת   יִשְׂרָאֵל   בְּנֵי   וַיַּעֲשׂוּ]

TN 255x, e.g.

Exod. 9:5   בְּאַרְעָא   הֲדֵין   פִּתְגָּמָא   ה'   יַעְבֵּד   מְחַר   לְמֵימַר   **זְמַן**   ה'   וְשַׁוִּי
[~   בָּאָרֶץ   הַזֶּה   הַדָּבָר   ה'   יַעֲשֶׂה   מָחָר   לֵאמֹר   **מוֹעֵד**   ה'   וַיָּשֶׂם]

TPJ 256x, e.g.

Deut. 16:6   מִמִּצְרַיִם   פּוּרְקָנְכוֹן   שֵׁירוּת   **זְמַן** ... תֵּיכְלוּנֵיהּ   שִׁימְשָׁא   יַת   בְּמֵיעַל
[~   מִמִּצְרָיִם   צֵאתְךָ   **מוֹעֵד**   הַשֶּׁמֶשׁ   כְּבוֹא]

TJ 136x, e.g.

1 Sam. 13:11	יומיא	**לזמן**	אתיתא	לא	ואת	מעלוי	עמא אתבדר
[~	הַיָּמִים	**לְמוֹעֵד**	בָאתָ	לֹא	וְאַתָּה	מֵעָלַי	הָעָם נָפַץ

Independent Use

Heb.

BS (B) 43:7	בם מועד **וזמני** חוק זחפץ עתה בתקופתו
NḤ 45:28–29 (Yardeni I p. 115)	...ואדם תבע עד סוף **הזמן** הלז
M Ber. 2:1	היה קורא בתורה והגיע **זמן** המקרא
M Shab. 17:7	ר׳ ליעזר או׳: פקק החלון, **בזמן** שהוא קשור ותלוי
	פוקקים בו ואם לאו אין פוקקים בו
M RoshH 3:8	"ויאמר ה׳ אל משה עשה לך שרף ושים" וגו׳
	(במ׳ כא 8). וכי נחש ממית ומחיה? אלא כל **זמן** שהיו
	ישר׳ מיסתכלים כלפי למעלן ומשעבדים את לבם
	לאביהם שבשמים היו מתרפים ואם לאו היו נימוקים
Sifre Deut. 75 (p. 140)	מה קדשים **בזמן** אף חולין **בזמן**

Aram.

TAD II 8.9:4	ז[א שנתא לא עד **זמנא** יביל להם למומא על זנה [טעמא]
4Q206 f1xxii:2–3	עד יום די יתדֿינן ועד **זמן** יום קצא ד[י] דינא רבא
Cooke 96:5–6 (Nab.)	...די שלטו **זמנין** תרין
Cooke 102:5 (Nab.)	...אחֹר **זמן** אבני מחרמתא קדמיתא די עבד בנהבל
BT BB 171b	**דזמנין** דיזיף מיניה בתשרי וכתיב ליה **זמנא** דשטרא לניסן

COMMENTS

a. "All occurrences of the root זמן in the Bible are postexilic—no earlier than the fifth century.... Some scholars argue that the noun is traced ultimately to Old Persian; others say it is borrowed from Akkadian. Whatever its origin, it is clear that the word came into Late Biblical Hebrew from Aramaic no earlier than the second half of the fifth century BCE. Preexilic Biblical Hebrew uses the noun מוֹעֵד with the same meaning" (Seow 1996: 652).

b. The word's vocalization in the MT, with *a qamatz* rather than a *pataḥ*, is due merely to its pausal status and should not be considered a member of the qᵉṭāl nominal pattern, which is also a characteristic late linguistic feature of BH (on this, see ibid.).

c. In the Masada scroll of BS 43:7 we find וממנו instead of וזמני (which is also a variant reading recorded in the margin of MS B).

BIBLIOGRAPHY

BDB 273b • *HALOT* I 273b • GB 200 • Ben-Iehuda III 1354b • Kaddari 254a
Barton 1908: 103 • Bendavid 1967–71: I 64 • Bergey 1983: 150–151 • Delitzsch 1877: 190–196 •
Dihi 2004: 226–228 • S. R. Driver 1913: 553 note * • du Plessis 1971: 169 • Eskhult 2003: 12,
22 • Fredericks 1988: 197–198 • Ginsburg 1861: 304 • Gordis 1968: 229 • Polzin 1976: 136 •
Schoors 1992–2001: I 60–61; II 382 • Seow 1996: 652; 1997: 13 • Tal 1975: 186 • Tyler 1988:
151–154 • R. M. Wright 2005: 117–119

זַן n. m. *kind, species*: Ps. 144:13 מְזָוֵינוּ מְלֵאִים מְפִיקִים מִזַּן אֶל זַן (see comment **b** below); 2 Chron. 16:14 בְּשָׂמִים וּזְנִים מְרֻקָּחִים בְּמִרְקַחַת מַעֲשֶׂה

BA זַן Dan. 3:5, 7, 10, 15 פְּסַנְתֵּרִין וְסוּמְפֹּנְיָה וְכֹל זְנֵי זְמָרָא

CBH ALTERNATIVES

מִין, e.g.

| Gen. 1:12 | וַתּוֹצֵא הָאָרֶץ דֶּשֶׁא ... לְמִינֵהוּ וְעֵץ עֹשֶׂה פְּרִי ... לְמִינֵהוּ |
| [~ Ps. 144:13 | אֶל זַן   מִזַּן   מְזָוֵינוּ מְלֵאִים מְפִיקִים] |

EXTERNAL POST-CLASSICAL SOURCES
Renderings/Paraphrases/Glosses

TO 30x, e.g.

| Lev. 11:22 | ית | גובא | **לזניה** ... | וית | חרגלא | **לזנוהי** | וית | חגבא | **לזנוהי** |
| [~ | | | הָאַרְבֶּה לְמִינוֹ ... | וְאֶת | הַחַרְגֹּל | לְמִינֵהוּ | וְאֶת | הֶחָגָב | לְמִינֵהוּ] |

TPJ 46x, e.g.

| Gen. 1:24 | תהנפק גרגישתא | דארעא | נפשת | ברייתא | **ליזנה** |
| [~ | תּוֹצֵא | הָאָרֶץ | נֶפֶשׁ | חַיָּה | לְמִינָהּ] |

Other Sources

FTP Gen. 1:25

| FTP Gen. 1:25 | ית | חיתא | דארעא | **לזנה** | וית | בעירא | **לזנה** |
| [~ | וְאֵת | חַיַּת | הָאָרֶץ | לְמִינָהּ | וְאֶת | הַבְּהֵמָה | לְמִינָהּ] |

Independent Use
Heb.

| BS (B) 37:28 | כי לא הכל לכל טוב, לא כל נפש כל זן תבחר |
| BS (B) 49:8 | יחזקאל ראה מראה ויגד זני מרכבה |

Aram.

| TAD I 6.1 (= Cowley 17): 3 | [...] מפרש זן זן [י]רֹח בירח הוו שלחן עלי אף נשתונא כתיב יהיב לן |

COMMENTS

a. Although זַן is not found either in the Qumran scrolls or Rabbinic literature, its Biblical distribution (in Hebrew and Aramaic), the existence of a CBH alternative (מִין), and the suspected Persian origin of the word (see Kaddari; on Persian loanwords in general, see entry [גֶּנֶז], comment **b**) strongly support its lateness. "[T]he Chronicler employs ... new words even in cases where they are out of place, as being entirely anachronistic.... [T]hese new words replace obvious synonyms that are found in similar situations in the texts from which he otherwise draws much of his material. There are several such instances. . . . In 2 Chron. 16.14 the word זַן . . ., and not מִין, is used in the expression 'spices of various kinds' in connection with King Asa's burial" (Eskhult 2003: 13; cf. גְּנְזָךְ, comment **b**).

b. The expression מִזַּן אֶל זַן in Ps. 144:13 is commonly interpreted 'of each kind' (cf. *HALOT* I 274b). On the linguistic status of Ps. 144, see Hurvitz 1972: 164–169 and the following statement: "The language used in [Ps. 144] vv. 12–15 makes it difficult to accept a pre-exilic dating for it (זַן 'kind', v 13; the relative שׁ 'who(se)', v 15)" (Allen 1983: 290).

BIBLIOGRAPHY

BDB 275a • *HALOT* I 274b • Kaddari 255b

Allen 1983: 290 • Dihi 2004: 228–231 • S. R. Driver 1913: 374 note †, 501 note *, 540 • Eskhult 2003: 13 • Hurvitz 1972: 16, 93, 164–169 • Nöldeke 1904: 92 §146 • Polzin 1976: 136 • F. Rosenthal 1961: 59 §189 • Seow 1996: 647 and note 25 • Wagner 1966: 49 no. 70 • R. M. Wright 2005: 113

√**חפה** vb. *cover, overlay, plate*: **Pi'el** 2 Chron. 3:5, 7–9 וְאֵת הַבַּיִת הַגָּדוֹל חִפָּה עֵץ בְּרוֹשִׁים וַיְחַפֵּהוּ זָהָב טוֹב...וַיְחַף אֶת הַבַּיִת הַקֹּרוֹת...וְדַלְתוֹתָיו זָהָב...וַיְחַפֵּהוּ זָהָב טוֹב...וְהָעֲלִיּוֹת חִפָּה זָהָב

CBH Alternatives
√צפה; e.g.

1 Kgs. 6:20	**וַיְצַפֵּהוּ** זָהָב	...וְעֶשְׂרִים אַמָּה רֹחַב...	...עֶשְׂרִים אַמָּה אֹרֶךְ...
[~ 2 Chron. 3:8	**וַיְחַפֵּהוּ** זָהָב	...אַמּוֹת עֶשְׂרִים וְרָחְבּוֹ...	...אָרְכּוֹ...]

External Post-Classical Sources
Renderings/Paraphrases/Glosses
TO 85x (53—*Pe'al*; 2—*Pa'el*; 2—*Etpe'el*; 1—questionable [Num. 7:3]), e.g.

Exod. 26:32	ותתין יתה על ארבעה עמודי שטין **מחפן** דהבא
[~	וְנָתַתָּה אֹתָהּ עַל אַרְבָּעָה עַמּוּדֵי שִׁטִּים **מְצֻפִּים** זָהָב]

TN 38x, e.g.

Deut. 7:25	לא תתחמדון כספא ודהבה **דמחפי** עליהון
[~	לֹא תַחְמֹד כֶּסֶף וְזָהָב עֲלֵיהֶם]

TPJ 65x, e.g.

Lev. 13:12	**ותחפי** סגירותא ית כל משך בישריה מרישיה ועד ריגלוי
[~	וְכִסְּתָה הַצָּרַעַת אֶת כָּל עוֹר הַנֶּגַע מֵרֹאשׁוֹ וְעַד רַגְלָיו]

TJ 81x (28-*Pa'el*), e.g.

Hab. 2:19	ייא דאמר לצלים אעא קום ... הא הוא **מחפי** ליה דהב וכסף
[~	הוֹי אֹמֵר לָעֵץ הָקִיצָה ... הִנֵּה הוּא **תָּפוּשׂ** זָהָב וָכֶסֶף]

Other Sources

BMM 7 (p. 181)	כיצד עשה בצלאל הארון? עשה שלש תיבות שתים של זהב ואחת של עץ; נתן של עץ בתוך של זהב ונתן של זהב בתוך של עץ **וחפה** שפתיו העליונות בזהב שנ' "וצפית אותו זהב טהור" (שמ' כה 11), שאין ת"ל "**תצפנו**" (שם) ומה ת"ל "**תצפנו**"? מלמד **שחופה** שפתיו העליונות בזהב

MekhRI Shira 5 (p. 132)	ומה ת"ל "תהומות **יכסיומו**" (שמ' טו 5) אלא מלמד שעלה תהום התחתון על תהום העליון **וחיפה** עליהם את הרקיע והקדיר עליהם את הכוכבים

BT Ḥag. 26b	...ותיפוק לי משום **ציפויייו**, דהא תנן: השולחן והדובלקי שנפחתו או **שחיפן** בשיש, אם נשתייר בו כדי הנחת כוסות טמא

Independent Use

Heb.

M Pe'ah 5:7 | העומר ששכיחוהו פועלים ולא שכחו בעל הבית ... עמדו
העניים בפניו או **שחיפוהו** בקש – הרי זה אינו שכחה

M Shev. 4:5 | המבקיע בזית לא **יחפה** בעפר אבל **מכסה** הוא באבנים או
בקש

Sifra Qedoshim 5:1 | וכי מה חטאת המשפחה? אילא ללמדך שאין לך משפחה
שיש בה מוכס – שכולם מוכסים; שיש בה ליסטוס – שכולם
ליסטים, מפני שכולם **מחפין** עליו

T Kil. 1:19 (Zer. p. 207) | שדה שעלו בה עשבים אין מחייבין אותו לופך, אלא חורש
בשעה **שמחפה** והופך

PT Ta'an. 4:5 (p. 730) | כל מי שהיה כשר וירא חט באותו הדור היה מביא את בכוֹ־
ריו ונותנן לתוך הסל **ומחפה** אותן קציעות

BT Ber. 10b | רבונו של עולם, מה שונמית שלא עשתה לפניך אלא קיר
אחֹ קטנה החיית את בנה – אבי אבא **שחיפה** את ההיכל
כולו בטבלאות של זהב, על אחת כמה וכמה

Aram.

4Q206 f4i:15 | וערבא **חפית** וכסית

4Q206 f4i:18 | ו[אֹ]נה הוית חזה עד ארעא **חפית** מין

11Q18 f10i:5–6 | ... כול אבניהון [...] וֹך **חפא** דהב

PT Shev. 9:2 (p. 210) | אייתי טביין **וחפי** קרנתהון בכסף ושלחון לאפריקי

Comments

a. √חפה appears in BH (including CBH) in the following verbal forms: the *Qal*
form is always combined with רֹאשׁ/פָּנִים (חָפוּ רֹאשָׁם, חֲפוּ רֹאשׁ, חָפוּ רֹאשָׁם, וּפְנֵי הָמָן חָפוּ)—
most probably meaning *cover the head* (in token of grief or shame). This usage
is attested 6x in the books of Samuel, Jeremiah, and Esther and is therefore by
no means indicative of any particular style, genre, or historical age; the *Niph'al*
form נֶחְפָּה בַכֶּסֶף (*silver-plated*) in Ps. 68:14 is a *hapax* in BH and is unknown in
epigraphic inscriptions or RH (excluding quotations of the above verse) and,
consequently, is not helpful for dating purposes; the *Pi'el* form, in contrast, is
found only as a technical term in the building account of Solomon's Temple,
as recorded in 2 Chron. (5x—preceded and followed by verses that use the
standard צִפָּה). The parallel version in Kings is unfamiliar with חִפָּה and resorts
exclusively to the alternative term צִפָּה (12x), as does Exodus, which uses it consistently (26x) in the descriptions of the Tabernacle. Furthermore, חפה/א (in
both *Qal* and *P'iel/ Pa'el*) is the standard term for *overlay* in RH and Aramaic—
including Targumic Aramaic, which regularly renders the Biblical צִפָּה by חפא.

All this clearly indicates that חֻפָּה reflects the linguistic milieu of the Second Temple period.

b. חֻפָּה *covering, canopy* belongs in the morphological pattern *qull* (ע″ע roots) with the feminine ending (e.g., סֻכָּה, חֻקָּה [see JM 241 §88B, *i*]) and is thus regularly associated with √חפף, and not √חפה (see Lexicons).

c. BMM 7 שחופה, וחפה (*Qal*) appear in various manuscripts as שחיפה, וחיפה (*Pi'el*); cf. Kirschner 1992: 181. In both cases, however, RH √חפה replaces BH √צפה.

BIBLIOGRAPHY

BDB 342a • JM 241 §88B, *i* • Kaddari 330a

Bendavid 1967–71: I 69, 333, 360 • Curtis and Madsen 1910: 326 • Hurvitz 1974a: 32–33 • Japhet 1987: 28–29; 1993: 554 • Kirschner 1992: 181

טֵבֵת pr. n. name of 10th month, derived from Akkad. *ṭebētum*: Esth. 2:16
הָעֲשִׂירִי הוּא חֹדֶשׁ טֵבֵת

Cf. אֲדָר

CBH ALTERNATIVES

Months are generally named by their numerical order, e.g., 1 Kgs. 12:32
בַּחֹדֶשׁ הַשְּׁמִינִי; in a few cases they follow the Canaanite pattern, e.g., 1 Kgs. 8:2
בְּיֶרַח הָאֵתָנִים. Only in the LBH corpus do we find both (the older) numerical system and (the more recent) Mesopotamian names side by side in one and the same verse, e.g., Esth. 3:7 לְחֹדֶשׁ שְׁנֵים עָשָׂר הוּא חֹדֶשׁ אֲדָר.

2 Kgs. 25:1   וַיְהִי בִשְׁנַת הַתְּשִׁיעִית לְמָלְכוֹ **בַּחֹדֶשׁ הָעֲשִׂירִי**
[~ Esth. 2:16   **בַּחֹדֶשׁ הָעֲשִׂירִי** הוּא חֹדֶשׁ **טֵבֵת** בִּשְׁנַת שֶׁבַע
לְמַלְכוּתוֹ

EXTERNAL POST-CLASSICAL SOURCES
Renderings/Paraphrases/Glosses
TPJ 1X
Gen. 8:22   בתקופת תמוז   וחומא   **טבת**   וקורא בתקופת...
[~   וָחֹם   וְקֹר...]

Other Sources
T Soṭ. 6:10 (Nash. p. 189)   זה עשרה **בטבת** שבו סמך מלך (19 ח׳ זכ׳) – "צום **העשירי**"
בבל על ירושלם

Independent Use
Heb.
M Taʿan. 4:5   באחד **בטבת** שבו בני פרעוש שנייה. באחד **בטבת**
לא היה בו מעמד, שהיה בו הלל קרבן מוסף קרבן
עצים

T Taʿan. 1:7 (Moʿed p. 325)   חצי תשרי מרחשון וחצי כסליו – זרע. חצי כסליו
טבת וחצי שבט – חורף. חצי שבט אדר וחצי ניסן –
קור. חצי ניסן אייר וחצי סיון – קציר. חצי סיון תמוז
וחצי אב – קיץ. חצי אב אלול וחצי תשרי – חום

Beth Alpha (Naveh 1978:   תקופת ניסן תקופת תמוז תקופת תישרי תקופת
no. 45): 13–16   **טבת**

ʿEin Gedi (Naveh 1978: no. 70):   ניסן אייר סיון תמוז אב אילול תשרי מרחשון כסליו
5–7   **טבית** שבט ואדר

PT Eruv. 5:1 (p. 474)

אם אין יודע לכוין את הרוחות, צא ולמד מן התקופה.
ממקום שהחמה זורחת באחד בתקופת תמוז עד
מקום שהיא זורחת באחד בתקופת **טבת** – אילו
פני מזרח. ממקום שהחמה שוקעת באחד בתקופת
טבת עד מקום שהיא שוקעת באחד בתקופת תמוז
– אילו פני המערב. והשאר צפון ודרום.

Aram.

Cooke 80:1–3 (Nab.)

דנה כפרא די עבדו כמכם ברת ואלת ברת חרמו וכליבת
ברתה לנפשהם ואחרהם בירח **טבת** שנת תשע לחרתת
מלך נבטו רחם עמה ...

EN 46:1–3 (Idum.)

ב 13 **לטבת** דבר עבדאדה מן קדם עזיזו ולעדאל חיון 4:
דכר 1 אמרן 2 רחל 1

Pap. Starcky (+ NḤ 36):10
(Yardeni I p. 265)

... עשרין **לטבת** [שנ]ת ארבע למנכו מלכא מלך נבטו

BT Taʻan. 6b

ואמ' רב חסדא: טובה דשתא **דטבת** ארמלתא

1 Tg. Esth 3:7

בכן שרי שמשי (ס)פרא לצבעא פייסא דעדבין קדם
המן ... ושרי בירחיא. בניסן ולא על מן בגלל זכותא
דפיסחא ... **בטבת** לא על מן בגלל דביה סליק נבוכד נצר
רשיעא על ירושלם ומיסת הוי לעוקתא ההיא ... כד מטא
לסוף תריסר ירחי שתא דאיהוא ירחא דאדר ...

COMMENTS

a. See the entry אֲדָר for general comments on month-names and the bibliography there. See also BDB 372a.

b. Josephus (*Ant.* 11.148) writes that the Hebrews call this month Ξένιος (ἐν τρισὶν ἡμέραις εἰκάδι τοῦ ἐνάτου μηνός ὃς κατὰ μὲν Ἑβραίους Ξένιος κατὰ δὲ Μακεδόνας Ἀπελλαῖος καλεῖται), trying, perhaps, to derive the name טבת etymologically from the Heb. טוב.

חשׁ√ vb. **Hitp** *be enrolled by genealogy*: Ezra 2:62 אֵלֶּה בִּקְשׁוּ כְתָבָם הַמִּתְיַחְשִׂים וְלֹא נִמְצָאוּ ;8:1, 3; Neh. 7:5 וָאֶקְבְּצָה אֶת הַחֹרִים וְאֶת הַסְּגָנִים וְאֶת הָעָם לְהִתְיַחֵשׂ וָאֶמְצָא סֵפֶר הַיַּחַשׂ, 64; 1 Chron. 4:33; 5:1, 7, 17; 7:5, 7, 9, 40; 9:1 וְכָל יִשְׂרָאֵל הִתְיַחְשׂוּ וְהִנָּם כְּתוּבִים עַל סֵפֶר מַלְכֵי יִשְׂרָאֵל, 22; 2 Chron. 12:15; 31:16–19

Cf. יַחַשׂ

CBH ALTERNATIVES

ילד Hitp

| Num. 1:18 | **וַיִּתְיַלְדוּ** | עַל מִשְׁפְּחֹתָם | לְבֵית אֲבֹתָם |
| [~ 2 Chron. 31:17 | **הִתְיַחֵשׂ** וְאֶת | הַכֹּהֲנִים | לְבֵית אֲבוֹתֵיהֶם |

| Josh. 19:8 | **לְמִשְׁפְּחֹתָם** שִׁמְעוֹן ... זֹאת נַחֲלַת ... הֶעָרִים סְבִיבוֹת ... הַחֲצֵרִים וְכָל |
| [~ 1 Chron. | **וְהִתְיַחְשָׂם** זֹאת מוֹשְׁבֹתָם ... הֶעָרִים סְבִיבוֹת ... חַצְרֵיהֶם וְכָל |
| 4:33 |

EXTERNAL POST-CLASSICAL SOURCES
Renderings/Paraphrases/Glosses

TO 1X

| Num. 1:18 | ולעילא שנין עסרין מבר ... אבהתהון לבית זרעיתהון עַל **ואתיחסו** |
| [~ | וָמָעְלָה שָׁנָה עֶשְׂרִים מִבֶּן ... אֲבֹתָם לְבֵית מִשְׁפְּחֹתָם עַל **וַיִּתְיַלְדוּ**] |

TN 1X

| Num. 1:18 | לעיל שנין עשרין בר מן ... אבהתהון לבית זרעייתהון עַל **ואתייחסו** |
| [~ | וָמָעְלָה שָׁנָה עֶשְׂרִים מִבֶּן ... אֲבֹתָם לְבֵית מִשְׁפְּחֹתָם עַל **וַיִּתְיַלְדוּ**] |

TPJ 5x: 1—as TO above; 4—independent of MT, e.g.

| Num. 3:1 | ...משה עם ה' דמליל ביומא **דאתיחסו** ומשה אהרן ייחוסי ואיליין |
| [~ | ...מֹשֶׁה אֶת ה' דִּבֶּר בְּיוֹם ... וּמֹשֶׁה אַהֲרֹן תּוֹלְדֹת וְאֵלֶּה] |

Other Sources

MekhRI Pisḥa 5 (p. 15)

כשם **שמיחסן** בירידתן שנאמר "ראובן שמעון לוי ויהודה" (שמ' א 2), כך **מייחסן** בעלייתן ראובן שמעון לוי ואו' "ויתילדו על משפחותם לבית אבותם וגו' (במ' א 18)

Independent Use

Heb.

Sifre Num. 48 (p. 52)	נחשון בן עמינדב למטה יהודה **ייחסו** הכתוב על שם שבטו
Sifre Deut. 355 (p. 420)	כשהיו שבטים **מתייחסין** זה אומר שלי היא לויה וזה אומר
	שלי היא לויה, אמר להם: אם מראובן הכתוב **מייחס** שלי
	היא לויה ואם מבנימין הכתוב **מייחס** של לוי היא לויה
T Peʾah 4:11 (Zer. p. 58)	אמרו: משפחת בית נבטלה היתה בירושלם והיתה **מתיחסת**
	עם בני ארנון היבוסי
BT Shab. 55b	אמ׳ רב: פינחס לא חטא שנא׳ ״ואחיה בן אחיטוב אחי
	איכבוד בן פינחס בן עלי״ וגו׳ (שמ״א יד 3)–איפשר חטא
	בא לידו והכתוב **מיחסו**
PT Yev. 2:5 (p. 839)	ר׳ יוחנן אמ׳: גוים יש להם יחסים. ר׳ שמעון בן לקיש אמ׳:
	גוים אין להן יחסין. והא כת׳ ״בעת ההיא שלח מרודך בלאדן
	בן בלאדן מלך בבל ספרים ומנחה אל חזקיהו״ (יש׳ לט 1)?
	על ידי שכיבד זקינו זכה **להתייחס**

Aram.

BT Yev. 62a	. . . **דיחסינהו** בשמיהו ובשמא דאבוהי

COMMENTS

a. "The penchant for pedigrees and genealogical registers, made up from a mixture of genealogico-historical and ethnologico-statistical elements, is a characteristic feature of Judaism; along with the thing the word [יחש] also first came into use during the later times. Compendious histories are written in the form of [תלדות] and [יוחשין]" (Wellhausen 1885: 148).

b. LBH ספר-(ה)יחש linguistically occupies an intermediate stage between CBH ספר-תולדת and RH מגלת-יחסים/יוחסין. In ספר-(ה)יחש, the older תולדת is replaced by post-Classical יחש, but the traditional ספר is still retained. In the post-Biblical מגלת-יחסים/יוחסין, however, ספר is substituted by the later מגלה (Hurvitz 1996: 41*).

c. 1 Chron. 5:1, which directly relates to Jacob's parting words to Reuben in Gen. 49:3–4, uses √יחש in this connection. Although common in the book of Chronicles, this technical term makes no appearance in the Genesis version of the story:

1 Chron. 5:1	וּבְנֵי רְאוּבֵן בְּכוֹר יִשְׂרָאֵל . . . וּבְחַלְּלוֹ יְצוּעֵי אָבִיו נִתְּנָה בְּכֹרָתוֹ . . . וְלֹא **לְהִתְיַחֵשׂ** לַבְּכֹרָה
[~ Gen. 49:3–4	רְאוּבֵן בְּכֹרִי אַתָּה . . . אָז חִלַּלְתָּ יְצוּעִי עָלָה]

d. In contrast to Biblical literature, the verbal forms of √יחס in Rabbinic literature are much less frequent than its nominal forms.

e. √יחש is both infrequent and of unclear context in the DSS. Three possible usages in this corpus are:

4Q266 f5ii:14	ביחֹש{ֹי}ם
4Q275 f3:2	[. . .] יעלו ביחוש
4Q279 f5:3	. . . וכבירות יחוס עָלָֹיו

f. Although verbal forms of √יחש are attested in BH only in *hitpaʿel*, it is the root itself that should be considered a neologism (cf. יחש n.). Therefore, verbal forms from other conjugations as well are presented above in both Hebrew and Aramaic.

g. יחש/יחס does not seem to be attested in non-Jewish sources. Even if the Arabic root adduced in *HALOT* II 408a is etymologically related to יחש, semantically it does not have the specific genealogical meaning found in the Jewish texts.

BIBLIOGRAPHY

HALOT II 408a • Kaddari 422b

Batten 1913: 96 • Curtis and Madsen 1910: 30 no. 49 • S. R. Driver 1913: 535 no. 1 • Hurvitz 1996: 41* • Mosis 1990: 57 • Wellhausen 1885: 148 • Williamson 1977a: 45–46

יַחַשׂ n. m. *genealogy, genealogical list*: Neh. 7:5 סֵפֶר הַיַּחַשׂ

Cf. √יחשׂ

CBH Alternatives

תולדת, e.g.

Gen. 5:1   סֵפֶר   **תּוֹלְדֹת אָדָם**

[~ Neh. 7:5   הַיַּחַשׂ הָעוֹלִים בָּרִאשׁוֹנָה   סֵפֶר]

External Post-Classical Sources
Renderings/Paraphrases/Glosses

TN 22X, e.g.

Gen. 5:1	ית אדם	די ברא ה'	ביומא	דאדם	תלדוותה	**יחוס**	ספר	דין
[~	אָדָם	בָּרָא אֱלֹהִים	בְּיוֹם	אָדָם	תּוֹלְדֹת		סֵפֶר	זֶה]

TPJ 41X, e.g.

Num. 1:24	אבהתהון	לבית	לגניסתהון	**ייחוסיהון**	דגד	לבנוי
[~	אֲבֹתָם	לְבֵית	לְמִשְׁפְּחֹתָם	**תּוֹלְדֹתָם**	גָד	לִבְנֵי]

Deut. 32:26	דוכרנהון	אנוש	**מספר ייחוס**	אבטל
[~	זִכְרָם	מֵאֱנוֹשׁ		אַשְׁבִּיתָה]

Other Sources

FTV Gen. 25:19	(ד)יצחק	תולדתיה	**ואילי' יחוס**
[~	יִצְחָק	תּוֹלְדֹת	וְאֵלֶּה]

Tg. Ps 96:7	עמיא	**ייחוסי**	קדם ה'	איהבו זמר
[~	עַמִּים	**מִשְׁפְּחוֹת**	לַה'	הָבוּ]

PT Qid. 4:5 (p. 1183)   ר' שמואל בר נחמן בשם ר' יונתן: כת' "וְהַתְיַחְשָׂם בצבא
במלחמה" (דה"א ז 40) – זכות יחסיהם עומדת להם במלחמה

Independent Use
Heb.

4Q275 f3:1–2	והזקנים עמו . . . יעלו **ביחוש** (cf. √יחשׂ, comment e)
4Q279 f5:3	וכבירות **יחוס** עליו (cf. √יחשׂ, comment b)
M Yev. 4:13	אמ' ר' שמעון בן עזיי: מצאתי מגילת **יחסים** בירושלם
	וכתוב בה איש פלוני ממזר מאשת איש
T Ḥag. 2:9 (Moʿed p. 384)	ושם יושבין ובודקין **יחסי** כהונה **יחסי** לויה

Gen. Rab. 37:7 (p. 349)	ר' יוסי א': הראשונים על ידי שהיו מכירים **יחסיהם** היו מוציאים לשם המאורע. אבל אנו שאין אנו יודעין את **יחסינו** אנו מוציאין לשם אבותינו
Gen. Rab. 82:11 (p. 989)	קשה לפני הקב"ה לעקר שלשלת **יחסים** ממקומן ... "ובני ראובן בכור ישראל" (דה"א ה 1)... אמור מעתה, בכורת ממון ניטלה ממנו ולא בכורת **יחסים**
Sifre Num. 116 (p. 133)	"ולמבית לפרוכת" (במ' יח 7) – מיכן אמרו: מקום היה אחורי בית לפרוכת ששם בודקים **ייחוסי** כהונה
BT Pes. 62b	אמר ראמי בר רב יוד[!] אמר רב: מיום שנגנז ספר **יוחסין** תשש כוחן שלחכמים וכהה מאור עיניהם
BT BB 15a	עזרא כתב ספרו **ויחס** בדברי הימים עד לו

Aram.

| Tg. 1 Chron. 1:1 | דין ספר **יחוסיא** פתגמי יומיא דמן יומי עלמא |

COMMENTS

See √יחשׂ.

BIBLIOGRAPHY

See √יחשׂ.

יְרוּשָׁלַיִם (plene spelling) g.n. *Yerušalayim* (= *Jerusalem*): Jer. 26:18; Esth. 2:6
;וְשֵׁם אִמּוֹ יְהוֹעַדָּן מִירוּשָׁלָיִם ‎1 Chron. 3:5; 2 Chron. 25:1; אֲשֶׁר הָגְלָה מִירוּשָׁלַיִם
שָׁלַח סַנְחֵרִיב מֶלֶךְ אַשּׁוּר עֲבָדָיו יְרוּשָׁלַיְמָה ‎32:9

1QIsaᵃ 2:7	**וירושלים**	יהודה	על	אמוץ	בן	ישעיה	חזה	אשר	הדבר
[~ Isa. 2:1	**וִירוּשָׁלָם**	יְהוּדָה	עַל	אָמוֹץ	בֶּן	יְשַׁעְיָהוּ	חָזָה	אֲשֶׁר	הַדָּבָר]

11QPsᵃ 3:9		לו	שחברה	כעיר	הבנויה	**ירושלים**
[~ Ps. 122:3	יַחְדָּו	לָהּ	שֶׁחֻבְּרָה	כְּעִיר	הַבְּנוּיָה	**וִירוּשָׁלַם**]

CBH ALTERNATIVES
ירושלם, e.g.

2 Sam. 5:14	וּשְׁלֹמֹה	וְנָתָן	וְשׁוֹבָב	שַׁמּוּעַ	**בִּירוּשָׁלָ͏ִם**	לוֹ	הַיְלָדִים	שְׁמוֹת	וְאֵלֶּה
[~ 1 Chron. 3:5	וּשְׁלֹמֹה	וְנָתָן	וְשׁוֹבָב	שִׁמְעָא	**בִּירוּשָׁלָיִם**	לוֹ	נוּלְדוּ		וְאֵלֶּה]

Isa. 36:2	חִזְקִיָּהוּ	הַמֶּלֶךְ	אֶל	**יְרוּשָׁלְמָה**	רַב שָׁקֵה ...	אֶת ... וַיִּשְׁלַח
[~ 2 Chron. 32:9	יְחִזְקִיָּהוּ	עַל	...	**יְרוּשָׁלִַמָה**	עֲבָדָיו	סַנְחֵרִיב ... שָׁלַח]

Mic. 3:12	יָעַר	לְבָמוֹת	הַבַּיִת	וְהַר	תִּהְיֶה	עִיִּין	**וִירוּשָׁלַם**	תֶחָרֵשׁ	שָׂדֶה	צִיּוֹן
[~ Jer. 26:18	יָעַר	לְבָמוֹת	הַבַּיִת	וְהַר	תִּהְיֶה	עִיִּים	**וִירוּשָׁלַיִם**	תֵּחָרֵשׁ	שָׂדֶה	צִיּוֹן]

EXTERNAL POST-CLASSICAL SOURCES
Renderings/Paraphrases/Glosses

4Q176 f1–2i:5	**ירושלים**	לב	על	דברו
[~ Isa. 40:2	**יְרוּשָׁלָם**	לֵב	עַל	דַּבְּרוּ]

BT Ket. 8a	קול ששון וקול שמחה	**ירושלים** ובחוצות יהודה בערי	ישמע ...
[~ Jer 33:10–11	קוֹל שָׂשׂוֹן וְקוֹל שִׂמְחָה ...	**יְרוּשָׁלַם** וּבְחֻצוֹת יְהוּדָה בְּעָרֵי ... יִשָּׁמַע עוֹד]

Independent Use
Heb.

1QM 1:3	בשוב גולת בני אור ממדבר העמים לחנות במדבר **ירושלים**
4Q162 2:10	היא עדת אנשי הלצון אשר **בירושלים**
Masada (Meshorer 1989: 101, no. 1320 ff.)	**ירושלים** הקדושה
PT Meg. 1:8 (p. 751)	אנשי ירושלם היו כותבין **ירושלים ירושלימה**, ולא היו מקפידין

COMMENTS

a. "ירושלם appears in the Bible some 640 times spelled this way—without the *yod*—and only 5 times (three times in Chron., once in Jeremiah and once in the book of Esther) as ירושלים—with the *yod*. On the coins of the first Revolt against the Romans in 66–70 CE (immediately preceding the destruction of the Second Temple) we find both ירושלים and ירושלם, and this is the case in Mishnaic Hebrew also. Now in the Scrolls we also find the spelling ירושלים used concurrently with ירושלם. The spelling of over 40 proper nouns differs in the Scrolls and the Masoretic Text. It can be proven in over 25 of these (each one of which appears dozens of times) that the Scroll's reading is secondary in relation to that of the Masoretic Text" (Kutscher 1974: 5).

b. The antiquity of the MT spelling ירושלם is corroborated by extra-Biblical sources from the second and first millennia BCE: "the cuneiform equivalents *Urusalim* (EA) and *Ursalimmu* (Sennacherib prism) obviously presuppose the reading *yᵉrûšālēm*. The writing *r( )w-u-š( )l-m-m* in the Egyptian Execration texts probably represents the form *Urušalimum*. Etymologically, the name may mean something like 'foundation (→ ירה *yārâ* I) of the god Shalem'. This would be a pre-Israelite name" (Ringgren 1990: 348).

c. It has been suggested that the new ending of the name ירושלים represents the dual morpheme -*ayim* and that it reflects the eighth-century BCE territorial expansion of the city covering two different topographical areas (Derby 1997: 241–245). Whatever the meaning and function of the ending -*ayim* in the place-name Jerusalem, its distribution in the OT is clearly characteristic of LBH (4x in Esther and Chronicles), as the name does not appear in the Bible prior to the book of Jeremiah (1x).

d. Beside the distinctive LBH corpus, the sole Biblical occurrence of the extended form ירושלים is in the book of Jeremiah. Since this book chronologically embraces the end of the First Temple period and the beginning of the Exile, it should come as no surprise that certain post-Classical innovations found their way into Jeremiah as forerunners of LBH proper. Indeed, "the language called Rabbinic Hebrew first began to be used in writing step by step and little by little. Grammatical features characteristic of RH . . . first appear in writing in the book of Jeremiah, and from there [spread] to the distinctive Second Temple books, like Chronicles, Ezra-Nehemiah, and Esther. . . . The spelling ירושלים with a *yod*, which long before the appearance of vocalization testifies to the expansion of the vowel in the last syllable to a diphthong, occurs [only] once here" (Bar-Asher 1985: 93–94 [= 2009: 123]).

e. As noted, both forms (with and without the second *yod*) appear in the DSS, in Rabbinic literature, and the Targumim. It is not always clear when, where, and why each of the competing forms gained the upper hand. Regarding

Rabbinic literature and the Targumim, the place name ירושלים (with the second *yod*) appears extensively throughout the texts. However, it is methodologically problematic to make diachronic judgments based on the orthography
of the extant manuscripts of these sources, and for this reason the examples
adduced above reflect primarily ancient texts that were not subject to the pre-
cariousness of scribal transmission.

BIBLIOGRAPHY

Bar-Asher 1985: 93–94 (= 2009: 123–124) • Bergey 1983: 43–45 • Demsky 2002: 17 • Derby
1997: 241–245 • Fohrer 1972: 296 • Kutscher 1974: 5; 1982: §§118, 153 • Meshorer 1982: I 109,
plates 17–19; 1989: 101 • Qimron 1986: 91 • Ringgren 1990

יֵשׁוּעַ pr. g.n. *Jeshua*: Ezra 2:2, 6, 36, 40; 3:2, 8–9; 4:3; 8:33; 10:18; Neh. 3:19; 7:7, 11, 39, 43; 8:7, 17; וִישׁוּעַ בֶּן אֲזַנְיָה 10:10; מִימֵי יֵשׁוּעַ בֶּן נוּן 9:4–5; וְיֵשׁוּעַ 11:26 וּבִישׁוּעַ וּבְמוֹלָדָה וּבְבֵית פָּלֶט (see comment c below); 12:1, 7, 8, 10, 24 וְיֵשׁוּעַ בֶּן קַדְמִיאֵל, 26; 1 Chron. 24:11; עֵדֶן וּמִנְיָמִן וְיֵשׁוּעַ וּשְׁמַעְיָהוּ 2 Chron. 31:15

BA

Ezra 5:2		בַּר יוֹצָדָק	וְיֵשׁוּעַ	בַּר שְׁאַלְתִּיאֵל	זְרֻבָּבֶל
[~ Hag. 1:12		בֶּן יְהוֹצָדָק	וִיהוֹשֻׁעַ	בֶּן שַׁלְתִּיאֵל	[זְרֻבָּבֶל

CBH Alternatives

יְהוֹשֻׁעַ, יְהוֹשׁוּעַ, e.g.

Judg. 2:7	וְכֹל יְמֵי הַזְּקֵנִים	וַיַּעַבְדוּ הָעָם אֶת ה׳ כֹּל יְמֵי **יְהוֹשֻׁעַ**
	אֲשֶׁר הֶאֱרִיכוּ יָמִים אַחֲרֵי **יְהוֹשׁוּעַ**	
1 Kgs. 16:34	בֶּן נוּן	...כִּדְבַר ה׳ אֲשֶׁר דִּבֶּר בְּיַד **יְהוֹשֻׁעַ**
[~ Neh. 8:17	בֶּן נוּן כֵּן בְּנֵי יִשְׂרָאֵל עַד הַיּוֹם הַהוּא	מִימֵי **יֵשׁוּעַ** כִּי לֹא עָשׂוּ]

External Post-Classical Sources
Renderings/Paraphrases/Glosses

LXX 277x, e.g.

Deut. 34:9	καὶ Ἰησοῦς υἱὸς Ναυη	ἐνεπλήσθη πνεύματος συνέσεως
[~	מָלֵא רוּחַ חָכְמָה	[**וִיהוֹשֻׁעַ** בֶּן נוּן

Independent Use
Heb.

BS (B) 51:30   עד הנה דברי שמעון בן **ישוע** שנקרא בן סירא. חכמת שמעון בן **ישוע** בן אלעזר בן סירא

4Q175 1:21–23   בעת אשר כלה **ישוע** להלל ולהודות בתהלותיהו ויאמר: ארור היש אשר יבנה את העיר הזות, בבכורו ייסדנה ובצעירו יציב דלתיה

4Q378 f22i:2	משה	עבדך	משרת	ביד **ישוע**
[~ Num. 11:28	מֹשֶׁה	בֶּן נוּן מְשָׁרֵת	**יְהוֹשֻׁעַ**	וַיַּעַן]

Mur. 42:1–2 (Yardeni I p. 155)   מן הפרנסין של בית משכו מן **ישוע** ומן אלעזר **לישוע** בן גלגולא רו/יש המחניה שלום

T Ḥul. 2:22 (p. 503)   מעשה בר׳ אלעזר בן דמה שנשכו נחש ובא יעקב איש כפר סמא לרפאותו משום **ישוע** בן פנטרא ולא הניחו ר׳ ישמעאל

BT San. 43a   בערב הפסח תלאוהו **לישוע** הנצרי, וכרוז יוצא לפניו
(not found in the Vilna edition)   ארבעים יום: **ישוע** הנצרי יוצא להיסקל ...

Aram.

NḤ 22:8 (Yardeni I p. 149)	ישוע בר ישוע שהד
Rahmani 9:1 (Yardeni I p. 235)	ישוע בר יהוסף
NḤ 54:13–15 (Yardeni I p. 171)	וית **ישוע** בֹר תדמריה תחדון תשגרון לי באספליה
PT Ter. 8:4 (p. 247)	ר' חנניה ור' **ישוע** בן לוי, חד אמ' ישן מותר וחרנה
	אמ' ישן אסור

Comments

a. "In the Second Temple period יהושע became ישוע, possibly as a result of dissimilation: *yəhōšūʿ > yōšūʿ > yēšūʿ*; this is the form of the name in late biblical books (in both Hebrew and Aramaic) and Qumran writings, not only as the name of contemporaries but even of the biblical figure ישוע בן נון (33x). In Ben-Sira, on the other hand, according to the manuscripts available, historical names appear in their Classical form; thus יהושע בן נון (46:1) is differentiated from Ben-Sira's own name, שמעון בן ישוע (2:27; 51:30). ישוע is extant in Hebrew and Aramaic extra-Biblical writings from Second Temple times [n. 46 ad loc.: In the writings from Qumran, Naḥal Ḥever, and Wādi Murabbaʿāt, and in the area of Jerusalem, even in the shortened form ישו], as well as in epigraphic materials from the Tannaitic period. It also occurs in manuscripts of the Mishnah ..." (D. Talshir 1998: 374–375).

b. "Dissimilation. Certain vowels cannot be explained except in terms of a tendency to avoid a sequence of two vowels of identical or similar timbre. The first vowel in רֵאשׁוֹן (from רֹאשׁ) is due to dissimilation; analogously חִיצוֹן from חוּץ, תִּיכוֹן from cst. תּוֹךְ, ... יֵשׁוּעַ for *יוֹשׁוּעַ from יְהוֹשׁוּעַ (proper noun)" (JM 92 §29 *h*).

c. ישוע in Neh. 11:26 also denotes a geographical name, but the same linguistic development is evident in both the personal and geographical application of the name.

d. The newer form, ישוע, did not completely supplant its earlier counterpart, יהושע; both forms are documented in the later period. For instance, within the LBH corpus Haggai and Zechariah invariably read יהושע בן יהוצדק, whereas Ezra and Nehemiah record the same name ישוע בן יוצדק (or BA ישוע בר יוצדק). Similarly, in Rabbinic writings we find both forms of the name, e.g., a passage that appears twice in the PT spells Joshua ben Levi in two different ways:

PT Ter. 8:4 (p. 247)	ר' חנניה ור' **ישוע** בן לוי, חד אמ' ישן מותר וחרנה אמ' ישן אסור
[~ PT AZ 2:3 (p. 1386)	ר' חנינה ר' **יהושע** בן לוי, חד אמ' ישן מותר וחד אמ' ישן אסור

BIBLIOGRAPHY

BDB 221b • JM 92 §29 *h*

Foerster 1972: 284 • Liver 1965: 895 • Loewenstamm 1965: 895 • Sawyer 1990: 443 •
D. Talshir 1988: 186–187 note 68; 1992: 233–234; 1998: 374–379

√**ישט** vb. *extend, stretch out* : **Hiph** Esth. 4:11; 5:2; 8:4 וַיּוֹשֶׁט הַמֶּלֶךְ לְאֶסְתֵּר אֵת שַׁרְבִט הַזָּהָב

CBH Alternatives

√שלח (יד), e.g.

וַיִּשְׁלַח מַלְאַךְ ה'	אֶת קְצֵה הַמִּשְׁעֶנֶת	אֲשֶׁר בְּיָדוֹ	וַיִּגַּע ...	Judg. 6:21
וַיִּשְׁלַח	אֶת קְצֵה הַמַּטֶּה	אֲשֶׁר בְּיָדוֹ ...		1 Sam. 14:27
[**וַיּוֹשֶׁט** הַמֶּלֶךְ לְאֶסְתֵּר אֵת	שַׁרְבִיט הַזָּהָב אֲשֶׁר בְּיָדוֹ ... וַתִּגַּע ...			[~ Esth. 5:2

לְהִשְׁתַּחֲוֺת לוֹ	**וְשָׁלַח**	אֶת יָדוֹ ...	2 Sam. 15:5
[וַתִּפֹּל לִפְנֵי רַגְלָיו ... **וַיּוֹשֶׁט** הַמֶּלֶךְ לְאֶסְתֵּר אֵת שַׁרְבִט הַזָּהָב			[~ Esth. 8:3–4

External Post-Classical Sources
Renderings/Paraphrases/Glosses

TO 13x, e.g.

לא **תושיט** ידך בעולימא ולא תעביד ליה מדעם	Gen. 22:12
[אַל תִּשְׁלַח יָדְךָ אֶל הַנַּעַר וְאַל תַּעַשׂ לוֹ מְאוּמָה	[~

אושיט ידך ואחוד בדנביה **ואושיט** ידיה ואתקיף ביה	Exod. 4:4
[שְׁלַח יָדְךָ וֶאֱחֹז בִּזְנָבוֹ **וַיִּשְׁלַח** יָדוֹ וַיַּחֲזֶק בּוֹ	[~

TN 1x

ויקרב ... לוות דייניא אין לא **שלח** ידי⟨ה⟩ במקמתא דחבריה	Exod. 22:7
(דלא **תושיט** בעבידת׳)	(in marg.
[וְנִקְרַב ... אֶל הָאֱלֹהִים אִם לֹא **שָׁלַח** יָדוֹ בִּמְלֶאכֶת רֵעֵהוּ	[~

TPJ 14x, e.g.

ואושיטו גוברייא ית ידיהון והנעילו ית לוט לוותהון לביתה	Gen. 19:10
[**וַיִּשְׁלְחוּ** הָאֲנָשִׁים אֶת יָדָם וַיָּבִיאוּ אֶת לוֹט אֲלֵיהֶם הַבָּיְתָה	[~

TJ 28x, e.g.

ידה לסכתא **אושיטת** וימינה לארזפתא למתבר רשיעין ואנוסין	Judg. 5:26
[יָדָהּ לַיָּתֵד **תִּשְׁלַחְנָה** וִימִינָהּ לְהַלְמוּת עֲמֵלִים	[~

ארי דמנזיק לכון כיד **מושיט** ידיה למקרב בגלגלי עינוהי	Zech. 2:12
[כִּי הַנֹּגֵעַ בָּכֶם נֹגֵעַ בְּבָבַת עֵינוֹ	[~

Other Sources

Tg. Ruth 2:14	ויתיבת מסטר חצודיא **ואושיט** לה קמח קלי ואכלת
[~	[וַתֵּשֶׁב מִצַּד הַקּוֹצְרִים **וַיִּצְבָּט** לָהּ קָלִי וַתֹּאכַל

Sifra Beḥuqotai 1:3 "ושעשע יונק על חור וגו' [פתן ועל מאורת צפעוני גמול ידו **הדה**]
(יש' יא 8) – מלמ' שתינוק מישר' עתיד להיות **מושיט** אצבעו לתוך
גלגל עינו שלציפעוני ומוציא מרה מתוך פיו

Independent Use

Heb.

BS (C) 4:31	אל תהי ידך **מושטת** לשאת ובעת השב קפודה
BS (B) 34:18	וגם אם בין רבים ישבת לפני רע אל **תושט** יד
M Tam. 7:3	בזמן שכהן גדול רוצה להקטיר היה עולה בכבש ...הגיע
	למחצית הכבש, אחז הסגן בימינו והעלהו. **הושיט** לו הראשון
	הראש והרגל וסמך עליהן וזרקן, **והושיט** השני לראשון ונתן
	לכהן גדול וסמך עליהן וזרקן. נשמט השני והלך לו. כך היו
	מושיטין לו ושאר כל האיברין הוא סומך עליהן וזורקן
T Demai 2:24 (Zer. p. 72)	לא **יושיט** ישראל אבר מן החי לבני נח ולא כוס יין לנזיר

Aram.

Ruth Rab. 3:4	נפק וצלי בהדי אולוסיס דטבריא וחמא ידא **מושטא** ליה חדא
	מרגלית
PT BM 2:2 (p. 1218)	שמעון בר ווה הוה מהלך חורי ר' לעזר. נפל מיניה דינר. **אושטיה**
	ליה שמע' בר ווה. אמ' ליה: כבר נתייאשתי מיניה
TM 4:1100–1101	"ואין מידי מציל" (דב' לב 39) – ...הן **התושטת** יד סהד וקטל
(p. 301)	זכי–"ואין מידי מציל", ולא יתפרק מני

COMMENTS

a. "... √ישט, and its usage in the *hiph'il* (*aph'el*) and *hoph'al* conjugations, are attested in the Second Temple Biblical corpus, Ben-Sira, Rabbinic literature, and in [both] eastern and western Middle and Late Aramaic. Since in Hebrew [√ישט] occurs only in the Hebrew of the Second Temple period, whereas in the Hebrew of the First Temple period other roots conveying similar meanings were employed [and since] ... in Targumic Aramaic [√ישט] is freely employed as a rendering of various Hebrew roots (particularly as a translation of the verb √שלח), it would seem that this root penetrated Hebrew from Aramaic" (Dihi 2004: 322). See also Bendavid (1967–73: I 62): "The book of Esther is unparalleled in the richness of its Aramaic words, cast in their original native mould: יְקָר (instead of כבוד)...שלט (instead of משל), הושיט ידו (instead of שלח) ... and an abundance of Persian words."

b. In all three LBH occurrences, ישׁט is tied to שׁרביט (also widely classified as an LBH word).

BIBLIOGRAPHY

BDB 445a • *HALOT* II 446b

Bendavid 1967–73: I 62 • Bergey 1983: 123–124 • Dihi 2004: 321–323 • S. R. Driver 1913: 484 • Eskhult 2003: 14 • Paton 1908: 62–63, 223 • Rabin 1962: 1075 • Wagner 1966: 63 no. 122

וְאִם ‎**כְּאֶחָד** adv. *together* (lit., *as one*); *jointly*; *simultaneously*: Isa. 65:25; Qoh. 11:6; כִּי הִטַּהֲרוּ הַכֹּהֲנִים וְהַלְוִיִּם כְּאֶחָד כֻּלָּם טְהוֹרִים; Ezra 2:64; 3:9; 6:20; שְׁנֵיהֶם כְּאֶחָד טוֹבִים; כָּל הַקָּהָל כְּאֶחָד אַרְבַּע רִבּוֹא אֲלָפַיִם שְׁלֹשׁ מֵאוֹת וְשִׁשִּׁים 2 Chron. 5:13 Neh. 7:66

BA כַּחֲדָה Dan. 2:35 בֵּאדַיִן דָּקוּ כַחֲדָה פַּרְזְלָא חַסְפָּא נְחָשָׁא כַּסְפָּא וְדַהֲבָא

CBH Alternatives

כְּאִישׁ אֶחָד, יַחַד, יַחְדָּו, e.g.

וַיָּקָם	כָּל הָעָם	**כְּאִישׁ אֶחָד**	Judg. 20:8
[וַיַּעֲמֹד יֵשׁוּעַ בָּנָיו וְאֶחָיו . . .		**כְּאֶחָד**	[~ Ezra 3:9

Isa. 11:6–9

וְגָר זְאֵב עִם כֶּבֶשׂ
וְנָמֵר עִם גְּדִי יִרְבָּץ
וְעֵגֶל וּכְפִיר וּמְרִיא **יַחְדָּו** . . . וּפָרָה וָדֹב תִּרְעֶינָה
יַחְדָּו יִרְבְּצוּ יַלְדֵיהֶן
וְאַרְיֵה כַּבָּקָר יֹאכַל תֶּבֶן . . . וְלֹא יַשְׁחִיתוּ . . .
[זְאֵב וְטָלֶה יִרְעוּ **כְאֶחָד** וְאַרְיֵה כַּבָּקָר יֹאכַל תֶּבֶן . . . וְלֹא יַשְׁחִיתוּ . . . ~ Isa. 65:25]

וַיַּעֲנוּ כָל הָעָם		**יַחְדָּו**	Exod. 19:8
כָּל קְצִינַיִךְ נָדְדוּ יַחַד . . .			Isa. 22:3
כָּל נִמְצָאַיִךְ אֻסְּרוּ יַחְדָּו			
[כָּל הַקָּהָל	**כְּאֶחָד** אַרְבַּע רִבּוֹא . . .		~ Neh. 7:66]

External Post-Classical Sources
Renderings/Paraphrases/Glosses

TO 18x, e.g.

Deut. 22:10	**כחדא**	ובחמרא	בתורא	תרדי	לא
[~	**יַחְדָּו**	וּבַחֲמֹר	בְּשׁוֹר	תַחֲרֹשׁ	לֹא]

TN 33x, e.g.

Gen. 13:6 ולא אסחנ(ת)⟨![⟩ יתהון ארעא למשרי **כחדה** . . . ולא הוון יכלין למשרי **כחדא**
[וְלֹא נָשָׂא אֹתָם הָאָרֶץ לָשֶׁבֶת **יַחְדָּו** וְלֹא יָכְלוּ לָשֶׁבֶת **יַחְדָּו** ~]

TPJ 46x, e.g.

Gen. 22:6 ונסיב אברהם ית קיסי דעלתא ושוי עילוי יצחק בריה . . . ואזלו תרוויהום **כחדא**
[וַיִּקַּח אַבְרָהָם אֶת עֲצֵי הָעֹלָה וַיָּשֶׂם עַל יִצְחָק בְּנוֹ . . . וַיֵּלְכוּ שְׁנֵיהֶם **יַחְדָּו** ~]

TJ 70x, e.g.

1 Sam. 17:10   וַאמר   פלשתאה ... איתו לי גברא ונגיח קרבא **כחדא**

[~   וַיֹּאמֶר הַפְּלִשְׁתִּי ... תְּנוּ לִי אִישׁ וְנִלָּחֲמָה **יָחַד**

Other Sources

FTP Exod. 19:8   ועניין כל עמא **כחדא** ואמרו כל דמליל   מימרא דה׳ נעביד

[~   וַיַּעֲנוּ כָל הָעָם **יַחְדָּו** וַיֹּאמְרוּ כֹּל אֲשֶׁר דִּבֶּר   ה׳   נַעֲשֶׂה

11QTgJob 30:4–5   במזהר **כחדא** כוכבי צפר ויזעק[ו]ן **כחדה** כל מלאכי אלהא

[~ Job 38:7   בְּרָן **יַחַד** כֹּוכְבֵי בֹקֶר וַיָּרִיעוּ   כָּל בְּנֵי   אֱלֹהִים

1QApGen 21:25   כול אלן אזדמנו **כחדא** לקרב לעמקא די סדיא

[~ Gen. 14:3   כָּל אֵלֶּה חָבְרוּ   אֶל עֵמֶק   הַשִּׂדִּים הוּא יָם הַמֶּלַח

Independent Use
Heb.

M Teh. 5:5   שני שבילין אחד טמא ואחד טהור, הילך באחד מהן ועשה
טהרות ובא חבירו והילך בשיני ועשה טהרות, ר׳ יהודה או׳:
אם נשאלו זה בפני עצמו וזה בפני עצמו טהורין, אם נשאלו
שניהן **כאחת** טמאין

T Bekh. 2:7 (p. 536)   רחילה שלא ביכרה וילדה שני זכרים ויצא ראשיהן **כאחד**, ר׳
יוסי הגלילי אומר: שניהן לכהן

MekhRI Nez. 9 (p. 279)   הפיל שתי שיניו **כאחת**, סימא שתי עיניו **כאחת**: הרי זה יוצא בן
חורין ואינו נוטל כלום, תלמוד לומר עין שן שן

MekhRS 15:11
(p. 93)   שלא כמדת בשר ודם מדת המק׳, בשר ודם אין יכול לדבר
שני דברים **כאחד** אבל מי שאמר והיה העולם אינו כן אלא אמ׳
עשר דברות בדיבור אחד

Sifra Tzav 3:1   יכול אהרן ובניו **כאחת** יהוא מביאין קרבן זה? תל׳ לו׳ ״אהרן
ובניו אשר יקריבו״ (וי׳ ו 13). הא כיצד? אהרן מביא לעצמו
ובניו מביאין לעצמן

BT Giṭ. 77b   גיטה וידה באין **כאחד**, הכא נמי גיטה וחצירה באין **כאחד**

Aram.

TAD II 1.1: 5–6   חמר קבל חמר פר[ס קבל]פרס טבא ולחיא נפלג **כחדה**

TAD II 2.11 (= Cowley 28):2–3   אנחנה אשתוין **כחדה** ופלגן עלין עבדיה זי מבטחיה אמן

1QApGen 21:34–22:1	וְשֹׁבִ֖י לוֹט . . . דִי הוא יתב בסודם **כחדא** עמהון וכול נכסוהי		
[~ Gen. 14:12	[וַיִּקְחוּ אֶת לוֹט . . . וְהוּא יֹשֵׁב בִּסְדֹם		

PT Ḥag. 2:2 (p. 787)   תרין חסידין הוון באשקלון, אכלין **כחדא** ושתי **כחדא** ולעיי באוריתא **כחדא**

Gen. Rab. 35:2 (pp. 328–329)   אליהו זכור לטוב ור׳ יהושע ⟨בן לוי⟩ הוון יתבין תניין **כחדא** . . .

COMMENTS

a. "In early Heb. כאיש אחד is used to express joint action. . . . The text [i.e., Ezra 2:64] shows a late usage. The mng. required here is 'combined', which in early Heb. would be יחדו" (Batten 1913: 98). Cf. also the following statements: "כאחד, which was not understood by the LXX, is an Aramaism (= כַּחֲדָא, Dan. 2:35; כחדא, Targum on Gen. 13:6) occurring in late Hebrew and meaning 'together, altogether'. . . . Here [i.e., Qoh 11:6] it is used to denote 'equally, lit. like one another'" (Gordis 1968: 333); "This phrase appears in II Chr 5.13 and elsewhere only in Qoh 11.6, Ezr 2.64 (= Neh 7.66), 3.9, 6.20, and Is 65.25. Compare the Aramaic *kaḥ*ᵃ*dā*ʾ and also mheᵎ [= Mishnaic Hebrew of the Tannaim], where this idiom is frequently attested. We can consider it a very probable LBH idiom, perhaps of Aramaic origin" (Polzin 1976: 139). In summary, "all passages in which Hebrew כאחד appears are dated to the exilic/postexilic period. . . . For the original Hebrew, כאיש אחד, see Num 14:15; Judg 6:16; 20:1 . . ." (Polak 2006a: 603 note 62).

b. This entry should not be confused with the earlier CBH usage in Gen. 49:16 (כְּאַחַד (שִׁבְטֵי יִשְׂרָאֵל = *as one (out) of (many)*, wrongly translated in the Targumim (TO, TN, and TPJ) כחדא, under the influence of the LBH meaning *together*.

c. "[Isaiah 65²⁵] . . . is a condensed quotation from 11⁶⁻⁹, . . . where יחדו, the common Hebrew word for *together*, is replaced by כאחד, an expression modeled upon the Aram. כחדא, and occurring besides only in the latest books of the OT" (S. R. Driver 1913: 240).

d. Whereas LBH makes use of כאחד, RH employs both כאחד (m.) and כאחת (f.). The meaning of the two forms is synonymous and fulfills the same adverbial function, but there seems to have been a certain preference in RH for the f. כאחת with feminine nouns and the m. כאחד with masculine nouns (see the RH quotations above).

e. For the Akkadian parallels (*kima ištēn*, *kī ištēn*), see Kutscher 1963–64: 122 (= 1977: 398).

BIBLIOGRAPHY

BDB 25b • *HALOT* I 30a

Barton 1908: 194 • Batten 1913: 98 • Delitzsch 1877: 190–196 • S. R. Driver 1913: 240, 475 no. 8 • Fredericks 1988: 199, 228 • Gordis 1968: 333 • Hurvitz 1983: 215 • Kaddari 1976: 75 note 56 • Kutscher 1963–64: 122 [= 1977: 398] • Polak 2006a: 603 note 62 • Polzin 1976: 139 • Rabin 1962: 1075 • Schoors 1992–2004: II 278 • Seow 1996: 652 • Wagner 1966: 63 no. 124

כִּסְלֵו pr. n. name of 9th month, derived from Akkad. *Kislimu*: Neh 1:1 וַיְהִי בְחֹדֶשׁ
בְּאַרְבָּעָה לַחֹדֶשׁ הַתְּשִׁיעִי בְּכִסְלֵו 7:1 Zech; כִּסְלֵיו (ק׳) שְׁנַת עֶשְׂרִים

Cf. אֲדָר

CBH ALTERNATIVES
Months are generally named by their numerical order, e.g., 1 Kgs. 12:32 בַּחֹדֶשׁ
הַשְּׁמִינִי; in a few cases they follow the Canaanite pattern, e.g., 1 Kgs. 8:2 בְּיֶרַח
הָאֵתָנִים. Only in the LBH corpus do we find both (the older) numerical system
and (the more recent) Mesopotamian names side by side in one and the same
verse, e.g., Esth. 3:7 לְחֹדֶשׁ שְׁנֵים עָשָׂר הוּא חֹדֶשׁ אֲדָר.

Jer. 36:9	בַּחֹדֶשׁ הַתְּשִׁעִי	בַּשָּׁנָה הַחֲמִשִׁית לִיהוֹיָקִים... מֶלֶךְ יְהוּדָה
[~ Zech. 7:1	בְּאַרְבָּעָה לַחֹדֶשׁ הַתְּשִׁיעִי בְּכִסְלֵו	[בִּשְׁנַת אַרְבַּע לְדָרְיָוֶשׁ הַמֶּלֶךְ...

EXTERNAL POST-CLASSICAL SOURCES
Renderings/Paraphrases/Glosses
TJ 1x

Zech. 7:1	**בכסלו** תשיעאה לירחא בארבעה... ה׳ קדם מן נבואה פתגם הוה		
[~	**בְּכִסְלֵו** הַתְּשִׁיעִי לַחֹדֶשׁ בְּאַרְבָּעָה... ה׳		דְּבַר הָיָה]

Other Sources

Tg. 1 Chron. 27:12	**דכסליו**	לירחא	תשיעאה
[~	**הַתְּשִׁיעִי**	לַחֹדֶשׁ	הַתְּשִׁיעִי]

Independent Use
Heb.

NḤ 45: 1–3	בשנים **לכסלו** שנת שלוש, לשמעון בן כוסבא נשיא ישראל בעין גדי
M RoshH 1:3	על ששה חדשים שלוחים יוצאים: על ניסן מפני הפסח... על **כסליו** מפני החנוכה
T Taʻan. 1:7 (Moʻed p. 325)	חצי תשרי מרחשון וחצי **כסליו** – זרע. חצי **כסליו** טבת וחצי שבט – חורף. חצי שבט אדר וחצי ניסן – קור. חצי ניסן אייר וחצי סיון – קציר. חצי סיון תמוז וחצי אב – קיץ. חצי אב אלול וחצי תשרי – חום
ʻEin Gedi (Naveh 1978: no. 70): 5–7	ניסן אייר סיון תמוז אב אילול תשרי מרחשון **כסליו** טבת שבט ואדר
BT Pes. 94b	בארבעה שבילין חמה מהלכת... תשרי מרחשון **וכסלו** בימים כדי ליבש את הנהרות...

Aram.

PAT 0285 (= Cooke 127):5	שנת 574 בירח **כסלול**[!]
EN 63:1–3 (Idum.)	ב 11 **לכסלו** שנת 2 חבותו לבני גורו שערן סאן עשר
	ותמ[נ]ה קב חד
Meg. Ta'an. 3 Kislev (p. 98)	בתלתא **בכסלו** אתנטלו סמואתא מן דרתא
FTP Exod. 12:2	**כסלו** ענא ואמר: בי אינון מתפרקין
1 Tg. Esth. 3:7	בכן שרי שמשי (ס)פרא לצבעא פייסא דעדבין קדם
	המן . . . ושרי בירחיא. בניסן ולא על מן בגלל זכותא
	דפיסחא . . . **בכסלו** לא על מן בגלל דביה איתיסר בית
	מוקדשא . . . כד מטא לסוף תריסר ירחי שתא דאיהוא
	ירחא דאדר . . .

Greek (LXX)

1 Macc. 4:52   καὶ ὤρθρισαν τὸ πρωὶ τῇ πέμπτῃ καὶ εἰκάδι τοῦ μηνὸς τοῦ ἐνάτου
(οὗτος ὁ μὴν Χασελευ) τοῦ ὀγδόου καὶ τεσσαρακοστοῦ καὶ
ἑκατοστοῦ ἔτους

COMMENTS

a. See the entry אֲדָר for general comments on month-names and the bibliography there.

See also BDB 493a; Kaddari 523b.

√כעס vb. *be angry*: Qal Ezek. 16:42 וְשָׁקַטְתִּי וְלֹא אֶכְעַס עוֹד; Ps. 112:10 רָשָׁע יִרְאֶה וְכָעָס;
(see comment **a** below); Qoh. 5:16; 7:9 אַל תְּבַהֵל בְּרוּחֲךָ לִכְעוֹס; Neh. 3:33 וַיִּחַר לוֹ
2 Chron. 16:10 וַיִּכְעַס אָסָא אֶל הָרֹאֶה . . . כִּי בְזַעַף עִמּוֹ עַל זֹאת; וַיִּכְעַס הַרְבֵּה

CBH Alternatives

√קצף, חרה, (אַף) √אנף, e.g.

Gen. 40:2–3	אֶל בֵּית הַסֹּהַר	וַיִּתֵּן אֹתָם בְּמִשְׁמַר . . .	וַיִּקְצֹף פַּרְעֹה עַל שְׁנֵי סָרִיסָיו . . .
Judg. 2:14	וַיִּשְׁסּוּ אוֹתָם	וַיִּתְּנֵם בְּיַד שֹׁסִים	וַיִּחַר אַף ה' בְּיִשְׂרָאֵל
[~ 2 Chron. 16:10	בֵּית הַמַּהְפֶּכֶת	וַיִּתְּנֵהוּ	וַיִּכְעַס אָסָא אֶל הָרֹאֶה

Gen. 4:5	וַיִּפְּלוּ פָּנָיו	מְאֹד	וַיִּחַר לְקַיִן
[~ Neh. 3:33	וַיִּלְעַג עַל הַיְּהוּדִים	וַיִּכְעַס הַרְבֵּה	וַיִּחַר לוֹ

External Post-Classical Sources
Renderings/Paraphrases/Glosses

TPJ 1x (pass. ptc.)

Gen. 38:15	והוה מדמיה באנפוי כנפקת ברא ארום **כעיסת** אפין הות בביתיה דיהודה
[~	וַיַּחְשְׁבֶהָ לְזוֹנָה כִּי כִסְּתָה פָּנֶיהָ

Other Sources

MekhRI Shira 9
(pp. 146–147)

"שמעו עמים **ירגזון**" (שמ' טו 14) – כיון ששמעו האומות שהקדוש
ברוך הוא מגביה קרנן של ישראל ומכניסן לארץ התחילו **מתרגזין**.
אמר להם הקדוש ברוך הוא: שוטים שבעולם, כמה מלכים מלכו
מכם ולא **כעסו** ישראל, שנ' "ואלה המלכים אשר מלכו בארץ אדום"
(בר' לו 31), וכמה שלטונות שלטו מכם ולא **כעסו** ישראל, שנ' "אלוף
לוטן אלוף שובל" (שם, 29) ועכשו אתם **כעסים**! אף אני אתן לכם
כעס שאין בו רצון, שנ' "ה' מלך **ירגזו** עמים" (תה' צט 1)

MekhRI Vayassaʿ 4 (p. 167)

"**ויקצף** עליהם משה" (שמ' טז 20) –
כעס עליהם ואמר להם: מפני מה עשיתם כן

PesiqRK 17 (pp. 282–283)

"אם **קפץ באף** רחמיו סלה" (תה' עז 10) –
אף על גב דהוא **כעס** רחמיו קריבין

BT Pes. 66b

אמר ריש לקיש: כל אדם **שכועס**, אם חכם הוא חכמתו מסתלקת; אם נביא
הוא נבואתו מסתלקת ממנו; אם חכם הוא חכמתו מסתלקת ממנו, דכת'
"**ויקצף** משה על פקודי החיל" וג' (במ' לא 14)

Independent Use

Heb.

M Avot 5:11	ארבע מידות בדעות: נוח **לכעוס** ונוח לרצות – יצא שכרו בהפסדו. קשה **לכעוס** וקשה לרצות – יצא הפסדו בשכרו. קשה **לכעוס** ונוח לרצות – חסיד. נוח **לכעוס** וקשה לרצות – רשע
T Suk. 2:6 (Mo'ed pp. 262–263)	בזמן שהמאורות לוקין סימן רע לאומות העולם. משל למלך בשר ודם שבנה פלטרין ושכללה והתקין בה את הסעודה ואחר כך הכניס את האורחין. **כעס** עליהן, אמ' לשמש ונטל את הנר מלפניהן ונמצאו כולן יושבין בחשיכה
MekhRI Pisḥa 1 (p. 5)	שכל שלשים ושמונה שנה שהיה **כועס** על ישראל לא היה מדבר עמו
Sifra Milu'im 1:2	כיון שראה אהרן שקרבו כל הקרבנות ונעשו כל המעשים ולא ירדה שכינה לישר' היה עומד ומצטער. א': יודע אני **שכעס** עלי המקום ובשבילי לא ירדה שכינה לישר'

Aram.

Gen. Rab. 80:1 (p. 951)	. . . שמע ר' **וכעס**. בפתי רמשא על ר' שמעון בן לקיש משאל בשלמיה ומפייסיה עלוי
Qoh. Rab. 3:11 (3)	דילמא תבע הוא גבי בר נש כלום ולא יהיב **וכעס** עלוי וקטיל ליה
PT Pe'ah 8:9 (pp. 113–114)	אמ' ליה: לא **יכעוס** מרי עלי בגין . . . דלא אכלית עמך יומא דין. אמ' ליה: אתה פייסת למאן דמיתחמי ולא חמי. דין דחמי ולא מיתחמי יקבל פייוסך
PT Ber. 7:2 (p. 57)	שמע ינאי מלכא **וכעס**. דחל שמעון בן שטח וערק
PesiqRK 17 (p. 284)	מאן **דכעיס**, סופא מתרציא

Comments

a. The root כעס, whose basic meaning is *vexation, anger* (of both God and man), is quite common in CBH, where it is attested as a noun (כַּעַס) and a verb in the *hiph'il* (הִכְעִיס) and *pi'el* (כִּעֵס), conveying a transitive sense (*to vex, provoke anger*). However, in the *Qal* (כָּעַס *to be vexed, angry*), its distribution pattern is clearly indicative of the late period (on the linguistic status of Ps. 112, see Hurvitz 1972: 174). This late Biblical usage is in line with its external counterparts in RH (כָּעַס) and Aramaic (כְּעַס). In contrast, the notion of *being vexed, angry* is expressed in CBH by קָצַף, חָרָה (אַף), הִתְאַנַּף, אָנַף (see also the ninth-century BCE Mesha' inscription, lines 5–6: כי יאנף כמש בארצה = *because Kᵉmôš was angry with his land* [Aḥituv 2008: 392–394]). כָּעַס (*qal*) should therefore be classified as an LBH element.

b. The old CBH counterparts of כָּעַס "had not altogether vanished, for they appear in some late sources. However, they are nothing more than ancient survivals or archaizing devices, inherited from a previous phase of the language. The late distribution of *kāʿas* within the Bible faithfully reflects an actual linguistic situation" (Hurvitz 1982: 116).

Bibliography

Aḥituv 2008: 392–394 • Bendavid 1967–71: I 361 • Hurvitz 1972: 174 note 303; 1982: 115–116 • Rooker 1990: 147–148 • Milgrom 1991–2001: I 609–610.

(עשה√) כִּרְצוֹן *as pleases, according to one's will*: Esth. 1:8 לַעֲשׂוֹת כִּרְצוֹן אִישׁ וָאִישׁ;
9:5; Dan. 8:4 וְאֵין מַצִּיל מִיָּדוֹ וְעָשָׂה כִרְצֹנוֹ וְהִגְדִּיל; 11:3, 16, 36; Neh. 9:24 וַתִּתְּנֵם בְּיָדָם וְאֶת
וְעַל גְּוִיָּתֵנוּ מֹשְׁלִים וּבִבְהֶמְתֵּנוּ כִּרְצוֹנָם 37, מַלְכֵיהֶם . . . לַעֲשׂוֹת בָּהֶם כִּרְצוֹנָם

BA Ezra 7:18 כִּרְעוּת אֱלָהֲכֹם תַּעַבְדוּן

EXTERNAL POST-CLASSICAL SOURCES
Renderings/Paraphrases/Glosses
TO 1X,
Gen. 6:6   ואמר למתבר תוקפהון   **כרעותיה**
[~   וַיִּתְעַצֵּב   אֶל   **לִבּוֹ**   ]

TPJ 1X
Deut.   ארום תיעול . . . בכרמא דחברך ותיכול   **כרעוות** נפשך עד דתיסבע
23:25
[~   שָׂבְעֶךָ   **כְנַפְשְׁךָ**   וְאָכַלְתָּ עֲנָבִים   רֵעֶךָ   בְּכֶרֶם   תָבֹא   כִּי]

TJ 10X, e.g.
1 Sam. 2:35   **וכרעותי יעביד** דכמימרי   מהימן קדמי כהן ואקים
[~   **יַעֲשֶׂה**   **וּבְנַפְשִׁי** כַּאֲשֶׁר בִּלְבָבִי נֶאֱמָן כֹּהֵן לִי וַהֲקִימֹתִי]

Jer. 5:9   **כרעותי** מנהון אתפרע לא עובדוהי דכדין עמא מן ואם
[~   **נַפְשִׁי**   תִּתְנַקֵּם לֹא   כָּזֶה אֲשֶׁר בְּגוֹי וְאִם]

Independent Use
Heb.
BS (B) 50:22   עתה ברכו נא את ה' . . . . המגדל אדם מרחם **ויעשהו כרצונו**
11QT 59:19–20   ונתתי את כול אויביו לפניו ומשל בהמה **כרצונו** והמה לוא ימשולו בו
M Men. 10:8   אנשי יריחו קוצרין **כרצון** חכמ' וגודשין שלא **כרצון** חכמ'
Lam. Rab. Pet. 24   בודאי זהו ביתי וזהו מנוחתי שבאו אויבים **ועשו בו כרצונם**

Aram.
4Q541 f9i:3   מאמרה כמאמר שמין ואלפונה **כרעות אל**
4Q542 f1ii:2–3   די הוא אלה עלסיה ומרא כול סעבדיא ושליט בכולא
למעבד בהון כרעותה
Qaddish (liturg.; Genizah   יתגדל ויתקדש שמיה רבא. ויגיבון: אמן. בעלמא די ברא
fragment CUL T-S H18.20)   **כרעותיה** וימלך מלכותיה
2 Tg. Esth. 4:13   ומאן דעבד לישראל נסין בכל עדן ועדן הוא ימסר שנאנא
בידנא **ונעביד** ביה **כרעות נפשנא**

COMMENTS

a. "In SBH רָצוֹה means 'to be content', while חָפוֹץ means 'to wish'. In LBH רָצוֹה is already approaching the meaning of חָפוֹץ 'to wish'. That is why in Esther 1, 8 we find לַעֲשׂוֹת כִּרְצוֹן כָּל אִישׁ וָאִישׁ 'to do as every man desired'. In MH רָצוֹה is practically the only verb which survives with this meaning" (Kutscher 1982: 83 §123).

"It is well known that the principal meaning of רצה in the Bible is 'to be satisfied, pleased', whereas the usual meaning in Modern Hebrew, 'to want', is late and is characteristic specifically of RH; (לומר) רוצה in RH (and in Modern Hebrew) is equivalent to (לאמר) חפץ in BH. This semantic shift apparently occurred under the influence of Aramaic רעה. In any event, this development is evident in the Bible in the later books, particularly in light of the use of the expression לעשות כרצון, which is found only in the books of Daniel, Esther, and Nehemiah" (Hurvitz 1972: 73–74).

BIBLIOGRAPHY

Ben-Iehuda XIII 6696b note 2; XIV 6707 note 2

Bendavid 1967–71: II 6, 62 • Bergey 1983: 153–155 • Hurvitz 1972: 73–78, 110, 126 note 155, 175 • Kutscher 1982: 83 §123 • Qimron 1986: 94, 95 • Sáenz-Badillos 1993: 127 • van Peursen 2004: 253 note 73 • R. M. Wright 2005: 75–77

כְּתָב n. m. *writing, document, register, letter, edict*: Ezek. 13:9 לֹא בִכְתָב בֵּית יִשְׂרָאֵל
פַּתְשֶׁגֶן הַכְּתָב לְהִנָּתֵן דָּת 14, מְדִינָה וּמְדִינָה כִּכְתָבָהּ וְעַם וָעַם כִּלְשׁוֹנוֹ 3:12; Esth. 1:22; יִכָּתְבוּ
9:27; 8:8 ,4:8; ... אֵין לְהָשִׁיב בְּשֵׁם הַמֶּלֶךְ נִכְתָּב אֲשֶׁר כְתָב כִּי, 13 ,9; בְּכָל מְדִינָה וּמְדִינָה
וּכְתָב הַנִּשְׁתְּוָן כָּתוּב אֲרָמִית 4:7; Ezra 2:62; אַגִּיד לְךָ אֶת הָרָשׁוּם בִּכְתָב אֱמֶת Dan. 10:21
וַיֹּאמֶר חוּרָם מֶלֶךְ צֹר בִּכְתָב 2 Chron. 2:10; 1 Chron. 28:19; Neh. 7:64; וּמְתֻרְגָּם אֲרָמִית
35:4; וַיִּשְׁלַח אֶל שְׁלֹמֹה

BA Ezra 6:18 רְשִׁים כְּתָבָא 8 ,Dan. 5:7; וְלָא כָהֲלִין כְּתָבָא לְמִקְרֵא 6:9–11, 15–17, 24–25; BA Dan. 5:7, 8
(perhaps also 7:22) וַהֲקִימוּ כָהֲנַיָּא בִּפְלֻגָּתְהוֹן ... כִּכְתָב סְפַר מֹשֶׁה

CBH Alternatives

ספר, e.g.

Exod. 32:32–33	כָּתַבְתָּ	אֲשֶׁר	מְחֵנִי נָא מִסִּפְרְךָ
			מִי אֲשֶׁר חָטָא לִי אֶמְחֶנּוּ מִסִּפְרִי
[~ Ezek. 13:9	יִכָּתֵבוּ	לֹא	וּבִכְתָב בֵּית יִשְׂרָאֵל]

Deut. 30:10	בְּסֵפֶר הַתּוֹרָה הַזֶּה	הַכְּתוּבָה	לִשְׁמֹר מִצְוֹתָיו וְחֻקֹּתָיו
[~ Dan 10:21	בִּכְתָב אֱמֶת	הָרָשׁוּם	אַגִּיד לְךָ אֶת]

1 Kgs. 5:22	אֶל שְׁלֹמֹה		וַיִּשְׁלַח חִירָם
2 Kgs. 5:5	מֶלֶךְ אֲרָם לְךָ בָּא וְאֶשְׁלְחָה סֵפֶר	אֶל מֶלֶךְ יִשְׂרָאֵל	וַיֹּאמֶר
[~ 2 Chron. 2:10	בִּכְתָב וַיִּשְׁלַח אֶל שְׁלֹמֹה		וַיֹּאמֶר חוּרָם מֶלֶךְ צֹר]

External Post-Classical Sources
Renderings/Paraphrases/Glosses

TO 11x, e.g.

Exod. 39:30	... מפרש כתב עלוהי וכתבו ... דקודשא כלילא ציצא ית ועבדו
[~	חוֹתָם ... פִּתּוּחֵי מִכְתַּב עָלָיו וַיִּכְתְּבוּ ... הַקֹּדֶשׁ נֵזֶר צִיץ אֶת וַיַּעֲשׂוּ]

TN 13x, e.g.

Lev. 19:28	בכון תשווׄן לא חקיק וכתב בבשרכון תתנון לא ... ושרט(ה)
[~	בָּכֶם תִּתְּנוּ לֹא קַעֲקַע וּכְתֹבֶת בִּבְשַׂרְכֶם תִתְּנוּ לֹא ... וְשֶׂרֶט]

TPJ 13x, e.g.

Exod. 32:16	לוחיא על ומפרש חקיק הוא דה׳ כתבא וכתבא
[~	הַלֻּחֹת עַל חָרוּת הוּא אֱלֹהִים מִכְתַּב מִכְתָּב וְהַמִּכְתָּב]

TJ 7x, e.g.
Isa. 38:9

כתב אודאה . . . לחזקיה מלך . . . יהודה כד מרע ואתסי ממרעיה

[~   מֶחֱלְיֹו   וַיְחִי   בַּחֲלֹתֹו   יְהוּדָה   מֶלֶךְ   לְחִזְקִיָּהוּ   [מִכְתָּב]

Other Sources

Pesh. Deut. 24:3   דשובקנא   **כתבא**   לה   ונכתוב

[~   כְּרִיתֻת   סֵפֶר   לָהּ   וְכָתַב

Pesh. Deut. 29:20   הנא   דנמוסא   **בכתבא**   דכתיבן . . .

[~   הַזֶּה   הַתֹּורָה   **בְּסֵפֶר**   הַכְּתוּבָה . . .]

Independent Use

Heb.

BS (B) 39:32   והתבוננתי התיצבתי מראש כן על **ובכתב** הנחתי

3Q15 12:11–13   משנא הכתב הזא ופרושיו ומשחותיהם ופרוט כל [. . .] אחד ואח[ד]

M Shab. 16:1   כל **כתבי** הקדש מצילין אותן מפני הדליקה, בין שקורים בהן ובין שאינן קורין בהם

M Ket. 2:4   זה או׳: זה **כתב** ידי וזה **כתב** ידו שלחבירי, וזה אומ׳: זה **כתב** ידי וזה **כתב** ידו של חבירי, הרי אילו נאמנים

Sifra Beḥukotai 2:7   "והתורות" (וי׳ כו 46)-מלמ׳ ששתי תורות ניתן להם ליש׳, אחת **בכתב** ואחת בפה

Aram.

TAD IV 23.16C:6   לספרא זי כתב **כתבא** דנה

PAT 1624:1–4   בירח אלול שנת חמש מאה ועשרין וחמש יולים אורליס ידיעבל די מתקרא מזבנא בר יולים אורליס אנינוס אשאלת **כתב** ידי ליולים בר אורליס עגילו בר אפרחת בר חרי זבדבול בדיל די לא ידע ספר

Cooke 79:2–3 (Nab.)   . . . ולמן די ינפק בידה **כתב** תקף מן יד עידו

Cooke 80:9–10 (Nab.)   . . . מן די ינפק בידה **כתב** מן יד כמכם או כליבת ברתה

4Q536 f2ii:12   מן יכתוב מלי אלה **בכתב** די לא יבלא

PT Ter. 8:11 (p. 252)   דיקלוט חזירא, מחוניה טליי דר׳ יודה נשייא. איתעביד מלך. נחת לפמייס שלח **כתבין** בתר רבנין: תיהוון גביי במפקי שובתא מיד. אמ׳ ליה לשלוחיא: לא תתן להון **כתבין** אלא בערובתא עם מטמעי שמשא

Qoh. Rab. 5:8 (5)   ר׳ יצחק ב״ר אלעזר הוה מטייל על שונייתא דימא דקיסרין. ראה קולית אחת מתגלגלת ובאה, והוה מצנע לה והיא מתגלגלת. אמ׳: זו מוכנת לעשות שליחותה. לבתר יומין עבר חד בלדר מן מלכותא. אתגלגלא ביני רגלוהי ונכשל ונפל ומת. אזלין פשפשוניה בשקיה, אשכחון יתיה טעין **כתבין** בישין על יהודאי דקיסרין

COMMENTS

a. Although the root כתב is used extensively throughout BH, the lexeme כְּתָב is attested exclusively in post-Classical compositions in the Bible (17x in Hebrew [Ezekiel; Esther; Daniel; Nehemiah; Chronicles] and 12x in Aramaic [Daniel; Ezra]). Furthermore, the קְטָל noun pattern of כְּתָב is a morphological hallmark of RH and the post-Biblical Aramaic dialects current during and after the Second Temple period, clearly indicating that כְּתָב ought to be classified as an LBH element that was imported from the Aramaic scribal formulary in the Persian period. In other words, "the form כְּתָב . . . reflects the language of the period" (Qimron 2003: 390).

b. "The Masoretes always knew well how to preserve the ancient Aramaic *qamaṣ* within Hebrew (i.e., in loanwords borrowed from Aramaic). Cf. זְוִית, כְּתָב, etc." (Kutscher 1982: 75 §103).

c. The pair of terms, בִּכְתָב *in writing / in a written text* and בְּעַל-פֶּה *orally / in an oral tradition*, is common in RH. Although in Rabbinic sources בִּכְתָב (vis-à-vis its counterpart, בְּעַל-פֶּה, which is not found in the Bible) conveys a later semantic nuance than that appearing in the Hebrew Bible, it is noteworthy that the biblical form בִּכְתָב is employed exclusively in the LBH corpus, which in various passages heralds the emergence of subsequent Rabbinic terms such as בֵּית מִדְרָשׁ, מִקְדָּשׁ, and עֲזָרָה (see the relevant entries).

d. In summary, "[i]n view of the manner of use of the word כְּתָב in the Bible (only in late books), its high frequency in RH and Aramaic (including BA), the existence of an alternative word serving in its place in CBH (סֵפֶר), and also in view of the fact that the period of Ezekiel heralds the transition to LBH . . . it must be acknowledged that a late word that penetrates the language, may find its way into all genres of literature current during that late period, including the elevated language of prophecy" (Hurvitz 1972: 58–59).

BIBLIOGRAPHY

BDB 508a • *HALOT* II 504b • GKC 231–232 §84ᵃn, 274 §94ww • JM 226 §88E, *c* • Kaddari 539b

Bauer and Leander 1922: 470*la* • Bendavid 1967–71: I 62, 149; II 444 § 26 note □ • Bergey 1983: 103–105 • Dihi 2004: 347–351 • Hurvitz 1972: 58–59; 2000b: 185 note 17 • Kautzsch 1902: 70 • Kutscher 1982: 75 §103 • Polzin 1976: 139 • Qimron 1986: 66, 91–92, 116; 2003: 390 • Rabin 1962: 1075 • Rooker 1990: 139–141 • Strauss 1900: 21 • Wagner 1966: 69 no. 141 • Zevit 1984: 43–44

לְאֵין adv. ל + negative particle) *without*: Ezra 9:14 הֲלוֹא תֶאֱנַף בָּנוּ עַד כַּלֵּה לְאֵין
וַיִּרְדְּפֵם אָסָא . . . וַיִּפֹּל 14:12 .Chron 2 ;וַעֲצֵי אֲרָזִים לְאֵין מִסְפָּר 22:4 .Chron 1; שְׁאֵרִית וּפְלֵיטָה
וַיָּבֹא יְהוֹשָׁפָט וְעַמּוֹ לָבֹז אֶת שְׁלָלָם . . . וַיִּנָּצְלוּ לָהֶם לְאֵין 20:25 ;מִכּוּשִׁים לְאֵין לָהֶם מִחְיָה
מַשָׂא 21:18; נֶגְפוֹ ה' בְּמֵעָיו לָחֳלִי לְאֵין מַרְפֵּא 36:16 on) עַד לְאֵין מַרְפֵּא, cf. עַד ל)

Cf. עַד ל

CBH ALTERNATIVES
אין

Gen. 41:49		**אֵין**	מִסְפָּר	. . . הַרְבֵּה מְאֹד עַד כִּי חָדַל לִסְפֹּר כִּי
Ps. 40:13		**אֵין**	מִסְפָּר	כִּי אָפְפוּ עָלַי רָעוֹת עַד
[~ 1 Chron. 22:4		**לְאֵין**	מִסְפָּר	וַעֲצֵי אֲרָזִים]

Deut. 28:31	מוֹשִׁיעַ	לְךָ	**וְאֵין**	צֹאנְךָ נְתֻנוֹת לְאֹיְבֶיךָ . . . חֲמֹרְךָ גָּזוּל
[~ 2 Chron. 14:12	מִחְיָה	לָהֶם	**לְאֵין**	וַיִּרְדְּפֵם אָסָא . . . עַד לִגְרָר וַיִּפֹּל מִכּוּשִׁים]

Jer. 14:19	מַרְפֵּא	לָנוּ	**וְאֵין**	הִכִּיתָנוּ
[~ 2 Chron. 21:18	מַרְפֵּא	לָחֳלִי	**לְאֵין**	נֶגְפוֹ ה' בְּמֵעָיו]

EXTERNAL POST-CLASSICAL SOURCES
Renderings/Paraphrases/Glosses

1QM 11:1		קובר	**לאין**		פגריהם	ובכוח ידכה רוטשו
[~ 2 Kgs. 9:10	קֹבֵר	**וְאֵין**	יִזְרְעֶאל	בְּחֵלֶק	הַכְּלָבִים יֹאכְלוּ	וְאֶת אִיזֶבֶל]
[~ Ps. 79:3	קוֹבֵר	**וְאֵין**	יְרוּשָׁלָ͏ִם	סְבִיבוֹת	דָּמָם כַּמַּיִם	שָׁפְכוּ]

1QS 2:14–15		סליחה	**לאין**	ונספתה רוחו הצמאה עם הרווה
[~ Deut. 29:18–19	לוֹ	סְלֹחַ	**לֹא יֹאבֶה ה'** אֶת הַצְּמֵאָה:	לְמַעַן סְפוֹת הָרָוָה אֶת]

Independent Use
Heb.

BS (B) 51:4	**לאין** פחה[!]	וממצוקות שלהבת . . . מכבות אש
1QHᵃ 11:21	**לאין** חקר	ואתהלכה במישור
1QHᵃ 14:9–10	**לאין** עול	וֹלהתהלך בדרך לבכה
1QM 18:2	**לאין** קום	ונפלו בני יפת

MekhRI BaḤodesh 6 (p. 227)	כשם שמידת פורענות לארבעה דורות – כך מדת הטוב לארבעה דורות, תלמוד לומר "לאלפים" (שמ' ג 6). אי "לאלפים", שומע אני מיעוט אלפים שנים, תלמוד לומר "לאלף דור" (דב' ז 9) – **לאין** חקר ואין מספר

COMMENTS

a. "In LBH and QH we find לאין + (abstract) noun or infinitive in the sense of 'without, so that not', e.g. 1 Chron. 22:4 לאין מספר 'without number'; 2 Chron. 20:25 לאין משא 'so that there was no carrying away'; 1QS 2:7 לאין רחמי֗ם 'without mercy'. In Ben Sira we find in 51:4 (b) מכבות אש לאין פחה '(You saved me) from burning fire, without a trace of it remaining'" (van Peursen 1999: 237). "This construction occurs some 40 times in the DSS. . . . It is characteristic of the Second Temple period; no similar construction is found in First Temple texts" (Qimron 1986: 77).

c. "In 1QS 2:14–15 ונספתה רוחו הצמאה עם הרווה לאין סליחה the addition to Deut 29:18 למען ספות הרוה את הצמאה reflects the popularity of *l'ēn* + NP [=noun phrase] in QH and in Late Biblical Hebrew" (Baasten 2000: 8–9).

d. The lateness of the construction לְאֵין is confirmed by the evidence of LBH and QH. However, this phrase apparently fell into disuse in post-DSS times, since it is hardly ever documented in RH texts (the isolated appearance of לאין in the Mekhilta [see above] seems to be a mere literary remnant rather than an independent linguistic usage).

e. The form לְאֵין is also attested in the following verses, but clearly with an entirely different meaning, i.e., *'to him who has no/who is not'*:

Isa. 40:29	וּלְאֵין אוֹנִים עָצְמָה יַרְבֶּה = ". . . and *to him who has no* might he increases strength" [RSV];
Neh. 8:10	וְשִׁלְחוּ מָנוֹת לְאֵין נָכוֹן לוֹ = ". . . and send portions *to him for whom nothing* is prepared" [RSV];
2 Chron. 14:10	אֵין עִמְּךָ לַעְזוֹר בֵּין רַב לְאֵין כֹּחַ = "it is all the same to You to help the numerous and the powerless" [= *to him who has no power*] [NJPS].

BIBLIOGRAPHY

BDB 35a

Baasten 2000: 8–9 • Curtis and Madsen 1910: 36 no. 132 • S. R. Driver 1913: 539 no. 43 • Hurvitz 1972: 39 • Qimron 1986: 77 • van Peursen 1999: 237

לְהַרְבֵּה (מְאֹד) adv. phr. *abundantly, exceedingly*: Neh. 5:18 יַיִן לְהַרְבֵּה; 2 Chron. 11:12
לְרֶכֶב וּלְפָרָשִׁים לְהַרְבֵּה מְאֹד 16:8; וַיְחַזְּקֵם לְהַרְבֵּה מְאֹד

Cf. לָרֹב מְאֹד

CBH ALTERNATIVES

רַב (מְאֹד), הַרְבֵּה (מְאֹד), e.g.

וַיִּצְבֹּר יוֹסֵף	בַּר כְּחוֹל הַיָּם **הַרְבֵּה מְאֹד**		Gen. 41:49
לַעֲשִׁיר	הָיָה	צֹאן וּבָקָר **הַרְבֵּה מְאֹד**	2 Sam. 12:2
וַיֵּצְאוּ . . . עַם רָב . . .	וְסוּס וָרֶכֶב **רַב מְאֹד**		Josh. 11:4
[הַכּוּשִׁים וְהַלּוּבִים הָיוּ	לְחַיִל לָרֹב	לְרֶכֶב וּלְפָרָשִׁים **לְהַרְבֵּה מְאֹד**	[~ 2 Chron. 16:8

COMMENTS

a. "[W]e find the phrase *l*ᵉ*harbēh* in only three passages in the OT: II Chr 11.12,
16.8, and Neh 5.18, in contrast to the 42 times that *harbēh* is used. Apparently,
[the late] *l*ᵉ*harbēh* and [the classical] *harbēh* are both used in the late language.
What can be said here is that *l*ᵉ*harbēh* . . . indicate[s] and emphasize[s] the late
language's preference for idioms containing the preposition *l*ᵉ" (Polzin 1976:
141). Thus, although this term did not take root in the available post-Biblical
sources, it may still be maintained that its appearance in the Hebrew Bible
reflects LBH.

b. The phrase לְהַרְבֵּה is found in Gen. Rab. 69:7 (p. 797) אמר ר' אחא: עתיד השער
הזה להפתח **להרבה** צדיקים כיוצא בך. However, syntactically, לְהַרְבֵּה here is not an
adverbial phrase.

BIBLIOGRAPHY

BDB 547a; 915b • Kaddari 984b

S. R. Driver 1913: 539 no. 44 • Polzin 1976: 141 • Shin 2007: 124–125

לְרֹב מְאֹד adj. phr. *abundant, of large quantity*: זָהָב וָכֶסֶף וּבְגָדִים לְרֹב Zech. 14:14 24:24; וּבְשָׂמִים לְרֹב מְאֹד 9:9; וַיַּעַשׂ שְׁלֹמֹה כָּל הַכֵּלִים הָאֵלֶּה לְרֹב מְאֹד 4:18 Chron. 2; מְאֹד וַיֵּאָסְפוּ יְרוּשָׁלַם עַם רָב...קָהָל לְרֹב מְאֹד 30:13; וַה' נָתַן בְּיָדָם חַיִל לְרֹב מְאֹד

Cf. (מְאֹד) לְהַרְבֵּה

CBH ALTERNATIVES

הרבה מאד, e.g.

בִּנְכָסִים רַבִּים שׁוּבוּ אֶל אָהֳלֵיכֶם... בְּכֶסֶף וּבְזָהָב... וּבִשְׂלָמוֹת **הַרְבֵּה מְאֹד** Josh. 22:8
[וְאָסַף חֵיל כָּל הַגּוֹיִם סָבִיב זָהָב וָכֶסֶף וּבְגָדִים **לְרֹב מְאֹד** [~ Zech.
14:14

וַתִּתֵּן לַמֶּלֶךְ מֵאָה וְעֶשְׂרִים כִּכַּר זָהָב וּבְשָׂמִים **הַרְבֵּה מְאֹד** 1 Kgs. 10:10
[וַתִּתֵּן לַמֶּלֶךְ מֵאָה וְעֶשְׂרִים כִּכַּר זָהָב וּבְשָׂמִים **לְרֹב מְאֹד** [~ 2 Chron.
9:9

לְרֹב, e.g.

וַיִּזְבַּח שׁוֹר וּמְרִיא וְצֹאן **לְרֹב** 1 Kgs. 1:19
[וַיֵּאָסְפוּ יְרוּשָׁלַם עַם רָב... קָהָל **לְרֹב** **מְאֹד** [~ 2 Chron. 30:13

COMMENTS

a. "The expression לרב מאד is not attested in the extra-biblical sources—but its distribution and linguistic contrast strongly support its suggested lateness. It may well be regarded that לרב מאד is a late 'blend' of the synonymous Classical expressions לרב and הרבה מאד, caused by the analogy to the late expression להרבה מאד" (Shin 2007: 125). In a slightly different manner, לרב מאד (like להרבה מאד; cf. this entry above) represents a typologically tautological—and secondary— linguistic innovation that is chronologically later than the CBH standard לרב. Since the appearance of לרב מאד in the Hebrew Bible is limited exclusively to the late books of Zechariah and Chronicles (including the "parallel passages"; see 2 Chron. 9:9, quoted above), it may be classified as a neologism of the LBH vocabulary.

BIBLIOGRAPHY

BDB 547a; 914a
Shin 2007: 124–125

מִ...וּלְמַעְלָה *from… and upwards*: Ezek. 1:27 וָאֵרֶא כְּעֵין חַשְׁמַל...מִמַּרְאֵה מָתְנָיו
‎2 Chron. 43:15; 8:2; 1 Chron. 23:27 מִסְפַּר בְּנֵי לֵוִי מִבֶּן עֶשְׂרִים שָׁנָה וּלְמַעְלָה; 2 Chron.
‎31:16–17

CBH ALTERNATIVES

מ...ומעלה, e.g.

Num. 1:18	**וָמַעְלָה**	שָׁנָה	עֶשְׂרִים	מִבֶּן	בְּמִסְפַּר שֵׁמוֹת	...כָּל הָעֵדָה...
[~ 1 Chron.	**וּלְמַעְלָה**	שָׁנָה	עֶשְׂרִים	מִבֶּן	בְּנֵי לֵוִי	מִסְפַּר	הֵמָּה]

‎23:27

1 Sam. 9:2	**וָמַעְלָה**		מִשִּׁכְמוֹ
[~ Ezek. 1:27	**וּלְמַעְלָה**	מָתְנָיו	מִמַּרְאֵה]

EXTERNAL POST-CLASSICAL SOURCES
Renderings/Paraphrases/Glosses

TO 38x, e.g.

Num. 1:20	חילא	נפיק	כל	**ולעילא**	שנין	עסרין	מבר
[~	צְבָא	יֹצֵא	כָּל	**וָמַעְלָה**	שָׁנָה	עֶשְׂרִים	מִבֶּן]

TN 38x, e.g.

Lev. 27:7	**ולעיל**	שנין	אשתין	בר	מן
[~	**וָמַעְלָה**	שָׁנָה	שִׁשִּׁים	מִבֶּן]

TPJ 38x, e.g.

Num. 4:3	לחילא	דאתי	כל	שנין	חמשין	בר	ועד	**ולעילא**	שנין	תלתין	מבר
[~	לַצָּבָא	בָּא	כָּל	שָׁנָה	חֲמִשִּׁים	בֶּן	וְעַד	**וָמַעְלָה**	שָׁנָה	שְׁלֹשִׁים	מִבֶּן]

TJ 11x, e.g.

1 Sam. 9:2	עמא	מכל	רם	**ולעילא**	מכתפיה	מניה	דשפיר	...גברא	ולית
[~	הָעָם	מִכָּל	גָּבֹהַּ	**וָמַעְלָה**	מִשִּׁכְמוֹ	מִמֶּנּוּ	טוֹב	...אִישׁ	וְאֵין]

1 Sam. 16:13	**ולעילא**	ההוא	מיומא	דוד	על	ה׳	קדם	מן	גבורא	רוח	ושרת
[~	**וָמָעְלָה**	הַהוּא	מֵהַיּוֹם	דָּוִד	אֶל	ה׳			רוּחַ	וַתִּצְלַח]

Other Sources

4Q365 f27:4	**וּלְמַעְל[ה...]**	חודש	זכר	מבן	כול	שמות	במספר
[~ Num. 3:28	**וָמָעְלָה**	חֹדֶשׁ	מִבֶּן	זָכָר	כָּל	בְּמִסְפַּר]

Independent Use

Heb.

11QT 39:10–11	אחר יבואו מבֶן עשׂרים **שׁנָּה ולמעלה**
	(see comment **b** below)
M Shev. 9:2	מכפר חננייה **ולמעלן**, כל שאינו מגדל שיקמים – גליל העליון.
	מכפר חננייה ולמטן, כל שהוא מגדל שיקמים – גליל התחתון
M Suk. 4:8	אבל מוריד הוא את הכלים **מן** המנחה **ולמעלן** בשביל כבוד
	יום טוב האחרון
T Ber. 5:1 (Zer. p. 25)	לא יאכל אדם בערב שבת **מן** המנחה **ולמעל׳** כדי שיכנס
	לשבת כשהוא תאוה
MekhRI Pisḥa 5 (p. 17)	מנין ראיה ל״בין הערבים״ (שמ׳ יב 6) שהוא **משש שעות**
	ולמעלה? אף על פי שאין ראיה לדבר זכר לדבר...
Sifra Negaʿim 2:1	מקרום ביצה **ולמעלן** – טמא, ומיצטרפין זה עם זה

Aram.

PT Shev. 6:1 (p. 197)	ר׳ הוה בעכו. חמא חד בר נש סלק **מן** כיפתא **ולעייל**
BT Ber. 59b	הרואה פרת אגושרא דבבל אומ׳: ברוך עושה בראשית...האידנא
	דדליוה פרסאי – **מבי** שבור **ולעייל**

Comments

a. "The expression מ...ולמעלה is attested in BH exclusively in Ezekiel and Chronicles, and is prevalent in RH and in Aramaic [ולעילא (ן)מ]. In the earlier Biblical books מ...ומעלה is employed (it is encountered also in Chronicles). Note that in the DSS the earlier idiom is utilized as well (11QT 17:8; 11QM 2:4). The addition of the extra ל stems from the collapse of the directional ה in the later language (Bendavid 1971: II 452)" (Qimron 1980: 248).

b. ולמעלה does not appear in Yadin's edition of the Temple Scroll, but according to Qimron, "it is clearly visible in the scroll itself."

Bibliography

Hornkohl 2012: 225 and note 1081 • Hurvitz 1974a: 36–39; 1982: 107–109 • Qimron 1980: 248

מַאֲמַר מָרְדֳּכַי 2:20; מַאֲמַר הַמֶּלֶךְ **[מַאֲמָר]** n. m. *word, command*: only cstr. Esth. 1:15;
מַאֲמַר אֶסְתֵּר 9:32

Cf. פִּתְגָם

BA Dan. 4:14 כְּמֵאמַר כָּהֲנַיָּא דִי; Ezra 6:9 בִּגְזֵרַת עִירִין פִּתְגָמָא וּמֵאמַר קַדִּישִׁין שְׁאֵלְתָא
בִּירוּשְׁלֶם

CBH ALTERNATIVES

דבר (cf. BS 37:16 below), e.g.

2 Sam. 24:4	וַיֶּחֱזַק **דְּבַר** הַמֶּלֶךְ אֶל יוֹאָב וְעַל שָׂרֵי הֶחָיִל		
[~ Esth. 1:15	אֲשֶׁר לֹא עָשְׂתָה אֶת **מַאֲמַר** הַמֶּלֶךְ... בְּיַד הַסָּרִיסִים		

EXTERNAL POST-CLASSICAL SOURCES
Renderings/Paraphrases/Glosses

TO (see comment **d** below), e.g.

Exod. 15:8	אזליא	כשור	קמו	מיא	חכימו	פומך	**ובמימר**
[~	נֹזְלִים	נֵד	כְמוֹ	נִצְּבוּ	מַיִם	נֶעֶרְמוּ	אַפֶּיךָ **וּבְרוּחַ**]

אִם... תְּקַבֵּל **לְמֵימְרָא** דַה' אֱלָהָך... כָּל מַרְעִין... לָא אֲשַׁוִּינוּן עֲלָך Exod.
15:26

[אִם... תִּשְׁמַע **לְקוֹל** ה' אֱלֹהֶיךָ... כָּל הַמַּחֲלָה... לֹא אָשִׂים עָלֶיךָ]

TN (see comment **d** below), e.g.

Deut. 33:9	זהירין אינון ואורייתך וגזרתך **פומך** **מימר** נטרו ארום
[~	יִנְצֹרוּ וּבְרִיתְךָ **אִמְרָתֶךָ** שָׁמְרוּ כִּי]

TPJ (see comment **d** below), e.g.

Exod. 34:27	קיים עמך גזרית האילין פיתגמיא **מימר** על ארום
[~	בְּרִית אִתְּךָ כָּרַתִּי הָאֵלֶּה הַדְּבָרִים **פִּי** עַל כִּי]

Num. 4:27	גרשון בני פולחן כל יהי ובנוי דאהרן **מימרא** על
[~	הַגֵּרְשֻׁנִּי בְּנֵי עֲבֹדַת כָּל תִּהְיֶה וּבָנָיו אַהֲרֹן **פִּי** עַל]

TJ (see comment **d** below), e.g.

Josh. 22:2	יתכון דפקידית לכל **למימרי** וקבילתון
[~	אֶתְכֶם צִוִּיתִי אֲשֶׁר לְכֹל **בְּקוֹלִי** וַתִּשְׁמְעוּ]

Other Sources

Tg. Ps. 78:1	פמי	**למימרי**	אודניכון	אצלון	אורייתי	עמי	אציט
[~	פִּי	**לְאַמְרֵי**	אָזְנְכֶם	הַטּוּ	תּוֹרָתִי	עַמִּי	[הַאֲזִינָה

11QTgJob 33:8–9	קנ[ה]	יְרִֹים	וְעוֹזָֹא	נִשְֹרָא	יתגבֹה	**מאמרך**	על	או
[~ Job 39:27	קִנּוֹ	יָרִים	וְכִי	נֶשֶׁר	יַגְבִּיהַּ	**פִּיךָ**	עַל	[אִם

Pesh. Gen. 4:23	**למאמרי**	צותין	למד	נשי
[~	**אִמְרָתִי**	הַאֲזֵנָּה	לֶמֶךְ	[נְשֵׁי

Independent Use

Heb.

BS 3:8 (A)	בני **במאמר** ובמעשה כבד אביך
BS 37:16 (D)	ראש כל מעשה **מאמר** לפני כל פעל היא מחשבת
BS 37:16 (B – marg.)	ראש כל מעשה **מאמר** לפני כל פועל היא מחשבת
[~ BS 37:16 (B)	[ראש כל מעשה **דבר** וראש כל פועל היא מחשבת

4Q271 f3:13-15   אל יקחה איש כי אם [בראות נשים] נאמנות וידעות ברורות **ממאמר**
המבֹקֹרֹ אשר על [הרבים]

M Yev. 5:4   עשה **מאמר** בזו **ומאמר** בזו צריכות שני גיטים וחליצה

BT Ber. 59a   הרואה קשת אומ': ברוך נאמן בבריתו וקיים **במאמרו**

Aram.

4Q542 fii:7-8   אחדו **בממר** יעקֹוב אבוכון ואתקפו בדיני אברהם ובֹצדקת לוי
ודילי

NŞ 13:9–12 (Yardeni I   וקים עלה אנה שלמצין כֹּוֹל די על בֹ[ת]בֹ שלמצין ברת יהוסף על
p. 134)   נפשה שאלה כתב מֹתֹת בֹ[ר] שמעון **ממרא**

ND:8–10 (Yardeni I   ...וחתמוֹי בגוה שאול בר רבן על נפשה כתב...בר חזקיה
p. 20)   **ממרה**

COMMENTS

a. Although אמר is one of the most common roots in BH (especially in verbal, but also in nominal, derivatives—אֹמֶר, [אֵמֶר], [אֶמְרָה/אִמְרָה]), "[t]he word מַאֲמָר, 'command', occurs in Biblical Hebrew only in Esther (3 times). In the Standard Biblical Hebrew and elsewhere in Late Biblical Hebrew the sense 'command' in a royal context is expressed by דבר or מצוה" (Bush 1996: 341). It has further been suggested that "*ma'amar*...always means human 'directive', the 'expression of the will' to which the person(s) addressed must accommodate himself. . . . The two examples from Biblical Aramaic are to be understood basically in the same way. . . . Here also, one will be correct in translating 'rule' or 'regulation'" (Wagner 1974: 344).

b. The antiquity of דְּבַר הַמֶּלֶךְ (2 Sam. 24:4; see CBH Alternatives above) is corroborated by the pre-Exilic epigraphic discovery from Arad: ודבר המלך אתכם בנבשכם (Arad 24 [Dobbs-Allsopp et al. p. 48] reverse: 6–7). See also the entry פִּתְגָם, comment **c.**

c. "The noun מאמר is shared by the late Biblical books of (Esther), Ben Sira, the DSS, Rabbinic literature and Aramaic. . . . In the late Biblical books and in the DSS it is employed in the sense of 'command'. In Ben Sira it is employed in the sense of 'utterance'. In Rabbinic literature and in Aramaic both meanings, 'command' and 'utterance', are used. Due to the fact that the noun appears for the first time in Hebrew only in the book of Esther . . . while in the Biblical books from the First Temple period there are other words that have this same meaning . . . it seems that the noun penetrated into Hebrew from Aramaic" (Dihi 2004: 365).

d. The word מימר in Tg. Aram. is used by and large as a "theological buffer" added to God's name (מימרא דה'), occurring hundreds of times throughout the Targums, and therefore does not have a direct Hebrew equivalent. For this reason, the statistics of its occurrences in the different Targums have not been provided above.

BIBLIOGRAPHY

BDB 57b • *HALOT* II 540a • GB 393
Bergey 1983: 100–101 • Bush 1996: 341 • Dihi 2004: 363–365 • S. R. Driver 1913: 484 • Paton 1908: 62–63 • Wagner 1974: 342–345

מַדָּע n. m. *knowledge, thought*: Qoh. 10:20 גַּם בְּמַדָּעֲךָ מֶלֶךְ אַל תְּקַלֵּל; Dan. 1:4 ...וְיֹדְעֵי
11, 12 חָכְמָה וּמַדָּע תֶּן לִי; 2 Chron. 1:10 נָתַן לָהֶם הָאֱלֹהִים מַדָּע וְהַשְׂכֵּל 17, דַעַת וּמְבִינֵי מַדָּע
הַחָכְמָה וְהַמַּדָּע נָתוּן לָךְ

BA Dan. 2:21 וּמַנְדְּעָא לְיָדְעֵי בִינָה; 4:31 וְהַב חָכְמְתָא לְחַכִּימִין וּמַנְדְּעָא לְיָדְעֵי בִינָה; 5:12, 33 רוּחַ וּמַנְדַּע עִלֵּי יְתוּב
יַתִּירָה וּמַנְדַּע וְשָׂכְלְתָנוּ

CBH Alternatives

חכמה ,דעת ,דעה ,בינה

1 Kgs. 3:12	לְפָנֶיךָ	לֹא הָיָה	...אֲשֶׁר	**וְנָבוֹן**	לֵב חָכָם	נָתַתִּי לְךָ
[~ 2 Chron. 1:12	לְפָנֶיךָ	לֹא הָיָה כֵן...	אֲשֶׁר	נָתוּן לְךָ...	**וְהַמַּדָּע**	הַחָכְמָה	]

Jer. 3:15	**דֵעָה** וְהַשְׂכֵּיל	וְרָעוּ אֶתְכֶם	כְּלִבִּי	רֹעִים לָכֶם	וְנָתַתִּי
[~ Dan. 1:17	**מַדָּע** וְהַשְׂכֵּל	בְּכָל סֵפֶר וְחָכְמָה	הָאֱלֹהִים	נָתַן לָהֶם	...וְהַיְלָדִים הָאֵלֶּה]

Exod. 36:1	**וּתְבוּנָה**	בָּהֵמָּה	חָכְמָה	ה'	נָתַן	...וְכֹל אִישׁ אֲשֶׁר
1 Kgs. 5:9	**וּתְבוּנָה** הַרְבֵּה מְאֹד	לִשְׁלֹמֹה	חָכְמָה	אֱלֹהִים	וַיִּתֵּן	עַתָּה]
[~ 2 Chron. 1:10	**וּמַדָּע** תֶּן לִי		חָכְמָה			

External Post-Classical Sources

Renderings/Paraphrases/Glosses

TO 6x, e.g.

Deut. 4:41–42	בלא **מדעיה**	...דיקטול קטולא לתמן	...למעירק	תלת קרוין...
[~	בִּבְלִי **דַעַת**	...אֲשֶׁר יִרְצַח	רוֹצֵחַ שָׁמָּה	לָנֻס ...שָׁלֹשׁ עָרִים]

TJ 19x, e.g.

Isa. 11:9	דה'	דחלתא	ית	**מדע**	ארעא	תתמלי	אֲרִי	...יבאשון לא
[~	ה'		אֶת	**דֵעָה**	הָאָרֶץ	מָלְאָה	כִּי	...יָרֵעוּ לֹא]

Other Sources

Lev. Rab. 32:2 "גם **במדעך** מלך אל תקלל..." (כה' י 20) – אמ' ר' אבין: לא **במדע**
(p. 736) שנתתי לך יותר מן הבהמה חיה ועוף תהא מחרף ומגדף לפניי

Independent Use

Heb.

BS (A) 3:12–13   בני התחזק בכבוד אביך...וגם אם יחסר **מדעו** עזוב לו
BS (A) 13:8   השמר אל תרהב מאד ואל תדמה בַחֲסִירֵי **מַדָּע**

1QS 7:5	ואשר ידבר את רעהו במרו/ים או יעשה רמיה **במדעו** ונענש ששה חודשים
BT Mak. 23a	אין מעמידין בדיינים אלא חסירי כח ויתירי **מדע**. ר' יהודה אומ': יתירי כוח וחסירי **מדע**

Aram.

NḤ 17: 1	קבלת מן בֹּבֹתֹא] אנ]תי **במנדע** יעקוב אֹדֹוֹנֹה
FTP Num. 22:30	ווי לך בלעם רשיעא חסר דעתא כל חוכמתא **ומדע** לא אישתכח גבך
TM 3:664 (p. 201)	אמר **מדעה** ללבה: שמעת אלין מליה. ענתה לבה: אה **מדעה**, זלין אנן מנך ...

COMMENTS

a. *"madda'*, 'knowledge, thought', is undoubtedly a late Hebrew word, appearing only in II Chr 1.10.11.12, Dn 1.4.17 and Qoh 10.20. It also occurs in Ben Sira 3.13 and three times in *Sérek hayáḥad*: VI, 9, VII, 3.5 ... [E]arlier Hebrew would rather have used *bînāh, da'at, dē'āh*, or the like. *madda'* may reflect Aramaic influence" (Polzin 1975: 141 no. 49).

b. The nominal pattern *maqtal* is well attested in the vocabulary of CBH, as is the root ידע (in both verbal and nominal usages). However, the specific noun מַדָּע—in which √ידע is cast morphologically in the *maqtal* pattern—is not found in the stock of Classical writings. In addition, since its counterpart מַ(נְ)דַּע is frequent—during and after the exile—in various Aramaic dialects (including BA), the Hebrew מַדָּע is widely regarded as a late Aramaism within BH. Furthermore, "the conjugation of [this] פ״י form like the פ״נ form is most likely an indication of the word's Aramaic provenance" (Dihi 2004: 369).

c. Note that some commentators emend במדעך in Qoh. 10:20 to במצעך; cf. Ben-Iehuda VI 2814a note 2.

BIBLIOGRAPHY

BDB 396a • *HALOT* II 550a • JM 236 §88L, *e*

Barton 1908: 52–53, 179 • Braver 1976: 158–159 • Collins 1993: 21, 127 • Crenshaw 1988: 177 • Curtis and Madsen 1910: 317 • Delitzsch 1877: 190–196 • Dihi 2004: 366–369 • S. R. Driver 1913: 506 no. 5 • Gordis 1968: 59 note 7 (p. 373) • Keil 1877: 44 note 2 • Magnanini 1968: 372–373 • Montgomery 1927: 126 • Polzin 1976: 141 no. 49 • Qimron 1986: 92 • Qimron and Strugnell 1994: §3.5.2.18 • Rabin 1962: 1075 • Schoors 1992–2004: II 392 • Williamson 1982: 196 • C. H. H. Wright 1883: 495

[מִדְרָשׁ] n. m. *a written composition; study/exegesis (of a written [sacred] text)*:
only cstr. 2 Chron. 13:22 מִדְרַשׁ הַנָּבִיא עִדּוֹ; 24:27 מִדְרַשׁ סֵפֶר הַמְּלָכִים

Cf. √דרש

CBH Alternatives
ספר

1 Kgs. 15:7	וְיֶתֶר דִּבְרֵי אֲבִיָּם וְכָל אֲשֶׁר עָשָׂה הֲלוֹא הֵם כְּתוּבִים עַל **סֵפֶר** דִּבְרֵי הַיָּמִים לְמַלְכֵי יְהוּדָה
[~ 2 Chron. 13:22	וְיֶתֶר דִּבְרֵי אֲבִיָּה וּדְרָכָיו וּדְבָרָיו כְּתוּבִים **בְּמִדְרַשׁ** הַנָּבִיא עִדּוֹ
2 Kgs. 12:20	...וְיֶתֶר דִּבְרֵי יוֹאָשׁ הֲלוֹא הֵם כְּתוּבִים עַל **סֵפֶר** דִּבְרֵי הַיָּמִים לְמַלְכֵי יְהוּדָה
[~ 2 Chron. 24:27	...וּבָנָיו...וִיסוֹד בֵּית הָאֱלֹהִים הִנָּם כְּתוּבִים עַל **מִדְרַשׁ** סֵפֶר הַמְּלָכִים

External Post-Classical Sources
Renderings/Paraphrases/Glosses

TN 7x, e.g.

| Gen. 25:22 | ואזלת לבית **מדרשא**... למתבע רחמין מן קדם ה' |
| [~ | וַתֵּלֶךְ לִדְרֹשׁ אֶת ה' |

TPJ 17x, e.g.

| Num. 24:5 | כמא יאוון הינון **בתי מדרישיכון במשכנא** די שמיש בהון יעקב אבוכון |
| [~ | מַה טֹּבוּ אֹהָלֶיךָ יַעֲקֹב |

TJ 1x

| Judg. 5:24 | תתברך... יעל... כחדא מנשיא דמשמשן **בבתי מדרשין**... |
| [~ | תְּבֹרַךְ... יָעֵל... מִנָּשִׁים בָּאֹהֶל... |

Other Sources

| Tg. Ps. 43:3 | יעלון יתי לטור בית מוקדשא **ולמדרשי בית שכינתך** |
| [~ | יְבִיאוּנִי אֶל הַר קָדְשְׁךָ וְאֶל **מִשְׁכְּנוֹתֶיךָ** |

MekhRI Yitro 1 (p. 193)   "וַיָּבֹאוּ הָאֹהֱלָה" (שמ' יח 7) – זה בית המדרש

Independent Use

Heb.

BS (B) 51:23 — פנו אלי סכלים ולינו בבית **מדרשי**

1QS 8:14–16 — כאשר כתוב "במדבר פנוֹ דרך ה׳ ישרו בערבה מסלה לאלוהינו"
(יש׳ מ 3) – היאה **מדרש התורה** א[ש]רׄ צוה ביד מושה לעשות
ככול הנגלה עת בעת וכאשר גלו הנביאים ברוח קודשו

CD 20 (= CDᵇ 2:6–7) — ובהופע מעשיו כפי **מדרש התורה** אשר יתהלכו בו אנשי תמים
הקדש...

4Q249 f1V title:1 — **מדרש** ספרׄ מושה

Dabbura (Naveh 1978: no. 6) — זה **בית מדרשו** שהלרבי אליעזר הקפר

M Avot 1:17 — ולא **המדרש** הוא העיקר אלא המעשה

M Ned. 4:3 — ומלמדו **מדרש** הלכות ואגדות, לא ילמדינו מקרא

T Soṭ. 7:21 (Nash. p. 200) — "הָכֵן בחוץ מלאכתך" (מש׳ כד 27) – זו מקרא. "וְעַתְּדָהּ בשדה
לך" (שם) – זו משנה. "אחר וּבָנִיתָ ביתך" (שם) – זה **מדרש**

Aram.

Lev. Rab. 5:4 (p. 113) — ר׳ חייה בר אבא עביד פסיקא למיתן בהדין **בי מדרשא** דטיבריא

Qoh. Rab. 8:1 (4) — ר׳ הוה דריש **במדרשא**: מנן שאין ממירין בבכור?

PT Ber. 7:5 (p. 59) — ר׳ ברכיה מוקים לאמוריה על תרעא מציעיא **דבי מדרשא**

BT Ber. 16a — אדהכי ואכי איזיל ואישמע מילתא **בי מדרש׳** ואיתי ואימ׳ לכו

COMMENTS

a. "The term *Midrash* occurs only here [2 Chron. 24:27] and 13²² in the OT, though it is common in post-Biblical literature. דרש is to *search out, investigate, explore* as applied to Scripture, to discover or develop a thought not apparent on the surface,—for instance, the hidden meaning of a word, or the particulars implied by an allusion.... The Midrash may be defined as an imaginative development of a thought or theme suggested by Scripture, especially a didactic or homiletic exposition, or an edifying religious story" (S. R. Driver 1913: 529).

b. "It is hard to imagine that two attestations of the term מדרש occur merely by chance expressly in the book of Chronicles, whose manner of thinking and writing is so close to Midrash in its commonly accepted sense" (Seeligmann 1979–80: 23 note 29).

c. "The derivative *midhrash*, which is to be defined grammatically as an Aramaic infinitive of the qal, is used as a noun in the construct in the two passages in which it appears in the OT (2 Ch. 13:22; 24:27). In the LXX this term is translated *epí biblíō*, 'in the book of,' in the former passage, and *epí tén graphén*, 'in the writing of,' in the latter, while the Vulgate has *in libro*, 'in the book of,' in both places.... Exegetically both passages refer to a historical source...."

Since 'midrash' in postbiblical Judaism means approximately the same thing as 'exposition,' 'explanation,' 'commentary' (of [or on] a scriptural passage), the reference might already be to the cited interpretation of a source in these very late biblical texts in Chronicles" (Wagner 1978: 305–306).

d. The Rabbinic technical term מדרש belongs in the semantic field of *inquiry/ reading/investigation* and denotes *study/textual interpretation*. Similarly, the verb דרש in Rabbinic writings has the meaning of *examine/interpret/expound* (cf. entry √דרש). Thus, in both its nominal and verbal usages the root דרש signifies the intellectual activity of reading and studying—which is directly related to *written* sacred texts. The same is true of the linguistic situation reflected in the DSS, where we find the combination מדרש/דרש√ + תורה—a combination completely missing in CBH (for differences in the terminological usages of √דרש/מדרש in Rabbinic literature and the Qumran writings, see Schiffman 1975: 54–60). In other words, whatever the precise semantic nuance of מדרש and √דרש in the relevant passages of Ezra (7:10), Chronicles (1 Chron. 28:8; 2 Chron. 13:22; 24:27), and Psalms (119:45, 94, and 155; cf. √דרש, comment a), their very appearance (see comment f below) in the Bible in association with the written Pentateuchal Law and commandments (תּוֹרָה, מִצְוֹת, חֻקִּים, פִּקוּ־ דִים) suggests a relatively late linguistic stage, heralding post-Biblical (QH, RH) halakhic terminology.

e. Mention should be made here of 2 Chron. 31:20–21 וַיַּעַשׂ...יְחִזְקִיָּהוּ...הַטּוֹב וְהַיָּשָׁר...וּבְכָל מַעֲשֶׂה אֲשֶׁר הֵחֵל בַּעֲבוֹדַת בֵּית הָאֱלֹהִים וּבַתּוֹרָה וּבַמִּצְוָה לִדְרֹשׁ לֵאלֹהָיו בְּכָל לְבָבוֹ עָשָׂה וְהִצְלִיחַ. Although תורה and מצוה are not used here syntactically as accusatives of √דרש, all three lexemes are bound together in the same verse; note, again, that this verse is found in the late book of Chronicles.

f. The widespread Rabbinic expression בֵּית מִדְרָשׁ is documented already in BS 51:23. Even if this construct state idiom in Ben-Sira does not yet function as a fixed technical term denoting *school, academy* (lit., *house of study*), its very appearance in our sources (see comment d above) decisively reflects the Second Temple linguistic milieu (for a detailed discussion of the term, see Schiffman 1975: 54–57).

g. According to a well-known homily in Rabbinic literature, the biblical word אֹהֶל is interpreted anachronistically as בית מדרש. "This Midrashic homily, – אהל בית מדרש, is not very ancient ... but nevertheless it is so common in Midrashic and Talmudic literature that the word אֹהֶל invokes immediately an association with the study of Torah ... as if the equation אהל = בית מדרש is taken for granted" (Sarfatti 1969: 89). Hence the frequent rendering of the Biblical אהל by בית מדרשא in Targumic Aramaic (cf. the examples quoted above).

BIBLIOGRAPHY

BDB 205b

S. R. Driver 1913: 529 • Hurvitz 1972: 133–134; 1995a: 1–10 • Jeffery 1938: 128–129 • Kutscher 1982: 89 §134 • Sarfatti 1969 • Schiffman 1975: 54–60 • Wagner 1978: 293–307 • Seeligmann 1979–80

מַלְכוּת, pl. **מַלְכָיּוֹת** n. f. *kingdom*: 91x in 82vv.: Num. 24:7; 1 Sam. 20:31; 1 Kgs. 2:12; Jer. 10:7; 49:34; 52:31; Ps. 45:7; 103:19; 145:11, 12, 13 מַלְכוּתְךָ מַלְכוּת כָּל עֹלָמִים; Qoh. 4:14; Esth. 1:2, 4, 7, 9 בֵּית הַמַּלְכוּת, 11, 14, 19, 20; 2:3, 16, 17 כֶּתֶר מַלְכוּת; 3:6, 8; 4:14; 5:1, 3, 6; 6:8; 7:2; 8:15; 9:30; Dan. 1:1, 20; 2:1; 8:1, 22 אַרְבַּע מַלְכָיּוֹת, 23; 9:1; 10:13; 11:2, 4, 9, 17, 20, 21; Ezra 1:1; 4:5, 6; 7:1; 8:1; Neh. 9:35; 12:22; 1 Chron. 11:10; 12:24; 14:2; 17:11, 14; 22:10; 26:31; 28:5 כִּסֵּא מַלְכוּת ה', 7; 29:25, 30; 2 Chron. 1:1, 18; 2:11; 3:2; 7:18; 11:17; 12:1; 15:10, 19; 16:1, 12; 20:30; 29:19; 33:13; 35:19; 36:20, 22

BA מַלְכוּ 57x in 43vv.: Dan. 2:37, 39–42, 44 מַלְכְוָתָא; 3:33 מַלְכוּת עֹלָם מַלְכוּתֵהּ; 4:14, 15, 22, 23, 26 דָּא הִיא בָּבֶל רַבְּתָא דִּי אֲנָה בֱנַיְתַהּ לְבֵית מַלְכוּ 27 הֵיכַל מַלְכוּתָא 28, 29, 31, 33; 5:7, 11, 16, 18, 20 סָרְכֵי מַלְכוּתָא, 21, 26, 28, 29; 6:1, 2, 4, 5, 8 כָּרְסֵא מַלְכוּתֵהּ, 27, 29; 7:14, 18, 22–24, 27; Ezra 4:24; 6:15; 7:13, 23

CBH Alternatives

מלוכה, ממלכה, e.g.

2 Sam. 7:12 — וַהֲקִימֹתִי אֶת זַרְעֲךָ אַחֲרֶיךָ אֲשֶׁר יֵצֵא מִמֵּעֶיךָ וַהֲכִינֹתִי אֶת **מַמְלַכְתּוֹ**

[~ 1 Chron. 17:11 — וַהֲקִימוֹתִי אֶת זַרְעֲךָ אַחֲרֶיךָ אֲשֶׁר יִהְיֶה מִבָּנֶיךָ וַהֲכִינוֹתִי אֶת **מַלְכוּתוֹ**

2 Sam. 7:13 — הוּא יִבְנֶה בַיִת לִשְׁמִי וְכֹנַנְתִּי אֶת כִּסֵּא **מַמְלַכְתּוֹ** עַד עוֹלָם

[~ 1 Chron. 22:10 — הוּא יִבְנֶה בַיִת לִשְׁמִי... וַהֲכִינוֹתִי כִּסֵּא **מַלְכוּתוֹ** עַל יִשְׂרָאֵל עַד עוֹלָם

2 Sam. 7:16 — וְנֶאְמַן בֵּיתְךָ **וּמַמְלַכְתְּךָ** עַד עוֹלָם לְפָנֶיךָ כִּסְאֲךָ יִהְיֶה נָכוֹן עַד עוֹלָם

[~ 1 Chron. 17:14 — וְהַעֲמַדְתִּיהוּ בְּבֵיתִי **וּבְמַלְכוּתִי** עַד הָעוֹלָם וְכִסְאוֹ יִהְיֶה נָכוֹן עַד עוֹלָם

1 Kgs. 9:5 — וַהֲקִמֹתִי אֶת כִּסֵּא **מַמְלַכְתְּךָ**... כַּאֲשֶׁר דִּבַּרְתִּי עַל דָּוִד אָבִיךָ

[~ 2 Chron. 7:18 — וַהֲקִימוֹתִי אֶת כִּסֵּא **מַלְכוּתֶךָ** כַּאֲשֶׁר כָּרַתִּי לְדָוִיד אָבִיךָ

Deut. 17:20   יִשְׂרָאֵל בְּקֶרֶב וּבָנָיו הוּא **מַמְלַכְתּוֹ** עַל יָמִים יַאֲרִיךְ לְמַעַן

[~11QT 59:21   אחריו ובניו הוא **מלכותו** על רבים ימים ויארך]

1 Kgs. 1:46   **הַמְּלוּכָה** כִּסֵּא עַל שְׁלֹמֹה יָשַׁב וְגַם

[~ Esth. 5:1   **מַלְכוּתוֹ** בְּבֵית **מַלְכוּתוֹ** כִּסֵּא עַל יוֹשֵׁב וְהַמֶּלֶךְ]

EXTERNAL POST-CLASSICAL SOURCES
Renderings/Paraphrases/Glosses
TO 26x, e.g.

Gen. 10:10   וכלנה ואכד וארך בבל **מלכותיה** ריש והות

[~   וְכַלְנֶה וְאַכַּד וְאֶרֶךְ בְּבֶל **מַמְלַכְתּוֹ** רֵאשִׁית וַתְּהִי]

Exod. 15:18   ולעלמי עלמיא לעלמא **מלכותיה** ה'

[~   וָעֶד לְעֹלָם **יִמְלֹךְ** ה']

TN 51x, e.g.

Deut. 3:10   בבותנין דעוג **מלכותה** **בית** קורי

[~   בַּבָּשָׁן עוֹג **מַמְלֶכֶת** עָרֵי]

TPJ 47x, e.g.

Gen. 20:9   רבא חובא **מלכותי** ועל עלי אייתיתא ארום ...לנא עבדת מה

[~   גְדֹלָה חֲטָאָה **מַמְלַכְתִּי** וְעַל עָלַי הֵבֵאתָ כִּי ...לָּנוּ עָשִׂיתָ מֶּה]

TJ 290x, e.g.

1 Kgs. 11:35   לך ואתנה בריה מיד **מלכותא** ואסב

[~   לָךְ וּנְתַתִּיהָ בְּנוֹ מִיַּד **הַמְּלוּכָה** וְלָקַחְתִּי]

Other Sources
Pesh. Deut. 17:18   **דמלכותה**... כורסיא על דיתב ומא

[~   **מַמְלַכְתּוֹ**... כִּסֵּא עַל כְּשִׁבְתּוֹ וְהָיָה]

Independent Use

Heb.

BS (A) 10:8	בגלל חמס גאוה תסוב מגוי אל גוי **מלכות**
[~ 1 Kgs. 2:15	[לִי הָיְתָה הַמְּלוּכָה... וַתִּסֹּב הַמְּלוּכָה וַתְּהִי לְאָחִי

4Q252 5:3–4	עד בוא משיח הצדק צמח דויד כי לו ולזרעו נתנה ברית **מלכות** עמו עד דורות עולם
4Q388a f7ii:4	בימו אשבור את **מלכות** מצרים
M Ber. 2:5	איני שומע לכם לבטל ממני **מלכות** שמים שעה אחת
M RoshH 4:6	אין פוחתים מעשר מעשר **מַלְכִיוֹת** ומעשרה זכרונות מעשרה שופרות
M Giṭ. 8:5	כתב לשם **מלכות** שאינה הוגנת, לשם **מלכות** מדי ולשם **מלכות** יון...תצא מזה ומזה צריכה גט מזה ומזה
MekhRI Pisḥa 1 (p. 2)	עד שלא נבחר דוד היו כל ישראל כשרים **למלכות**. משנבחר דוד יצאו כל ישראל
PT Ber. 3:1 (p. 26) = PT Naz. 7:1 (p. 1124)	מצוה לראות גדולי **מלכות**, לכשתבוא **מלכות** בית דוד יהא יודע להפריש בין **מלכות למלכות**

Aram.

TAD III 1.1:79 (= Cowley, Ahiqar 95)	אף לאלהן יק[י]רה הי...**מלכותא** בשמ[י]ן שימה הי כי בעל קדשן נשא[ה]
Wadi Daliyeh 1:1 (Yardeni I p. 380)	ב 20 לאדר שנת 2 ראש **מלכות**] ד[ריהוש מלכא בשמרי]ן]
4Q246 f1ii:5	**מלכותה מלכות** עלם וכל ארחתה בקשוט
Gen. Rab. 78:12 (p. 931)	ר׳ שמעון בן לקיש סליק למשאל בשלמיה דרבנו. אמר ליה צלי עלי דהדא **מלכותה** בישה סגין

QH – Biblical Scrolls		מלוכה/ממלכה	מלכות
Num.	4Q23	1	–
Deut.	4Q31	1	–
Sam.	4Q51	1	1
	4Q52	1	–
Kgs.	5Q2	1	–
Isa.	1QIsᵃ	17	–
	1Q8	3	–
	4Q55	2	–
	4Q56	1	–
	4Q57	1	–
Amos	Mur. 88	1	–
Obad.	Mur. 88	1	–
Mic.	Mur. 88	1	–
Nah.	Mur. 88	1	–
Ps.	11Q5	–	2
Dan.	4Q112	–	1
	4Q114	–	2
	6Q7	–	1
Ezra	4Q117	–	1
	Total:	33	8

CBH	מלוכה/ממלכה	מלכות
Gen.	2	–
Exod.	1	–
Num.	2	1
Deut.	7	–
Josh.	2	–
1 Sam.	11	1
2 Sam.	8	–
1 Kgs.	19	–
2 Kgs.	6	–
Isa.	16	–
Amos	3	–
Mic.	1	–
Nah.	1	–
Zeph.	1	–
Total:	80	2

Transitional and/or Uncertain	מלוכה/ממלכה	מלכות
Jer.	18	3
Ezek.	6	–
Obad.	1	–
Ps.	7	6
Lam.	1	–
Total:	33	9

Non–Biblical Scrolls	מלוכה/ממלכה	מלכות
1QSᵇ	–	3
1QM	1	4
1QHᵃ	1	1
1Q25	1	–
4Q160	1	–
4Q169	1	1
4Q172	–	1
4Q174	1	–
4Q176	1	–
4Q200	–	1
4Q252	–	2
4Q286	–	1
4Q299	–	1
4Q301	–	1
4Q365	–	1
4Q378	1	–
4Q381	–	1
4Q382	1	–
4Q387	3	–
4Q388ᵃ	–	1
4Q389	1	–
4Q390	1	–
4Q392	2	–
4Q393	1	–
4Q400	–	5
4Q401	2	3
4Q403	1	6
4Q405	3	7
4Q416	1	–
4Q418	1	–
4Q448	2	–
4Q458	–	1
4Q462	1	–
4Q491	1	–
4Q492	–	1
4Q509	–	1
4Q510	–	1
4Q521	–	1
4Q524	–	1
6Q9	1	–
11Q16	1	–
11QT	–	2
Total:	31	48

	LBH	
	מלוכה/ממלכה	מלכות
Hag.	2	–
Qoh.	–	1
Esth.	–	26
Dan.	1	16
Ezra	1	6
Neh.	1	2
1 Chron.	4	11
2 Chron.	19	17
Total:	28	79
	מלוכה/ממלכה	מלכות
Ben-Sira	3	2

The division between Biblical and non-Biblical scrolls in QH is intended for purposes of comparison to the MT, but does not necessarily reflect the status of these different texts by the Qumran community. Compositions categorized as *transitional/uncertain* show a preference for the traditional form.

COMMENTS

a. "Instead of SBH ממלכה or מלוכה 'kingdom', LBH prefers מלכות which is used about 30 times in Chronicles and also in Ezra, Nehemiah, Esther and Daniel . . . the noun pattern with the derivational suffix ־וּת becomes more and more prevalent in the course of the history of BH and MH" (Kutscher 1982: 84 §123).

b. Although מלכות is found sparingly in books not belonging to the distinctive LBH corpus (see particularly Num. 24:7; 1 Sam. 20:31; 1 Kgs. 2:12), its general distribution pattern is indeed "chiefly late" (BDB 574b). In Aramaic, מַלְכוּ(ת) is attested (defective spelling, מלכת חל = *a kingdom of sand*) already in the eighth century BCE (*KAI* 222 A 25); its massive expansion in LBH texts is clearly due to the influence of Imperial Aramaic in post-exilic times (note its extensive use in BA [more than 50x]).

c. The form מַמְלָכוּת (Josh. 13:12, 21, 27, 30, 31; 1 Sam. 15:28; 2 Sam. 16:3; Jer. 26:1; Hos. 1:4) may be interpreted as a *forma mixta* of מַמְלָכָה and מַלְכוּת; cf. Kutscher 1977: 131–133.

d. Arab. ملكوت is also regarded as a loanword from Aramaic (Jefferey 1938: 270–271).

e. Note that neither מלוכה nor ממלכה are found in BA, which makes use of מלכות alone (see above). This holds true for the other Aramaic dialects as well.

BIBLIOGRAPHY

BDB 574b • *HALOT* II 592b

Bendavid 1967–71: I 63, 67, 68, 181 • Bergey 1983: 31–34, 157–159 • Collins 1993: 21 • Curtis and Madsen 1910: 31 no. 67, 133, 208, 316 • Davila 1991: 823 • Dihi 2004: 373–375 • S. R. Driver 1913: 506 no. 1, 536 no. 9 • Eshel, Eshel, and Yardeni 1992: 209–210 • Hadas-Lebel 1995: 111 • Hurvitz 1972: 79–88, 110–113, 175–176 • Jefferey 1938: 270–271 • Kutscher 1977: 131–133; 1982: 43 §65, 81 §121, 84 §123 • Montgomery 1927: 117, 353 • Naveh and Greenfield 1984: 121 (= Greenfield 2001: I 238) • Polak 2006b: 121 note 23 • Polzin 1976: 142 • Qimron 1986: 66, 92 • Rendsburg 1991: 363–364 • Rooker 1990: 56–57 • Sáenz-Badillos 1993: 117 • Seybold, Ringgren, and Fabry 1997: 360 • Williamson 1977a: 43 • R. M. Wright 2005: 135–137 • Yoder 2001: 30

מְעַטִּים adj. (pl. of מְעַט)*few*: Ps. 109:8 יִהְיוּ יָמָיו מְעַטִּים (cf. comment a); Qoh. 5:1 עַל
כֵּן יִהְיוּ דְבָרֶיךָ מְעַטִּים

CBH Alternatives

מעט, e.g.

Gen. 47:9	וְרָעִים הָיוּ יְמֵי שְׁנֵי חַיַּי	**מְעַט**
[~ Ps. 109:8	[יִהְיוּ יָמָיו	**מְעַטִּים**

External Post-Classical Sources
Renderings/Paraphrases/Glosses

BT Ber. 61a — לעולם יהיו דבריו של אדם **מועטין** לפני הב״ה, שנא׳ ״אל תבהל על פיך
ולבך אל ימהר להוציא דבר [לפני האלהים כי האלהים בשמים ואתה על
הארץ על כן יהיו דבריך **מעטים**״] (קה׳ ה 1) [see comment b below]

Independent Use
Heb.

CD 10:10–11	אל ירחץ איש במים צואים ו**מעוטים** מדי מרעיל
M Eruv. 7:8	בזמן שהן מרובים – מזון שתי סעודות לכלם, בזמן שהן **מועטים** – כגרוגרת להוצאת שבת לכל אחד ואחד
M Pes. 5:7	קראו את ההלל. אם גמרו – שנו, ואם שנו – שילשו אפעלפי שלא שילשו מימיהם. ר׳ יהודה או׳: מימיה של כת השלישית לא היגיעה ל״אהבתי כי ישמע ה׳ ״ (תה׳ קטז 1) מפני שעמה מ**מועטים**
M Ḥag. 1:5	מי שיש לו...אוכלים **ממועטים** ונכסים מרובים מביא עולות מרובות ושלמים מ**מועטים**
T Ḥag. 2:6 (Mo‘ed, p. 382)	לא היו ימים **מועטים** עד שנסתלק בן זומא
T Yev. 1:5 (Nash. p. 1)	נמצאת או׳: כל זמן שאחין מרובין צרות מרובו׳, אחים **מועטין** צרות **מועטות**
T Soṭ. 15:2 (Nash. p. 239)	בראשונה כל עיר שהיו טלליה רבים מחברותיה פירותיה היו מרובין, עכשיו מ**מועטין**
Sifre Num. 102 (p. 100)	מדת בשר ודם כשהוא יוצא למלחמה יוצא בבני אדם מרובים וכשהוא יוצא לשלום אינו יוצא אלא בבני אדם **מועטין**
Sifre Deut. 40 (p. 81)	היו רשעים בראש השנה ונגזרו עליהם גשמים **מועטין** וחזרו בהם...
BT Ket. 91a–b	כשם שמרובין ונתמעטו זכו בהן יורשין – כך **מועטים** ונתרבו זכו בהן יורשין

COMMENTS

a. The plural form מְעַטִּים is documented only twice in the Hebrew Bible—once in Qohelet, whose language is widely assigned to post-exilic times, and once in Ps. 109, whose language betrays imprints of lateness (see Hurvitz 1972: 171–174). Compare the following statements: "The older language forms no plur. from the subst. מְעַט (fewness) used as an adv.; but the more recent treats it as an adj., and forms from it the plur. מְעַטִּים" (Delitzsch 1877: 286); "מעטים, as a plural predicate ... occurs elsewhere [besides Qoh 5:1] only in Ps. 109[8]. It is a late and rare usage" (Barton 1908: 125).

b. The emergence of the pl. מעטים in LBH may well be associated with the extensive use of its RH by-forms מועטים / ממועטים and RA זעירין in the linguistic milieu of the Second Temple period—LBH מעטים possibly being a forerunner of RH מועטים.

BIBLIOGRAPHY

Ben-Iehuda VI 3158b • Kaddari 641a

Barton 1908: 125 • Crenshaw 1988: 116 • Delitzsch 1877: 193, 286 • Hurvitz 1972: 171–174

מַעֲרָב n. m. *west*: Isa. 43:5 מִמִּזְרָח אָבִיא זַרְעֶךָ וּמִמַּעֲרָב אֲקַבְּצֶךָּ; 45:6 מִמִּזְרַח שֶׁמֶשׁ; 59:19 וּמִמַּעֲרָב; Ps. 75:7; 103:12 כִּרְחֹק מִזְרָח מִמַּעֲרָב; 107:3 (cf. comment **b** below on citations from Ps.); Dan. 8:5 וְהִנֵּה צְפִיר הָעִזִּים בָּא מִן הַמַּעֲרָב; 1 Chron. 7:28; 12:16; 26:16, 18, 30; 2 Chron. 32:30; 33:14 מֵעֵבֶר לַיַּרְדֵּן מַעֲרָבָה

CBH ALTERNATIVES

מבוא (השמש), אחור, ים, e.g.

בֵּין בֵּית אֵל וּבֵין הָעַי	**מִיָּם**	לָעִיר	Josh. 8:12
]	לְמַטָּה **מַעֲרָבָה**	לְעִיר דָּוִיד	[~ 2 Chron. 32:30

הַכְּנַעֲנִי	מִמִּזְרָח	**וּמִיָּם**	Josh. 11:3
אֲרָם	מִקֶּדֶם	וּפְלִשְׁתִּים **מֵאָחוֹר**	Isa. 9:11
[וְלַמִּזְרָח	נַעֲרָן	**וְלַמַּעֲרָב** גֶּזֶר וּבְנֹתֶיהָ	[~ 1 Chron. 7:28

בְּעֵבֶר	הַיַּרְדֵּן	**יָמָּה**	Josh. 12:7
[מֵעֵבֶר	לַיַּרְדֵּן	**מַעֲרָבָה**	[~ 1 Chron. 26:30

אֵל אֱלֹהִים ה׳ דִּבֶּר וַיִּקְרָא אָרֶץ מִמִּזְרַח שֶׁמֶשׁ **עַד מְבֹאוֹ**	Ps. 50:1
[לְמַעַן יֵדְעוּ מִמִּזְרַח שֶׁמֶשׁ וּמִמַּעֲרָבָה כִּי אֶפֶס בִּלְעָדָי	[~ Isa. 45:6

EXTERNAL POST-CLASSICAL SOURCES
Renderings/Paraphrases/Glosses

TO 19x, e.g.

ממדנח לבית אל... בית אל **ממערבא** ועי ממדנחא	Gen. 12:8
[מִקֶּדֶם לְבֵית אֵל... בֵּית אֵל **מִיָּם** וְהָעַי מִקֶּדֶם	[~

מן נהרא נהרא פרת ועד ימא **מערבאה** יהי תחומכון	Deut. 11:24
[מִן הַנָּהָר נְהַר פְּרָת וְעַד הַיָּם **הָאַחֲרוֹן** יִהְיֶה גְּבֻלְכֶם	[~

TN 16x, e.g.

טול כען עיניך וחמי... לצפונה ולדרומה ומדנחה **ומערבה**	Gen. 13:14
[שָׂא נָא עֵינֶיךָ וּרְאֵה... צָפֹנָה וָנֶגְבָּה וָקֵדְמָה **וָיָמָּה**	[~

TPJ 22x, e.g.

ותמשחון מברא לקרתא... וית רוח **מערבא** תרין אלפין גרמידי	Num. 35:5
[וּמַדֹּתֶם מִחוּץ לָעִיר... וְאֵת פְּאַת **יָם** אַלְפַּיִם בָּאַמָּה	[~

TJ 62x, e.g.

ארם ממדנחא ופלשתאי **ממערבא** ובזו ית נכסי ישראל	Isa. 9:11
[אֲרָם מִקֶּדֶם וּפְלִשְׁתִּים **מֵאָחוֹר** וַיֹּאכְלוּ אֶת יִשְׂרָאֵל	[~

Other Sources

Pesh. Deut. 11:30	**שמשא**	**במערבי**	אורחא	בסתר
[~	הַשֶּׁמֶשׁ	מִבוֹא	דֶּרֶךְ	[אַחֲרֵי

MekhRI Amalek 2 (p. 184)   ומנין שהראהו את כל **המערב** כלו? ת״ל ״עד הים
האחרון״ (דב׳ לד 2)

Independent Use
Heb.

11QT 46:13–16	ועשיתה להמה מקום יד חוץ מן העיר אשר יהיו יוצאים שמה לחוץ
	לצפון **המערב** לעיר, בתים ומקורים ובורות אשר תהיה
	הצואה יורדת אל תוכמה ולוא תהיה נראה לכול, רחוק מן העיר
	שלושת אלפים אמה
3Q15 3:9–10	ביאתא תחת הפנא **המערבית**
M RoshH 2:8	מעשה שבאו שנים ואמרו: ראינוהו שחרית במזרח וערבית **במערב**
T Soṭ. 13:7 (Nash.	כל זמן שהיה שמעון הצדיק קיים היה נר **מערבי** תדיר. משמת הלכו
p. 232)	ומצאוהו שכבה
PT Eruv. 5:1	ממקום שהחמה שוקעת באחד בתקופת טבת עד מקום שהיא
(p. 474)	שוקעת באחד בתקופת תמוז – אילו פני **המערב**

Aram.

TAD II 3.11 (= Krael.	ודנה תחומוהי מועה שמש לה אוצר מלכא...**מערב שמש** לה הו
10): 3–5	בבא זילך למנפק ושוק מלכא בינים
PAT 2743:4–6	ואסק חמרא עתיקא לכמריא שתא כלה מן ביתה וחמר בזקין לא
	איתי מן **מערבא**
4Q209 f23:3–7	[וקרין לקדימא קדים בדי הוא] קׄדמיה וקרין לדרומא דרום בדיל
	לתמן דׄאׄ רבא...ולרוחא רבא רוח **מערבא** בדי תמן [אתין כו]
	כׄבי שמיא מאין ערבין ומאין עללין וכלהון כוכבן ובדכן קרין
	מעדׄבא
NṢ 8:4 (Yardeni I	...תחמי אתריה [אלך]: מדנחה – דרתה; **מערבה** – דרת בית
p. 67)	מנו/י רבתה; דרומה – נזמה] צפו]נה...
PT Suk. 3:4 (p. 646)	ר׳ יסא כד סלק להכא חמתון מבחרין הדסה. אמ׳: למה **בני מערבא**
	[= אנשי ארץ ישראל] מבחרין הדסה?

COMMENTS

a. מַעֲרָב signifies a natural phenomenon, namely the direction in which the setting of the sun takes place. The root ערב means *enter* and the sun is perceived as entering the sea.

b. מַעֲרָב appears in three psalms (75:7; 103:12; 107:3) whose date is debatable. Note, however, that Pss. 103 and 107 exhibit some other possibly late elements; see Hurvitz 1972: 113, 173.

c. מַעֲרָב in Ezekiel (27:9, 13, 17, 19, 25, 27, 33–34) denotes *merchandise, imported goods*, and, therefore, is not included here (cf. Lexicons).

d. Note that in Aramaic itself מערב is attested as early as the eighth century BCE:

KAI 215:13–14   ...מֹן מוקא שמש ועד **מערב**...ובנת מוקא שמש יבל **מעֹרֹב** ובנת
מעֹרֹב יבל מו[קא ש]מש

However, the distribution pattern of מערב in BH strongly suggests that the emergence of the word is a late phenomenon on the Biblical scene. Cf. קום, comment **g**.

BIBLIOGRAPHY

BDB 788a

Curtis and Madsen 1910: 33 no. 93 • Hurvitz 1972: 113, 173 • Montgomery 1927: 331 • Sommer 1998: 261 • Williamson 1977a: 42 • R. M. Wright 2003: 142–144; 2005: 97–100

נְבוּאָה n. f. *prophecy, prophetic utterance/writing*: Neh. 6:12 כִּי הַנְּבוּאָה דִּבֶּר עָלָי;
2 Chron 9:29 וּשְׁאָר דִּבְרֵי שְׁלֹמֹה...הֲלֹא הֵם כְּתוּבִים עַל דִּבְרֵי נָתָן הַנָּבִיא וְעַל נְבוּאַת אֲחִיָּה
15:8 וְכִשְׁמֹעַ אָסָא הַדְּבָרִים הָאֵלֶּה וְהַנְּבוּאָה עֹדֵד הַנָּבִיא; הַשִּׁילוֹנִי וּבַחֲזוֹת יֶעְדּוֹ (ק') הַחֹזֶה
הִתְחַזַּק

BA Ezra 6:14 וְשָׂבֵי יְהוּדָיֵא בָּנַיִן וּמַצְלְחִין בִּנְבוּאַת חַגַּי נְבִיָּא (ק') וּזְכַרְיָה בַּר עִדּוֹא

CBH Alternatives

מַחֲזֶה, חָזוֹן, דָּבָר, e.g.

לְמַעַן הָקִים אֶת **דְּבָרוֹ** אֲשֶׁר	דִּבֶּר ה' בְּיַד	אֲחִיָּה הַשִּׁילֹנִי...	1 Kgs. 12:15	
[וּשְׁאָר דִּבְרֵי שְׁלֹמֹה...הֲלֹא הֵם כְּתוּבִים עַל **דִּבְרֵי** נָתָן הַנָּבִיא...			[~ 2 Chron. 9:29	
וְעַל **נְבוּאַת** אֲחִיָּה הַשִּׁילוֹנִי...				

חֲזוֹן יְשַׁעְיָהוּ בֶן אָמוֹץ...			Isa. 1:1
דִּבְרֵי יִרְמְיָהוּ בֶּן חִלְקִיָּהוּ...			Jer. 1:1
[הֲלֹא הֵם כְּתוּבִים עַל **דִּבְרֵי** נָתַן הַנָּבִיא...			[~ 2 Chron. 9:29
וְעַל **נְבוּאַת** אֲחִיָּה הַשִּׁילוֹנִי...			

לֹא שְׁלַחְתִּים... **חֲזוֹן** שֶׁקֶר... הֵמָּה מִתְנַבְּאִים לָכֶם			Jer. 14:14
[לֹא אֱלֹהִים שְׁלָחוֹ כִּי **הַנְּבוּאָה** דִּבֶּר עָלָי			[~ Neh. 6:12

External Post-Classical Sources
Renderings/Paraphrases/Glosses

TO 9x, e.g.

בָּתַר פִּתְגָמַיָּא הָאִלֵּין הֲוָה פִּתְגָמָא דַה' עִם אַבְרָם **בִּנְבוּאָה** לְמֵימַר			Gen. 15:1
[אַחַר הַדְּבָרִים הָאֵלֶּה הָיָה דְבַר ה' אֶל אַבְרָם **בַּמַּחֲזֶה** לֵאמֹר			[~

TN 8x נְבוּאָה, 12x נְבוּ, e.g.

וְאַף **בִּנְבוּאָתָךְ** מֹשֶׁה עַבְדִי יְהֵמְנוּן לְעָלַם			Exod. 19:9
[וְגַם **בְּךָ** יַאֲמִינוּ לְעוֹלָם			[~

TPJ 18x נְבוּאָה, 9x נְבוּ, e.g.

וְאַשְׁלִים עִמֵּיהּ **רוּחַ נְבוּאָה** מִן קֳדָם ה' בְּחוּכְמְתָא			Exod. 35:31
[וַיְמַלֵּא אֹתוֹ **רוּחַ** אֱלֹהִים בְּחָכְמָה			[~

וּנְטַל מְתַל **נְבוּתֵיהּ** וַאֲמַר			Num. 23:18
[וַיִּשָּׂא מְשָׁלוֹ וַיֹּאמַר			[~

TJ 236x, e.g.

| Jer. 43:8 | למימר | בתחפנחס | ירמיה | עם | ה׳ | קדם | מן | **נבואה** | פתגם | והוה |
| [~ | לֵאמֹר | בְּתַחְפַּנְחֵס | יִרְמְיָהוּ | אֶל | ה׳ | | | | דְּבַר | [וַיְהִי |

| Hab. 1:1 | נביא | חבקוק | דאתנבי | **נבואתא** |
| [~ | הַנָּבִיא | חֲבַקּוּק | אֲשֶׁר חָזָה | [הַמַּשָּׂא |

| Hab. 2:2 | דאוריתא | ספרא | על | ומפרשא | **נבואתא** | כתיבא | ואמר |
| [~ | הַלֻּחוֹת | עַל | וּבָאֵר | חָזוֹן | כְּתוֹב | [וַיֹּאמֶר |

Independent Use
Heb.

BS 44:3 (B)	היועצים בתבונתם וחזי כל **בנבואתם**
BS 46:1 (B)	גבור בן חיל יהושע בן נון משרת משה **בנבואה**
11QPsᵃ 27:11	כול אלה דבר **בנבואה** אשר נתן לו מלפני העליון
M San. 11:5	...אבל הכובש את **נבואתו** והמוותר על דברי הנביא ונביא שעבר על דברי עצמו מיתתו בידי שמים
T Edu. 1:1 (p. 454)	שנ׳ "לכן הנה ימים באים...ונע׳ מים ועד ים ומצפון ועד מזרח ישוטטו לבקש את דבר ה׳ ולא ימצאו" (עמוס ח 11–12). "דבר ה׳" – זו **נבואה**
MekhRI Amalek 2 (p. 198)	"ואתה תחזה מכל העם" (שמ׳ יח 12) – תחזה להם **בנבואה**
Sifre Deut. 357 (p. 430)	"ולא קם נביא עוד בישראל כמשה" (דב׳ לד 10) – בישראל לא קם אבל באומות העולם קם. ואיזה זה? זה בלעם בן בעור. אלא הפרש יש בין **נבואתו** של משה **לנבואתו** של בלעם: משה לא היה יודע מי מדבר עמו ובלעם היה יודע מי מדבר עמו

Aram.

Qoh. Rab. 11:3 (1)	תרגם עקילס הגר: "ועל העבים אצוה מהמטיר עליו מטר" (יש׳ ה 6) – ועל נביאיא הפקד דלא יתנבון להון **נבואתא**
PesiqRK 13 (p. 228)	"ויצא ירמיה מירושלם ללכת" וג׳ (יר׳ לז 12) – רב אמר: ליטול מחלקו יצא. ר׳ בנימן בן לוי אמ׳: למשריה תמן **נבואן סגין**, "דבר ירמיה" אין כת׳ כן אלא "דברי ירמיהו"
TM 5:120–124 (p. 313)	"וזאת הברכה אשר ברך משה"..."איש האלהים את בני ישר׳ לפני מותו" (דב׳ לג 1) – **נביזתה** משררה אקרי זכותה

COMMENTS

a. The root נבא is common in both verbal (הִתְנַבֵּא, נִבָּא) and nominal (נָבִיא) forms throughout BH. "From the noun nāḇî, the Chronicler's history derives the technical term nᵉḇû'â, 'oracle' (2 Ch. 15:8; Ezr. 6:14 [Aram.]; Neh. 6:12) or 'story of a prophet' (2 Ch. 9:29). The term appears later in Sir. 44:3 (parallel *tbwntm*, 'their understanding'); 46:1, 13, 20 as an abstract noun meaning 'prophecy'. It is also found in the Dead Sea Scrolls, and it undergoes a rich semantic development in Middle Hebrew. Its parallel in Jewish Aramaic is nᵉḇûʾâ, 'prophecy'" (Müller 1998: 134).

b. Various CBH expressions for "prophetic utterance" (e.g., משא, חזון/חזיון, דבר) are still to be found in LBH—probably with certain different nuances in meaning. Yet, the decisive fact for dating purposes in the present discussion is "that the appearance of the—abstract—noun נְבוּאָה in biblical literature specifically in the books of Ezra, Nehemiah, and Chronicles marks a late stage of development in the history of BH. It signals the birth of a new religious term, which was to become a distinctive characteristic of post-biblical Hebrew" (Hurvitz 2000a: 152).

c. Ben Sira 46:1 (B), משרת משה בנבואה, clearly alludes to various Biblical passages about Joshua (cf. מְשָׁרֵת מֹשֶׁה in Num 11:28; Josh 1:1). Yet, the term נבואה in BS is not to be found in the relevant Biblical verses and it reflects the late linguistic milieu of Ben Sira's days.

BIBLIOGRAPHY
BDB 612b • KB 587b • Kaddari 689a
Dihi 2004: 405–407 • Hurvitz 1997a: 74–77; 2000a: 151–152 • Müller 1998: 134

√נדב vb. **Hitp** *to obligate oneself freely, to volunteer oneself* Judg. 5:2, 9 (cf. note
a below); Ezra 1:6; 2:68; 3:5 'מִתְנַדֵּב נְדָבָה לַה; Neh. 11:2; 1 Chron. 29:5, 6–9 וַיִּתְנַדְּבוּ שָׂרֵי
הָאָבוֹת וְשָׂרֵי שִׁבְטֵי יִשְׂרָאֵל... וַיִּתְּנוּ לַעֲבוֹדַת בֵּית הָאֱלֹהִים זָהָב כִּכָּרִים חֲמֵשֶׁת אֲלָפִים... וַיִּשְׂמְחוּ
אֲנִי בְּיֹשֶׁר לְבָבִי הִתְנַדַּבְתִּי כָל אֵלֶּה 17, 14, הָעָם עַל הִתְנַדְּבָם כִּי בְּלֵב שָׁלֵם הִתְנַדְּבוּ לַה';
עֲמַסְיָה בֶן זִכְרִי הַמִּתְנַדֵּב לַה' 2 Chron. 17:16

כְּסַף 15, כָל מִתְנַדַּב בְּמַלְכוּתִי מִן עַמָּה יִשְׂרָאֵל... לְמְהָךְ לִירוּשְׁלֶם עִמָּךְ יְהָךְ BA Ezra 7:13
וְכֹל כְּסַף וּדְהַב דִּי תְהַשְׁכַּח... עִם הִתְנַדָּבוּת 16, וּדְהַב דִּי מַלְכָּא וְיָעֲטוֹהִי הִתְנַדַּבוּ לֶאֱלָהּ יִשְׂרָאֵל
עַמָּא וְכָהֲנַיָּא מִתְנַדְּבִין לְבֵית אֱלָהֲהֹם דִּי בִירוּשְׁלֶם

CBH Alternatives

√נדב Qal (+ לֵב/רוּחַ), נשא√ Qal (+ לֵב), e.g.

מֵאֵת כָּל אִישׁ אֲשֶׁר **יִדְּבֶנּוּ** לִבּוֹ		תִּקְחוּ אֶת תְּרוּמָתִי	Exod. 25:2
כָּל אִישׁ אֲשֶׁר **נְשָׂאוֹ** לִבּוֹ			Exod. 35:21
וְכֹל אֲשֶׁר **נָדְבָה** רוּחוֹ אֹתוֹ הֵבִיאוּ אֶת תְּרוּמַת ה'		Exod. 35:29
כָּל אִישׁ... אֲשֶׁר **נָדַב** לִבָּם אֹתָם... הֵבִיאוּ... **נְדָבָה** לַה'		

versus

...]וּלְכֹל	**מִתְנַדֵּב** **נְדָבָה** לַה'	[~Ezra 3:5
[וַיִּשְׂמְחוּ הָעָם עַל **הִתְנַדְּבָם** כִּי בְּלֵב שָׁלֵם **הִתְנַדְּבוּ** לַה'	[~ 1 Chron. 29:9
[בְּיֹשֶׁר לְבָבִי **הִתְנַדַּבְתִּי**...רָאִיתִי... **לְהִתְנַדֶּב** לָךְ	[~ 1 Chron. 29:17

External Post-Classical Sources
Renderings/Paraphrases/Glosses

TN 12X, e.g.

דן קרבנה דִי **אתנדב** וקרב מן נכסי גרמיה... אליאב בר חלן			Num. 7:29
[זֶה קָרְבַּן אֱלִיאָב בֶּן חֵלֹן			[~

TJ 1X

כל כסף **דמתנדב** גבר בלביה לאיתאה לבית מקדשא דה'	2 Kgs. 12:5
[כָּל כֶּסֶף אֲשֶׁר יַעֲלֶה עַל לֵב אִישׁ לְהָבִיא בֵּית ה'	[~

Other Sources

Tg. Ps. 110:3   עמך בית ישראל **דמתנדבין** לאוריתא ביום אגחותך קרבא

[~   [עַמְּךָ   **נְדָבֹת**   בְּיוֹם   חֵילֶךָ

Independent Use

Heb.

M Men. 12:3   הרי עלי מנחה מן השעורין – יביא מן החיטין. קמח – יביא סלת...ר'
שמעון פוטר שלא **ניתנדב** כדרך **המיתנדבין**

M Men. 12:5   **מיתנדבין** יין ואין **מיתנדבין** שמן, דבר' ר' עקיבה. ר' טרפון או':
מיתנדבין שמן

MekhRI Kaspa 19   נוטלין מעות מן ההקדש ולוקחין בהן בהמה מן החולין ומתרחמות
(p. 320)   עליה ומניקות אותן, אף על פי שאמרו אחרים **מתנדבין** היו על
מנת כן

Kh. Susiya (Naveh   זכור לטובה קדושת מרי רבי איסי הכהן המכובד בירבי שעשה
1978: no. 75): 1–6   הפסיפוס הזה וטח את כותליו בסיד מה **שנתנדב** במשתה רבי יוחנן
הכהן הסופר בירבי בנו שלום על ישראל אמן

Aram.

Tiberias (Naveh 1978: no.   [הֹון ו]...[ ] סגין[...]בנ[...]והֹ...דהי[נון...]**לֹאתנדב**]
25)

Beth Alpha (Naveh 1978:   [הדין פסי[פֹוסה אתקבע בשתה]...ל[מֹלכותה דיוסטינוס
no. 43)   מלכהֹ...[סאין](?)...ד[**אתנדבון** כל בני ק[רתה]...

COMMENTS

a. √נדב, whose basic meaning is *to make a voluntary decision* (*HALOT* II 671b), appears in the *hithpa'el* conjugation already in the Song of Deborah (Judg. 5:2, 9). However, in texts dealing with the religious cultic center (the Tabernacle, the Jerusalem Temple), התנדב is employed in BH exclusively in the books of Ezra, Nehemiah, and Chronicles (12x). The earlier sources make use of other verbal and nominal forms derived from √נדב (נְדָבָה; נָדַב) in such contexts, but not of התנדב (Driver 1913; Curtis and Madsen 1910; Hurvitz 1974a; Williamson 1977a; D. Talshir 1988; Dimant 2007). "The semantic development that took place between the Torah text and the *Chronicler's* account is exemplified by the fact that the voluntary offerings to the Tabernacle are described by the verb √נדב in the *qal*, whereas the *Chronicler* has recourse only to the *hithpa'el* forms. The *hithpa'el* forms come in a similar context and carry a similar emphasis in *Ezra's* description of the returnees from Babylon. Again the *hithpa'el* of the verb √נדב designates the voluntary offer of materials and animals by those who prepared to return to Judaea, as well as those who stayed behind in Babylon (*Ezra* 1:6). The same use and context recur in *Ezra's* account in 2:68–69 of how the heads of the families contributed money and priestly vestments. In *Ezra* 3:5 the reference is explicitly to the cultic sacrifices made on the re-established altar, including voluntary offerings (המתנדבים נדבה). Even the single mention in *Neh* 11:2 of '*mitnadevim* to settle in Jerusalem' may not be purely secular, but may have been connected with some cultic function. Obviously, in later biblical times the *hithpa'el* of √נדב acquired the special sense of free-will initiatives related to the cultic sphere" (Dimant 2007: 238).

b. The linguistic consistency of RH נ/הִתְנַדֵּב versus BH נָדַב may be vividly illustrated by the following Rabbinic midrash on the Biblical account that describes the preparations for the construction of the Tabernacle:

> Why here were the Princes first to donate (להתנדב) while at the construction of the Tabernacle they were not first to donate (נתנדבו)? For the Princes said thus: Let the community donate (יתנדבו) whatever they donate (מה שמתנדבים), and whatever is missing we will complete (Sifre Num. 45 [p. 51]).

c. In Ezra 3:5 and 1 Chron. 29:5-6 we observe another late development. In contrast to the standard *intransitive* or *reflexive* functions of the *hitpa'el*, in these verses התנדב assumes a *transitive* sense and is followed by a direct object (as in M Men. 12:5 quoted above); its meaning here is "to make a voluntary contribution, with acc[usative]" (*HALOT* II 671b). This linguistic usage is likewise attested in BA (see above, Ezra 7:15–16) and in the ancient synagogue inscriptions of Beth Alpha and Kh. Susiya (see above).

d. QH makes use of התנדב, but not to describe the donation of objects in the cultic realm; cf. 1QS 5:1 וזה הסרך לאנשי היחד המתנדבים לשׁוב מכול רע ולהחזיק בכול and 4Q258 2:1–2 ואת מעשיהם בתורה על פי בני אהרון המתנדבים להקים את אשר צוה. For בריתו ולפקוד את כל חקיו אשר צוה לעשות על פי רוב ישראל המתנדבים לשוב ביחד further details on the use of √נדב in the *hitpa'el* at Qumran, see Dimant 2007; and on the sectarians' concept of נדבה, see Licht 1965.

e. In summary, the lateness of התנדב is observable in both semantics (a technical term used exclusively in the vocabulary of cult and temple) and grammar (a shift from the *qal* conjugation to the *hitpa'el*).

BIBLIOGRAPHY

Kaddari 696b

Curtis and Madsen 1910: 31 no. 70 • Dimant 2007: esp. 237–238, 245 • S. R. Driver 1913: 537 no. 23 • Hurvitz 1974a: 29–32 • Licht 1965: 108–109 • Polzin 1976: 135–136 • Qimron 1986: 92 • D. Talshir 1988: 188 no. 57, note 73 • Williamson 1977a: 48

נִיסָן pr. n. name of 1st month, derived from Akkad. *nissanu*: Esth. 3:7 בַּחֹדֶשׁ
הָרִאשׁוֹן הוּא חֹדֶשׁ נִיסָן ;Neh. 2:1 וַיְהִי בְּחֹדֶשׁ נִיסָן שְׁנַת עֶשְׂרִים לְאַרְתַּחְשַׁסְתְּא הַמֶּלֶךְ

Cf. אֲדָר

CBH ALTERNATIVES

Months are generally named by their numerical order, e.g., 1 Kgs. 12:32 בַּחֹדֶשׁ
הַשְּׁמִינִי; in a few cases they follow the Canaanite pattern, e.g., 1 Kgs. 8:2 בְּיֶרַח
הָאֵתָנִים. Only in the LBH corpus do we find both (the older) numerical system
and (the more recent) Mesopotamian names side by side in one and the same
verse, e.g., Esth. 3:7 לַחֹדֶשׁ שְׁנֵים עָשָׂר הוּא חֹדֶשׁ אֲדָר.

| Exod. 40:17 | בַּשָּׁנָה הַשֵּׁנִית ... | **בַּחֹדֶשׁ הָרִאשׁוֹן** |
| [~ Esth. 3:7 | הָרִאשׁוֹן הוּא חֹדֶשׁ נִיסָן בִּשְׁנַת שְׁתֵּים עֶשְׂרֵה ... | [**בַּחֹדֶשׁ** |

EXTERNAL POST-CLASSICAL SOURCES
Renderings/Paraphrases/Glosses

TO 2x, e.g.

| Num. 9:5 | ועבדו ית פסחא **בניסן** בארבעת עסרא יומא לירחא בין שמשיא |
| [~ | [וַיַּעֲשׂוּ אֶת הַפֶּסַח **בָּרִאשׁוֹן** בְּאַרְבָּעָה עָשָׂר יוֹם לַחֹדֶשׁ בֵּין הָעַרְבָּיִם |

TN 2x, e.g.

| Exod. 12:2 | ירחא הדין **ניסן** לכון ריש ירחין קדמיי הוא לכון ... |
| [~ | [הַחֹדֶשׁ הַזֶּה לָכֶם רֹאשׁ חֳדָשִׁים רִאשׁוֹן הוּא לָכֶם ... |

TPJ 26x, e.g.

| Gen. 8:22 | דרועא בתקופת תשרי וחצדא בתקופת **ניסן** וקורא בתקופת טבת |
| [~ | [זֶרַע וְקָצִיר וְקֹר |

| Num. 28:16 | ובירחא **דניסן** בארביסר יומין לירחא ניכסת פיסחא קדם ה' |
| [~ | [וּבַחֹדֶשׁ הָרִאשׁוֹן בְּאַרְבָּעָה עָשָׂר יוֹם לַחֹדֶשׁ פֶּסַח לַה' |

TJ 3x, e.g.

| Joel 2:23 | ומחית לכון מטר בכיר בעדניה ולקישא **בירח ניסן** |
| [~ | [וַיּוֹרֶד לָכֶם גֶּשֶׁם מוֹרֶה וּמַלְקוֹשׁ **בָּרִאשׁוֹן** |

Independent Use

Heb.

M RoshH 1:1 — ארבעה ראשי שנים הן. באחד **בניסן** ראש שנה למלכים
ולרגלים...

T Er. 4:6 (Mo'ed
p. 106) — תקופת **ניסן** ותקופת תשרי חמה יוצאה בחצי מזרח ושוקעת
בחצי מערב

T Ta'an. 1:7 (Mo'ed
p. 325) — חצי תשרי מרחשון וחצי כסליו – זרע. חצי כסליו טבת וחצי
שבט – חורף. חצי שבט אדר וחצי **ניסן** – קור. חצי **ניסן** אייר
וחצי סיון – קציר. חצי סיון תמוז וחצי אב – קיץ. חצי אב אלול
וחצי תשרי – חום

MekhRI VaYasa' 1
(p. 159) — **ניסן** שיצאו בו ישראל ממצרים אירע להיות בחמישי בשבת.
השלים **ניסן**. אירע אייר להיות בשבת. חסר אייר. אירע סיון
להיות באחד בשבת

Sifra Milu'im 1:1 — באחד **בניסן** שלמו המלואים

Beth Alpha (Naveh
1978: no. 45): 13–16 — תקופת **ניסן** תקופת תמוז תקופת תישרי תקופת טבת

'Ein Gedi (Naveh
1978: no. 70): 5–7 — **ניסן** אייר סיון תמוז אב אילול תשרי מרחשון כסליו טבית שבט
ואדר

Aram.

Cooke 79:4–5 (Nab.) — ...בירח **ניסן** שנת תשע לחרתת מלך נבטו רחם עמה...

EN 163:1–2 (Idum.) — ב 8 ל**ניסן** קוסעני...גרגרן 53

Meg. Ta'an. 1–8 Nisan (p. 57) — מן רש ירחא ד**ניסן** עד תמניא ביה איתוקם תמידא

1 Tg. Esth. 3:7 — בכן שרי שמשי (ס)פרא לצבעא פייסא דעדבין קדם
המן...ושרי בירחיא. **בניסן** ולא על מן בגלל זכותא
דפיסחא

Greek

LXX Esth. 1:1a — Ἔτους δευτέρου βασιλεύοντος Ἀρταξέρξου τοῦ μεγάλου τῇ
μιᾷ τοῦ Νισα ἐνύπνιον εἶδεν Μαρδοχαῖος ὁ τοῦ Ιαΐρου τοῦ
Σεμεΐου τοῦ Κισαιου ἐκ φυλῆς Βενιαμιν

4 Bar. 5:34 — ὁ δὲ Ἱεπε Νισσάν ὁ ἐστιν Ἀβίβ

Ant. 1:80–81 — Συνέβη δὲ τοῦτο τὸ πάθος κατὰ τὸ ἑξακοσιοστὸν ἔτος ἤδη
Νώχου τῆς ἀρχῆς ἐν μηνὶ δευτέρῳ Δίῳ μὲν ὑπὸ Μακεδόνων
λεγομένῳ Μαρσουάνῃ δ' ὑπὸ Ἑβραίων οὕτω γὰρ ἐν
Αἰγύπτῳ τὸν ἐνιαυτὸν ἦσαν διατεταχότες. Μωυσῆς δὲ τὸν
Νισὰν ὅς ἐστι Ξανθικός μῆνα πρῶτον ἐπὶ ταῖς ἑορταῖς ὥρισε
κατὰ τοῦτον ἐξ Αἰγύπτου τοὺς Ἑβραίους προαγαγών

COMMENTS

a. See the entry אֲדָר for general comments on month-names and the bibliography there.

See also BDB 1a; 644b; *HALOT* I 4b; Kaddari 714a.

וַיִּשְׂאוּ √נשׂא + אִשָּׁה idiom. *take a wife*: **Qal** Judg. 21:23 (cf. comment **b**); Ruth 1:4; וּבְנֹתֵיהֶם אַל תִּשְׂאוּ לִבְנֵיכֶם (cf. comment **b** below); Ezra 9:2, 12 לָהֶם נָשִׁים מֹאָבִיּוֹת כִּי נָשִׁים שְׁמוֹנֶה עֶשְׂרֵה; Neh. 13:25; 2 Chron. 11:21 נָשִׂאוּ (ק׳) נָשִׁים נָכְרִיּוֹת 10:44; כָּל אֵלֶּה נָשְׂאוּ (ק׳) וַיִּשָּׂא לוֹ יְהוֹיָדָע נָשִׁים שְׁתָּיִם 24:3; 13:21; נָשָׂא

CBH ALTERNATIVES
√לקח (אשה), e.g.

Gen. 4:19	שְׁתֵּי נָשִׁים	לֶמֶךְ	לוֹ	**וַיִּקַּח**
[~ 2 Chron. 24:3	נָשִׁים שְׁתָּיִם	יְהוֹיָדָע	לוֹ	**וַיִּשָּׂא**]

Gen. 34:9	**תִּקְחוּ** לָכֶם	וְאֶת בְּנֹתֵינוּ	לָנוּ	תִּתְּנוּ	בְּנֹתֵיכֶם
[~ Ezra 9:12	לִבְנֵיכֶם **תִּשְׂאוּ** אַל	וּבְנֹתֵיהֶם	לִבְנֵיהֶם	תִּתְּנוּ	אַל	בִּנוֹתֵיכֶם]

EXTERNAL POST-CLASSICAL SOURCES
Renderings/Paraphrases/Glosses

11QT 57:15–19 — ואשה לוא **ישא** מכול בנות הגויים כי אם מבית אביהו **יקח** לו אשה ממשפחת אביהו. ולוא **יקח** עליה אשה אחרת כי היאה לבדה תהיה עמו כול ימי חייה. ואם מתה, **ונשא** לו אחרת מבית אביהו ממשפחתו

Gen. Rab. 65:1 (p. 713) — ...וכיון שהגיע לארבעים שנה דימה עצמו לאביו. אמר: מה אבא **נשא** בן ארבעים אף אני **נושא** אשה בן ארבעים שנה. הה״ד ״ויהי עשו בן ארבעים שנה **ויקח** אשה״ וגו׳ (בר׳ כו 34)

M Yev. 6:4	אלמנה	**ישא**	לא	גדול	כהן
[~ Lev. 21:10–14	**יקח**... אַלְמָנָה... הַגָּדוֹל... וְהַכֹּהֵן]

Sifra Aḥare 8:3 — ״ואיש...אשר **יקח** את אשה ואת אמה״ (וי׳ כ 14) – בכולו הוא אומר שכיבה וכן [= וכאן] הוא או׳ **לקיחה**. ללמדך שלעולם אינו חייב אילא על **הניסואין**

Sifre Num. 78 (p. 74)	למואב״ (דה״א ד 22) –	**אשר בעלו**
	מואביות	נשים	**שנשאו**

Independent Use
Heb.

BS (A) 7:23 — בנים לך יסיר אותם **וְשָׂא** לָהֶם נשים בנעוריהם

M Mo'edQ 1:7 — אין **נושאים** נשים במועד, לא בתולות ולא אלמנות, ולא מיבמין

M Yev. 1:4 — אף על פי שאילו פוסלין ואלו מכשירין לא נימנעו בית שמי **מלישא** נשים מבית הלל ולא בית הלל מבית שמי

M Ket. 2:1	האשה שנתאלמנה או שנתגרשה – היא אומרת: בתולה **נְשָׂאתַי**,
	והוא אומ׳: לא כי אלא אלמנה **נשאתיך**...
T Yoma 2:6	ובדבר הזה מזכירין אותן [את בית אבטינס] לשבח: שלא יצאת מהן
(Mo'ed p. 233)	אשה מבוסמת מעולם, ולא עוד אלא כשהיו **נושׂאין** אשה ממקום
	אחר היו פוסקין "על מנת שלא תתבסמי" – כדי שלא יאמרו: מפטום
	הקטרת הן מתבסמות
Sifre Deut. 253	אני גר מצרי **ונסׂוי** אני אשה גיורת מצרית והריני הולך **להסׂיא** את בני
(pp. 279–280)	אשה בת גיורת מצרית כדי שיהא בן בני ראוי לבוא בקהל

COMMENTS

a. "[T]he verb for 'to marry' . . . in SBH . . . is expressed by the phrase לִקוֹחַ אִשָּׁה, while in LBH this phrase is . . . replaced by נָשׂוֹא אִשָּׁה. . . . How are we to account for this change? The only explanation seems to be in the fact that . . . לִקוֹחַ in SBH is mainly used with the meaning 'to take', but in MH it is used mainly with the meaning 'to buy'. . . . Therefore, to avoid misunderstanding, the verb נָשׂוֹא . . . was employed" (Kutscher 1982: 83 §123). Note, however, that occurrences of the older idiom לקח + אשה may still be found in LBH as survivals of the CBH linguistic usage (see Ezra 2:61; Neh. 7:63; 1 Chron. 7:15).

b. The combination נשא + אשה appears twice outside the distinctive LBH corpus—in Judg. 21:23 and Ruth 1:4. Regarding Judges, the meaning of the phrase does not necessarily imply the expression's technical sense *take as a wife, marry*. נשא in this context may well be rendered *carry away, secure* (S. R. Driver 1913: 455) or *seize* [*a woman without her/her family's consent*], as the entire story deals with this incident in terms of violent seizure: חטף√ v. 21, גזל√ v. 23, ריב√ v. 22. Regarding Ruth, those who consider this composition as late may indeed consider the phrase נשא אשה as evidence for the lateness of the book's language; those who assign an early date to the book, on the other hand, will insist that נשא in Ruth 1:4 is no more than an isolated occurrence within our pre-Exilic corpus and, therefore, indecisive for dating purposes. In other words, "although the expression occurred occasionally in the pre-exilic period, it was rare and unproductive. It was not until the post-exilic period that this alternative expression for 'acquire a wife' began to replace SBH לקח אשה" (R. M. Wright 2005: 72 note 66).

c. The above mentioned Temple Scroll passage is an exception in DSS linguistic usage; generally, the earlier idiom, לקח אשה, is retained (ibid., 74).

d. The linguistic antiquity of the phrase לקח אשה is further corroborated by its attestation in Ugaritic (see Olmo Lete and San Martín 2003: II 503)—which is totally unfamiliar with its LBH and RH counterpart נשא אשה (ibid., 648–649).

BIBLIOGRAPHY

BDB 671b • *HALOT* II 726a

Curtis-Madsen 1910: 72 no. 76, 370 • S. R. Driver 1913: 454–455, 540, 553 note * • Eskhult 2003: 15–16 • Freedman, Willoughby, Fabry, Ringgren 1999: 38–39 • Hadas-Lebel 1995: 110 • Japhet 1993: 672 • Joosten 2000: 125–126 • Kutscher 1966: 22–23 (= 1977: 352–353); 1982: 83 §123 • Olmo Lete and Sanmartín 2003: II 503, 648–649 • Polzin 1976: 146 • Qimron 1986: 93 • Williamson 1977a: 52 • R. M. Wright 2005: 71–74, 127

סוֹף n. m. *end*: Joel 2:20 פָּנָיו אֶל הַיָּם הַקַּדְמֹנִי וְסֹפוֹ אֶל הַיָּם הָאַחֲרוֹן; Qoh. 3:11 וּמְצָאתֶם אֹתָם בְּסוֹף הַנַּחַל 2 Chron. 20:16 סוֹף דָּבָר; 12:13; 7:2; סוֹף

BA Dan. 4:8, 19 וּרְבוּתָךְ רְבָת וּמְטָת לִשְׁמַיָּא וְשָׁלְטָנָךְ לְסוֹף אַרְעָא 7:26; 6:27 לְהַשְׁמָדָה סוֹפָא דִי מִלְּתָא 28, וּלְהוֹבָדָה עַד סוֹפָא

CBH Alternatives

אחרית, קץ, קצה

Amos 9:1	**וְאַחֲרִיתָם** בַּחֶרֶב אֶהֱרֹג	כֻּלָּם	בְּרֹאשׁ	וּבְצַעַם
Deut. 11:12	וְעַד **אַחֲרִית שָׁנָה**	מֵרֵשִׁית הַשָּׁנָה	תָּמִיד עֵינֵי ה׳ אֱלֹהֶיךָ בָּהּ	
[~ Qoh. 3:11	וְעַד **סוֹף**	מֵרֹאשׁ		]

Josh. 15:8	**בְּקָצֵה** עֵמֶק רְפָאִים צָפֹנָה	אֲשֶׁר	הָהָר...	רֹאשׁ	אֶל...
Josh. 18:19	נֶגְבָּה	הַיַּרְדֵּן	אֶל **קְצֵה**	יָם הַמֶּלַח צָפוֹנָה	לְשׁוֹן	אֶל...
[~ 2 Chron. 20:16	**בְּסוֹף** הַנַּחַל			בְּמַעֲלֵה הַצִּיץ...	]

External Post-Classical Sources
Renderings/Paraphrases/Glosses

TO 36x, e.g.

Deut. 8:16	**בְּסוֹפָךְ**	לָךְ	לְאֵיטָבָא	לְנַסָּיוּתָךְ	וּבְדִיל
[~	**בְּאַחֲרִיתֶךָ**		לְהֵיטִבְךָ	נַסֹּתְךָ	וּלְמַעַן]

TN 60x, e.g.

Exod. 32:1	**בְּסוֹפָה**	הֲוָה	מַה	יָדְעִין	אֲנָן	לֵית...	גַּבְרָא	מֹשֶׁה	דֵּן אֲרוּם
[~	**לוֹ**	הָיָה	מֶה	יָדַעְנוּ	לֹא	...הָאִישׁ	מֹשֶׁה	זֶה	כִּי]

TPJ 64x, e.g.

Exod. 12:41	שְׁנִין... אַרְבַּע מְאָה... נְפַקוּ... מֵאַרְעָא דְמִצְרַיִם	תְּלָתִין	**מִסּוֹף**	וַהֲוָה
[~	שָׁנָה וְאַרְבַּע מֵאוֹת שָׁנָה... יָצְאוּ... מֵאֶרֶץ מִצְרָיִם	שְׁלֹשִׁים	**מִקֵּץ**	וַיְהִי]

TJ 73x, e.g.

Hos. 3:5	יוֹמַיָּא	**בְּסוֹף**	לְהוֹן דַּיְתִי טוּבָיָה וּסְגֵי	דה׳	לְפוּלְחָנָא	וִיתֻנְהוֹן
[~	הַיָּמִים	**בְּאַחֲרִית**	טוּבוֹ וְאֶל	ה׳	אֶל	וּפָחֲדוּ]

Other Sources

11QTgJob 28:3–4	**סוֹף** לָא דִי שְׁנוֹהִי וּמִנְיָן נַ[נ]דְע[לָא] סַגִּיא... הוּא רַב אֱלָהָא
[~ Job 36:26	**חֵקֶר** וְלֹא שָׁנָיו מִסְפַּר נֵדַע וְלֹא שַׂגִּיא אֵל]

Independent Use

Heb.

BS (A) 11:27	וְסוֹף אדם יגיד עליו
4Q171	פשרו על כול הרשעה לסוֹף ארבעים השנה אשר יתמו ולוא ימצא
f1-2ii:6–8	בארץ כול איש [ר]שע
4Q268 f1:2	...איזה תחלתו ואיזה סוֹפו...
Mur. 24e:8–9	תעפר הלז חכרתי המך מן היום עד סוֹף ערב השמטה
(Yardeni I p. 107)	
M Ber. 1:1	מאמתי קורין את שמע בערבים? משעה שהכהנים נכנסים לאכל
	בתרומתן עד סוֹף האשמורת הראשונה
T Par. 2:1 (p. 631)	ר' יהודה אומר: משמרין אותה שלא לעבוד בה בכל עבודה. אמרו
	לו: אם בן![!] אין לדבר סוֹף
MekhRI Pisḥa 15	יש פרשיות שהוא כולל בתחלה ופורט בסוֹף, פורט בתחלה וכולל
(p. 52)	בסוֹף

Aram.

1QApGen 20:18	ולסוֹף תרתין שנין תקפו וגברו עלוהי מכתשיא ונגדיא
4Q530 f2ii+6–12:20	עד כה סוֹף חלמא
Beth She'arim 2	דקביר בהדין שמעון בר יוחנן ובשבועה דכל דיפתח
(Naveh 1992: 195): 1–6	עלוי יהי מאית בסוֹף ביש
BT BQ 117a	מעיקרא סבור כדר' אבין...ולבסוֹף סברוה כדר' ירמיה

COMMENTS

a. "The noun סוֹף, which is found in Qoh. 3,11; 7,2; 12,13, is a late word in BH. The verb סוּף, 'come to an end' is good classical Hebrew.... Besides the attestations in Qoh, however, the noun occurs only in Joel 2,20 and 2 Chr 20,16. It is also found in Sir..., Qumran...and Murabba'at...and it is common in MH....[T]he noun is [also] common in Official Aramaic, including BA...and later Aramaic dialects, and there are the Hebrew synonyms קץ and אחרית. Therefore, quite a number of scholars rightly regard it as an Aramaism. According to Aalders, it is not necessarily a late word in BH, since it occurs in Joel 2,20, the date of the book of Joel being completely uncertain.... Tyler and Fredericks doubt that it is late because of the older use of the verb סוּף and because of the presence in Qoh of the early synonym קץ. Neither of these objections, however, is convincing, since [1] a noun is not a verb and [2] the emergence of a neologism does not necessarily stop the use of the older synonym" (Schoors 1992–2004: II 339–340).

b. Whatever the date of composition of the book of Joel, the single occurrence of סוֹף in it does not constitute sufficient grounds for disqualifying the term as an element especially characteristic of the Second Temple linguistic milieu. Even if Joel is pre-Exilic, its use of סוֹף proves only that the word was available and admissible during the First Temple period, but in no way demonstrates that its use was prevalent or typical of CBH, which consistently employs its Classical alternatives. The late Biblical and extra-Biblical evidence, on the other hand, points conclusively to the word being among the distinguishing markers of LBH, late extra-Biblical Hebrew, and late Aramaic. It should also be noted that the solitary instance of סוֹף in Joel does not prove, in and of itself, the book's late provenance, as such a conclusion should be based on an accumulation of late features in Joel. (On the possibility of such an accumulation, see S. R. Driver 1913: 313; Hurvitz 1983: 216).

BIBLIOGRAPHY

BDB 693a • *HALOT* II 747a • Kaddari 750b

Barton 1908: 105, 200 • Davila 1991: 823 • Delitzsch 1877: 190–196 • Dihi 2004: 473–475 • S. R. Driver 1913: 313, 475 no. 11 • Gordis 1968: 354 • Hadas-Lebel 1995: 111 • Hurvitz 1983: 216; 2003b: 281–284 • Joosten 2000: 121 • Kutscher 1982: 75–76 §105 • Magnanini 1968: 374 • Nebe 1997: 151 • Polzin 1976: 146–147 • Qimron 1986: 93 • Sæbø 1999: 188 • Schoors 1992–2004: II 339–340 • C. H. H. Wright 1883: 494 • R. M. Wright 2005: 101–103, 131

סִיוָן pr. n. name of 3rd month, derived from Akkad. *simanu*: Esth. 8:9 בְּחֹדֶשׁ
הַשְּׁלִישִׁי הוּא חֹדֶשׁ סִיוָן

CBH ALTERNATIVES

Months are generally named by their numerical order, e.g., 1 Kgs. 12:32 בְּחֹדֶשׁ
הַשְּׁמִינִי; in a few cases they follow the Canaanite pattern, e.g., 1 Kgs. 8:2 בְּיֶרַח
הָאֵתָנִים. Only in the LBH corpus do we find both (the older) numerical system
and (the more recent) Mesopotamian names side by side in one and the same
verse, e.g., Esth. 3:7 לְחֹדֶשׁ שְׁנֵים עָשָׂר הוּא חֹדֶשׁ אֲדָר.

Exod. 19:1	לָצֵאת בְּנֵי יִשְׂרָאֵל מֵאֶרֶץ מִצְרָיִם	**הַשְּׁלִישִׁי**	**בַּחֹדֶשׁ**
[~ Esth. 8:9	חֹדֶשׁ סִיוָן	הוּא	הַשְּׁלִישִׁי	בַּחֹדֶשׁ]

EXTERNAL POST-CLASSICAL SOURCES
Renderings/Paraphrases/Glosses
TPJ 2x, e.g.

Gen. 30:14	חִינְטִין	חֲצַד	בִּזְמַן	בְּיוֹמֵי **סִיוָן**	רְאוּבֵן	וַאֲזַל
[~	חִטִּים	קְצִיר		בִּימֵי	רְאוּבֵן	וַיֵּלֶךְ]

Other Sources
PesiqRK 10 (p. 210)

א"ר עזריה: מה תפוח הזה אינו גומר פירותיו אלא **בסיון** כך
לא נתנו ישר' ריח טוב בעולם אלא בסיני[!]. אימתי? "בחדש
השלישי" (שמ' יט 1)

Independent Use
Heb.

M Sheq. 3:1

בשלושה פרקים בשנה תורמים את הלשכה...בן עזי או':
בעשרים ותשעה באדר, באחד **בסיון**, בעשרים ותשעה באלול.
ר' לעזר ור' שמעון או': באחד בניסן, באחד **בסיון**, באחד
בתשרי

MekhRI VaYasa' 1
(p. 159)

ניסן שיצאו בו ישראל ממצרים אירע להיות בחמישי בשבת.
השלים ניסן. אירע אייר להיות בשבת. חסר אייר. אירע **סיון**
להיות באחד בשבת

Gen. Rab. 33:7
(p. 312)

"ותנח התבה בחדש השביעי..." (בר' ח 4) – זה **סיון** שהוא
שביעי לירידת גשמים

T Ta'an. 1:7 (Mo'ed
p. 325)

חצי תשרי מרחשון וחצי כסליו – זרע. חצי כסליו טבת וחצי
שבט – חורף. חצי שבט אדר וחצי ניסן – קור. חצי ניסן אייר
וחצי **סיון** – קציר. חצי **סיון** תמוז וחצי אב – קיץ. חצי אב אלול
וחצי תשרי – חום

'Ein Gedi (Naveh 1978:
no. 70): 5–7

ניסן אייר **סיון** תמוז אב אילול תשרי מרחשון כסליו טבת שבט
ואדר

Aram.

Eshel-Kloner 1–3   בירח **סיון** שנת 136 סִיֹלֹב[קוס מלכא] קוסרם בר קוסיד הו
בחדות לבבה [...] אמר[...] לקוסיד בר קוסיהב...

Cooke 129:5–6   ...בירח **סיון** די שנת 575
(Palm.)

EN 33:1–2 (Idum.)   היתי חלפת ב 15 **לסיון** ש כרן 2...

NṢ 13:1–2 (Yardeni I   בעשרין **לסיון** שנת תלת לחרת ישראל לשם שמע[ו]ן בר כסבה
p. 134)   נ[שי]א ישראל

BT Shab. 87b   הוה ליה ריש ירחא דאייר מעלי שבתא וריש ירחא ד**סיון** שבתא

1 Tg. Esth. 3:7   בכן שרי שמשי (ס)פרא לצבעא פייסא דעדבין קדם
המן...ושרי בירחיא. בניסן ולא על מן בגלל זכותא דפיסחא.
באייר ולא על מן בגלל דביה נחת מונא. ב**סיון** לא על מן בגלל
דביה איתיהיבת אוריתא בסיני...כד מטא לסוף תריסר ירחי
שתא דאיהוא ירחא דאדר...

Greek (LXX)

Bar. 1:8   ἀποστρέψαι εἰς γῆν Ιουδα τῇ δεκάτῃ τοῦ Σιουαν

COMMENTS

a. See the entry אֲדָר for general comments on month-names and the bibliography there.

See also BDB 695b.

סֵפֶר מֹשֶׁה n. m. (fixed phrase) *the Torah* (lit., *the book of Moses*): Neh. 13:1 בַּיּוֹם
35:12 ;הַהוּא נִקְרָא בְסֵפֶר מֹשֶׁה 2 Chron. 25:4 ;כַּכָּתוּב בַּתּוֹרָה בְסֵפֶר מֹשֶׁה
כַּכָּתוּב בְּסֵפֶר מֹשֶׁה

BA Ezra 6:18 וַהֲקִימוּ כָהֲנַיָּא בִּפְלֻגָּתְהוֹן...כִּכְתָב סְפַר מֹשֶׁה

CBH Alternatives

e.g., תורת משה, ספר תורת משה, ספר תורה

כַּכָּתוּב	בְּסֵפֶר	תּוֹרַת	**מֹשֶׁה**...　וּבָנִים לֹא יוּמְתוּ עַל אָבוֹת 2 Kgs. 14:6
[כַּכָּתוּב		בַּתּוֹרָה	**בְּסֵפֶר** **מֹשֶׁה**...　וּבָנִים לֹא יָמוּתוּ עַל אָבוֹת 2~] Chron. 25:4

לִשְׁמֹר	...חֻקֹּתָיו	כַּכָּתוּב	**בְּתוֹרַת**	מֹשֶׁה	1 Kgs. 2:3
[וַיָּסִירוּ	...הָעֹלָה	כַּכָּתוּב	**בְּסֵפֶר**	מֹשֶׁה	2~] Chron. 35:12

External Post-Classical Sources
Independent Use
Heb.

2Q25 f1:3	כן כתוב בספר מוש[ה]
4Q249 f1Vtitle:1	מדרש סֵפֶר מֹושֶׁה
4Q397 f14–21:10	[כתב]נֹו אליכה שתבין **בספר מושֹה** [ו]בספר[י הנ]בִיאים ובדוי[ד

Greek (LXX)

1 Esdr. 1:12	προσενεγκεῖν τῷ κυρίῳ κατὰ τὰ γεγραμμένα ἐν βιβλίῳ **Μωυσῆ**
1 Esdr. 5:48	προσενέγκαι ἐπ' αὐτοῦ ὁλοκαυτώσεις ἀκολούθως τοῖς ἐν τῇ **Μωυσέως βίβλῳ** τοῦ ἀνθρώπου τοῦ θεοῦ διηγορευμένοις
1 Esdr. 7:6	καὶ ἐποίησαν οἱ υἱοὶ Ισραηλ...ἀκολούθως τοῖς ἐν τῇ **Μωυσέως βίβλῳ**
1 Esdr. 7:9	καὶ ἔστησαν οἱ ἱερεῖς καὶ οἱ Λευῖται ἐστολισμένοι κατὰ φυλάς...ἀκολούθως τῇ **Μωυσέως βίβλῳ**
Tob. (Sinaiticus) 6:13	...ὀφειλήσειν θάνατον κατὰ τὴν κρίσιν τῆς **βίβλου Μωυσέως**...

Tob. (Sinaiticus)
7:12–13

… κατὰ τὴν κρίσιν τῆς βίβλου Μωυσέως … κατὰ τὴν κρίσιν τὴν γεγραμμένην ἐν τῇ βίβλῳ Μωυσέως δοῦναί σοι τὴν γυναῖκα

Mark 12:26

οὐκ ἀνέγνωτε ἐν τῇ βίβλῳ Μωϋσέως ἐπὶ τοῦ βάτου πῶς εἶπεν αὐτῷ ὁ θεὸς λέγων …

COMMENTS

a. "This phrase is typical only of sources from the Second Temple period" (Qimron 1986: 93). "One can see its prevalence in the later period from the modification made in the … parallel texts: בספר תורת משה (2Kgs 14:6); בתורה (2Chr 25:4)" (Qimron and Strugnell 1994: 93–94). Or, in a slightly different formulation, once the phrase ספר משה had been coined, we observe that "[t]he terms תורה, ספר משה, and תורת משה were used interchangeably in the later biblical books" (Pfann 1999: 2 note 6).

b. "The phrase is not found in MH, but perhaps only out of theological concerns concerning divine authorship …; likewise תורת משה is found in LBH and QH, but only rarely in MH" (Qimron and Strugnell 1994: 94). In any event, the late provenance of the pattern χ-סֵפֶר (χ denoting a proper name) as a designation for various Biblical compositions is clearly corroborated by QH; e.g.:

4Q163 f8–10:8	כתו[ב֫ בֹ בספר זכריה
4Q174 f1–2i:15	אשר כתוב בספרֹ ישעיה הנביא לאחרית ה[ה]ימים
4Q174 f1–3ii:3	אש[ר כתוב בספר דניאל הנביא
4Q176 f1–2i:4	ומן ספר ישעיה
4Q177 f7:3	אש[רׄ כֹתׄוב בספר יחזקאל הנ]ביא

c. תורת משה, ספר תורת משה, ספר התורה—all referring to *the Instruction/Law [of Moses]*—are widely assigned in scholarly literature (Weinfeld 1972: 339) to the phraseology of the Deuteronomist's editorial layer, whose chronological *terminus post quem* is generally associated with the destruction of the First Temple. Be that as it may, the decisive fact for the present discussion is that the Deuteronomist is completely unfamiliar with the distinctive LBH idiom ספר משה and that this term is not recorded in the books of the Pentateuch and the Prophets, even though these compositions make frequent reference to "The Instruction/Law [of Moses]". Thus, "the emergence of the term ספר משה in the books of Chronicles and Ezra-Nehemiah definitely indicates a [linguistic] innovation in the history of Biblical terminology related to the Torah" (Hurvitz 1997b: 43*).

BIBLIOGRAPHY

Baillet 1962: 90 • Hurvitz 1997b: 43* • Pfann 1999: 2 note 6 • Qimron 1986: 93 • Qimron and Strugnell 1994: 93–94 • Weinfeld 1972: 339

עַד לְ... comp. prep. *until, as much as*: 1 Kgs. 18:29 (cf. comment **d** below); Ezra
3:13; 9:4, 6; 10:14; 1 Chron. 4:39 וַיֵּלְכוּ לְמָבוֹא גְדֹר עַד לְמִזְרָח וְהַקּוֹל נִשְׁמַע עַד לְמֵרָחוֹק;
וַיֵּלֶךְ שְׁמוֹ 26:8; 5:9; 12:17, 23; 23:25; 28:7, 20; 2 Chron. 14:12; 16:12, 14; 17:12; 24:10; הַגַּיְא
עַד 36:16; 15–16, 28:9; 29:28, 30; 31:1, 10; 32:24, עַד לְבוֹא מִצְרַיִם כִּי הֶחֱזִיק עַד לְמָעְלָה
לְאֵין מַרְפֵּא

CBH ALTERNATIVES

עד, e.g.

Gen. 14:15			חוֹבָה	**עַד**		וַיִּרְדְּפֵם
[~ 2 Chron. 14:12			לִגְרָר	**עַד**	אָסָא וְהָעָם אֲשֶׁר עִמּוֹ	[וַיִּרְדְּפֵם]

Gen. 27:33	מְאֹד	**עַד**	גְּדֹלָה	חֲרָדָה	יִצְחָק	וַיֶּחֱרַד
[~ 2 Chron. 16:14	לִמְאֹד	**עַד**	גְּדוֹלָה	שְׂרֵפָה	לוֹ	[וַיִּשְׂרְפוּ]

2 Sam. 7:13	עוֹלָם	**עַד**	מַמְלַכְתּוֹ	כִּסֵּא	אֶת	וְכֹנַנְתִּי
[~ 1 Chron. 28:7	לְעוֹלָם	**עַד**	מַלְכוּתוֹ		אֶת	[וַהֲכִינוֹתִי]

EXTERNAL POST-CLASSICAL SOURCES
Renderings/Paraphrases/Glosses

TN 13x, e.g.

Gen. 13:15 יָת כָּל אַרְעָא דִי אַתְּ חָמֵי לָךְ אַתֵּן יָתַהּ וְלִבְנַיִךְ **עַד לְעָלַם**
[~ אֶת כָּל הָאָרֶץ אֲשֶׁר אַתָּה רֹאֶה לְךָ אֶתְּנֶנָּה וּלְזַרְעֲךָ **עַד** עוֹלָם]

TPJ 2x, e.g.

Gen. 3:22 אִין אָכֵיל הוּא מִנַּהּ הֱוֵי חַי וְקַיָּים **עַד לְעָלְמִין**
[~ וְאָכַל וָחָי **לְעֹלָם**]

TJ 4x, e.g.

Isa. 57:9 וַאֲמַאִיכַת תַּקִּיפֵי עַמְמַיָּא **עַד לִשְׁאוֹל**
[~ וַתַּשְׁפִּילִי **עַד** שְׁאוֹל]

Independent Use
Heb.

1QHᵃ 12:28 ובי האירותה פני רבים ותגבר **עד** **לאין** מספר
[~ Job 5:9 עֹשֶׂה גְדֹלוֹת וְאֵין חֵקֶר נִפְלָאוֹת **עַד** אֵין מִסְפָּר]

4Q378 f26:6 **ועד לעלמיה** זכור

M Ket. 9:1 אין לי בנכסייך ובפירותיהן ובפירי פירותיהם **עד לעולם**

Sifra Metzoraʿ 1:1 נמצאתה מרבה והולך **עד לעולם**

BT Shab. 7a (= 7b)

נעץ קנה ברשות היחיד וזרק ונח על גביו חייב, ואפי׳
גבוה מאה אמה, מפני שרשות היחיד עולה **עד** לרקיע

Scholion Meg. Ta'an. 25
Sivan (p. 72)

אמ׳ להם אלסכנדרוס: מה אתם משיבים להם? אמרו לו:
תן לנו זמן **עד** למחר

Aram.

TAD III 1.1 (= Cowley, Ahiqar): 52
TAD IV 22.27:1–3

אל תקטלני בלני לב[י׳][תך ע]תד[ד] ליומן אחרנן
בריך רבה תרכמנא...ובריך תרבמי...זי אתו
עד לפנה

BT Shab. 136a

אי אתרחיתו **עד** לאורתא, הוה אכלינן מיניה

Comments

a. עַד לְ is "a strengthened form for עַד, found chiefly in Ch Ezr" (BDB), "where the older language would find עַד or לְ alone sufficient" (S. R. Driver 1913: 538 no. 38). This construction is found "(a) before a *subst.* . . . (b) before an *inf.* . . ." (ibid.) and it is used: "1. [O]f *space* . . . 2. Of *time* . . . 3. Of *degree*" (BDB).

b. A superfluous לְ is found in several phrases and expressions attested in post-Classical writings, cf. the entries לְהַרְבֵּה, לְאַיִן, and לְרֹב מְאֹד. It has been noted that "Chronicles in general illustrates the late practice of multiplying the usage of *lᵉ* whenever possible" (Polzin 1976: 69).

c. Both phrases, עַד לְאֵין-χ and לְאֵין-χ, function as synonymous expressions in LBH and QH, with no clear distinction between them. See:

2 Chron. 21:18	מַרְפֵּא	לְאֵין		לָחֳלִי	בְּמֵעָיו	ה׳	נְגָפוֹ
2 Chron. 36:16	מַרְפֵּא	לְאֵין	עַד		בְּעַמּוֹ	ה׳	חֲמַת	עֲלוֹת	עַד

It may be suggested, therefore, either that עַד לְאֵין is a secondary expansion of the shorter לְאֵין, or, vice versa, that לְאֵין is an abbreviated form of the longer עַד לְאֵין. Whatever the case, both expressions belong to the distinctive vocabulary of LBH.

d. 1 Kgs. 18:29 וַיִּתְנַבְּאוּ עַד לַעֲלוֹת הַמִּנְחָה is the only occurrence of עַד לְ in BH that is outside the distinctive LBH corpus.

e. עַד לְבוֹא חֲמָת (Josh. 13:5; Judg. 3:3; 1 Chron. 13:5) is to be excluded from our discussion, since the לְ is not a preposition, but an integral component of the place name לְבוֹא חֲמָת (see, e.g., Amos 6:14 וְלָחֲצוּ אֶתְכֶם מִלְּבוֹא חֲמָת עַד נַחַל הָעֲרָבָה; 1 Kgs. 8:65; 2 Kgs. 14:25; 2 Chron. 7:8; Ezek. 47:20; see Mazar 1962: 417; Rainey 2007: 16; *pace* S. R. Driver 1913: 538 no. 38, BDB 725a; and *HALOT* II 787a).

f. Note that the CBH formula עַד + *temporal phrase* without לְ is also attested in the contemporaneous Arad and Lachish ostraca, e.g.:

Arad 7 (Dobbs- לחֹדֶשׁ   השׁשׁה **עַד** לחדש   לעשרי ב1
Allsopp et al.
p. 22): 3–5
[cf. Exod. 12:18   בָּרִאשֹׁן בְּאַרְבָּעָה עָשָׂר יוֹם לַחֹדֶשׁ... **עַד** יוֹם הָאֶחָד וְעֶשְׂרִים לַחֹדֶשׁ]

Lachish 18 (Dobbs-   הערב   **עד**
Allsopp et al.
p. 332): 2   [...] שׁלֹם יִשׁלח עֹבֹדְךָ הֹספר
[cf. Josh. 7:6   הָעֶרֶב   **עַד**   [וַיִּפֹּל עַל פָּנָיו אַרְצָה לִפְנֵי אֲרוֹן ה']
[~ Ezra 9:4   הָעֶרֶב לְמִנְחַת   **עַד**   [וַאֲנִי יֹשֵׁב מְשׁוֹמֵם]

g. Although לעלמיה in 4Q378 appears in a Hebrew passage, its form (יה-) seems to be Aramaic. *DJD* XXII (p. 261, line 6) renders 'its ages', but the orthography יֵה- (pronominal suffix of the 3rd person m. sg.) is not characteristic of DSS Aramaic and becomes common only in later Aramaic.

BIBLIOGRAPHY

BDB 725a • *HALOT* II 787a

S. R. Driver 1913: 538 no. 38 • Mazar 1962: 417 • Polzin 1976: 69, 141 • Qimron 1980: 249; 1986: 93 • Rainey 2007: 16 • Sáenz-Badillos 1993: 119, 122 • van Peursen 2004: 235–236

עֲזָרָה n. f. *court, enclosure* (*of the Temple precincts*): 2 Chron. 4:9 וַיַּעַשׂ חֲצַר הַכֹּהֲנִים
כִּי עָשָׂה שְׁלֹמֹה כִּיּוֹר נְחֹשֶׁת וַיִּתְּנֵהוּ בְּתוֹךְ הָעֲזָרָה 6:13; וְהָעֲזָרָה הַגְּדוֹלָה וּדְלָתוֹת לָעֲזָרָה

CBH ALTERNATIVES

חצר (cf. comment **d** below).

EXTERNAL POST-CLASSICAL SOURCES

Renderings/Paraphrases/Glosses

TJ 8x, e.g.

Isa. 1:12	**עזרתי**	תדושון	למיתי לא	מידכון	דא	תבע	מן
[~	**חֲצֵרָי**	רְמֹס		מִיֶּדְכֶם	זֹאת	בִקֵּשׁ	מִי]

Isa. 10:32	דבירושלם **עזרתא** ועל	דבציון	מקדשא בית	טור על	בידיה	... מוביל
[~	יְרוּשָׁלָ‍ם **גִּבְעַת**	צִיּוֹן	(ק') בַּת הַר	יָדוֹ	יָנֹפֵף]

Ezek. 43:8	**עזרתי**	בסטר	ובניניהון	מקדשי בית	ספי	כקביל	ספיהון	במתנהון
[~	**מְזוּזָתִי**	אֵצֶל	וּמְזוּזָתָם		סִפִּי	אֶת	סִפָּם	בְּתִתָּם]

Independent Use

Heb.

BS (B) 50:11	בעלותו על מזבח הוד ויהדר **עזרת** מקדש
M Suk. 5:4	הלוים בכינורות ובנבלים ובמצלתים ובכל כלי שיר בלא מספר על חמש עשרה מעלות היורדות **מעזרת** ישראל **לעזרת** הנשים
Sifra Nedava 6:2	איזה הוא צפון? מקירו שלמזבח הצפוני ועד כותל **העזרה** צפוני ועד כנגד מזבח

Aram.

Meg. Ta'an. 23 Marḥeshvan (p. 45)	בעשרים ותלתא למרחשון סתור סורגיא מן **עזרתא**

TJ 1 Sam. 3:3	דה' מהיכלא אשתמע וקלא ליואי **בעזרת** שכיב ושמואל
[~	ה' בְּהֵיכַל	שֹׁכֵב	וּשְׁמוּאֵל]

COMMENTS

a. The עֲזָרָה dealt with in this entry is not to be equated with the technical term עֲזָרָה which denotes the "ledge surrounding Ezekiel's altar" (BDB 741b; see Ezek. 43:14, 17, 20; 45:19; see also 11 QT 23:13–14).

b. "The term עזרה, usually translated 'temple court'... is considered to be the later equivalent for the more frequent חצר... [I]t is more widespread in later Hebrew, notably in the Mishnah and Tosefta.... עזרה is also attested in the

Aramaic Targum … to translate MT חצר …. It is clear that the term עזרה should be considered a late lexeme in BH which became preferred over חצר in the post-biblical period. In the Bible the term is restricted to LBH … " (Rooker 1990: 170–171).

c. In Aramaic, עזרה/עזרתא is a distinctive characteristic of JA, hence the suggestion (see Tal 1975: 167) that it is borrowed in Aramaic from Second-Temple Hebrew terminology. The proposed existence of a cognate root in OSA (see *HALOT* II 812b) does not rule out *a priori* the possibility that in Aramaic this term may have arrived as a (late) loanword via Hebrew.

d. In the synoptic description of Solomon's Temple in 1 Kings and 2 Chronicles, the word עֲזָרָה is to be found only in the latter book. Its first appearance is attested in 2 Chron. 4:9 as an expansion of 1 Kings:

1 Kgs. 7:38–40	וַיַּעַשׂ עֲשָׂרָה כִירוֹת … וַיִּתֵּן … חָמֵשׁ … מִיָּמִין וְחָמֵשׁ … מִשְּׂמֹאלוֹ
[~ 2 Chron. 4:6–11	וַיַּעַשׂ כִּיּוֹרִים עֲשָׂרָה וַיִּתֵּן חֲמִשָּׁה מִיָּמִין וַחֲמִשָּׁה מִשְּׂמֹאול

1 Kgs.	וַיַּעַשׂ חִירוֹם אֶת הַכִּירוֹת
2 Chron.	חֲצַר הַכֹּהֲנִים **וְהָעֲזָרָה** הַגְּדוֹלָה וּדְלָתוֹת **לָעֲזָרָה** וַיַּעַשׂ חוּרָם אֶת הַסִּירוֹת]

We cannot determine precisely the meaning of Chronicles' עֲזָרָה, but it clearly denotes an enclosure/courtyard of the Temple precincts. The parallel CBH term that seems to fulfill this function is חָצֵר, e.g.:

1 Kgs. 7:12	בֵּית ה'	וְהֶחָצֵר הַגְּדוֹלָה סָבִיב שְׁלֹשָׁה טוּרִים גָּזִית … וְלַחֲצַר הַפְּנִימִית וּלְאֻלָם הַבָּיִת
1 Kgs. 8:64	בֵּית ה'	הֶחָצֵר אֲשֶׁר לִפְנֵי בַּיּוֹם הַהוּא קִדַּשׁ הַמֶּלֶךְ אֶת תּוֹךְ

The older חָצֵר and more recent עֲזָרָה appear together in 2 Chron. 4:9. This should come as no surprise, for often the emergence of a neologism does not completely or systematically supplant its predecessor(s). Therefore, the coexistence of an LBH term and its CBH counterpart is quite common in Late Biblical writings. Consequently, even if certain architectural and/or functional differences existed between חָצֵר and עֲזָרָה in the Temple's cultic terminology, the very appearance of עֲזָרָה in the Bible is a clear indicator of linguistic lateness. Ascribing an עֲזָרָה to Solomon's Temple is thus an anachronism reflecting the linguistic milieu—and historical reality—of the Chronicler's period (cf. גנזך).

BIBLIOGRAPHY

GB 579a

Dihi 2004: 501–502 • Gesenius 1815: 29 • Howie 1950: 57 • Hurvitz 1982: 78–81 • Japhet 1993: 567 • Polzin 1976: 147 • Qimron 1986: 93 • Rooker 1990: 170–171; 1997 • Strauss 1900: 24 • Tal 1975: 167 • Zimmerli 1979: II 426

פִּתְגָם n. m. *decree, word*: Qoh. 8:11 אֲשֶׁר אֵין נַעֲשָׂה פִתְגָם מַעֲשֵׂה הָרָעָה מְהֵרָה ;Esth.
1:20 וְנִשְׁמַע פִּתְגָם הַמֶּלֶךְ אֲשֶׁר יַעֲשֶׂה בְּכָל מַלְכוּתוֹ

Cf. מַאֲמָר

BA פִּתְגָם Dan. 3:16; 4:14 בְּגֵזֵרַת עִירִין פִּתְגָמָא וּמֵאמַר קַדִּישִׁין שְׁאֶלְתָּא ;פִּתְגָמָא Ezra 4:17
כָּל אֱנָשׁ דִּי יְהַשְׁנֵא 6:11 ;פִּתְגָמָא הֲתִיבוּנָא לְמֵמַר 5:7, 11; שְׁלַח מַלְכָּא עַל רְחוּם בְּעֵל טְעֵם
פִּתְגָמָא דְּנָה יִתְנְסַח אָע מִן בַּיְתֵהּ

CBH Alternatives
דבר, e.g.

2 Sam. 24:4	אֶל יוֹאָב וְעַל שָׂרֵי הֶחָיִל	הַמֶּלֶךְ	**דְּבַר**	וַיֶּחֱזַק	
[~ Esth. 1:20	אֲשֶׁר יַעֲשֶׂה בְּכָל מַלְכוּתוֹ	הַמֶּלֶךְ	**פִּתְגָם**	וְנִשְׁמַע]	

External Post-Classical Sources
Renderings/Paraphrases/Glosses
TO 229x, e.g.

Gen. 22:1	אברהם	ית	נסי	וה׳	האילין	**פתגמיא**	בתר	והוה
[~	אַבְרָהָם	אֶת	נִסָּה	וְהָאֱלֹהִים	הָאֵלֶּה	**הַדְּבָרִים**	אַחַר	וַיְהִי]

Gen. 45:3	קדמוהי	מן	אתבהילו	ארי	יתיה	**פתגם**	לאתבא	אחוהי	יכילו	ולא
[~	מִפָּנָיו	נִבְהֲלוּ	כִּי	אֹתוֹ	לַעֲנוֹת	אֶחָיו	יָכְלוּ	וְלֹא]

TN 156x, e.g.

Num. 22:8	**פתגם**	יתכון	ואתיב	וליליא	הדין	יומא	הכה	אביתו
[~	**דְּבַר**	אֶתְכֶם	וַהֲשִׁבֹתִי	הַלַּיְלָה	פֹּה	לִינוּ]

TPJ 247x, e.g.

Num. 36:6	צלפחד	לבנת	...׳ה	דפקיד	**פתגמא**	דין
[~	צְלָפְחָד	לִבְנוֹת	ה׳	אֲשֶׁר צִוָּה	**הַדָּבָר**	זֶה]

TJ 852x, e.g.

Judg. 21:11	תגמרון	...דכורא	כל	דתעבדון	**פתגמא**	ודין
[~	תַּחֲרִימוּ	...זָכָר	כָּל	אֲשֶׁר תַּעֲשׂוּ	**הַדָּבָר**	וְזֶה]

1 Kgs. 17:8	למימר	עמיה	ה׳	קדם	מן	נבואה	**פתגם**	והוה
[~	לֵאמֹר	אֵלָיו	ה׳	**דְּבַר**	וַיְהִי]

Other Sources

11QTgJob 34:2–3	**פתגם**	והתיבני	אשאלנך	חלציך	כגבר	נא	אסר	
[~ Job 40:7		וְהוֹדִיעֵנִי	אֶשְׁאָלְךָ	חֲלָצֶיךָ	כְּגֶבֶר	נָא	אֱזָר־]	

Independent Use
Heb.

BS 5:11 (A)   היה ממהר להאזין ובארך רוח השב **פתגם**

BS 8:9 (A)   אל תמאס בשמיעת שבים אשר שמעו מאבתם כי ממנו תקח שכל
בְּעַת צֹ[רך] להשיב **פתגם**

4Q161 5–6:10   **פתגם** לאחרית הימים לבוא

4Q420 f1aii–b2   בארוך אפים ישיב **פתגם**

Aram.

TAD A6.8 (= Driver 4):   הן פסמש[ד] אחר קבלת מנך ישלח עלי חסן תשתאל וגסת
3–4   **פתגם** יתעבד לך

TAD D7.39:8   ושלח לי **פתגם**

4Q242 f1–3:1–2   מלי צ[ל]תא די צלי נֹבֹני מלך [בב]ל מלֹ֯[א] רבא כדי כתיש
הוא[ן] בשחנא באישא **בפתגם** א[ל]ה[א]

BT BB 136a   בין אקנייה וקנינא מיניה, בין קנינא מיניה ואקנייה – לֹא צריך,
בדוכרן **פתגמי** דהוה באנפנא פליגי

COMMENTS

a. "The noun is of Persian origin... and was adopted in Official Aramaic...,
BA..., Qumran-Aramaic..., JA... and Syriac. That it is an Aramaism, in
the sense that the Persian lexeme entered Hebrew through the medium of
Aramaic, can hardly be doubted" (Schoors 1992–2004: II 413) in light of its
distribution pattern (only in Daniel and Qoheleth) and etymology (a Persian
loanword [see Proleg. §II.3 Linguistic Affinities, *Persian Loanwords*], and [גֶּנֶז],
comment b]). It is of interest to note, however, that פתגם apparently did not
take root in post-Biblical Hebrew—neither in QH (where it is sparsely documented [2x according to Abegg's concordance of non-Biblical material: 4Q161
f5-6:10; 4Q420 f1aii-b:2]) nor in RH (where it is virtually not to be found).

b. "In Est 1,20, the word denotes an edict or decree. In the two instances in Sir,
it functions in the phrase השיב פתגם, 'give an answer' (cf. in BA: Dan 3,16; Ezr 5,
11), the equivalent of SBH השיב דבר. Thus the noun appears to mean 'word', a
general meaning that can be further specified according to the context and is
mostly in the public realm" (Schoors 1992–2004: II 413).

c. The linguistic contrast established in the Hebrew Bible between CBH דבר
המלך and LBH פתגם המלך, demonstrated above, is further corroborated by the
pre-Exilic Arad letters, which—as expected—employ the earlier phrase ודבר

הַמֶּלֶךְ אתכם בנבשכם (Arad 24 [Dobbs-Allsopp et al. p. 48] reverse: 6–7). See also מאמר, comment **b**.

Bibliography

BDB 834a • *HALOT* III 984a • Ben-Iehuda XI 5296b note 1 • Kaddari 890a
Barton 1908: 52–53, 155–156 • Bergey 1983: 102 • Delitzsch 1877: 190–196 • Dihi 2004: 571–573 • S. R. Driver 1913: 475 no. 12, 484–485 • Ginsberg 1969: 52 • Ginsburg 1861: 402 • Gordis 1968: 59 note 6 (p. 373), 296 • Kutscher 1982: 88, §131 • Naveh and Greenfield 1984: 121 (= Greenfield 2001: I 238) • Paton 1908: 65, 160 • Qimron 1986: 94 • Rabin 1962: 1079 • Schoors 1992–2004: II 413–414 • Torczyner 1938: 7 • Wagner 1966: 96 no. 241 • C. H. H. Wright 1883: 498 • R. M. Wright 2005: 114, 119–220

[**צוּרָה**] n. f. *form; drawing, plan*: 4x in Ezek. 43:11 ... (ק׳) וְכָל צוּרֹתָיו ... צוּרַת הַבַּיִת
וְכָל צוּרֹתוֹ (ק׳)... כָּל צוּרֹתָיו

CBH Alternatives

תבנית, דמות, מעשה, e.g.

...אֵת	**תַּבְנִית**	הַמִּשְׁכָּן	Exod. 25:9
וְאֵת	**תַּבְנִית**	כָּל כֵּלָיו	
וְזֶה	**מַעֲשֵׂה**	הַמְּכוֹנָה	1 Kgs. 7:28
	כְּמַעֲשֵׂה	אוֹפַן הַמֶּרְכָּבָה	1 Kgs. 7:33
[מִכֹּל אֲשֶׁר עָשׂוּ **צוּרַת**		הַבַּיִת	~ Ezek. 43:11]

וַיִּשְׁלַח הַמֶּלֶךְ אָחָז אֶל אוּרִיָּה הַכֹּהֵן אֶת	**דְּמוּת** הַמִּזְבֵּחַ		2 Kgs. 16:10
	וְאֵת **תַּבְנִיתוֹ**	לְכָל מַעֲשֵׂהוּ	
[הוֹדַע אוֹתָם וּכְתֹב לְעֵינֵיהֶם... אֵת כָּל **צוּרֹתוֹ**		וְאֵת כָּל חֻקֹּתָיו	~Ezek. 43:11]

External Post-Classical Sources
Renderings/Paraphrases/Glosses

TO 5x, e.g.

Deut. 4:16	נוקבא	או	דכר	דמות	**צורא**	כל	דמות	צלמא
[~	נְקֵבָה	אוֹ	זָכָר	תַּבְנִית	כָּל **סֶמֶל**	תְּמוּנַת	[פֶּסֶל

TN 7x (all seven appearances have been censored; cf. MS Neophyti), e.g.

Exod. 20:4	{**צלם וצורה**}	לכון	תעבדון	לא
[~	**פֶּסֶל**	לְךָ	תַעֲשֶׂה	[לֹא

TPJ 15x, e.g.

Exod. 25:9	מנוי	כל	**צורת**	וית	**צורת**	ית
[~	כֵּלָיו	כָּל	**תַּבְנִית**	וְאֵת	**תַּבְנִית**	[אֵת

Deut. 10:1	דקמאי	**כצורתהון**	מרמירא	לוחי	תרי	לך	פסל	
[~	כָּרִאשֹׁנִים		אֲבָנִים	לוּחֹת	שְׁנֵי	לְךָ	[פְּסָל	

TJ 15x, e.g.

Ezek. 28:12	בשופריה	ומשכלל	בחכמתא	דמתקן	**דצורתא**	**למנא**	דמי	את
[~	יֹפִי	וּכְלִיל	חָכְמָה	מָלֵא	**תָּבְנִית**	**חוֹתֵם**		[אַתָּה

Other Sources

1QM 7:10–11	מעשה חושב	רוקמה	**וצורת**	וארגמן...	תכלת	משוזר	שש
[~ Exod. 39:29	רֹקֶם	**מַעֲשֵׂה**	וְאַרְגָּמָן	וּתְכֵלֶת...	מָשְׁזָר	שֵׁשׁ

Independent Use

Heb.

1QM 5:5	והמגן מוסב מעשי גדיל שפה **וצורת** מחברת מעשה חושב
M Eruv. 1:1	מבויי...הרחב מעשר אמות ימעט. אם יש לו **צורת** הפתח, אפעלפי שהוא רחב מעשר אמות אינו צריך למעט
M AZ 3:3	המוציא כלים ועליהם **צורת** החמה, **צורת** הלבנה, **צורת** הדרקון – יוליבם[!] לים המלח
T Shab. 11:3 (Mo'ed p. 46)	הצר **צורה** – עד שיצור את כולה
MekhRI Shira 8 (p. 144)	מדת בשר ודם אינו יכול לצור **צורה** במים, אבל הקב״ה צר **צורה** במים, שנ' "ויאמר אלהים" (בר' א 20). מדת בשר ודם אינו יכול לצור **צורה** בעפר, והקב״ה צר **צורה** בעפר, שנ' "לא נכחד עצמי ממך אֲשֶׁר עֻשֵּׂיתִי בַסֵּתֶר רֻקַּמְתִּי בְּתַחְתִּיּוֹת אָרֶץ" (תה' קלט 15)

Aram.

4Q552 f1ii:2–3	ואמר֯ [...] **צורתא** ואמרת אן אחזא ואתב[ונ]ן ב[ה]
PAT 1091:1–7	דכירין ובריכין...אנשיא דצירי[ן]...[ד]י צרו **צורתא** הד[א]...
BT Pes. 104a	ואמאי קרו ליה בן בנן שלקדושים? דאפילו **בצורתא** דזוזי לא מיסתכלי
BT BM 45b	מאי טע' דמאן דאמ' אין מטבע נעשה חליפין? משום דדעתיה **אצורתא**, **וצורתא** עבידא דבטלה

COMMENTS

a. Deut. 4:16 contains four different CBH nouns belonging to the semantic field of form/image (פֶּסֶל, תְּמוּנָה, סֶמֶל, תַּבְנִית); צוּרָה is not listed among them (in TO to this verse, צוּרָא is rendered for Heb. סֶמֶל, whereas in TPJ to Exod. 25:9 צורת is rendered for Heb. תַּבְנִית—see above).

b. Note that Arabic صورة is regarded as a loan from Aramaic (Fraenkel 1886: 272–273).

Bibliography

Kaddari 907a

Fraenkel 1886: 272–273 • Howie 1950: 58 • Hurvitz 1982: 82–84, 161–162 • Qimron 1986: 94 • Zunz 1892: 169

צָפִיר n. m. *he-goat*: Dan. 8:5 וְהַצָּפִיר קֶרֶן חָזוּת בֵּין עֵינָיו...וְהִנֵּה צְפִיר הָעִזִּים בָּא, 8, 21;
בְּנֵי הַגּוֹלָה הִקְרִיבוּ עֹלוֹת...צְפִירֵי חַטָּאת שְׁנֵים עָשָׂר Ezra 8:35; וְהַצָּפִיר הַשָּׂעִיר מֶלֶךְ יָוָן
וּצְפִירֵי עִזִּים שִׁבְעָה לְחַטָּאת 2 Chron. 29:21

וְהַקְרִבוּ...וּצְפִירֵי עִזִּין לְחַטָּאָה (ק') עַל כָּל יִשְׂרָאֵל תְּרֵי עֲשַׂר לְמִנְיָן שִׁבְטֵי יִשְׂרָאֵל BA Ezra 6:17

CBH Alternatives
שעיר (cf. Dan. 8:21 above); e.g.

Num. 28:15	לְחַטָּאת	אֶחָד	עִזִּים	**וּשְׂעִיר**
[~ 2 Chron. 29:21	לְחַטָּאת	שִׁבְעָה	עִזִּים	**וּצְפִירֵי**

External Post-Classical Sources
Renderings/Paraphrases/Glosses
TO 84x, e.g.

Gen. 37:31	בִּדְמָא	כִּתּוּנָא	יָת	וְטַבְלוּ	עִזֵּי	בַּר	**צְפִירָא**	וּנְכַסוּ
[~	בַּדָּם	הַכֻּתֹּנֶת	אֶת	וַיִּטְבְּלוּ	עִזִּים		**שָׂעִיר**	וַיִּשְׁחֲטוּ]

Num. 28:30	עֲלֵיכוֹן	לְכַפָּרָא	חַד	עִזִּין	בַּר	**צְפִיר**	
[~	עֲלֵיכֶם	לְכַפֵּר	אֶחָד	עִזִּים		**שָׂעִיר**]	

TN 61x, e.g.

Lev. 4:24	יָ(ת/)יה	וְיִכּוּס	**דִּצְפִירָה**	רֵישָׁהּ	עַל	יְדֵיהּ	וְיִסְמוֹךְ
[~	אֹתוֹ	וְשָׁחַט	**הַשָּׂעִיר**	רֹאשׁ	עַל	יָדוֹ	וְסָמַךְ]

TPJ 57x, e.g.

Lev. 16:20	חַיָּא	**צְפִירָא**	יָת	וִיקָרֵב
[~	הֶחָי	**הַשָּׂעִיר**	אֶת	וְהִקְרִיב]

TJ 3x, e.g.

Ezek. 43:25	לְיוֹמָא	דַּחַטָּתָא	**צְפִירָא**	תַּעֲבֵיד	יוֹמִין	שַׁבְעָה
[~	לַיּוֹם	חַטָּאת	**שָׂעִיר**	תַּעֲשֶׂה	יָמִים	שִׁבְעַת]

Other Sources

Pesh. Lev. 16:15	דְּעַמָּא	דַּחַטְהָא	**צְפִירָא**		וּנְכוּס
[~	אֲשֶׁר לָעָם	הַחַטָּאת	**שָׂעִיר**	אֶת	וְשָׁחַט]

Independent Use

Aram.

BT AZ 28b   והני מילי פיקעא עילאה, אבל פיקעא תתאה ניתי תרבא **דצפירדתא**

דלא פתח וניפשר ונישדי בה

BT Yoma 66b   תנא: מאשי **צפירא** זעיר חוביה דדרא סגיאין

(relates to the Heb. שעיר of Lev. 16)

COMMENTS

a. The expression שְׂעִיר עִזִּים is quite common in the cultic terminology of P, where it is found some 25 times. P is entirely unfamiliar with צָפִיר עִזִּים, which is attested exclusively in the LBH corpus (Daniel, Ezra, Chronicles). In a non-cultic context in the book of Genesis we find שְׂעִיר עִזִּים, but not its later counterpart צָפִיר עִזִּים: "... then they ... slaughtered a kid (שְׂעִיר עִזִּים), and dipped the tunic in the blood" (Gen. 37:31 [NJPS]).

b. צפיר did not take root in RH and is seldom used outside the Targumim; nevertheless, it is attested only in LBH and, consequently, is widely regarded as a late Aramaism.

c. It is highly questionable whether Ug. and Phoen. צפר (*HALOT* III 1048b) is etymologically related to the Biblical צפיר.

d. Dan. 8:21 וְהַצָּפִיר הַשָּׂעִיר may be a doublet/gloss.

BIBLIOGRAPHY

BDB 862a • *HALOT* III 1048b

Collins 1993 • S. R. Driver 1913: 507 no. 19 • Montgomery 1927: 331 • Polzin 1976: 149 • Rabin 1962: 1075 • Wagner 1966: 99 no. 248 • Williamson 1977a: 44

וַאֲנַחְנוּ נִכְרֹת עֵצִים מִן הַלְּבָנוֹן כְּכָל צָרְכֶּךָ וּנְבִיאֵם לָךְ 2 Chron. 2:15 *need* n. m. ‏[צֹרֶךְ]

CBH ALTERNATIVES

חפץ, e.g.

אֲנִי אֶעֱשֶׂה אֵת כָּל חֶפְצְךָ בַּעֲצֵי אֲרָזִים 1 Kgs. 5:22

‏[~ 2 Chron. 2:15] וַאֲנַחְנוּ נִכְרֹת עֵצִים מִן הַלְּבָנוֹן כְּכָל צָרְכֶּךָ

EXTERNAL POST-CLASSICAL SOURCES
Renderings/Paraphrases/Glosses

TO 5x, e.g.

מרוד באנשא הוא יהי צריך לכולא ואף אנשא יהי צריך ליה Gen. 16:12

‏[~ פֶּרֶא אָדָם יָדוֹ בַכֹּל וְיַד כֹּל בּוֹ

אֲרֵי ה׳ ... אֱלָהָךְ ... סופיק לך צורכך במהכך ית מדברא רבא הדין Deut. 2:7

‏[~ כִּי ה׳ אֱלֹהֶיךָ ... יָדַע לֶכְתְּךָ אֶת הַמִּדְבָּר הַגָּדֹל הַזֶּה

TN 13x, e.g.

ותזופון לאומין סגין ואתון עמי לא תצרכון למיזף Deut. 15:6

‏[~ וְהַעֲבַטְתָּ גּוֹיִם רַבִּים וְאַתָּה לֹא תַעֲבֹט

לא תעצי אגריה דמסכינה וצריכה מן אחיכון או מן גיוריכון Deut. 24:14

‏[~ לֹא תַעֲשֹׁק שָׂכִיר עָנִי וְאֶבְיוֹן מֵאַחֶיךָ אוֹ מִגֵּרְךָ

ארום תיעול כאריס בכרמייה דחברך ותאכל ענבים דצורכה ותשבע Deut. 23:25

‏[~ כִּי תָבֹא בְּכֶרֶם רֵעֶךָ וְאָכַלְתָּ עֲנָבִים כְּנַפְשְׁךָ שָׂבְעֶךָ

TPJ 27x, e.g.

הא יהיבת לכון ית כל עיסבא... וית כל אילני סרקא לצרוך Gen. 1:29
ביניינא ולאסקותא

‏[~ הִנֵּה נָתַתִּי לָכֶם אֶת כָּל עֵשֶׂב... וְאֶת כָּל הָעֵץ

ית דאתון צריכין למיפא מחר...וית דאתון צריכין למבשלא מחר... Exod. 16:23

‏[~ אֵת אֲשֶׁר תֹּאפוּ... וְאֵת אֲשֶׁר תְּבַשֵּׁלוּ...

TJ 47x, e.g.

1 Kgs. 5:23	ואת תטול ואת תסופיק ית **צרכי** למתן מזון לאנש ביתי
[~	וְאַתָּה תִשָּׂא וְאַתָּה תַעֲשֶׂה אֶת **חֶפְצִי** לָתֵת לֶחֶם בֵּיתִי
Isa. 54:12	ואשוי כמרגלין אעך ותרעך לאבני גמר וכל תחומך לאבני **צרוך**
[~	וְשַׂמְתִּי כַּדְכֹד שִׁמְשֹׁתַיִךְ וּשְׁעָרַיִךְ לְאַבְנֵי אֶקְדָּח וְכָל גְּבוּלֵךְ לְאַבְנֵי **חֵפֶץ**
Isa. 58:13	אם תתיב משבתא רגלך למעבד **צרכך** ביומא דקודשי... ומלסופקא **צורכך**
[~	אִם תָּשִׁיב מִשַּׁבָּת רַגְלֶךָ עֲשׂוֹת **חֲפָצֶיךָ** בְּיוֹם קָדְשִׁי... מִמְּצוֹא **חֶפְצְךָ**
Isa. 60:19	לא **תצטרכין** עוד לניהור שמשא ביממא ואף לזיהור סיהרא בליליא
[~	לֹא יִהְיֶה לָּךְ עוֹד הַשֶּׁמֶשׁ לְאוֹר יוֹמָם וּלְנֹגַהּ הַיָּרֵחַ לֹא יָאִיר לָךְ

Independent Use

Heb.

BS 15:12 (A)	כי אין **צורך** באנשי חמס
~ (B)	כי אין לי **חפץ** באנשי חמס
BS 39:16 (B)	...וכל **צורך** בעתו יספיק
~ (marg. B)	לכל **צריך** ב׳ יספיקו

4Q372 f1:17–18	ואין אתה **צריך** לכל גוי ועם לכל עזרה
11QT 47:7–10	כול עור בהמה טהורה אשר יזבחו בתוך עריהמה לוא יבי/ואו לה כי בעריהמה יהיו עושים בהמה מלאכתמה לכול **צורכיהמה** ואל עיר מקדשי לוא יבי/ואו
M Shab. 18:3	כל **צורכי** מילה עושין בשבת
MekhRI BaḤodesh 6 (p. 224)	היה לו של זהב **וצרך** לו–עשאו של כסף. ⟨היה לו של כסף⟩ **וצרך** לו–עשאו של נחשת. היה לו של נחשת **ונצרך** לו– עשאו של ברזל או מעופרת
MekhRS 6:2 (p. 6)	וכי למה **הוצרך** הדבר ⟨לומר⟩ אם לקח עמרם אשה אם לא לקח? אלא להודיע לכל באי העולם זכותו של עמרם הצדיק
Sifre Deut. 343 (p. 395)	ואף שמנה עשרה ברכות שתיקנו נביאים הראשונים שיהו ישראל מתפללים בכל יום, לא פתחו **בצורכן** של ישראל עד שפתחו בשבחו של מקום

Aram.

PT Ter. 9:7 (p. 254)	לפום כן **צרכינן** מימר דר׳ שמעון היא
PT BM 2:4 (p. 1219)	לא דהבך ולא כספך אנא **צריך**
BT Eruv. 12a	ואתא לקמיה דרב יהודה ולא **אצרכיה** אלא פס אחד

COMMENTS

a. "Quite a few Hebrew roots which are very common in MH first appear in LBH, e.g., the root of MH צָרִיךְ 'to need', in צָרְכְּךָ 'your need' (II Chron. 2, 15)" (Kutscher 1982: 83 §123).

b. "It is noteworthy that BH lacks an unequivocal lexeme for the concept צֹרֶךְ.... By and large the imperative is used in this sense: אַתֶּם הֵאָסְרוּ (= *You must stay in prison* [Gen 42:16]); [or] the regular future, e.g., וּמִפָּנֶיךָ אֶסָּתֵר (= *I need to remain hidden* (*from you*) [Gen 4:14]); and likewise וְעָלַי לָתֶת לְךָ עֲלִי: (= *I should have given you* [2 Sam 18:11]). In contrast to BH, the late language found it necessary to coin an unequivocal word to signify this notion, and thus the root צרך became widespread" (Kutscher 1961: 78).

c. Regarding the etymology and semantic range of √צרך, it is generally maintained that "its basic meaning is *to be needy/poor*; this is indeed the sense of the corresponding root in Arabic.... and it is also extant in our [Rabbinic] source.... How did this root spring up in the late literature?... The consonantal form of the root צרך and its presence in Ugaritic suggest a Hebrew origin. Yet, the grammatical form [צריך] and its frequency in the Aramaic dialects point to an Aramaic provenance.... [W]e can only postulate... that Aramaic assimilated this root at an early date from one of the Canaanite dialects... and there the root became increasingly widespread" (Kutscher 1961: 78). Be that as it may, "we must assume that Aramaic was the determining factor for the widespread diffusion of the root צרך in RH" (Moreshet 1980: 313 note 18**). Note further that חֵפֶץ״ (40x)—the parallel of צורך in the early books (1 Kgs 5:22)—was pushed aside by the word under discussion and became diminished in Rabbi's [= Rabbi Judah's] Mishnah" (Gluska 1999: 58).

d. In addition to nouns, this entry also includes some post-Biblical (Hebrew and Aramaic) verbal forms that reflect the wide distribution and versatility of the root in later periods.

BIBLIOGRAPHY

BDB 863b • *HALOT* III 1056a

Dihi 2004: 605 • Gluska 1999: 58 • Kutscher 1961: 77–78; 1982: 83 §123 • Moreshet 1980: 312–313

√**קבל** vb. *accept, receive, take*: **Pi'el** Prov. 19:20 שְׁמַע עֵצָה וְקַבֵּל מוּסָר (cf. comment a below); Job 2:10 ...וְאֶת הָרָע לֹא נְקַבֵּל גַּם אֶת הַטּוֹב נְקַבֵּל (cf. Prol. §II.4); Esth. 4:4 ...וְלֹא קִבֵּל;27 ,9:23 וַתִּשְׁלַח בְּגָדִים לְהַלְבִּישׁ אֶת מָרְדֳּכַי; הַיְּהוּדִים (ק') קִיְּמוּ וְקִבְּלוּ ;1 Chron. עֲלֵיהֶם...לִהְיוֹת עֹשִׂים Ezra 8:30 וְקִבְּלוּ הַכֹּהֲנִים וְהַלְוִיִּם מִשְׁקַל הַכֶּסֶף וְהַזָּהָב; 12:19 וַיְקַבְּלֵם דָּוִיד וַיִּתְּנֵם בְּרָאשֵׁי הַגְּדוּד;22 ,2 Chron. 29:16 וַיְקַבְּלוּ הַכֹּהֲנִים אֶת הַדָּם; 21:11

BA Dan. 2:6 וְהַדַּר יְקָר וּמְדָאָה (ק') קַבֵּל מַלְכוּתָא מִן קֳדָמָי...וִיקָר שַׂגִּיא תְּקַבְּלוּן מִן קֳדָמַי; 6:1 מַתְּנָן...; 7:18 וִיקַבְּלוּן מַלְכוּתָא קַדִּישֵׁי עֶלְיוֹנִין

CBH Alternatives

√לקח, e.g.

וַיִּקַּח	מֹשֶׁה חֲצִי הַדָּם...	וַחֲצִי	הַדָּם	זָרַק	עַל	הַמִּזְבֵּחַ	Exod. 24:6
וְלָקַחְתָּ		אֶת	דָּמוֹ	וְזָרַקְתָּ	עַל	הַמִּזְבֵּחַ	Exod. 29:16
[**וַיְקַבְּלוּ**	הַכֹּהֲנִים	אֶת	הַדָּם	וַיִּזְרְקוּ		הַמִּזְבֵּחָה	~ 2 Chron. 29:22]

וַיִּקַּח...	אֶת		הַזָּהָב...	וַיָּבִאוּ	אֹתוֹ	אֶל אֹהֶל מוֹעֵד	Num. 31:54
[**וְקִבְּלוּ**...	מִשְׁקַל	הַכֶּסֶף	וְהַזָּהָב...	לְהָבִיא	לִירוּשָׁלַם	לְבֵית אֱלֹהֵינוּ	~ Ezra 8:30]

External Post-Classical Sources

Renderings/Paraphrases/Glosses

TO 221x, e.g.

Exod. 11:9	פרעה	מנכון	**יקביל**	לא	
[~	פַּרְעֹה	אֲלֵיכֶם	**יִשְׁמַע**	לֹא]	

Lev. 17:16	חוביה	**ויקביל**	יסחי	לא	ובסריה	יצבע	לא ואם
[~	עֲוֹנוֹ	**וְנָשָׂא**	יִרְחָץ	לֹא	וּבְשָׂרוֹ	יְכַבֵּס	לֹא וְאִם]

TN 140x, e.g.

Exod. 30:16	ישראל	בני	מן לוות	פורקניה	כסף	ית **ותקבל**
[~	יִשְׂרָאֵל	בְּנֵי	מֵאֵת	הַכִּפֻּרִים	כֶּסֶף	אֶת **וְלָקַחְתָּ**]

Deut. 16:19	שחוד	**תקבלון**	ולא	בדינה	אפין תסבון ולא בדינה תסטון לא
[~	שֹׁחַד	**תִקַּח**	וְלֹא	פָּנִים	תַכִּיר לֹא מִשְׁפָּט תַטֶּה לֹא]

TPJ 252x, e.g.

Num. 1:2	ישראל	דבני	כנישתא	כל	חושבן	ית **קבילו**
[~	יִשְׂרָאֵל	בְּנֵי	עֲדַת	כָּל	רֹאשׁ	אֶת **שְׂאוּ**]

TJ 439x, e.g.

עבדך	דיצלי	צלותא		**לקבלא**
עַבְדְּךָ	אֲשֶׁר יִתְפַּלֵּל	הַתְּפִלָּה	אֶל	[~ **לִשְׁמֹעַ**

1 Kgs. 8:29

אציתא	לפולחני	וכנשתי	עמי	למימרי	**קבילו**
הַאֲזִינוּ	אֵלַי	וּלְאוּמִּי	עַמִּי	אֵלַי	[~ **הַקְשִׁיבוּ**

Isa. 51:4

Other Sources

יקבל	מידך	מא	או	לה	תתן	מא	זכי]ת	[הן
יִקָּח	מִיָּדְךָ	מַה	אוֹ	לוֹ	תִּתֶּן	מַה	צָדַקְתָּ	[אִם

11QTg Job 26:1–2

[~ Job 35:7

"ולקח" (וי׳ יד 14) – יכול בכלי? תל׳ לו' "**ולקח** הכהן...ונתן הכהן" Sifra Metzoraʿ 3:2 (שם). מה נתינה בעצמו שלכהן אף **קבלה** בעצמו שלכהן

	בימינו	**מקבל**		דם אשמו של מצורע
הַכֹּהֵן מִדַּם הָאָשָׁם		**וְלָקַח**		]

T Zev. 1:10 (p. 480)

[~ Lev. 14:14

Independent Use

Heb.

BS (A) 15:2 וקדמתהו כאם וכאשת נעורים **תקבלנו**

BS (B) 50:12 **בקבלו** נתחים מיד אחיו והוא נצב על מערכות

1QSa 1:11 ובכן **תקבל** להעיד עליו משפטות התורא ולהתיצׄב במשמע משפטים

4Q171 f1–2ii:8–9 וענוים ירשו ארץ והתענגו על רוב שלום – פשרו על עדת האביונים אשר **יקבלו** את מועד התענית/התעות

M Ber. 2:7 וכשמת טבי עבדו **קיבל** עליו תנחומים. אמרו לו: לא לימדתנו שאין **מקבלין** תנחומין על העבדים? אמ׳ להם: אין טבי עבדי כשאר כל העבדים – כשר היה

M Peʾah 2:6 אמר נחום הליבלר: **מקובל** אני מרבי מיישא **שקיבל** מאבא **שקיבל** מן הזוגות **שקיבלו** מן הנביאים הלכה למשה מסיני

Aram.

4Q550 f2:7 ...**ותקבל** עבידת אבוך

NṢ 8:5 (Yardeni I p. 67) ותקלי כספה אנה **מקבל** דמין גמרין

Gen. Rab. 49:4 (p. 502) אין **מקבל** עלוי לברך הוה אכיל ושתי ואזיל ליה. ואין לא **יקבל** הוה אמר ליה: הב מה דעלך

Lam. Rab. 1:4 תו נעביד בינגא דלא **נקבל** חד מנהון

COMMENTS

a. Eliahu Levita (Bachur; 1468/1469–1549) wrote about the verb קבל: "This is Aramaic. For this reason it is not to be found other than in the exilic [/post-exilic] books and in addition once in Proverbs and twice, in one verse, in Job; but it is not to be found neither in the Torah nor in the Prophets" (Levita 1847: 438). This view is widely accepted in modern scholarship, e.g., "לקבל = 'to receive, take' is widely used in post-Exilic Hebrew, in Tannaitic and Talmudic literature alike. It is also very common in the Aramaic sources: earlier and later, western and eastern. In BH, however, the usage of לקבל is clearly characteristic of the post exilic writings: out of 9 occurrences outside [the post-Classical narrative framework of] Job [which contains 2 examples], 8 are found in Esther, Ezra and Chronicles—all of which are known to have been written in the Persian period at the earliest. Once (XIX 20) לקבל also appears in the chronologically disputable book of Proverbs—which, therefore, cannot bear upon our discussion—but never does it occur in any of the biblical compositions which were without doubt written in pre-exilic times" (Hurvitz 1974b: 20–21).

b. "In SBH 'to receive' is לָקוֹחַ.... In LBH the Aramaic loan קַבֵּל is used instead.... the reason for the change is obvious. Because of the semantic change of לָקוֹחַ [which in RH had come to mean *buy*].... [a] new verb was urgently needed, so Aramaic קַבֵּל was 'accepted' by Hebrew and became very common in MH" (Kutscher 1982: 83–84 §123).

c. Note that the late Biblical expression דם + √קבל (2 Chron. 29:22) is widely attested as a technical sacrificial term in RH in both verbal and nominal forms (קיבל/ניתקבל/קיבול + דם).

d. Against Albright's (1943: 31 note 16) oft-echoed claim, that √קבל *receive* is to be found already in Amarna Canaanite, see Moran (1975: 149 note 1) and Rainey (2002: 51–52). Even if this individual case of an Akkadian proverb reflecting Canaanite √קבל *receive* is granted, it still does not change the fact that in Hebrew the verb in question became an unequivocal linguistic marker only in Second Temple times—most probably under Aramaic influence. We may, therefore, conclude as follows: "קבל (Piel) appears in Hebrew prose of post-exilic times; but it is not found in EBH where לקח is the standard lexeme. לקח remains the preferred form throughout LBH.... Also לקח is the more frequently used term of the two in the DSS. So from the literary evidence, it seems that קבל never thoroughly permeated the language until Tannaitic times. Nevertheless, its appearance in Esther, Ezra, and Chronicles is the earliest indication of this lexeme's penetration into the Hebrew literary sources, an entrance which was the harbinger of its gradually increased use as is evident especially in the Mishna" (Bergey 1983: 146–147; see also his instructive remarks in note 2).

Bibliography

BDB 867a, 1110a • *HALOT* III 1061b, V 1965a • Kaddari 929a

Albright 1943: 31 note 16 • Bendavid 1967–71: I 62, 411 • Bergey 1983: 145–147 • Curtis and Madsen 1910: 33 no. 103, 250 • Dihi 2004: 606–608 • S. R. Driver 1913: 536 no. 11 • Hurvitz 1974b: 20–23; 1982: 22 • Kutscher 1966: 22; 1982: 83–84 §123 • Levita 1847: 438 • Moran 1975: 149 note 1 • Paton 1908: 218, 298 • Polzin 1976: 149–150 • Rainey 2002: 51–52 • Strauss 1900: 25 • von Soden 1968: 264; 1977: 193 • Williamson 1977a: 43 • R. M. Wright 2003: 140–142; 2005: 103–106

√קום vb. Pi'el *confirm, establish, fulfill, sustain* Ezek. 13:6 לְקַיֵּם דְּבַר; Ps. 119:28
לְקַיֵּם כָּל דָּבָר 4:7 Ruth ;(below b comment .cf) נִשְׁבַּעְתִּי וָאֲקַיֵּמָה 106, קַיְּמֵנִי כִּדְבָרֶךָ
(cf. comment c below); Esth. 9:21, 27 קִיְּמוּ וְקִבְּלוּ (ק')...לִהְיוֹת עֹשִׂים, לְקַיֵּם אֶת 29
וּמַאֲמַר אֶסְתֵּר קִיַּם 32 ,31, אִגֶּרֶת הַפּוּרִים

BA Dan. 6:8 לְקַיָּמָה קְיָם מַלְכָּא וּלְתַקָּפָה אֱסָר (cf. Dan. 6:27 קְיָם and comment f)

CBH ALTERNATIVES
Usually √קום Hiph, e.g.

Num. 30:14	וְאִישָׁהּ יְפֵרֶנּוּ		**יְקִימֶנּוּ**	אִישָׁהּ...			כָּל נֵדֶר...
[~ Esth. 9:32		וְנִכְתָּב בַּסֵּפֶר	**קִיַּם**	...אֶסְתֵּר	וּמַאֲמַר		

1 Sam. 15:13		ה'	אֵת	דְּבַר	**הֲקִימֹתִי**	
[~ Ezek. 13:6				דְּבָר	**לְקַיֵּם**	חָזוּ שָׁוְא וְקֶסֶם כָּזָב...וְיִחֲלוּ]

Exod. 13:10	לְמוֹעֲדָהּ	הַזֹּאת	הַחֻקָּה	אֵת		**וְשָׁמַרְתָּ**
[~ Esth. 9:31	בִּזְמַנֵּיהֶם	הָאֵלֶּה	הַפֻּרִים	יְמֵי	אֵת	**לְקַיֵּם**

EXTERNAL POST-CLASSICAL SOURCES
Renderings/Paraphrases/Glosses
TO Pa'el 105x, Itpa'al 24x, e.g.

Gen. 26:3	אבוך	לאברהם	**דקיימית**	קימא	ית	וְאקִים
[~	אָבִיךָ	לְאַבְרָהָם	אֲשֶׁר נִשְׁבַּעְתִּי	הַשְּׁבֻעָה	אֶת	**וַהֲקִמֹתִי**]

Deut. 19:15	פתגמא	**יתקיים**	...סהדין	תרין	מימר		עַל
[~	דָּבָר	**יָקוּם**	...עֵדִים	שְׁנֵי	פִּי	עַל]	

TN Pa'el 123x, Itpa'al 7x, e.g.

Num. 30:12	יקום	נפשה	על	**קיימת**	די	קיימה וכל	ויקומון כל נדרה
[~	יָקוּם	נַפְשָׁהּ	עַל	אָסְרָה	אֲשֶׁר	אִסָּר וְכָל נְדָרֶיהָ	וְקָמוּ כָּל]

Gen. 19:20	נפשי **ותתקיים** היא זעירא הלא ...לתמן למיערק קריבא הדא קרתא				
[~	נַפְשִׁי **וּתְחִי** הוּא מִצְעָר הֲלֹא ...שָׁמָּה לָנוּס קְרֹבָה הַזֹּאת הָעִיר]				

TPJ Pa'el 113x, Itpa'al 31x, e.g.

Gen. 12:12	**יקיימון** ויתיך יתי ויקטלון ...מצראי ביד יסתכלון ארום ויהי			
[~	**יְחַיּוּ** וְאֹתָךְ אֹתִי וְהָרְגוּ ...הַמִּצְרִים אֹתָךְ יִרְאוּ כִּי וְהָיָה]			

לא **יתקיים** סהדן דחד בגבר... ועל מימר תרין סהדין... **יתקיים** פיתגמא Deut. 19:15

[~ דָּבָר **יָקוּם**... שְׁנֵי עֵדִים עַל פִּי... בְּאִישׁ אֶחָד עֵד **יָקוּם לֹא**]

TJ Pa'el 209x, Itpa'al 90x, e.g.

דא נעביד להון **ונקיים** יתהון... על קימא **דקיימנא** להון Josh. 9:20

[~ לָהֶם **נִשְׁבַּעְנוּ** אֲשֶׁר הַשְּׁבוּעָה עַל קֶצֶף... אוֹתָם וְהַחֲיֵה לָהֶם נַעֲשֶׂה זֹאת]

עוד **אקימיניך ותתקימין** כנשתא דישראל Jer. 31:4

[~ עוֹד **אֶבְנֵךְ וְנִבְנֵית** בְּתוּלַת יִשְׂרָאֵל]

Independent Use
Heb.

CD 20 (= CD^b2):
11–12 (but nowhere
else in DSS)

כי דברו תועה על חקי הצדק ומאסו בברית ואמנה אשר **קימו** בארץ דמשק והוא ברית החדשה

NŞ 49:7–12 (Yardeni
I p. 19)

תסלע הזוא אנמקבל המך שאפרך בכל זמן שת]ומ[ר לי ואשה את השטר הזא [וא]ם לא לא **יתקים** לי והתשלם [מן]ביתי ומן נכסי. **וקים** עלי כול שאש על השטר הזא...

M San. 4:5

וכל **המקים** נפש אחת מעלין עליו כילו קים **קיים** עולם מלא

M Avot 4:9

כל **המקים** את התורה מעוני, סופו **לקיימה** מעושר

M Shab. 12:1

זה הכלל: כל העושה מלאכה ומלאכתו **מתקיימת** בשבת – חייב

M Neg. 9:3

חכם גדול אתה **שקיימתה** את דברי חכמ'

MekhRI Pisḥa 14
(p. 48)

כהרף עין נסעו בני ישראל מרעמסס לסוכות, **לקיים** מה שנאמר "ואשא אתכם על כנפי נשרים" וג' (שמ' יט 4)

Sifra Tzav 2:1

שני כתובין – אחד **מקים** עצמו **ומקיים** חבירו ואחד **מקים** עצמו ומבטל חבירו – תופשין את **המקיים** עצמו **ומקיים** חבירו ומניחין את **המקיים** עצמו ומבטל חבירו

BT Shab. 30a

מנהגו של עולם, מלך בשר ודם גוזר גזרה אחת – ספק **מקיימין** אותה, ספק אין **מקיימין** אותה. ואם תימצא לומ' **מקיימין** אותה – בחייו **מקיימין** אותה, במותו אין **מקיימין** אותה. ואילו משה רבנו גזר כמה גזירות ותיקן כמה תקנות מעצמו **ומקויימות** הן לעולם ולעולמי עולמים

Aram.

4Q201 f1ii:4–6	חזו דכל איל[ניה] כֹלהן מיבישין [ומנפילין כל עליהן ברא] מן ארבעת
	עסר אילֹנֹי[ן] דֹעֹליהן **מתקימי**ֹ [ולא מחדתין עליהן עד] דֹתרתין ותלת
	שנין [יעברן]
4Q462 f1:12	ויעבודו **ויתקימו** ויזעקו אל ה׳
NḤ 7:2 (Yardeni I p. 96)	בעשרין וארבעה בתמוז שנת עשר וחמש במחוז עגלתין יהב **ומקים** במלה **קימה** מתנת עלם די לא תעדה מן רעותי
NṢ 8:6–7 (Yardeni I p. 67)	ואנה יהונתן מזבנה וכול די איתי לי ודי אקנה אחראין וערבין **למקימה** [ולמרק]א אתריה] אל[ך] מכול חרר ותג]ר
Lev. Rab. 33:6 (p. 769)	אמ׳ להון: או דאתון **מקימין** רישיה דפסוקא או דאנא **מיקים** סופיה
PT Ber. 1:3 (p. 8)	הא דבית הלל **מקיימין** תרין קרייא. מה **מקיימין** דבית שמי "בשבתך ביתך ובלכתך בדרך" (דב׳ ו 7) ?

COMMENTS

a. "The formation of the conjugations *Pi'el*, *Pu'al* and *Hithpa'el* is, strictly speaking, excluded by the nature of verbs ע״ו. It is only in the latest books that we begin to find a few secondary formations, probably borrowed from Aramaic…" (GKC 197 §72m). In light of the close morphological connection between these three 'strong' conjugations, we have included some examples of *pu'al* and *hitpa'el* in the Hebrew post-Biblical examples above, as well as forms of *itpa'al* in Aramaic.

b. "We know of קֵיֵם in the Pi'el in the sense of 'confirm, perform, strengthen, validate', found in Biblical Hebrew already in books from the end of the First Temple period, and thereafter in the books actually composed during the Second Temple era, as illustrated by the following examples: ויחלו לְקַיֵם דבר 'and they would be able to confirm the word' (Ezek 13:6), לְקַיֵם כל דבר 'to confirm all things' (Ruth 4:[7]), קַיְּמֵנִי 'strengthen me' (Ps 119:28), וָאֲקַיֵמָה 'and I will perform' (Ps 119:106); כאשר קִיֵם עליהם מרדכי 'as Mordechai (…) had enjoined them' (Esth 9:31 and six further occurrences in this book)" (Bar-Asher 2003: 88–89).

c. לְקַיֵם in Ruth 4:7 "cannot be defended as old Hebrew … the word occurs in a verse which is not needed in the narrative, and has every appearance of being an *explanatory gloss*" (S. R. Driver 1913: 455). "[E]vidence for the lateness of the book as a whole depends, of course, upon whether one considers the digression that 4:7 represents to have been added to the text by the author of the rest of the book or by a later hand" (Bush 1996: 29).

d. Beside the late קִיֵם (*Pi'el* with a consonantal *yod*) in Ezekiel, this book often makes use of the Classical form הֵקִים (*Hiph'il*, with the *yod* functioning as a vowel letter). The simultaneous employment of both the old הֵקִים and its later equivalent קִיֵם in Ezekiel ought to be regarded as "a mark of transition from the classical to the later style" (Cooke 1936: 143). Similarly, "[t]he usage in the book of Ruth fits this transitional stage, for the *hiphil* לְהָקִים occurs in 4:5, 10, whereas the *piel* appears in 4:7" (Bush 1996: 27).

e. √קום in Ps. 119:106 נִשְׁבַּעְתִּי וָאֲקַיֵּמָה may echo the semantic nuance of 'making an oath', widely attested in Aramaic (see above the Targums to Gen. 26:3 and Josh. 9:20; and see Ben-Iehuda XII 5910a note 2).

f. Note that the prevalent RH adjective קיים (cf. the common divine epithet חי וקיים [attested already in the Aramaic of Dan. 6:27 אֱלָהָא חַיָּא וְקַיָּם לְעָלְמִין]) is morphologically related to the above *pi'el* form (it has been suggested that this Hebrew-Aramaic epithet also lies behind the Arabic الحي القيوم; see Jefferey 1938: 244–245).

g. Note that within Aramaic itself, √קום in *pa'el* is attested already in the Assur Ostracon (7th century BCE): *KAI* 233:9 ידיהם כתבת וקימת קדמי. However, its appearance on the Biblical scene in Hebrew is indicative of post-Exilic times. Cf. מערב, comment d.

BIBLIOGRAPHY

BDB 878b • *HALOT* III 1087b • GKC 197, §72m • JM 198 §80 *h* • Kaddari 939b Bar-Asher 2003: 86–93 • Bendavid 1967–71: I 62, II 481, 485 • Bergey 1983: 40–42 • Bush 1996: 27, 29 • Cooke 1936: 143 • Delitzsch 1871: 248 • S. R. Driver 1913: 454–455 • Hurvitz 1972: 34 note 73, 139–142; 1982: 32–35 • Jefferey 1938: 244–245 • Nebe 1997: 152 • Paton 1908: 294 • Paul 1984: 108–109 note 31 • Qimron 1986: 95 • Rooker 1990: 83–85 • Sáenz-Badillos 1993: 125 • van Peursen 2004: 34–35 • Wagner 1966: 137–138 • R. M. Wright 2005: 32–34 • Zimmerli 1979–83: I 22, 293

√קרה vb. *lay ceiling beams* (denominative from קוֹרָה *beam*): **Pi'el** Ps. 104:3 יְתֵּן לִי עֵצִים לִקְרוֹת אֶת שַׁעֲרֵי הַבִּירָה Neh. 2:8 ;הַמְקָרֶה בַמַּיִם עֲלִיּוֹתָיו הַשָּׂם עָבִים רְכוּבוֹ הֵמָּה קֵרוּהוּ וַיַּעֲמִידוּ דַּלְתֹתָיו, 6; 2 Chron. 34:11 3:3

CBH ALTERNATIVES

√ספן (?), e.g.

1 Kgs. 7:2–3	בָּאֶרֶז			**וְסָפַן** ... הַלְּבָנוֹן	יַעַר	בֵּית	אֶת	וַיִּבֶן
1 Kgs. 6:9	בָּאֲרָזִים	הַבַּיִת...	אֶת	**וַיִּסְפֹּן**	וַיְכַלֵּהוּ	הַבַּיִת	אֶת	וַיִּבֶן
[~ 2 Chron. 34:11	הַבָּתִּים	אֶת	**וְלִקְרוֹת** ... מַחְצֵב	אַבְנֵי				[לִקְנוֹת

(מְקַרְקַע הַבַּיִת עַד קִירוֹת הַסִּפֻּן **הַסִּפֻּן** 1 Kgs. 6:15 ספן n. cf. also)

EXTERNAL POST-CLASSICAL SOURCES

Renderings/Paraphrases/Glosses

MekhRI Shira 8 (p. 144)	מדת בשר ודם, כשהוא **מקרה מקרה** בעצים ובאבנים ובעפר...והקב״ה **קירה** עולמו במים, שנ' "**המקרה** במים עליותיו" (תה' קד 3)
M Mid. 2:5	וארבע לשכות היו בארבע מקצעות שלארבעים ארבעים אמה, לא היו **מְקֹורוֹת**..."ובארבעת מקצעות החצר חצירות קטורות" (יח' מו 22)...ואין "קטורות" אלא שאינן **מְקֹורוֹת**

Independent Use

Heb.

11QT 41:14–16	ורוחב פתחי השערים ארבע עשרה באמה וגובהמה שמונה ועשרים באמה עד המשקוף, **ומקורים** באדשכים עץ ארז ומצופים זהב
11QT 42:10–11	ועל גג השלישית תעשה עמודים **ומקורים** בקורות מעמוד אל עמוד
M Suk. 1:8	**הַמְקָרֶא** סוכתו בשפודים או בארוכות המטה, אם יש ריוח ביניהן כמותן – כשירה
M Mo'edQ 1:4	**וּמְקָרִים** את הפירצה במועד, ובשביעית בונה כדרכו
T BM 8:32 (Nez. p. 110)	המשכיר בית לחבירו ונפל – חייב להעמיד לו בית. היה **מקורה** בארזים – לא **יקרינו** בשקמים. בשקמים – לא **יקרינו** בארזים
[~ 1 Kgs. 6:9	[וַיִּבֶן אֶת הַבַּיִת וַיְכַלֵּהוּ **וַיִּסְפֹּן** אֶת הַבַּיִת גֵּבִים וּשְׂדֵרֹת בָּאֲרָזִים
BMM 2 (pp. 159–160)	כיצד היו **מקרין** המשכן? היו מביאין עשר יריעות של תכלת ושל ארגמן ושל תולעת שני ושל שש...והיה מחברן לחמשים קרסי זהב

COMMENTS

a. Apart from one occurrence in Ps. 104 (v. 3 הַמְקָרֶה בַמַּיִם עֲלִיּוֹתָיו 'who layeth the beams of his chambers in the waters' [KJV])—a psalm whose language exhibits features suggestive of late composition (Hurvitz 1972: 172–173)—"√קרה, 'to install a ceiling (תִּקְרָה)', appears in the Hebrew Bible also in Nehemiah (3x) and Chronicles [1x], as well as in the Temple Scroll... and

Rabbinic Hebrew. Thus, this verb and also some nouns derived from √קרה are characteristic of late Hebrew" (Qimron 1978: 150).

b. The near absence of this verb in Aramaic (it is apparently found only in the Talmudic phrase תיקרייה בסיפי בבא; see *DJPA* 1042a–b) may be explained by its suggested denominative origin from the Hebrew n. קוֹרָה—which is practically not documented in Aramaic.

BIBLIOGRAPHY

DJPA 1042a–b

Hurvitz 1972: 172–173 • Qimron 1978: 150

רָאוּי adj. (pass. ptc. Qal) *befitting, suitable, proper*: Esth. 2:9 וַיְבַהֵל אֶת...שֶׁבַע הַנְּעָרוֹת הָרְאֻיוֹת לָתֶת לָהּ

BA Dan. 3:19 לְמֵזֵא לְאַתּוּנָא חַד שִׁבְעָה עַל דִּי חֲזֵה לְמֵזְיֵהּ

EXTERNAL POST-CLASSICAL SOURCES
Renderings/Paraphrases/Glosses

TO 15x, e.g.

כגזירת	פסחא	**וכדחזי ליה**	כין	יעביד	
[כְּחֻקַּת	הַפֶּסַח	**וּכְמִשְׁפָּטוֹ**	כֵּן	יַעֲשֶׂה	~]

Num. 9:14

TN 12x, e.g.

	דלא	יפול	**מן דחמי לה**	למיפל	מניה
[כִּי	יִפֹּל			הַנֹּפֵל	מִמֶּנּוּ ~]

Deut. 22:8

TPJ 28x, e.g.

לדא	**חמי למיקרי**	איתא	ארום	מגבר	איתניסיבת	דא	
[לְזֹאת	**יִקָּרֵא**	אִשָּׁה	כִּי	מֵאִישׁ	לֻקֳחָה	זֹּאת	~]

Gen. 2:23

מן	בעירא	דהיא	**חזיא**	לכון	למיכול
[מִן	הַבְּהֵמָה	אֲשֶׁר הִיא		לָכֶם	לְאָכְלָה ~]

Lev. 11:39

TJ 26x, e.g.

מא	יהי	**דחזי**	לרביא	ומא	נעביד ליה
[מַה	יִּהְיֶה	**מִשְׁפַּט**	הַנַּעַר		וּמַעֲשֵׂהוּ ~]

Judg. 13:12

	ויוקדניה	באתר	**דחזי**	לביתא
[וְשָׂרְפוֹ		בְּמִפְקַד		הַבָּיִת ~]

Ezek. 43:21

Other Sources

	מאן	**חמי**	לימדר	במשכנך
[מִי			יָגוּר	בְּאָהֳלֶךָ ~]

Tg. Ps. 15:1

Independent Use
Heb.

11QT 66:8–10   כי יפתה איש נערה בתולה אשר לוא אורשה והיא **רויה** לו מן החוק ושכב עמה ונמצא

NH 44:11–13 (Yardeni I p. 113)   המקום שנקרה החפֿיר והמקום שנקרה הסלם והעפר הלבן שבהם ותכל אילן שבהם **כראוי** להֿם וכחזקתם

M Shab. 16:2	מצילים מזון שלוש סעודות. **הראוי** לאדם – לאדם. **והראוי** לבהמה – לבהמה
M Bez. 2:5	לא יחם אדם חמים לרגליו אלא אם כן היו **ראוים** לשתייה
M Ket. 6:6	יתומה שהשיאתה אמה ואחיה וכתבו לה מאה וחמשים זוז – יכולה היא משתתגדיל להוציא מידן מה **שראוי** להינתן לה
M BQ 6:1	הכונס צאן לדיר ונעל בפניה **כראוי** ויצתה והזיקה – פטור. לא נעל בפניה **כראוי** ויצתה והזיקה – חייב
T Pes. 10:4 (Moʻed p. 196)	מצוה על אדם לשמח בניו ובני ביתו ברגל. במה משמחן?...נשים **בראוי** להם וקטנים **בראוי** להם
MekhRI Pisḥa 1 (p. 2)	עד שלא נבחר בית עולמים היתה ירושלם **ראויה** לשכינה...עד שלא נבחר אהרן היו כל ישראל **ראוים** לכהונה...עד שלא נבחר דוד היו כל ישראל **ראויים** למלכות
MekhRI Nez. 17 (p. 308)	"מהור ימהרנה לו לאשה" (שמ׳ כב 15) – **בראויה** לו לאשה הכתוב מדבר, להוציא אלמנה לכהן גדול, גרושה וחלוצה לכהן הדיוט...
Sifra Milu'im 1:2	"וישא אהרן את ידיו אל העם ויברכם וירד מעשות" וג׳ (וי׳ ט 22) – זה מקרא מסורס, אילא **ראוי** לומר: וירד מעשות הח[טאת] והע[ולה] והש[למים] [ולמם] "וישא אהרן את ידיו אל העם ויברכם"

Aram.

Nṣ 8:7 (Yardeni I p. 67)	ובזמן די תמרון לי אחלף לך שטרה דנה כדי **חזה**
Nṣ 50:8–11 (Yardeni I p. 37)	אתרא דך בתחומה ובמצרה תאניא וכל די בה ודי **חזא** עלה מעלא ומפקא כדי **חזא** דך זבנת לכן בכסף זוזין שבעין ותמניה די המון סלעין תשע עסרה ותקל חד לחוד
NḤ 7:39–40 (Yardeni I p. 97)	תחומוהי למד[נ]חא [ג]רמאלה בר ערהזו ולמ[ערבא נ]הרא דכ[ר]א [וירתי יו]חנן בר בבא ולדרומא ולצ[פונ]אֹ [מ]נֹלס בר עותלה וענימיה כדי **חזא**
PT BM 5:2 (p. 1226)	אתא עובדא קומי ר׳ בא בר מינא. אמ׳ ליה: וקים ליה מה דהוה **חמי** למישרי
Gen. Rab. 65:13 (p. 724)	"תליך" (בר׳ כז 3) – אמר ליה: הרי ברכות תלויות. למאן **דחמי** ליה למתברכה – הוא מתברך
BT Ber. 50b	ולרבנן מאי **חזי**? א״ר זירא: **חזי** לקוריייטי

COMMENTS

a. "The word ראוי first occurs in LBH ... where it has the sense 'destined'.... It occurs frequently in MH, sometimes (as in QH) with a legal sense... [C]ompare the Aramaic כדחזי which is common in legal documents, and also appears as a translation of BH כמשפט (e.g., Lev 5:4)" (Qimron and Strugnell 1994: 95 §3.5.2.29a).

Bibliography

Dihi 2004: 628–629 • S. R. Driver 1913: 485 • Nebe 1997: 152 • Paton 1908: 63, 177 • Qimron 1986: 95 • Qimron and Strugnell 1994: 95 §3.5.2.29a

שְׁבָט pr. n. name of 11th month, derived from Akkad. *šabātu*: Zech. 1:7 בְּיוֹם עֶשְׂרִים
וְאַרְבָּעָה לְעַשְׁתֵּי עָשָׂר חֹדֶשׁ הוּא חֹדֶשׁ שְׁבָט

CBH Alternatives

Months are generally named by their numerical order, e.g., 1 Kgs. 12:32
בַּחֹדֶשׁ הַשְּׁמִינִי; in a few cases they follow the Canaanite pattern, e.g., 1 Kgs. 8:2
בְּיֶרַח הָאֵתָנִים. Only in the LBH corpus do we find both (the older) numerical
system and (the more recent) Mesopotamian names side by side in one and
the same verse; e.g., Esth. 3:7 לְחֹדֶשׁ שְׁנֵים עָשָׂר הוּא חֹדֶשׁ אֲדָר.

Deut. 1:3	בְּאֶחָד לַחֹדֶשׁ	**בְּעַשְׁתֵּי** **עָשָׂר** **חֹדֶשׁ**	שָׁנָה	בְּאַרְבָּעִים	וַיְהִי
[~ Zech. 1:7		**לְעַשְׁתֵּי** **עָשָׂר** **חֹדֶשׁ** הוּא חֹדֶשׁ **שְׁבָט**	וְאַרְבָּעָה	עֶשְׂרִים	בְּיוֹם

External Post-Classical Sources
Renderings/Paraphrases/Glosses

TPJ 1x

Deut. 1:3	בירחא	בחד	הוא ירחא **דשבט**	ירח	בחדסר	...והוה	
[~	בְּאֶחָד לַחֹדֶשׁ			חֹדֶשׁ עָשָׂר בְּעַשְׁתֵּי ...וַיְהִי]			

TJ 1x

Zech. 1:7	**שבט** ירחא הוא ירחין עסר לחד וארבעה עסרין ביום							
[~	**שְׁבָט** חֹדֶשׁ הוּא חֹדֶשׁ עָשָׂר לְעַשְׁתֵּי וְאַרְבָּעָה עֶשְׂרִים בְּיוֹם]							

Other Sources

Tg. 1 Chron. 27:14	ירחא **דשבט** בניה דמן פרעתון לחדסר חדסיראה				
[~	הַפִּרְעָתוֹנִי בְּנָיָה הַחֹדֶשׁ עָשָׂר לְעַשְׁתֵּי עָשָׂר עַשְׁתֵּי]				

Independent Use
Heb.

Mur. 24b:1–3
(Yardeni I p. 107)
[ב]עשרין **לשבט** שנת שתׁיׁם [ל]גאלת ישראל על יד[] ש[מעון בן
כוסבא נסיא ישרא]ל[

M RoshH 1:1
באחד **בשבט** ראש שנה לאילן כדברי בית שמי ובית הלל אומרין
בחמשה עשר בו

T RoshH 1:8
(Mo'ed p. 307)
ופירות נטיעה זו אסורין עד חמשה עשר **בשבט** אם ערלה ערלה
ואם רבעי רבעי

T Ta'an. 1:7
(Mo'ed p. 325)
חצי תשרי מרחשון וחצי כסליו – זרע. חצי כסליו טבת וחצי
שבט – חורף. חצי **שבט** אדר וחצי ניסן – קור. חצי ניסן אייר וחצי
סיון – קציר. חצי סיון תמוז וחצי אב – קיץ. חצי אב אלול וחצי
תשרי – חום

MekhRI Vayasaʿ 5 (pp. 172–173)	שבעים יום אכלו ישראל את המן אחר מיתתו של משה. הא כיצד? מת משה בשבעה **בשבט** ואכלו הימנו עשרים וארבעה של **שבט** ושלשים של אדר, ואותה שנה לא היתה מעוברת, וששה עשר של ניסן
ʿEin Gedi (Naveh 1978: no. 70): 5–7	ניסן אייר סיון תמוז אב אילול תשרי מרחשון כסליו טבית **שבט** ואדר

Aram.

Cooke 81:1–10 (Nab.)	דנה כפרא...די עבד חושבו בר כפיו...בירח **שבט** שנת עשר ותלת לחרתת מלך נבטו רחם עמה
EN 103:1–2 (Idum.)	ב 22 **לשבט** שנת 14 חנאל קמח חנטן...
Mur. 23:3–5 (Yardeni I p. 29)	ב 10 **לשבט** שנת...זֹבנת לך בכסֹף סֹלֹע[ין]...
1 Tg. Esth. 3:7	בכן שרי שמשי (ס)פרא לצבעא פייסא דעדבין קדם המן...ושרי בירחיא. בניסן ולא על מן בגלל זכותא דפיסחא...**בשבט** לא על מן בגלל דהוא ריש שתא לאילני דמנהון מתקרבין בכוריא. כד מטא לסוף תריסר ירחי שתא דאיהוא ירחא דאדר...

Greek (LXX)

1 Macc. 16:14	ἔτους ἑβδόμου καὶ ἑβδομηκοστοῦ καὶ ἑκατοστοῦ ἐν μηνὶ ἑνδεκάτῳ (οὗτος ὁ μὴν Σαβατ)

COMMENTS

a. See the entry אֲדָר for general comments on month-names and the bibliography there. See also BDB 987a.

√**שלט** vb. *have power over, dominate, rule*: **Qal** Qoh. 2:19 ;וְיִשְׁלַט בְּכָל עֲמָלִי
שְׁבְרוּ...לִשְׁלוֹט בָּהֶם...יִשְׁלְטוּ...בְּשֹׂנְאֵיהֶם, Esth. 9:1; שָׁלַט הָאָדָם בְּאָדָם לְרַע לוֹ 8:9;
Neh. 5:15 נַעֲרֵיהֶם שָׁלְטוּ עַל הָעָם. **Hiph** Ps. 119:133 וְאַל תַּשְׁלֶט בִּי כָל אָוֶן (cf. comment
e below); Qoh. 5:18; 6:2 וְלֹא יַשְׁלִיטֶנּוּ הָאֱלֹהִים לֶאֱכֹל מִמֶּנּוּ

Cf. שליט, שלטון

BA Pe'al Dan. 2:39 וְתַלְתִּי; 5:7 דִּי לָא שְׁלֵט נוּרָא בְּגֶשְׁמְהוֹן; 3:27 דִּי תִשְׁלַט בְּכָל אַרְעָא;
שְׁלְטוּ בְהוֹן אַרְיָוָתָא וְכָל גַּרְמֵיהוֹן הַדִּקוּ 6:25; וְתַלְתָּא בְמַלְכוּתָא תִּשְׁלַט 5:16; בְּמַלְכוּתָא יִשְׁלַט
Haph'el Dan. 2:38 וְהַשְׁלְטֵהּ עַל כָּל מְדִינַת בָּבֶל 2:48; וְהַשְׁלְטָךְ בְּכָלְּהוֹן

CBH Alternatives
√משל, √רדה, e.g.

Judg. 15:11			**מֹשְׁלִים**	בָּנוּ	פְּלִשְׁתִּים
[~ Esth. 9:1			שָׁבְרוּ אֹיְבֵי הַיְּהוּדִים **לִשְׁלוֹט** בָּהֶם]		

Lev. 26:17	**וְרָדוּ**...	בָּכֶם שֹׂנְאֵיכֶם
Isa. 14:2	**וְרָדוּ**...	בְּנֹגְשֵׂיהֶם
[~ Esth. 9:1	וְנַהֲפוֹךְ הוּא אֲשֶׁר **יִשְׁלְטוּ** הַיְּהוּדִים הֵמָּה בְּשֹׂנְאֵיהֶם]	

Post-Classical External Sources
Renderings/Paraphrases/Glosses
TO 18x, e.g.

Gen. 1:17–18	לְאַנְהָרָא	עַל	אַרְעָא	**וּלְמִשְׁלַט**	בִּימָמָא	וּבְלֵילְיָא
[~	לְהָאִיר	עַל	הָאָרֶץ	**וְלִמְשֹׁל**	בַּיּוֹם	וּבַלַּיְלָה]

TN 18x, e.g.

Gen. 1:28	תְּקוֹפוּ	וּסְגוֹן	וּמְלוֹן	יָת	אַרְעָא...	**וּשְׁלוֹטוּ**	בְּנוּנֵי	דִימָא
[~	פְּרוּ	וּרְבוּ	וּמִלְאוּ	אֶת	הָאָרֶץ...	**וּרְדוּ**	בִּדְגַת	הַיָּם]

TPJ 19x, e.g.

Exod. 7:28–29	וְירְבֵי	נַהְרָא	עוּרְדְעָנַיָּא...	וּבְכָל	עַבְדָּךְ	**יִשְׁלְטוּן** עוּרְדְעָנַיָּא
[~	וְשָׁרַץ	הַיְאֹר	צְפַרְדְּעִים...	וּבְכָל	עֲבָדֶיךָ	**יַעֲלוּ** הַצְּפַרְדְּעִים]

TJ 57x, e.g.

Jer. 10:25	אֲרֵי	**שְׁלִיטוּ**	בִּדְבֵית	יַעֲקֹב...	וְשֵׁיצִיאוּנוּן	וְיָת מְדוֹרֵיהוֹן אַצְדִיאוּ
[~	כִּי	**אָכְלוּ**	אֶת	יַעֲקֹב...	וַיְכַלֻּהוּ	וְאֶת נָוֵהוּ הֵשַׁמּוּ]

Cf. Dan. 6:25 above.

Independent Use
Heb.

BS 33:21 (E)   עד עודך חי ונשמה בך אל **תשלט** בך כל [...]
11QPsᵃ 19:15–16   אל **תשלט** בי שטן ורוח טמאה מכאוב ויצר רע אל ירשו בעצמי
M Men. 10:4   נתנוהו לאבוב, ואבוב היה מנוקב כדי שיהא האור **שולט** בכולן
MekhRI   כביכול איני מעמיד ואיני **משליט** עליכם אחרים אלא אני...איני
BaḤodesh 2   ממליך עליכם מאומות העולם אלא מכם
(p. 208)

PT Ber. 9:1 (p. 68)   ושולט ביבשה   בים   **שולט**   הקב״ה
[~ Ps. 89:10   הַיָּם   בְּגֵאוּת   **מוֹשֵׁל**   [אַתָּה

Aram.

TAD II 3.5   גבר אחרן אמי ואבי אח ואחה ואיש אחרן לא **ישלט** בביתה כלה
(= Krael. 4): 19-20   להן בני זי ילדתי לי
1QApGen 20:15   ואל **ישלט** בליליא דן לטמיא אנתתי מני
4Q544 f2:15   והוא **משלט** על כול חשוכה
Drijvers P1:15   ולא **אשתלט** למהפך במלי שטרא הנא
BT BM 85a   ר׳ זירא יתיב מאה תעניתא...לא הוה **שלטא** ביה נורא

COMMENTS

a. "The verb [שלט] does not occur in the Hebrew Bible, but [only] after
the Babylonian exile, under Aramaic influence" (Ben-Iehuda XIV 7152b
note 2). "While we find the root משל common throughout the Hebrew Bible,
and שלט in Qoheleth and in the Mishnah, there is no doubt as to the cause of
this linguistic change; and although the lexeme שליט occurs in Genesis (42:6),
by no means can it be maintained that the root שלט was native and early in
Hebrew usage: the root may be admissible in Hebrew, but it was isolated, rare,
and unproductive. The impetus to replace the word-group ימשל-ימשיל-ממשלה
with שלטון-ישליט-ישלט—this general change occurred only because of the
influence of Aramaic" (Bendavid 1967–71: I 127). In a slightly different formulation, it may also be said that "[i]n Qoheleth √שלט is the norm, whereas √משל
is the exception, and this is also an indication of lateness. In the Hebrew prior
to Qoheleth, Nehemiah, Esther and Rabbinic literature one finds the opposite"
(Ginsberg 1961: 29).

b. "Aramaic *šlṭ* is used to indicate possession of an item or power over it. It
is used in legal documents in the various Aramaic dialects.... In Aramaic
texts it is first attested in the Elephantine documents.... The Hebrew
use of *šlṭ* is obviously based on that of Aramaic" (Greenfield 1987: 39–40

[= 2001: I 415–416]). "[I]n early Biblical Hebrew there is one instance of the verb *mšl* (in legal context) clearly with the same meaning: *lō' yimšōl l^emokrāh* Ex 21:8, which recalls the expression *l' šlyt...lzbnh* (*AP* 9:6) as against *'ēn 'ādām šallīṭ...lik^elo' 'et hārū^aḥ*, Koh 8:8" (Kutscher 1954: 239 [= 1977: 43]).

c. שלט is regularly followed by the preposition ב; however, in Neh 5:15 we find על and in Qoh. 5:18; 6:2—an infinitive (לאכל).

d. The root שלט in various nominal and verbal forms is regarded as an Aramaic-oriented latecomer not only in BH, but in Akkadian and Arabic as well: "The rare N[eo-]A[ssyrian] and common N[eo-]B[abylonian] and L[ate-]B[abylonian] use of this verb in legal formulae is probably modeled after Aramaic usage, not the reverse" (Kaufman 1974: 99); "The material...from diverse periods of the Aramaic language shows that the verb *šlṭ* and even more so the noun *šallīṭ* was [!] used in legal and theological contexts. The use of the verb *šallaṭa* in the Qur'ān, in particular, and in the later Arabic sources should be seen as being influenced by this usage" (Greenfield 1987: 41 [= 2001: 417]).

e. For the linguistic status of Ps. 119, see Hurvitz 1972: 151–152; for a detailed discussion of √שלט, see ibid., 134–136.

BIBLIOGRAPHY

BDB 1020b; 1115b • *HALOT* IV 1521b • Ben-Iehuda XIV 7152b notes 1, 2 • Kaddari 1098b Barton 1908: 52–53, 95 • Bendavid 1967–71: I 127 • Bergey 1983: 140–141 • Delitzsch 1877: 191–192 • S. R. Driver 1913: 475 no. 13, 553 note * • Fensham 1982: 22–23 • Ginsberg 1961: 29 • Greenfield 1987: 39–41 (= 2001: 415–417) • Hadas-Lebel 1995: 111 • Hurvitz 1968: 239 note 27; 1972: 134–136 • Jeffery 1938: 176–177, esp. note 7 • Kaufman 1974: 98–99, esp. note 343 • Kutscher 1954: 239 (= 1977: 43) • Magnanini 1968: 378–379 • Paton 1908: 62–63, 285 • Qimron 1986: 96 • Tyler 1988: 131–137 • Schoors 1992–2004: II 246–247 • Seow 1996: 653–654; 1997: 13–15 • Strauss 1900: 26 • Wagner 1966: 113–114 nos. 306–309 • R. M. Wright 2005: 108–110, 131

שִׁלְטוֹן n. m. *authority, rule, dominion*: Qoh. 8:4 שִׁלְטוֹן מֶלֶךְ דְּבַר בַּאֲשֶׁר 8, שִׁלְטוֹן וְאֵין בְּיוֹם הַמָּוֶת

Cf. שַׁלִּיט, √שׁלט

BA שָׁלְטָן *dominion* Dan. 3:33; 4:19, 31 וְדָר דָּר עִם וּמַלְכוּתֵהּ עָלַם שָׁלְטָן שָׁלְטָנֵהּ; 6:27; 7:6, 12, 14 26, 27, וְלֵהּ יְהִיב שָׁלְטָן וִיקָר וּמַלְכוּ

[שִׁלְטֹן] *governor* Dan. 3:2, 3 מְדִינָתָא שִׁלְטֹנֵי (provincial *administrators*)

External Post-Classical Sources
Renderings/Paraphrases/Glosses

שולטן TO 3x, e.g.

Num. 21:30	מדיבון		עדא	**שולטן**	מלכו מחשבון פסקת
[~	דִּיבוֹן עַד				אָבַד חֶשְׁבּוֹן [וַנִּירָם

שלטון 7x, e.g.

Exod. 5:10	וסרכוהי	עמא	**שלטוני**	ונפקו
[~	וְשֹׁטְרָיו	הָעָם	**נֹגְשֵׂי**	[וַיֵּצְאוּ

שולטן TN 17x, e.g.

Deut. 11:25	באפיכון	**ושולטן מלך**	יקום	לא
[~	בִּפְנֵיכֶם	**אִישׁ**	יִתְיַצֵּב	[לֹא

שלטון 14x, e.g.

Exod. 10:6	**שלטונך**	כל	ובתי	בתיך	ויתמלון
[~	**עֲבָדֶיךָ**	כָּל	וּבָתֵּי	בָתֶּיךָ	[וּמָלְאוּ

שולטן TPJ 10x, e.g.

Gen. 24:3	ארעא על **דשולטניה** אלקא הוא מרומא בשמי דמותביה אלקא
[~	הָאָרֶץ וֵאלֹהֵי הַשָּׁמַיִם [אֱלֹהֵי

שלטן 3x, e.g.

Gen. 49:22	שורייא	על	מהלכן	**דשלטוניא**	בנתהון הוו
[~	שׁוּר	עֲלֵי	צָעֲדָה		] בָּנוֹת

שולטן TJ 24x, e.g.

Isa. 14:5	חייבין	**שלטן**	רשיעין	תקוף	ה'	תבר
[~	מֹשְׁלִים	**שֵׁבֶט**	רְשָׁעִים	מַטֵּה	ה'	[שָׁבַר

שלטון 87x, e.g.

Josh. 10:24	... וְאמר	**לשלטוני**	גברי	עבדי	קרבא
[~	[... וַיֹּאמֶר	אֶל קְצִינֵי	אַנְשֵׁי		הַמִּלְחָמָה

Judg. 5:3	שמעו	מלכיא	אציתו	**שלטוניא**
[~	[שְׁמְעוּ	מְלָכִים	הַאֲזִינוּ	**רֹזְנִים**

1 Kgs. 20:24	אעדי	מלכיא...	ומני	**שלטוניא**	חלופיהון
[~	[הָסֵר	הַמְּלָכִים...	וְשִׂים	**פַּחוֹת**	תַּחְתֵּיהֶם

Other Sources

MekhRI Shira 9 (p. 147)

וכמה **שלטונות** שלטו מכם ולא כעסו ישראל, שנ' "**אלוף** לוטן **אלוף** שובל" (בר' לו 29) ועכשו אתם כועסים!

Independent Use

Heb.

M Qid. 3:6

האומ' לאשה: הרי את מקודשת לי על מנת שאדבר עלייך **לשילטון** ואעשה עמיך בפועל, דבר עליה **לשלטון** ועשה עמה בפועל מקודשת ואם ליו אינה מקודשת

T AZ 1:4 (p. 460)

יחיד – אפילו יום המשתה שלו ויום שנעשה בו **שלטון**

MekhRI Vayeḥi 1 (p. 87)

ללמדך שהיה פרעה שולט מסוף העולם ועד סופו והיו לו **שלטונות** מסוף העולם ועד סופו בשביל כבודן של ישראל

Sifre Num. 131 (p. 171)

שוב מעשה ב**שלטון** אחד שבא ממדינת הים להשתחוות לפעור

Sifre Deut. 37 (p. 72)

"ואתן לך ארץ חמדה נחלת צבי צבאות גוים" (יר' ג 19) – ארץ שעשויה חוילאות חוילאות למלכים ול**שלטונים**, שכל מלך ו**שלטון** שלא קנה בארץ ישראל אומר: לא עשיתי כלום

Aram.

PAT 1666:1–8

דכיר אבגל ואחוהי ובני ביתה קדם ירחבול די יהב לאבגל **שלטנא** באתרא כלה לעלם

4Q550 f1:6

פתג[ם דר]יוש מלכא לעבדי **שלטנא** שלם

Comments

a. Both the verbal and nominal derivatives of √שלט are widely considered late Aramaisms in BH. "While we find the root משל common throughout the Hebrew Bible, and שלט in Qoheleth and in the Mishnah, there is no doubt as to the cause of this linguistic change; and although the lexeme שליט occurs in Genesis (42:6), by no means can it be maintained that the root שלט was native and early in Hebrew usage: the root may be admissible in Hebrew, but it was isolated, rare, and unproductive. The impetus to replace the word-group ימשל-ימשיל-ממשלה with ישלט-ישליט-שלטון—this general change occurred only because of the influence of Aramaic" (Bendavid 1967–71: I 127).

b. Not only is the root שלט a strong indicator of lateness, so, too, is the *qiṭlōn* nominal pattern (to be distinguished from *qiṭṭālōn*), which occurs sporadically in CBH, but much more frequently in RH (see du Plessis 1971: 164–167; Schoors 1992: I 62–64).

c. Note that שלטון is employed in various Aramaic sources and in RH not only as an abstract noun (meaning *rule*), but also as a concrete substantive (meaning *ruler*); cf. TN Deut. 11:25 (לֹא יִתְיַצֵּב אִישׁ בִּפְנֵיכֶם ~ לֹא יקום מלך ושולטן ושולטן באפיכון). It was further suggested that the Arabic *sulṭān* and Ethiopic *š/selṭān* were also influenced by the (late) Aramaic usage (Jeffery 1938: 176–177, esp. note 7).

BIBLIOGRAPHY

HALOT IV 1523b • Kaddari 1099a

Barton 1908: 52–53, 152 • Bendavid 1967–71: I 127 • Delitzsch 1877: 190–196 • Dihi 2004: 672–675 • S. R. Driver 1913: 475 no. 13 • du Plessis 1971: 164–167 • Gordis 1968: 59 note 7 (p. 373) • Hadas-Lebel 1995: 111 • Jeffery 1938: 176–177, esp. note 7 • Magnanini 1968: 378–379 • Podechard 1912: 44–46 • Sáenz-Badillos 1993: 124 • Schoors 1992–2004: I 63–64, II 246–247, 447 • Wagner 1966: 113–114 nos. 306–309 • Whitley 1979: 120 • C. H. H. Wright 1883: 500

שַׁלִּיט adj. *domineering*; n. m. *ruler*: Gen. 42:6 (cf. comment a below); Ezek. 16:30; אֵין אָדָם שַׁלִּיט בָּרוּחַ 8:8; Qoh. 7:19; מַעֲשֵׂה אִשָּׁה זוֹנָה שַׁלָּטֶת 10:5

Cf. √שלט, שלטון

BA Dan. 2:10 שַׁלִּיט עֲלָאָה (ק׳) 23, 29; בְּמַלְכוּת אֲנָשָׁא 15; 4:14, 22, כָּל מֶלֶךְ רַב וְשַׁלִּיט; מִנְדָּה בְלוֹ וַהֲלָךְ לָא שַׁלִּיט לְמִרְמֵא עֲלֵיהֹם 7:24; וְשַׁלִּיטִין בְּכֹל עֲבַר נַהֲרָה Ezra 4:20 5:21, 29;

CBH ALTERNATIVES
מושל (cf. TO below)

EXTERNAL POST-CLASSICAL SOURCES
Renderings/Paraphrases/Glosses

TO 10x, e.g.

Gen. 24:2	דליה	בכל	**דשליט**
[~	אֲשֶׁר לוֹ	בְּכָל	הַמֹּשֵׁל]

TN 46x, e.g.

Gen. 1:18	ובליליא	באיממא	**שליט**	ולמהוי
[~	וּבַלַּיְלָה	בַּיּוֹם	וְלִמְשֹׁל]	

TPJ 24x, e.g.

Deut. 28:44	הדיוטין	תהווי	ואתון	**שליט**	יהוי הוא
[~	לְזָנָב	תִּהְיֶה	וְאַתָּה	**לְרֹאשׁ**	יִהְיֶה הוּא]

TJ 16x, e.g.

Isa. 55:4	מלכותא	על כל	**ושליט**	מלך
[~	לְאֻמִּים		**וּמְצַוֵּה**	נָגִיד]

Other Sources

Pesh. Exod. 1:11	בישא	**שליטא**	עליהון	וסמו
[~	מִסִּים	**שָׂרֵי**	עָלָיו	וַיָּשִׂימוּ]

4Q252 5:1	ממשל לישראל בהיות יהודה משבט	**שליט**	יסור	לֹ[וֹא]
[~ Gen. 49:10	מיהודה	שֵׁבֶט		יָסוּר	לֹא]

"הַמֹּשֵׁל בְּכָל אֲשֶׁר לוֹ" (בר׳ כד 2) – שֶׁהָיָה **שַׁלִּיט** בְּיִצְרוֹ כְּמוֹתוֹ (Gen. Rab. 59:8 (p. 636

Independent Use
Heb.

MekhRI BaḤodesh 6 (p. 226)	"כי אנכי ה' אלהיך אל קנא" (שמ' כ 5) – ...אני **שליט** בקנאה ואין קנאה **שליטה** בי. אני **שליט** בנומה ואין הנומה **שליטה** בי
Sifre Deut. 306 (p. 333)	נמצינו למדים שהצדיקים **שליטין** בכל העולם כלו
Gen. Rab. 3:6 (pp. 22–23)	"וַיַּבְדֵּל" (בר' א 4) – אבדלה ממש. למלך שהיה לו שני איסטרטיגין. אחד **שליט** ביום ואחד **שליט** בלילה...
BT Ḥul. 59a	"את הגמל כי מעלה גרה הוא" (וי' יא 4) – **שליט** בעולמו יודע שאין לך דבר שמעלה גרה וטמא אלא גמל. לפיכך פרט לך הכת' "הוא"

Aram.

TAD II 2.3 (= Cowley 8): 8–11	ביתא זנך ארק אנה יהבתה לכי בחיי ובמותי אנתי **שליטה** בה מן יומא זנה ועד עלם ובניכי אחריכי למן זי רחמתי תנתנן לא איתי לי בר וברה אחרנן אח ואחה ואנתה ואיש אחרן **שליט** בארקא זך
1QApGen 20:13	אנתה מרה ו**שליט** על כולא ובכול מלכי ארעא אנתה **שליט** למעבד בכולהון דין
Drijvers As55(D1):2	אנא זרבין... **שליטא** דבירתא...
Drijvers As51(D9):1–5	הנא צלמא דעבד מענו בר מֹקמי לאבגר **שליטא** דֹערב
NḤ 7:61–63 (Yardeni I p. 98)	מן רעותי כתבת לכי מתנתא דא כדי עלא די תהוין אנתתי כקדמיתא ומשמשה יתי מן קצתה מתנתא֞ דא עד יום די אהך לבית עלמי ותהוין רשיה ו**שליטה** בכל די אש[בוק]

Comments

a. Both the verbal and nominal derivatives of √שלט are widely considered late Aramaisms in BH. "While we find the root משל common throughout the Hebrew Bible, and שלט in Qoheleth and in the Mishnah, there is no doubt as to the cause of this linguistic change; and although the lexeme שליט occurs in Genesis (42:6), by no means can it be maintained that the root שלט was native and early in Hebrew usage: the root may be admissible in Hebrew, but it was isolated, rare, and unproductive. The impetus to replace the word-group ימשל-ימשיל-ממשלה with ישלט-ישליט-שלטון—this general change occurred only because of the influence of Aramaic" (Bendavid 1967–71: I 127).

b. It is not entirely clear whether Ug. שליט is etymologically related to Heb.-Aram. √שלט; see, for instance, Gordon (1965: 490b): "possibly connected with Aram. ליט 'to curse' [in which case the initial ש of שליט is not part of the root, but the *šaph'el* prefix]; for a [potentially comparable] Š[aph'el] name, see Š'tqt."

In light of the normally defective spelling in Ugaritic, the *yod* here is probably consonantal.

BIBLIOGRAPHY

BDB 1020b • Ben-Iehuda XIV 7160b note 1 • Kaddari 1099a

Bendavid 1967–71: I 127 • Delitzsch 1877: 190–196 • Gordon 1965: 490b • Magnanini 1968: 378–379 • Rudman 1999 • Schoors 1992–2004: II 246–247 • Seow 1996: 653–654 and note 60 • Wagner 1966: 113–114 nos. 306–309

תַּכְרִיךְ n. m. *cloth wrapping, garment*: Esth. 8:15 וּמָרְדֳּכַי יָצָא מִלִּפְנֵי הַמֶּלֶךְ בִּלְבוּשׁ
מַלְכוּת תְּכֵלֶת וָחוּר וַעֲטֶרֶת זָהָב גְּדוֹלָה וְתַכְרִיךְ בּוּץ וְאַרְגָּמָן

CBH Alternatives
בגד (cf. comment **c** below)

External Post-Classical Sources
Renderings/Paraphrases/Glosses

TN 1x

דמית	ארון **ותכריכין** על נפש	מיניה	יהבנן	ולא
לְמֵת		מִמֶּנּוּ	נָתַתִּי	[וְלֹא

TPJ 1x

דמית	**תכריכין** לנפש	מיניה	יהבית	ולא
לְמֵת		מִמֶּנּוּ	נָתַתִּי	[וְלֹא

TJ 1x

ומרגלין	טבן	ואבנין	ובוץ	וציורין	דארגון	**בתכריכין**
וְכַדְכֹּד		וְרָאמֹת	ובוץ	וְרִקְמָה	אַרְגָּמָן	[**בְּנֹפֶךְ**

Other Sources

M Ma'asS 5:12 — "ולא נתתי ממנו למת" (דב' כו 14) – לא לקחתי ממנו ארון **ותכריכים** למת

Independent Use
Heb.

M Kel. 26:6 — עב כסות **ותכריך** כסות – מדרס. עב ארגמן **ותכריך** ארגמן: בית שמי או' מדרס, ובית הלל או' טמא מת

M BM 1:8 — מצא בחפיסה או בגלוסקמא **תכריך** של שטרות או אגודה של שטרות – הרי זה יחזיר

T BM 1:14 (Nez. p. 64) — אי זהו אגודה של שטר? שלשה קשורין זה בזה. אי זהו **תכריך** של שטר? כל שחוט או משיחה או דבר אחר כרוך עליו מבחוץ

PT Shab. 16:1 (p. 437) — מעשה באחד שהיה כותב ברכות והלך ר' ישמעאל לבודקו. כיון שהרגיש בקול פעמותיו שלר' ישמעאל נטל **תכריך** שלברכות וזרקן לתוך ספל של מים

Aram.

PT Shev. 4:2 (p. 190) — כד חמא גרמיה בסכנה אמ' לון: בחייכון, אמרון גו בייתיה דטרפון: עתדין ליה **תכריכין**

Qoh. Rab. 11:9 (1) — אי שדי זכי עם הדין מיתא דנזבין לה **תכריכין**

COMMENTS

a. "The [use of the] morphological pattern [of *taqṭīl*] expanded diachronically: it began in LBH and continued in the language of the halakhic *midrashim*; the forms added to this pattern were borrowed from Aramaic literature" (Gluska 1999: 269). See also תַּלְמִיד, תַּעֲנִית.

b. The lateness of תַּכְרִיךְ is clearly observable in the linguistic contrast between בִּגְדֵי־שֵׁשׁ (Gen. 41:42 [Joseph in the Egyptian court]) and תַּכְרִיךְ־בּוּץ (Esth. 8:15 [Mordechai in the Persian court])—both phrases being employed to describe royal apparel (cf. Bergey 1983: 139 and the entry בּוּץ, comment **b**).

c. √כרד *to wrap around* does not appear elsewhere in BH, but is found in various Aram. dialects and RH, in a variety of meanings and forms. For instance, כְּרַךְ/כְּרָךְ *a fortified city* (*surround by walls*); the verb כְּרַךְ/כָּרַךְ *to wrap around, encircle*; etc.

d. תכריך (Esth. 8:15) is rendered גלימא by 1 Tg. Esth., whereas 2 Tg. Esth. uses the participle מכריך.

BIBLIOGRAPHY

HALOT IV 1735b • Ben-Iehuda XVI 7759a note 1 • Kaddari 1169b

Bergey 1983: 139 • S. R. Driver 1913: 484 • Gluska 1999: 267–269 • Paton 1908: 62–63, 281

תַּלְמִיד n. m. *student, apprentice*: 1 Chron. 25:8 וַיַּפִּילוּ גּוֹרָלוֹת מִשְׁמֶרֶת לְעֻמַּת כַּקָּטֹן
כַּגָּדוֹל מֵבִין עִם תַּלְמִיד (|| קטן and opp. מבין)

CBH ALTERNATIVES
למוד(?), בן(?), נער(?) (cf. TJ below)

EXTERNAL POST-CLASSICAL SOURCES
Renderings/Paraphrases/Glosses

TO 1x
Num. 32:14   חייביא   גבריא   **תלמידי**   אבהתכון   בתר   קמתון   והא
[~   חַטָּאִים   אֲנָשִׁים   **תַּרְבּוּת**   אֲבֹתֵיכֶם   תַּחַת   קַמְתֶּם   וְהִנֵּה]

TN 1x (marg.)
Deut. 8:9   כנחשה   הי   חסינין   **ותלמידייהא**
[~   נְחֹשֶׁת   תַּחְצֹב   וּמֵהֲרָרֶיהָ]   (cf. TPJ ad loc.)

TPJ 6x, e.g.
Num.   **תלמידיהון**   כן הינון נהרין פרקטוני על שתילין כגנין והי
24:6   בבית מדרישיהון   חבורן חבורן
[~   נָהָר   עֲלֵי   כְּגַנֹּת]

TJ 18x, e.g.
2 Kgs. 4:1   נבייא   **תלמידי**   מנשי   חדא   ואתתא
[~   הַנְּבִיאִים   **בְּנֵי**   מִנְּשֵׁי   אַחַת   וְאִשָּׁה]

2 Kgs. 5:20   דאלישע   **תלמידא**   גיחזי   ואמר
[~   אֱלִישָׁע   **נַעַר**   גֵּיחֲזִי   וַיֹּאמֶר]

Other Sources
Tg. Qoh. 9:1   צדיקיא וחכימיא **ותלמידיהון** דמשעבדין להום על עיסק
אולפן אוריתא
[~   הַצַּדִּיקִים וְהַחֲכָמִים **וַעֲבָדֵיהֶם**]

Pesh. 1 Kgs. 19:3   **תלמידה**   תמן   ושבק   לברשבע...   ואתא
[~   שָׁם   **נַעֲרוֹ**   אֶת   וַיַּנַּח   בְּאֵר שֶׁבַע...   וַיָּבֹא]

Independent Use

Heb.

M Orlah 2:5   דוסתי איש כפר יתמה היה **מתלמידי** בית שמי

M Avot 4:12   יהי כבוד **תלמידך** חביב עליך ככבוד חבירך

MekhRI Pisḥa 1   וכן אתה מוצא בברוך בן נריה שהיה מתרעם לפני המקום: ...מה

(pp. 5–6)   נשתניתי אני מכל **תלמידי** הנביאים? יהושע שמש משה ושרתה עליו

                              רוח הקודש... מה נשתניתי אני מכל **תלמידי** הנביאים?

Sifra Milu'im 1:2   שבח לו **לתלמיד** שהוא מקיים עליו מצות רבו, שבח להן לבני אהרן

                              שקיימו עליהם מצות משה

Aram.

PT Ber. 2:1 (p. 14)   כולי עלמ' ידעין דר' אלעזר **תלמידיה** דר' יוחנן

Lev. Rab. 10:4 (p. 203)   אנטונינוס סליק לות רבנו, אשכחיה דיתיב **ותלמידיה** קמיה

Lam. Rab. 3:6   אתא ר' יהושע בן לוי לטבריה ואיתקבל גבי ר' חייא רבא, ויהב

                              לתלמידויי דר' יהושע דרכמונין ואמ' להון: זילו עבידו לרבכון כמנהגיה

COMMENTS

a. "The [use of the] morphological pattern [*taqṭīl*] was expanded diachronically, beginning in LBH and persisting in the language of the halakhic *midrashim*;
the forms supplemented to this pattern were borrowed from the Aramaic literature" (Gluska 1999: 269). See also תַּכְרִיךְ, תַּעֲנִית.

BIBLIOGRAPHY

BDB 541a • *HALOT* IV 1740b
Curtis and Madsen 1910: 31 no. 64, 280 • S. R. Driver 1913: 539 • Gluska 1999: 267–269 •
Hurvitz 1972: 138 note 185

קַמְתִּי מִתַּעֲנִיתִי Ezra 9:5 :*fast* [*ritual*] ,*self-affliction* .f .n [תַּעֲנִית]

CBH ALTERNATIVES
צום (cf. comment c below)

EXTERNAL POST-CLASSICAL SOURCES
Renderings/Paraphrases/Glosses
TJ 8x, e.g.

גזרו	תעני	ערעו	כנישא
[קַדְּשׁוּ	צוֹם	קְראוּ	עֲצָרָה

Joel 1:14 (first row), [~ (second row)

Other Sources

	מלי	דצומא	ודתעניתא
	[דִּבְרֵי	הַצֹּמוֹת	וְזַעֲקָתָם

2 Tg. Esth. 9:31 (first row), [~ (second row)

וגזר	תעני	על	כל	אנש	יהודה
[וַיִּקְרָא	צוֹם	עַל	כָּל		יְהוּדָה

Tg. 2 Chron. 20:3 (first row), [~ (second row)

Independent Use
Heb.

CD 6:18–19
ולשמור אֵת יום השבת כפרושה ואת המועדות ואת
יום התעניִת

4Q510 f1:6–8
בקץ ממשל[ת] רשעה ותעודות **תעניות** בני או[ר]...
לקץ **תעניות** פשע]

M Ta'an. 2:6
שלוש **תעניות** הראשונות אנשי משמר מתענים ולא משלימים,
ואנשי בית אב לא היו מתענים

M Meg. 1:3
מותרים בספד **ובתענית** ומתנות לאביונים

T Ta'an. 2:4
תענית צבור מתפללין עשרים וארבע ברכות מה שאין כן
(Mo'ed pp. 330–331)
בתענית יחיד

Aram.

Gen. Rab. 33:3
(p. 304)
ביומוי דר׳ תנחום׳ צרכון ישראל **לתעניתא**. אתון לגביה אמ׳ לו: ר׳,
גזור **תעניתא**. גזר תענית יום קדמיי ויום תניין ויום תליתיי ולא נחת
מטרא

PT Ta'an. 2:1
(p. 711)
אמ׳ ר׳ יוסה: הדא אמרה אילין **תענייתא** דאנן עבדין לית אינון **תעניין**.
למה? דלית נשייא עמן

PT Ta'an. 3:4
(p. 720)
ר׳ ליעזר עבד **תעני** ולא איתנחת מיטרא. עבד ר׳ עקיבא **תעני** ונחת
מיטרא

BT BM 85a
ר׳ זירא יתיב **תעניתא** דישתכח תלמודא דבבל מיניה

COMMENTS

a. The noun תענית is related etymologically and semantically to the verbs עָנָה, הִתְעַנָּה ,עִנָּה (= *oppress*; *do violence*; *afflict* — cf. Lev. 23:27 יוֹם הַכִּפֻּרִים הוּא מִקְרָא קֹדֶשׁ יִהְיֶה לָכֶם וְעִנִּיתֶם אֶת נַפְשֹׁתֵיכֶם). However, in contrast to the verbal forms, which appear throughout BH, the noun is attested only in Ezra 9:5. This Biblical *hapax* thus heralds the emergence of תענית as a halakhic term in post-Biblical, specifically Rabbinic, literature.

b. "The form תענית, which is an Aramaism in the Bible, increased considerably in frequency [in Tannaitic Hebrew].... The form צום, which is also found in Aramaic, survived in the language due only to its relatively high frequency in BH" (Gluska 1999: 358).

c. Both 2 Sam. 12:21 and Ezra 9:5 describe the conclusion of an individual's period of self-affliction/fasting with the verb קוּם, but they differ in the wording used to describe the affliction/fasting itself. 2 Sam. uses the verb צָמְתָּ (בַּעֲבוּר הַיֶּלֶד חַי צַמְתָּ וַתֵּבְךְּ וְכַאֲשֶׁר מֵת הַיֶּלֶד קַמְתָּ וַתֹּאכַל לָחֶם), whereas Ezra employs the noun תענית (קַמְתִּי מִתַּעֲנִיתִי) in this connection. Ezra does not make explicit mention of abstinence from food as part of one's תענית, but since the meaning of this noun in RH is first and foremost a religious fast, and since the aforementioned verse in Samuel employs the verb צוּם, it stands to reason that the meaning in Ezra is *fast* as well. In a slightly different formulation: "those who interpret the word תענית in Ezra 9:5 as *affliction* as opposed to *fast* ... reduce, of course, the linguistic affiliation between RH and the Biblical verse. Yet, in spite of the semantic nuance suggested by this interpretation for the term תענית in the book of Ezra, the basic line of our argument remains, i.e., that the very appearance of תענית in the Hebrew Bible is to be found only in a late composition" (Hurvitz 1972: 44 n. 108).

d. The lateness of the semantic shift 'affliction' > 'fasting' underlying the linguistic history of the noun תַּעֲנִית is further corroborated by the similar development of the verb ענה√: "In the Bible the *hitpa'el* of ענה√ with the meaning 'to fast' occurs only in Ezra 8:21 and Dan. 10:12 [cf. BDB 726b]. This is a late usage also common in RH.... And note also: the *pi'el* of ענה√ in the Bible does not mean 'to fast', but rather ענה + נפש ['to afflict the soul']" (Qimron 1980: 250).

e. The Biblical noun צוֹם is rendered in TJ by both צוֹמָא and תַּעֲנִיתָא, with no clear-cut distinction between the two. Interestingly, TJ translates the Hebrew word צוֹם in Zech. 7:5 with צום as well as תענ[ת].

f. The pattern of תַּעֲנִית is similar to that of תַּכְרִיךְ (Esth. 8:15) and תַּלְמִיד (1 Chron. 25:8; cf. these entries above), both of which are documented exclusively in late writings. Consequently, תַּעֲנִית may be regarded as a member of this category

(Segal 1927: 118 §265), though the final ת of תַּעֲנִית is not part of the lexeme's root (in contrast to the ך of תַּכְרִיך and the ד of תַּלְמִיד; see JM 239 §88L, *r*).

If a link between תַּעֲנִית and the nominal pattern תַּקְטִיל is granted, it may well be argued that the lateness of the specific word תַּעֲנִית in BH is indicated not merely by its exclusive appearance in Ezra 9:5, but also by the general intensified usage of *taqṭil* forms in the corpus of post-Classical sources (Aramaic, MH).

BIBLIOGRAPHY

Kaddari 1178a • Segal 1927: 118 §265 • JM 239 §88L, *r*

Gluska 1999: 358 • Hurvitz 1972: 44 • Qimron 1980: 250; 1986: 97; 2003: 386 • Rabin 1958a: 147 note 8; 1958b: 25 • Sáenz-Badillos 1993: 122

Bibliography: Works Cited in the *Lexicon*

A   Primary Sources

1   *The Hebrew Bible and Ancient Targums*

The Masoretic text (MT) of the Hebrew Bible is cited on the basis of BHS (*Biblia Hebraica Stuttgartensia*), which itself is based on Codex Leningrad. There may be a lack of agreement between the consonantal text and/or vocalization transmitted in BHS and other Masoretic editions (e.g., Ps. 122:5, where דָּוִיד in Codex Leningrad parallels the defective spelling דָּוִד in the Aleppo Codex). The versification used in the *Lexicon* is also identical to that of BHS. The Tetragrammaton in this volume appears as ה'.

In cases of *ketiv/qere*, i.e., instances in which the Masoretic text notes a difference between the consonantal text and the reading tradition, the word is cited according to the vocalized *qere* form, followed by ק', which stands for *qere*. For example, in Esth. 9:27, MT has the *ketiv* וקבל, whereas the *qere* calls for the pronunciation *weqibbelu*. In the *Lexicon*, this word appears as: (ק') וְקִבְּלוּ.

1.1   The Hebrew Bible (MT)

Elliger, K. and W. Rudolph 1997. *Biblia Hebraica Stuttgartensia*[5]. Stuttgart: Deutsche Bibelgesellschaft.

1.2   The Targums
1.2.1   *Septuagint (LXX)*

Rahlfs, A. 1971. *Septuaginta*. 2 vols. Stuttgart: Deutsche Bibelgesellschaft.

1.2.2   *Aramaic Targums*
1.2.2.1   Targum Onqelos (TO)

Sperber, A. 1959–73. 4 vols. *The Bible in Aramaic*. Leiden: Brill.

1.2.2.2   Targum Jonathan (TJ)

Sperber, A. 1959–73. 4 vols. *The Bible in Aramaic*. Leiden: Brill.

1.2.2.3   Targum Pseudo-Jonathan (TPJ)

Clarke, E. G. 1984. *Targum Pseudo-Jonathan of the Pentateuch*. Hoboken: KTAV.

1.2.2.4   Targum Neofiti (TN)

Díez Macho, A. 1968–79. *Neophyti I*. 6 vols. Madrid: Consejo Superior de Investigaciones Científicas.

1.2.2.5   Fragment Targums (FTP, FTV)

Ms. 110 of Bibliothèque Nationale de France, Paris (FTP); Ms. Vatican 440 (FTV)

Klein, M. L., ed. 1980. *The Fragment Targums of the Pentateuch*. 2 vols. Analecta Biblica
     76. Rome: Pontifical Biblical Institute.

1.2.2.6   Targum Psalms (Tg. Psalms)

Ms. Paris 110

Cohen, M., ed. 2003. *Tehillim*. 2 vols. *Miqra'ot Gedolot HaKeter*.

1.2.2.7   Targum Job (Tg. Job)

Stec, D. M., ed. 1994. *The Text of the Targum of Job: An Introduction and Critical Edition*.
     Leiden: Brill.

1.2.2.8   Targum Ruth (Tg. Ruth)

Sperber, A., ed. 1959–73. 4 vols. *The Bible in Aramaic*. Leiden: Brill.

1.2.2.9   Targum Rishon Esther (1 Tg. Esth.)

Ms. Paris 110

Katzenelnbogen, M. L., ed. 2006. *Megillat Esther*. Torat Ḥayyim. Jerusalem: Mosad
     Harav Kook.

1.2.2.10   Targum Sheni Esther (2 Tg. Esth.)

Ms. Vaticanus Urbinati Ebr. 1.

Katzenelnbogen, M. L., ed. 2006. *Megillat Esther*. Torat Ḥayyim. Jerusalem: Mosad
     Harav Kook.

1.2.2.11   Targum Qohelet (Tg. Qoh.)

Sperber, A., ed. 1959–73. 4 vols. *The Bible in Aramaic*. Leiden: Brill.

1.2.2.12   Targum Chronicles (Tg. 1 Chron.; Tg. 2 Chron.)

Ms. Codex Vaticanus Urbinati Ebr. 1

Le Déaut, R. and J. Roberts., eds. 1971. *Targum des Chroniques (Cod. Vat. Urb.
     Ebr. 1)*. 2 vols. Rome: Pontifical Biblical Institute.

1.2.3   *Peshiṭta (Pesh.)*

The Old Testament in Syriac, according to the Peshitta Version. Leiden: Brill, 1972–.

2   *Non-Transmitted Written Sources*

2.1   Various Inscriptions, Texts, and Documents
Aramaic material from Egypt is generally cited according to the numeration of *TAD*,
but for the benefit of the reader the relevant citations from Cowley 1923, G. R. Driver
1957, and Kraeling 1953 are also provided. Other material is cited according to the
numeration of the relevant edition (e.g., Cooke, EN, *KAI*, *PAT*).

Aggoula, B. 1985. *Inscriptions et graffites araméens d'Assour.* Annali dell'Istituto
    Universitario Orientale di Napoli, Supplement 43.
Aḥituv, S. 2008. *Echoes from the Past: Hebrew and Cognate Inscriptions from the Biblical
    Period.* Jerusalem: Carta (English translation of *HaKetav veHaMiktav: Handbook of
    Ancient Inscriptions from the Land of Israel and the Kingdoms beyond the Jordan from
    the Period of the First Commonwealth.* Jerusalem: Bialik, 2005 [Hebrew].
Cooke = Cooke, G. A. 1903. *A Text-Book of North-Semitic Inscriptions.* Oxford: Clarendon.
Cowley, A. E. 1923. *Aramaic Papyri of the Fifth Century B.C.* Oxford: Clarendon.
Dobbs-Allsopp et al. = Dobbs-Allsopp, F. W., J. J. M. Roberts, C. L. Seow, and R. E.
    Whitaker 2004. *Hebrew Inscriptions: Texts from the Biblical Period of the Monarchy.*
    New Haven: Yale University Press.
Drijvers = Drijvers, H. J. W. and J. F. Healey. 1999. *The Old Syriac Inscriptions of Edessa
    and Osrhoene: Texts, Translations and Commentary.* Handbook of Oriental Studies,
    Near and Middle East 42. Leiden: Brill.
Driver = Driver, G. R. 1957. *Aramaic Documents of the Fifth Century B.C.* Oxford:
    Clarendon.
Dupont-Sommer, A. 1979. "L'inscription araméenne." Pages 129–78, plates XVI–XXIII in
    Fouilles de Xanthos, Tome VI: La stèle trilingue de Létôon. Edited by H. Metzger. Paris:
    Klincksieck.
EN = Ephal, I. and J. Naveh. 1996. *Aramaic Ostraca of the Fourth Century B.C. from
    Idumaea.* Jerusalem: Magnes.
Eshel-Kloner = Eshel, E. and A. Kloner. 1996. "An Aramaic Ostracon of an Edomite
    Marriage Contract from Maresha, Dated 176 B.C.E." *Israel Exploration Journal* 46:
    1–22.
Frey, J.-B. 1936–52. *Corpus inscriptionum Judaicarum.* 2 vols. Vatican City: Pontifical
    Institute of Christian Archaeology.
KAI = Donner, H. and W. Röllig. 2002. *Kanaanäische und aramäische Inschriften.* 5 vols.
    Wiesbaden: Otto Harrassowitz.
Kraeling, E. G. 1953. *The Brooklyn Museum Aramaic Papyri.* New Haven: Yale University
    Press.

Magen et al. = Magen, Y., H. Misgav, and L. Tsfania 2004. *Mount Gerizim Excavations, vol. 1: The Aramaic, Hebrew and Samaritan Inscriptions.* Jerusalem: Staff Officer of Archaeology – Civil Administration of Judea and Samaria, Israel Antiquities Authority.

MPAT = Fitzmyer, J. A. and D. A. Harrington. 1978. *A Manual of Palestinian Aramaic Texts.* Rome: Biblical Institute.

Naveh, J. 1978. *On Stone and Mosaic: The Aramaic and Hebrew Inscriptions from Ancient Synagogues.* Tel-Aviv: Carta [Hebrew].

————. 1992. *On Sherd and Papyrus: Aramaic and Hebrew Inscriptions from the Second Temple, Mishnaic and Talmudic Periods.* Jerusalem: Magnes [Hebrew].

PAT = Hillers, D. and E. Cussini. 1996. *Palmyrene Aramaic Texts.* Baltimore: Johns Hopkins University Press.

TAD = Porten, B. and A. Yardeni. 1986. *Textbook of Aramaic Documents from Ancient Egypt, Newly Copied, Edited and Translated into Hebrew and English.* 4 vols. Jerusalem: Hebrew University, Department of the History of the Jewish People (see also Cowley, Driver, and Kraeling).

Vööbus, A. 1982. *The Syro-Roman Lawbook, vol.1: The Syriac Text with an Introduction.* Papers of the Estonian Theological Society in Exile 36. Stockholm: ETSE.

2.2 Documents from Qumran and the Judaean Desert and Related Sources

Quotations of the Dead Sea Scrolls and other documents from the Judaean Desert are generally cited according to the relevant *editio princeps* or the latest critical edition. As far as it was possible, comparison was made with photographs and/or drawings of the original text.

Qumran material is generally cited according to cave and text number, though certain texts better known by their (abbreviated) title are so cited (e.g., CD, 11QT, 11QTgJob, 11QPs^a). A given citation will thus include the cave number (appended to the letter Q), abbreviation or text number, column and/or fragment number in Arabic numerals (where appropriate), piece number in lowercase Roman numerals (where appropriate), colon (:), and line number in Arabic numerals. See the indices in Tov 2010 and in Parry and Tov 2004–5: XI–XXII, for the relevant abbreviations and text numbers. Non-Qumranic texts from the Judaean Desert are generally cited by location in accordance with the numeration in Yardeni 2000 (e.g., Mur., Nḥ, Nṣ). For the sources of texts not based on *DJD*, see below (it is worth noting that the vast majority of the references here conform to those of Parry and Tov 2004–5).

2.2.1 *General Collections*

Discoveries in the Judaean Desert (*DJD*). Oxford: Clarendon, 1955–.

Parry, D. W. and E. Tov. 2004–5. *The Dead Sea Scrolls Reader.* 6 vols. Leiden: Brill.

Tov, E. 2010. *Revised Lists of the Tests from the Judaean Desert*. Leiden: Brill.

Yardeni, A. 2000. *Textbook of Aramaic, Hebrew and Nabataean Documentary Texts from the Judaean Desert and Related Material*. 2 vols. Jerusalem: Ben-Zion Dinur Center for Research in Jewish History.

2.2.2   *Hebrew Texts*

2.2.2.1   Ben-Sira (BS)

Cited by manuscript (A, B, B-marg., C, D, E) and canonical chapter and verse.

The Book of Ben Sira: Text, Concordance and an Analysis of the Vocabulary. Jerusalem: Academy of the Hebrew Language and Shrine of the Book, 1973 [Hebrew].

2.2.2.2   Serakhim (1QS; 1QSa)

Qimron, E. 2010. *Megillot Midbar Yehuda: Ha-Ḥiburim ha-ʿIvriyim*. Jerusalem: Yad Izhak Ben-Zvi.

2.2.2.3   Copper Scroll (3Q15)

Lefkovits, J. K. 2000. *The Copper Scroll—3Q15: A Reevaluation: A New Reading, Translation and Commentary*. Studies on the Texts of the Desert of Judah 25. Leiden: Brill.

2.2.2.4   Damascus Covenant (CD)

Qimron, E. 2010. *Megillot Midbar Yehuda: Ha-Ḥiburim ha-ʿIvriyim*. Jerusalem: Yad Izhak Ben-Zvi.

2.2.2.5   The Hodayot (Thanksgiving) Scroll (1QHᵃ)

Stegemann, H., E. Schuller, and C. Newsom. 2009. *1QHodayotᵃ*. Discoveries in the Judaean Desert 40. Oxford: Clarendon.

2.2.2.6   The Great Isaiah Scroll (1QIsaᵃ)

Parry, D. W. and E. Qimron. 1998. *The Great Isaiah Scroll (1QIsaᵃ)*. Studies on the Texts of the Desert of Judah 32. Leiden: Brill.

2.2.2.7   Temple Scroll (11QT)

Qimron, E. 2010. *Megillot Midbar Yehuda: Ha-Ḥiburim ha-ʿIvriyim*. Jerusalem: Yad Izhak Ben-Zvi.

2.2.2.8   War Scroll (1QM)

Qimron, E. 2010. *Megillot Midbar Yehuda: Ha-Ḥiburim ha-ʿIvriyim*. Jerusalem: Yad Izhak Ben-Zvi.

2.2.2.9   The Psalms Scroll (11QPs^a [= 11Q5])
Sanders, J. A. 1965. *The Psalms Scroll of Qumrân Cave 11 (11QPs^a)*. Discoveries in the
    Judaean Desert 4. Oxford: Clarendon.

2.2.3   *Aramaic Texts*
2.2.3.1   Enoch (4Q201, 4Q206)
Milik, J. T. 1976. *The Books of Enoch: Aramaic Fragments of Qumrân Cave 4*. Oxford:
    Clarendon.

2.2.3.2   Genesis Apocryphon (1QApGen)
Fitzmyer, J. A. 2004. *The Genesis Apocryphon*³. Rome: Pontifical Biblical Institute.

2.2.3.3   Targum of Job (11QTgJob)
García Martínez, F. et al. 1998. *Qumran Cave 11, II*. Discoveries in the Judaean Desert 23.
    Oxford: Clarendon.

2.2.4   *Hebrew and Aramaic Documents from the Judaean Desert*
2.2.4.1   Naḥal Ḥever (NḤ)
Yardeni, A. 2000. *Textbook of Aramaic, Hebrew and Nabataean Documentary Texts from
    the Judaean Desert and Related Material*. 2 vols. Jerusalem: Ben-Zion Dinur Center
    for Research in Jewish History.

2.2.4.2   Naḥal Ṣeʾelim (NṢ)
Yardeni, A. 2000. *Textbook of Aramaic, Hebrew and Nabataean Documentary Texts from
    the Judaean Desert and Related Material*. 2 vols. Jerusalem: Ben-Zion Dinur Center
    for Research in Jewish History.

2.2.4.3   Wadi Murabbaʿat (Mur.)
Yardeni, A. 2000. *Textbook of Aramaic, Hebrew and Nabataean Documentary Texts from
    the Judaean Desert and Related Material*. 2 vols. Jerusalem: Ben-Zion Dinur Center
    for Research in Jewish History.

2.2.4.4   Wadi Daliyeh
Yardeni, A. 2000. *Textbook of Aramaic, Hebrew and Nabataean Documentary Texts from
    the Judaean Desert and Related Material*. 2 vols. Jerusalem: Ben-Zion Dinur Center
    for Research in Jewish History.

2.2.4.5   Rahmani Ossuary (Rahmani)

Yardeni, A. 2000. *Textbook of Aramaic, Hebrew and Nabataean Documentary Texts from the Judaean Desert and Related Material.* 2 vols. Jerusalem: Ben-Zion Dinur Center for Research in Jewish History.

3   *Rabbinic Sources*

Quotations of Rabbinic literature throughout the lexicon are cited as follows: The examined lemma is copied as it appears in what is considered to be the most reliable manuscripts for each Rabbinic work. Underlying this approach is the assumption that the more reliable the manuscript, the closer we can expect to preserve the original language of the cited work. Our choice of manuscripts and their readings are based on the textual database of *The Historical Dictionary of the Hebrew Language* of The Academy of Hebrew Language (http://hebrew-academy.huji.ac.il).

To afford easier referencing for the reader, the words surrounding the lemma are quoted according to the text appearing in the accepted editions (see details below, §§3.2–3.4, 3.6–3.11, 3.15, 3:17–3.19). For several reasons, exceptions were made for some works wherein the *full* quotation is cited according to the manuscripts alone: When citing the Mishnah (§3.1) and Sifra (§3.5) we relied upon manuscripts whose textual superiority over the current editions enjoys nearly unanimous academic consensus; when quoting from various *midrashim* (§§3.12–3.14, 3.16) and from tractates of the Babylonian Talmud (§§3.20–3.41) we used the most reliable manuscripts available since full critical editions of these corpora do not yet exist. The choice of these manuscripts was also based on *The Historical Dictionary*. In other words, all examined lemmas are cited according to reliable manuscripts, whereas the language of the rest of the quotation varies between the numerous Rabbinic works.

Wherever linear or intralinear corrections appear in manuscripts, the corrected version (i.e., the last "hand") was preferred. Parenthetical corrections or additions by editor(s) of the critical editions appear within angular brackets. Substitutions for the Tetragrammaton always appear as 'ה.

References and internal divisions of Rabbinic works (chapters, paragraphs, folios, etc.) always refer to the traditional editions, while parenthetical page numbers following the traditional reference refer to page numbers in critical editions, e.g.:

> T Shab. 11:3 (Mo'ed p. 46) עד שיצור את כולה – הצר צורה—i.e., Tosefta, Tractate Shabbat, chapter 11, halakhah 3 (per the traditional numbering); in parentheses: Order Mo'ed, page 46 (cited per Lieberman's critical edition, 1967–96); the citation itself.

The cited excerpts appear in most cases without vocalization points, however they have been punctuated and occasionally contain parenthetical glosses to facilitate understanding the passage.

The following manuscripts and editions were used for the Rabbinic quotations:

3.1 Mishnah (M)

Cited according to tractate, chapter, and mishnah (per *editio princeps*).

Ms. Budapest, Kaufmann A50 (including the so-called Kaufmann II pages that were added to the end of the codex).

3.2 Tosefta (T)

Cited according to tractate, chapter, and halakhah.

Ms. Vienna, Cod. Hebr. 20 ('Codex Vienna'); Berlin, Or. fol. 1220 ('Codex Erfurt').

Edd.: Tractates Ber.–BB: S. Lieberman 1967–96. *The Tosefta according to Codex Vienna, with Variants from Codices Erfurt, London, Geniza Mss. and Editio Princeps (Venice 1521), together with References to Parallel Passages in Talmudic Literature and a Brief Commentary.* New York: Jewish Theological Seminary of America;

Tractates San.–Yad.: M. S. Zuckermandel 2004. Repr. *The Tosefta, according to the Mss. Erfurt and Vienna.* Jerusalem: Wahrmann.

3.3 Mekhilta of R. Ishmael (MekhRI)

Cited according to tractate and *parashah*.

Ms. Oxford 151; Munich 117.

Ed. H. S. Horovitz and I. Rabin 1998. *Mekhilta de-Rabbi Yišma'el²*. Jerusalem: Bamberger and Wahrmann.

3.4 Mekhilta of R. Shimon b. Yoḥai (MekhRS)

Cited according to biblical chapter and verse.

Ms. St. Petersburg, Firkovitz 2 (A 268); Cambridge, T-S Misc. 36, 132.

Eds. J. N. Epstein and E. Z. Melamed, No date. *Mekhilta de-Rabbi Šim'on ben Yoḥai²*. Jerusalem: Yeshivat Sha'are Raḥamim.

3.5 Sifra

Cited by *parashah*, chapter, and paragraph.

Ms. Rome, Vatican 66; Rome, Vatican 31.

3.6 Sifre Numbers (Sifre Num.)

Cited by paragraph.

Ms. Rome, Vatican 32.

Ed. H. S. Horovitz 1917. *Sifre Numbers and Sifre Zuṭa.* Leipzig: J. Kaufmann.

3.7   Sifre Deuteronomy (Sifre Deut.)

Cited by paragraph.

Ms. Rome, Vatican 32; London 341; Oxford 151.

Ed. L. Finkelstein 1939. *Sifre 'al Sefer Devarim*. Berlin: Jüdischer Kulturbund in Deutschland E.V. Abteilung Verlag.

3.8   Baraita de-Melekhet ha-Mishkan (BMM)

Cited by paragraph.

Ms. Munich 95.

Ed. R. Kirschner, R. 1992. *Baraita de-Melekhet ha-Mishkan: A Critical Edition with Introduction and Translation*. Cincinnati: Hebrew Union College.

3.9   Talmud Yerushalmi (PT)

Cited by tractate, chapter, and halakhah per Venice printed edition.

Ms. Leiden, Scalliger 3 (Or. 4720).

Ed. 2005. *Talmud Yerushalmi*[2]. Jerusalem: Academy of the Hebrew Language.

3.10   Genesis Rabbah (Gen. Rab.)

Cited by *parashah* and paragraph.

Ms. Rome, Vatican 30; Rome, Vatican 60.

Eds. Y. Theodor and Ḥ. Albeck 1965. *Midrash Genesis Rabbah*. Repr. 2 vols. Jerusalem: Wahrmann.

3.11   Leviticus Rabbah (Lev. Rab.)

Cited by *parashah* and paragraph.

Ms. London, British Library Add. 27,169 (340).

Ed. M. Margulies 1993. *Midrash Leviticus Rabbah*[3]. 5 vols. (in 2). New York: Jewish Theological Seminary.

3.12   Lamentations Rabbah (Lam. Rab.)

Cited by *parashah* and paragraph.

Ms. Rome, Vatican 229.

3.13   Qohelet Rabbah (Qoh. Rab.)

Cited by biblical chapter, verse and paragraph.

Ms. Rome, Vatican 291.

3.14   Ruth Rabbah (Ruth Rab.)

Cited by *parashah* and paragraph.

Ms. Oxford 164.

3.15   Pesiqta de-Rav Kahana (PesiqRK)

Cited by number of *derashah*, according to the Table of Contents.

Ms. Oxford 151 .

Ed. B. Mandelbaum 1987. *Pesikta de Rav Kahana*. New York: Jewish Theological
    Seminary.

3.16   Tractate "Mourning" (Semaḥot)

Cited by chapter and halakhah.

Ms. Oxford 370.

3.17   'Avot de-Rabbi Natan (Vers. A) (ARN A)

Cited by chapter.

Ms. New York, Jewish Theological Seminary 25.

Ed. S. Schechter 1997. *Avot de-Rabbi Natan²*. New York and Jerusalem: Jewish
    Theological Seminary.

3.18   'Avot de-Rabbi Natan (Vers. B) (ARN B)

Cited by chapter.

Ms. Parma, de Rossi 327.

Ed. S. Schechter 1997. *Avot de-Rabbi Nathan²*. New York and Jerusalem: Jewish
    Theological Seminary.

3.19   Megillat Taʿanit (with Scholion) (Meg. Taʿan.)

Cited by date in the scroll.

Ms. Parma 117.

Ed. V. Noam, 2003. *Megillat Taʿanit: Ha-nosaḥim, pishram, toldotehem*. Jerusalem: Yad
    Izhak Ben-Zvi.

*All quotations from Babylonian Talmud are cited by folio and side (per Vilna printed
    edition):

3.20   Babylonian Talmud: Berakhot (BT Ber.)

Ms. Oxford 366.

3.21   Babylonian Talmud: Shabbat (BT Shab.)

Ms. Oxford 366.

3.22   Babylonian Talmud: ʿEruvin (BT Eruv.)

Ms. Rome, Vatican 109.

3.23   Babylonian Talmud: Pesaḥim (BT Pes.)
Ms. New York, Enelau 271.

3.24   Babylonian Talmud: Yoma (BT Yoma)
Ms. Munich 6.

3.25   Babylonian Talmud: Sukkah (BT Suk.)
Ms. Oxford e.51 (Neubauer 2677).

3.26   Babylonian Talmud: Rosh HaShanah (BT RoshH)
Ms. New York, Enelau 319.

3.27   Babylonian Talmud: Taʿanit (BT Taʿan.)
Ms. Jerusalem, Yad HaRav Herzog.

3.28   Babylonian Talmud: Megillah (BT Meg.)
Ms. New York, Columbia T-141.

3.29   Babylonian Talmud: Ḥagigah (BT Ḥag.)
Ms. Göttingen 3.

3.30   Babylonian Talmud: Yevamot (BT Yev.)
Ms. Munich 141.

3.31   Babylonian Talmud: Ketubot (BT Ket.)
Mss. St. Petersburg, Firkovitz 1, 187; Rome, Vatican 130.

3.32   Babylonian Talmud: Giṭṭin (BT Giṭ.)
Ms. Rome, Vatican 130.

3.33   Babylonian Talmud: Bava Qama (BT BQ)
Ms. Hamburg 165

3.34   Babylonian Talmud: Bava Metziʿa (BT BM)
Ms. Hamburg 165.

3.35   Babylonian Talmud: Bava Batra (BT BB)
Ms. Hamburg 165.

3.36   Babylonian Talmud: Sanhedrin (BT San.)
Ms. Jerusalem, Yad HaRav Herzog.

3.37   Babylonian Talmud: Makkot (BT Mak.)
Ms.: Jerusalem, Yad HaRav Herzog.

3.38   Babylonian Talmud: ʿAvodah Zarah (BT AZ)
Ms. Paris 1337

3.39   Babylonian Talmud: Zevaḥim (BT Zev.)
Ms. New York, Columbia T-141.

3.40   Babylonian Talmud: Ḥullin (BT Ḥul.)
Ms. Rome, Vatican 122.

3.41   Babylonian Talmud: Meʿilah (BT Meʿil.)
Ms. Florence II.I.7.

4   *Other Early Common Era Sources*

4.1   Greek New Testament
Holmes, M. W. (ed.). 2010. *The Greek New Testament: SBL Edition*. Atlanta-Bellingham:
     Society of Biblical Literature and Logos Bible Software.

4.2   Josephus
Niese, B. 1887–95. *Flavii Iosephi Opera*. 7 vols. Berlin: Weidmann.

4.3   Tibat Markeh (TM)
Cited by number of midrashic portion, according to Table of Contents and line number.
Ben-Ḥayyim, Z. 1988. *Tībåt Mårqe—A Collection of Samaritan Midrashim*. Jerusalem:
     Israel Academy of Sciences and Humanities.

B   Concordances, Lexicons, and Grammars

1   *Concordances*
Abegg, M. G., J. E. Bowley, and E. M. Cook, 2003. *The Dead Sea Scrolls Concordance, vol. 1:*
     The Non-Biblical Texts from Qumran. 2 vols. Leiden: Brill.

1.1 Lexicons

AHw = von Soden, W. 1965–81. *Akkadisches Handwörterbuch.* 3 vols. Wiesbaden: Otto Harrassowitz.

BDB = Brown, F., S. R. Driver, and C. A. Briggs. 1906. *A Hebrew and English Lexicon of the Old Testament.* Oxford: Clarendon.

Ben-Iehuda, E. 1947–59. *Thesaurus totius hebraitatis et veteris et recentioris.* 17 vols. Jerusalem: Le-ʿAm [Hebrew].

CDA = Black, J., A. George, and N. Postgate. 2000. *A Concise Dictionary of Akkadian*². Wiesbaden: Otto Harrassowitz.

CAD = *The Assyrian Dictionary of the Oriental Institute of the University of Chicago.* 21 vols. Chicago: Oriental Institute, 1956–2005.

GB = Gesenius, W. 1915. *Wilhelm Gesenius' hebräisches und aramäisches Handwörterbuch über das Alte Testament.* Edited by F. Buhl. Leipzig: Vogel.

HALOT = Koehler, L. and W. Baumgartner. 1994–2000. *Hebrew and Aramaic Lexicon of the Old Testament.* 5 vols. Revised by W. Baumgartner and J. J. Stamm. Leiden: Brill.

Kaddari = Kaddari, M. Z. 2006. *A Dictionary of Biblical Hebrew.* Ramat-Gan: Bar-Ilan University Press [Hebrew].

KB = Koehler, L. and W. Baumgartner. 1958. *Lexicon in Veteris Testamenti Libros.* Leiden: Brill.

Olmo Lete, G. del and J. Sanmartín. 2003. *A Dictionary of the Ugaritic Language in the Alphabetic Tradition*². 2 vols. Handbuch der Orientalistik 67. Leiden: Brill.

DJPA = Sokoloff, M. 1990. *A Dictionary of Jewish Palestinian Aramaic.* Ramat-Gan: Bar-Ilan University Press.

1.2 Grammars

Bauer, H. and P. Leander. 1922. *Historische Grammatik der hebräischen Sprache des Alten Testamentes.* Tübingen: Halle.

GKC = Kautzsch, E., ed. 1910. *Gesenius' Hebrew Grammar.* Translated by A. E. Cowley. Oxford: Clarendon.

JM = Joüon, P. 2006. *A Grammar of Biblical Hebrew*². Subsidia Biblica 27. Translated and edited by T. Muraoka. Rome: Pontifical Biblical Institute.

Segal, M. H. 1927. *A Grammar of Mishnaic Hebrew.* Oxford: Clarendon.

C Other Scholarly Literature

Abramson, Sh. 1985. "Biblical Hebrew in Mishnaic Hebrew." Pages 211–242 in *Language Studies* 1. Edited by M. Bar-Asher. Jerusalem: Hebrew University of Jerusalem and Institute for Jewish Studies [Hebrew].

Aharoni, Y. 1966. "Hebrew Ostraca from Tel Arad." *Israel Exploration Journal* 16: 1–7.

Albright, W. F. 1943. "An Archaic Hebrew Proverb in an Amarna Letter from Central Palestine." *Bulletin of the American Schools of Oriental Research* 89: 29–32.

Allen, L. C. 1983. *Psalms 101–150*. Word Biblical Commentary 21. Waco: Word Books.

Andersen, F. I. and A. D. Forbes. 1986. *Spelling in the Hebrew Bible: Dahood Memorial Lecture*. Biblica et Orientalia 41. Rome: Biblical Institute.

Avi-Yonah, M. 1954. *Jerusalem: The Saga of the Holy City*. Jerusalem: Universitas-Publishers.

Avi-Yonah, M. and J. Liver. 1962. "מטבע." Columns 816–825 in vol. 4 of *Encyclopaedia Biblica*. Jerusalem: Bialik Institute [Hebrew].

Baasten, M. F. J. 2000. "Existential Clauses in Qumran Hebrew." Pages 1–11 in *Diggers at the Well: Proceedings of a Third International Symposium on the Hebrew of the Dead Sea Scrolls and Ben Sira*. Edited by T. Muraoka and J. F. Elwolde. Studies on the Texts of the Desert of Judah 36. Leiden: Brill.

Baillet, M. 1962. "25. Document Juridique." Page 90 in *Les 'Petites Grottes' de Qumran*. Discoveries in the Judaean Desert 3. 2 vols. Edited by M. Baillet, J. T. Milik, and R. de Vaux. Oxford: Clarendon.

Bar-Asher, M. 1984. "The Different Traditions of Mishnaic Hebrew." *Tarbiz* 53: 187–220 (= Bar-Asher 2009: 76–108) [Hebrew].

———. 1985. "The Historical Unity of Hebrew and Mishnaic Hebrew Research." Pages 75–99 in *Language Studies* 1. Edited by M. Bar-Asher. Jerusalem: Hebrew University of Jerusalem and the Institute for Jewish Studies [Hebrew].

———. 2003. "On Several Linguistic Features of Qumran Hebrew." Pages 73–93 in *Hamlet on a Hill: Semitic and Greek Studies Presented to Professor T. Muraoka on the Occasion of His Sixty-Fifth Birthday*. Edited by M. F. J. Baasten and W. T. van Peursen. Leuven: Peeters.

———. 2009. *Studies in Mishnaic Hebrew*, vol. 1: *Introduction and Linguistic Investigations*. Jerusalem: Bialik Institute [Hebrew].

Barton, G. A. 1908. *A Critical and Exegetical Commentary on the Book of Ecclesiastes*. International Critical Commentary. Edinburgh: T & T Clark.

Batten, L. W. 1913. *A Critical and Exegetical Commentary on the Books of Ezra and Nehemiah*. International Critical Commentary. Edinburgh: T & T Clark.

Bendavid, A. 1967–71. *Biblical Hebrew and Mishnaic Hebrew*. 2 vols. Tel-Aviv: Dvir [Hebrew].

Bergey, R. L. 1983. "The Book of Esther: Its Place in the Linguistic Milieu of Post-Exilic Biblical Hebrew Prose: A Study in Late Biblical Hebrew." Ph.D. diss., Dropsie College for Hebrew and Cognate Learning.

Braver, A. Y. 1976. "The Meaning of the Noun מדע in Qohelet 10:20." *Beit Mikra* 21: 158–159 [Hebrew].

Brenner, A. 1980. "'White' Textiles in Biblical Hebrew and in Mishnaic Hebrew." *Hebrew Annual Review* 4: 39–44.

Breuer, Y. 2002. *The Hebrew in the Babylonian Talmud according to the Manuscripts of Tractate Pesahim.* Jerusalem: Magnes.

Bush, F. W. 1996. *Ruth, Esther.* Word Biblical Commentary 9. Dallas: Word Books.

Carmignac, J. 1974. "L'emploi de la négation אין dans la Bible et à Qumran." *Revue de Qumran* 31: 407–413.

Chazon, E. G. 2012. "Liturgy Before and After the Temple's Destruction: Change or Continuity?" Pages 371–392 in *Was 70 CE a Watershed in Jewish History?: On Jews and Judaism before and after the Destruction of the Second Temple.* Edited by D. R. Schwartz and Z. Weiss. Ancient Judaism and Early Christianity 78. Leiden: Brill.

Collins, J. J. 1993. *Daniel: A Commentary on the Book of Daniel.* Hermeneia 27. Minneapolis: Fortress.

Cooke, G. A. 1936. *A Critical and Exegetical Commentary on the Book of Ezekiel.* International Critical Commentary. Edinburgh: T & T Clark.

Crenshaw, J. L. 1988. *Ecclesiastes: A Commentary.* London: SCM.

Curtis, E. L. and A. A. Madsen. 1910. *A Critical and Exegetical Commentary on the Books of Chronicles.* International Critical Commentary. Edinburgh: T & T Clark.

Davila, J. R. 1991. Review of Fredericks 1988. *Journal of the American Oriental Society* 111: 821–824.

Delitzsch, F. 1871. *Biblical Commentary on the Psalms.* Vol. 5 of Commentary on the Old Testament. Translated by F. Bolton. Edinburgh: T & T Clark.

———. 1877. *Commentary on the Song of Songs and Ecclesiastes.* Edinburgh: T & T Clark.

Demsky, A. 2002. "Hebrew Names in the Dual Form and the Toponym 'Yerushalayim.'" Pages 11–20 in vol. 3 of *These Are the Names: Studies in Jewish Onomastics.* Edited by A. Demsky. Ramat-Gan: Bar-Ilan University Press.

Derby, J. 1997. "From Yerushalem to Yerushalayim." *Jewish Bible Quarterly* 25: 241–245.

de Vaux, R. 1965. *Ancient Israel.* 2 vols. New York: McGraw Hill.

Dihi, H. 2004. "Morphological and Lexical Innovations in the Book of Ben Sira." Ph.D. diss., Beer-Sheva: Ben-Gurion University of the Negev [Hebrew].

Dimant, D. 2007. "The Volunteers in the Rule of the Community: A Biblical Notion in Sectarian Garb." *Revue de Qumran* 23: 233–245.

Driver, G. R. 1953. "Hebrew Poetic Diction." Pages 26–39 in *Congress Volume, Copenhagen 1953.* Vetus Testamentum Supplement 1. Edited by G. W. Anderson. Leiden: Brill.

Driver, S. R. 1892. *A Treatise on the Use of the Tenses in Hebrew and Some Other Syntactical Questions*³. London: Oxford University Press.

———. 1913. *An Introduction to the Literature of the Old Testament.* Oxford: Clarendon.

du Plessis, S. J. 1971. "Aspects of Morphological Peculiarities of the Language of Qoheleth." Pages 164–180 in *De Fructu Oris Sui: Essays in Honour of Adrianus van Selms.* Edited by I. H. Eybers et al. Pretoria Oriental Series 9. Leiden: Brill.

Ehrensvärd, M. 2003. "Linguistic Dating of Biblical Texts." Pages 164–188 in *Biblical Hebrew: Studies in Chronology and Typology*. Edited by I. Young. London: T & T Clark.

Elitzur, Y. 2004. *Ancient Place Names in the Holy Land: Preservation and History*. Jerusalem: Magnes.

Elwolde, J. F. 2002. "3Q15: Its Linguistic Affiliation, with Lexicographical Comments." Pages 108–121 in *Copper Scroll Studies*. Edited by G. J. Brooke and P. R. Davies. London: Sheffield Academic.

Eshel, E., H. Eshel, and A. Yardeni. 1992. "A Qumran Composition Containing Part of Ps. 154 and a Prayer for the Welfare of King Jonathan and His Kingdom." *Israel Exploration Journal* 42: 199–229.

Eskhult, M. 2003. "The Importance of Loanwords for Dating Biblical Hebrew Texts." Pages 8–23 in *Biblical Hebrew: Studies in Chronology and Typology*. Edited by I. Young. London: T & T Clark.

Fassberg, S. E. 1994. *Studies in Biblical Syntax*. Jerusalem: Magnes [Hebrew].

———. 2000. "The Linguistic Study of the Damascus Document." Pages 53–67 in *The Damascus Document: A Centennial of Discovery*. Edited by J. M. Baumgarten, E. G. Chazon, and A. Pinnick. Studies in the Texts of the Desert of Judah 34. Leiden: Brill.

Fensham, F. C. 1982. *The Books of Ezra and Nehemiah*. New International Commentary on the Old Testament. Grand Rapids: Eerdmans.

Fishbane, M. 1985. *Biblical Interpretation and Ancient Israel*. Oxford: Clarendon.

Foerster, W. 1972. " Ἰησοῦς." Pages 284–293 in vol. 3 of *Theological Dictionary of the New Testament*. Edited by G. Kittel, G. Friedrich, and G. W. Bromiley. Grand Rapids: Eerdmans.

Fohrer, G. 1972. "Σιών, Ἰερουσαλήμ, Ἱεροσόλυμα, Ἱεροσολυμίτης." Pages 292–319 in vol. 7 of *Theological Dictionary of the New Testament*. Edited by G. Kittel, G. Friedrich, and G. W. Bromiley. Grand Rapids: Eerdmans.

Folmer, M. L. 1995. *The Aramaic Language in the Achaemenid Period: A Study in Linguistic Variation*. Leuven: Peeters.

Fraenkel, S. 1886. *Die aramäischen Fremdwörter im Arabischen*. Leiden: Brill.

Fredericks, D. C. 1988. *Qoheleth's Language: Re-Evaluating Its Nature and Date*. Ancient Near Eastern Texts and Studies 3. Lewiston, NY: Edwin Mellen.

Freedman, D. N. 1983. "The Spelling of the Name 'David' in the Hebrew Bible." *Hebrew Annual Review* 7: 89–104.

Freedman, D. N., B. E. Willoughby, H.-J. Fabry, and H. Ringgren. 1999. "נֶפֶשׁ." Pages 24–40 in vol. 10 of *Theological Dictionary of the Old Testament*. Edited by G. J. Botterweck, H. Ringgren, and H.-J. Fabry. Grand Rapids: Eerdmans.

Friedberg, A. D. 2000. "A New Clue in the Dating of the Composition of the Book of Esther." *Vetus Testamentum* 50: 561–563.

Gertner, M. 1962. "Terms of Scriptural Interpretation: A Study in Hebrew Semantics." *Bulletin of the School of Oriental (and African) Studies* 25: 1–27.

Gesenius, W. 1815. *Geschichte der hebräischen Sprache und Schrift*. Leipzig: Vogel; repr. Hildesheim: G. Olms, 1973.

Ginsberg, H. L. 1961. *Koheleth*. Tel-Aviv and Jerusalem: Neuman [Hebrew].

———. 1969. *The Five Megilloth and Jonah*. Philadelphia: Jewish Publication Society.

———. 1970. "The Northwest Semitic Languages." Pages 102–124 in vol. 2 [= Patriarchs] of *The World History of the Jewish People*. First Series: *Ancient Times*. Edited by Benjamin Mazar. Tel-Aviv: Massada [Hebrew].

Ginsburg, C. D. 1861. *Coheleth*. London: Longman, Green, Longman, and Roberts.

Gluska, I. 1999. *Hebrew and Aramaic in Contact during the Tannaitic Period: A Sociolinguistic Approach*. Tel-Aviv: Papyrus [Hebrew].

Gordis, R. 1968. *Koheleth: The Man and His World*³. New York: Schocken Books; first published: New York: Jewish Theological Seminary, 1951.

Gordon, C. H. 1965. *Ugaritic Textbook: Grammar, Texts in Transliteration, Cuneiform Selections, Glossary, Indices*. Rome: Pontifical Biblical Institute.

Greenfield, J. C. 1987. "The Verb *Sallaṭa* in the Qur'ān in the Light of Aramaic Usage." *Jerusalem Studies in Arabic and Islam* 9: 36–41; repr. pages 412–417 of vol. 1 in *'Al Kanfei Yonah: Collected Studies of Jonas C. Greenfield on Semitic Philology*. Edited by S. M. Paul, M. E. Stone, and A. Pinnick. Leiden: Brill; Jerusalem: Magnes, 2001.

———. 2001. *'Al Kanfei Yonah: Collected Studies of Jonas C. Greenfield on Semitic Philology*. 2 vols. Edited by S. M. Paul, M. E. Stone, and A. Pinnick. Leiden: Brill; Jerusalem: Magnes.

Grintz, Y. M. 1975a. "Archaic Terms in the Priestly Code I." *Lěšonénu* 39: 5–20 [Hebrew].

———. 1975b. "Archaic Terms in the Priestly Code II." *Lěšonénu* 39: 163–181 [Hebrew].

Hadas-Lebel, M. 1995. *Histoire de la langue hébraïque: Des origines à l'époque de la Mishna*. Collection de la Revue des Études Juives 13. Paris and Louvain: Peeters.

Hayneman, Y. 1946. "On the Development of Professional Terms for the Interpretation of Scripture." *Lěšonénu* 14: 182–189 [Hebrew].

Healey, J. F. 1996. "'May He Be Remembered for Good': An Aramaic Formula." Pages 177–186 in *Targumic and Cognate Studies: Essays in Honour of Martin McNamara*. Edited by K. J. Cathcart and M. Maher. Sheffield: Sheffield Academic.

Hill, A. E. 1981. "The Book of Malachi: Its Place in Post-Exilic Chronology Linguistically Reconsidered." Ph.D. diss. University of Michigan, Ann Arbor.

———. 1982. "Dating Second Zechariah: A Linguistic Reexamination." *Hebrew Annual Review* 6: 105–134.

Hornkohl, A. 2012. "The Language of the Book of Jeremiah and the History of the Hebrew Language." Ph.D. diss., Hebrew University of Jerusalem [Hebrew].

———. 2013. "Biblical Hebrew: Periodization." Pages 315–325 in vol. 1 of *Encyclopedia of Hebrew Language and Linguistics*. Edited by G. Khan. Leiden: Brill.

Howie, C. G. 1950. *The Date and Composition of Ezekiel*. Society of Biblical Literature Monograph Series 4. Philadelphia: Scholars.

Hurvitz, A. 1965. "Observations on the Language of the Third Apocryphal Psalm from Qumran." *Revue de Qumran* 5: 225–232.

———. 1967. "The Usage of שֵׁשׁ and בּוּץ in the Bible and Its Implication for the Date of P." *Harvard Theological Review* 60: 117–121.

———. 1968. "The Chronological Significance of Aramaisms in Biblical Hebrew." *Israel Exploration Journal* 18: 234–240.

———. 1972. *The Transition Period in Biblical Hebrew: A Study of Post-Exilic Hebrew and Its Implications for the Dating of Psalms*. Jerusalem: Bialik Institute [Hebrew].

———. 1974a. "The Evidence of Language in Dating the Priestly Code—A Linguistic Study in Technical Idioms and Terminology." *Revue Biblique* 81: 24–56.

———. 1974b. "The Date of the Prose-Tale of Job Linguistically Reconsidered." *Harvard Theological Review* 67: 17–34.

———. 1982. *A Linguistic Study of the Relationship between the Priestly Source and the Book of Ezekiel: A New Approach to an Old Problem*. Cahiers de la Revue Biblique 20. Paris: J. Gabalda.

———. 1983. "The Hebrew Language in the Persian Period." Pages 210–223, 306–309 in *The History of 'Am Israel, Shivat Tzion—The Period of Persian Rule*. Edited by Ch. Tadmor. Jerusalem: Peli and 'Am 'Oved [Hebrew].

———. 1990. Review of Fredericks 1988. *Hebrew Studies* 31: 144–154.

———. 1992. "בֵּית־קְבָרוֹת and בֵּית־עוֹלָם: Two Funerary Terms in Biblical Literature and Their Linguistic Background." *Maarav* 8: 59–68.

———. 1993. "בֵּית־(הָ)אוֹצָר—The History of a Biblical Administrative-Economic Term." *Eretz Israel* 24: 78–82 [Hebrew].

———. 1995a. "Continuity and Innovation in Biblical Hebrew—The Case of 'Semantic Change' in Post-Exilic Writings." Pages 1–10 in *Studies in Ancient Hebrew Semantics*. Abr-Nahrain Supplement 4. Edited by T. Muraoka. Leuven: Peeters.

———. 1995b. "Terms and Epithets Relating to the Jerusalem Temple Compound in the Book of Chronicles: The Linguistic Aspect." Pages 165–183 in *Pomegranates and Golden Bells: Studies in Honor of Jacob Milgrom*. Edited by D. P. Wright, D. N. Freedman, and A. Hurvitz. Winona Lake: Eisenbrauns.

———. 1996. "The Origins and Development of the Expression מְגִלַּת־סֵפֶר: A Study in the History of Writing-Related Terminology in Biblical Times." Pages *37–*46 in *Texts, Temples, and Traditions: A Tribute to Menahem Haran*. Edited by M. V. Fox, V. A. Hurowitz, A. Hurvitz, M. L. Klein, B. J. Schwartz, and N. Shupak. Winona Lake: Eisenbrauns [Hebrew].

———. 1997a. "The Linguistic Status of Ben Sira as a Link between Biblical and Mishnaic Hebrew: Lexicographical Aspects." Pages 72–86 in *The Hebrew of the Dead Sea Scrolls and Ben Sira: Proceedings of a Symposium Held at Leiden University, 11–14 December 1995*. Edited by T. Muraoka and J. F. Elwolde. Studies on the Texts of the Desert of Judah 26. Leiden: Brill.

———. 1997b. "On the Borderline between Biblical Criticism and Hebrew Linguistics: The Emergence of the Term סֵפֶר מֹשֶׁה." Pages 37*–43* in *Tehilla le-Moshe: Biblical and Judaic Studies in Honor of Moshe Greenberg*. Edited by M. Cogan, B. L. Eichler, and J. H. Tigay. Winona Lake: Eisenbrauns [Hebrew].

———. 2000a. "Can Biblical Texts Be Dated Linguistically? Chronological Perspectives in the Historical Study of Biblical Hebrew." Pages 143–160 in *Vetus Testamentum Supplements 80 Congress Volume Oslo 1998*. Edited by A. Lemaire and M. Saebø. Leiden: Brill.

———. 2000b. "Once Again: The Linguistic Profile of the Priestly Material in the Pentateuch and Its Historical Age—A Response to J. Blenkinsopp." *Zeitschrift für die alttestamentliche Wissenschaft* 112: 180–191.

———. 2003a. "Hebrew and Aramaic in the Biblical Period: The Problem of 'Aramaisms' in Linguistic Research on the Hebrew Bible." Pages 24–37 in *Biblical Hebrew: Studies in Chronology and Typology*. Edited by I. Young. London: T & T Clark.

———. 2003b. "ראש־דבר and סוף־דבר: Reflexes of Two Scribal Terms Imported into Biblical Hebrew from the Imperial Aramaic Formulary." Pages 281–286 in *Hamlet on a Hill: Semitic and Greek Studies Presented to Professor T. Muraoka on the Occasion of his Sixty-Fifth Birthday*. Edited by M. F. J. Baasten and W. T. van Peursen. Leuven: Peeters.

———. 2006. "The Recent Debate on Late Biblical Hebrew: Solid Data, Experts' Opinions, and Inconclusive Arguments." *Hebrew Studies* 47: 191–210.

———. 2013. "Hebrew Language, Late." Pages 329–338 in vol. 1 of *Encyclopedia of Hebrew Language and Linguistics*. Edited by G. Khan. Leiden: Brill.

Japhet, S. 1987. "Interchanges of Verbal Roots in Parallel Texts in Chronicles." *Hebrew Studies* 28: 9–50; Hebrew version: in *Lěšonénu* 31 (1966–67): 165–179, 261–279.

———. 1993. *I & II Chronicles*. Old Testament Library. Louisville: Westminster and John Knox.

Jeffery, A. 1938. *The Foreign Vocabulary of the Qurʾān*. Baroda, India: Oriental Institute.

Joosten, J. 1999. "Pseudo-Classicisms in Late Biblical Hebrew, in Ben Sira, and in Qumran Hebrew." Pages 146–159 in *Sirach, Scrolls, and Sages: Proceedings of a Second International Symposium on the Hebrew of the Dead Sea Scrolls and Ben Sira*. Edited by T. Muraoka and J. F. Elwolde. Studies on the Texts of the Desert of Judah 33. Leiden: Brill.

———. 2000. "The Knowledge and Use of Hebrew in the Hellenistic Period Qumran and the Septuagint." Pages 115–130 in *Diggers at the Well: Proceedings of a Third International Symposium on the Hebrew of the Dead Sea Scrolls and Ben Sira*. Edited by T. Muraoka and J. F. Elwolde. Studies on the Texts of the Desert of Judah 36. Leiden: Brill.

Kaddari, M. Z. 1976. *Parashiyot be-Taḥbir Leshon ha-Miqra*. Ramat-Gan: Bar-Ilan University.

Kaufman, S. A. 1974. *The Akkadian Influences on Aramaic*. Akkadian Studies 19. Chicago: University of Chicago Press.

Kautzsch, E. 1902. *Die Aramaismen im Alten Testament untersucht*. Halle: M. Niemeyer.

Keil, C. F. 1872. *The Books of the Chronicles*. Biblical Commentary on the Old Testament. Edinburgh: T & T Clark; New York: C. Scribner.

———. 1877. *The Book of the Prophet Daniel*. Biblical Commentary on the Old Testament. Edinburgh: T & T Clark.

Klein, R. W. 2006. *1 Chronicles: A Commentary*. Hermeneia. Minneapolis: Fortress.

Kogut, S. 1997. "A Proposed Solution to the Connection between the Textual Variants of II Sam. 6:14 and I Chron. 15:27." *Tarbiz* 66: 141–147 [Hebrew].

Kühlwein, J. "סָפַר". 1997. Pages 806–813 in vol. 2 of *Theological Lexicon of the Old Testament*. Edited by E. Jenni and C. Westermann. Peabody, Mass.: Hendrickson.

Kutscher, E. Y. 1937. "A Lexical Problem: מחוז = נמל." *Lěšonénu* 8: 136–145 (= 1977: 367–376) [Hebrew].

———. 1954. "New Aramaic Texts." *Journal of the American Oriental Society* 74: 233–248.

———. 1959. *The Language and Linguistic Background of the Isaiah Scroll (1QIsᵃ)*. Jerusalem: Magnes [Hebrew].

———. 1961. *Words and Their History*. Jerusalem: Kiryat Sefer [Hebrew].

———. 1963–64. "Aramaic Calque in Hebrew." *Tarbiz* 33: 118–130 [Hebrew] (= Kutscher 1977: 394–406 [Hebrew]).

———. 1966. "Marginal Notes to the Biblical Lexicon," *Lěšonénu* 30: 18–24 [Hebrew] (= Kutscher 1977: 348–354 [Hebrew]).

———. 1970. "Aramaic." Pages 347–412 in vol. 6 of *Current Trends in Linguistics*. Edited by T. A. Sebeok. The Hague: Mouton (= 1977: 90–155).

———. 1971. "Hebrew Language: The Dead Sea Scrolls." Columns 1583–1590 in vol. 16 of *Encyclopedia Judaica*. Edited by C. Roth. Jerusalem: Keter.

———. 1972. *A History of Aramaic*. Jerusalem: Academon [Hebrew].

———. 1974. *The Language and Linguistic Background of the Isaiah Scroll (1QIsᵃ)*. 2 vols. Studies in the Texts of the Desert of Judah 6–6a. Leiden: Brill.

———. 1977. *Hebrew and Aramaic Studies*. Edited by Z. Ben-Ḥayyim, A. Dotan, and G. B. Sarfatti. Jerusalem: Magnes [Hebrew].

———. 1982. *A History of the Hebrew Language*. Edited by R. Kutscher. Jerusalem: Magnes.

Lambdin, T. O. 1953. "Egyptian Loan Words in the Old Testament." *Journal of the American Oriental Society* 73: 145–155.

Lefkovits, J. K. 2000. *The Copper Scroll—3Q15: A Reevaluation: A New Reading, Translation, and Commentary*. Studies in the Texts of the Desert of Judah 25. Leiden: Brill.

Lemaire, A. and H. Lozachmeur. 1987. "La 'bîrtâ' en Méditerranée orientale." *Semitica* 43–44: 75–78.

Levita, E. 1847. *Sefer ha-Šorašim le-Rabbi David ben Yosef Qimḥi ha-Sefaredi*, with comments by Elias Levita. Edited by J. H. R. Biesenthal and F. Lebrecht. Berlin: G. Bethge.

Licht, J. 1965. *The Rule Scroll: A Scroll from the Wilderness of Judea, 1QS.1QSa.1QSb.*
Jerusalem: Bialik Institute [Hebrew].

Lieberman, S. 1935–36. "*Mekhilta.*" *Kiryat Sepher* 12: 54–65.

———. 1955–92 . *Tosefta ki-fshuṭah.* 8 vols. Jerusalem: Jewish Theological Seminary.

Liver, J. 1965. "יֵשׁוּעַ. 2." Column 895 in vol. 3 of *Encyclopaedia Biblica.* Jerusalem: Bialik
Institute [Hebrew].

Loewenstamm, S. E. 1962. "מכתב." Columns 966–967 in vol. 4 of *Encyclopaedia Biblica.*
Jerusalem: Bialik Institute [Hebrew].

———. 1965. "יֵשׁוּעַ. 1." Column 895 in vol. 3 of *Encyclopaedia Biblica.* Jerusalem: Bialik
Institute [Hebrew].

Magnanini, P. 1968. "Sull'origine letteraria dell'Ecclesiaste." *Annali dell'Istituto Orientale
di Napoli* 28: 363–384.

Mankowski, P. V. 2000. *Akkadian Loanwords in Biblical Hebrew.* Harvard Semitic Studies
47. Winona Lake: Eisenbrauns.

Margulis, B. 1969. "Gen. XLIX 10/Deut. XXXIII 2–3: A New Look at Old Problems." *Vetus
Testamentum* 19: 202–210.

Mazar, B. 1962. "לְבֹא חֲמָת, לְבוֹא חֲמָת." Columns 416–418 in vol. 4 of *Encyclopaedia
Biblica.* Jerusalem: Bialik Institute [Hebrew].

Meshorer, Y. 1982. *Ancient Jewish Coinage.* 2 vols. New York: Amphora.

———. 1989. "The Coins of Masada." Pages 70–132 and plates 61–81 in *Masada I: The
Yigael Yadin Excavations 1963–1965 Final Reports.* Jerusalem: Yigael Yadin Memorial
Fund, Hebrew University of Jerusalem, and Israel Exploration Society.

Milgrom, J. *Leviticus.* 1991–2001. Anchor Bible Commentary. 3 vols. New York: Doubleday.

Montgomery, J. A. 1927. *A Critical and Exegetical Commentary on the Book of Daniel.*
International Critical Commentary. Edinburgh: T & T Clark; repr. 1964.

Moore, C. A. 1971. *Esther.* Anchor Bible Commentary. Garden City, NY: Doubleday.

Morag, S. 1972. Review of Max Wagner 1966. *Journal of the American Oriental Society*
92: 298–300.

———. 1995. *Studies on Biblical Hebrew.* Jerusalem: Magnes.

Moran, W. L. 1975. "Amarna Glosses." *Revue d'assyriologie et d'archéologie orientale* 69:
147–158.

Moreshet, M. 1980. *A Lexicon of the New Verbs in Tannaitic Hebrew.* Ramat-Gan: Bar-Ilan
University [Hebrew].

Morgenstern, J. 1924. "The Three Calendars of Ancient Israel." *Hebrew Union College
Annual* 1: 13–78.

Mosis, R. 1990. "יָחַשׂ; יָחַשׂ." Pages 55–59 in vol. 6 of *Theological Dictionary of the Old Testament*. Edited by G. J. Botterweck, H. Ringgren, and H.-J. Fabry. Grand Rapids: Eerdmans.

Muffs, Y. 1969. *Studies in the Aramaic Legal Papyri from Elephantine*. Studia et documenta ad iura Orientis antiqui pertinentia 8. Leiden: Brill.

Müller, H.-P. 1998. "נָבִיא." Pages 129–150 in vol. 9 of *Theological Dictionary of the Old Testament*. Edited by G. J. Botterweck, H. Ringgren, and H.-J. Fabry. Grand Rapids: Eerdmans.

Mussies, G. 1992. "Languages (Greek)." Pages 195–203 in vol. 4 of *Anchor Bible Dictionary*. Edited by D. N. Freedman. New Haven: Yale University Press.

Naveh, J. and J. C. Greenfield. 1984. "Hebrew and Aramaic in the Persian Period." Pages 115–129 in vol. 1 of *The Cambridge History of Judaism*. Edited by W. D. Davies and L. Finkelstein. Cambridge: Cambridge University Press (= Greenfield 2001: I 232–246).

Nebe, G. W. 1997. "Die hebräische Sprache der Naḥal Ḥever Dokumente 5/6Ḥev 44–46." Pages 150–157 in *The Hebrew of the Dead Sea Scrolls and Ben Sira: Proceedings of a Symposium Held at Leiden University, 11–14 December 1995*. Edited by T. Muraoka and J. F. Elwolde. Studies on the Texts of the Desert of Judah 26. Leiden: Brill.

Nöldeke, T. 1903. Review of Kautzsch 1902. *Zeitschrift der Deutschen Morgenländischen Gesellschaft* 57: 412–420.

———. 1904. *Compendious Syriac Grammar*. London: Williams & Norgate.

———. 1910–11. "Semitic Languages." Pages 616–630 in vol. 24 of *Encyclopedia Britannica*[11]. Cambridge: Cambridge University Press.

Otzen, B. 1975. "בהל." Pages 3–5 in vol. 2 of *Theological Dictionary of the Old Testament*. Edited by G. J. Botterweck, H. Ringgren, and H.-J. Fabry. Grand Rapids: Eerdmans.

Paton, L. B. 1908. *A Critical and Exegetical Commentary on the Book of Esther*. International Critical Commentary. Edinburgh: T & T Clark; repr. 1961.

Paul, S. M. 1984. "Dan 6:8: An Aramaic Reflex of Assyrian Legal Terminology." *Biblica* 65: 106–110.

Pfann, S. 1999. "249. 4Qpap cryptA Midrash Sefer Moshe." Pages 1–24 in *Qumran Cave 4.XXV: Halakhic Texts*. Discoveries in the Judaean Desert 35. Edited by J. M. Baumgarten et al. Oxford: Clarendon.

Plesner, M. 1954. "גִּזְבָּר." Page 463 in vol. 2 of *Encyclopaedia Biblica*. Jerusalem: Bialik Institute [Hebrew].

Podechard, E. 1912. *L'Ecclésisaste*. Etudes Bibliques. Paris: Lecoffre.

Polak, F. H. 2003. "Style is More than the Person: Sociolinguistics, Literary Culture and the Distinction between Written and Oral Narrative." Pages 37–103 in *Biblical Hebrew: Studies in Chronology and Typology*. Journal for the Study of the Old Testament Supplement Series 369. Edited by I. Young. London: T & T Clark International.

————. 2006a. "Sociolinguistics and the Judean Speech Community in the Achaemenid Empire." Pages 589–528 in *Judah and the Judeans in the Persian Period*. Edited by O. Lipschits and M. Oeming. Winona Lake: Eisenbrauns.

————. 2006b. "Sociolinguistics: A Key to the Typology and the Social Background of Biblical Hebrew." *Hebrew Studies* 47: 115–162.

Polotsky, H. J. 1964. "Aramaic, Syriac, and Ge'ez." *Journal of Semitic Studies* 9: 1–10.

Polzin, R. 1976. *Late Biblical Hebrew: Toward an Historical Typology of Biblical Hebrew Prose*. Harvard Semitic Monographs 12. Missoula: Scholars.

Qimron, E. 1971. "The Psalms Scroll of Qumrân—A Linguistic Survey." *Lĕšonénu* 35: 99–116 [Hebrew].

————. 1978. "The Language of the Second Temple in the Book of Psalms." *Beit Mikra* 23: 139–150 [Hebrew].

————. 1980. "The Vocabulary of the Temple Scroll." *Shnaton: An Annual for Biblical and Ancient Near Eastern Studies* 4: 239–262. [Hebrew].

————. 1986. *The Hebrew of the Dead Sea Scrolls*. Atlanta: Scholars.

————. 2003. "Prayers for the Festivals from Qumran: Reconstruction and Philological Observations." Pages 383–393 in *Hamlet on a Hill: Semitic and Greek Studies Presented to Professor T. Muraoka on the Occasion of His Sixty-Fifth Birthday*. Edited by M. F. J. Baasten and W. T. van Peursen. Leuven: Peeters.

Qimron, E. and J. Strugnell. 1994. *Qumran Cave 4. V: Miqṣat Ma'aśe Ha-Torah*. Discoveries in the Judaean Desert 10. Oxford: Clarendon.

Rabin, Ch. 1958a. "The Historical Background of Qumran Hebrew." *Scripta Hiersolymitana* 4: 144–161.

————. 1958b. *The Zadokite Documents²*. Oxford: Clarendon.

————. 1960. "Semitic *ā* and Its Reflections in Hebrew." *Tarbiz* 30: 99–111 [Hebrew].

————. 1962. "מלים זרות." Columns 1070–1080 in vol. 4 of *Encyclopaedia Biblica*. Jerusalem: Bialik Institute [Hebrew].

————. 1970. "Hebrew." Pages 304–346 in vol. 4 of *Current Trends in Linguistics*. Edited by T. A. Sebeok. The Hague: Mouton.

————. 1971. "Hebrew [עברית]." Columns 51–73 in vol. 6 of *Encyclopaedia Biblica*. Jerusalem: Bialik Institute [Hebrew].

Rainey, A. F. 2002. "The 'Amârnah Texts a Century after Flinders Petrie." *Ancient Near Eastern Studies* 39: 44–75.

———— (with R. S. Notley). 2007. *Carta's New Century Handbook and Atlas of the Bible*. Jerusalem: Carta.

Rendsburg, G. A. 1990a. *Diglossia in Ancient Hebrew*. American Oriental Series 72. New Haven: Yale University Press.

————. 1990b. *Linguistic Evidence for the Northern Origin of Selected Psalms*. Society of Biblical Literature Monograph Series 43. Atlanta: Scholars.

————. 1991. "The Northern Origin of Nehemiah 9." *Biblica* 72: 348–366.

Rezetko, R. 2010. "The Spelling of 'Damascus' and the Linguistic Dating of Biblical Texts." *Scandinavian Journal of the Old Testament* 24: 110–128.

Ringgren, H. 1990. "יְרוּשָׁלִַם." Pages 347–348 in vol. 6 of *Theological Dictionary of the Old Testament*. Edited by G. J. Botterweck, H. Ringgren, and H.-J. Fabry. Grand Rapids: Eerdmans.

Robinson, G. L. 1895. "The Prophecies of Zechariah with Special Reference to the Origin and Date of Chapters 9–14." *American Journal of Semitic Languages and Literatures* 12: 1–92.

Rooker, M. F. 1990. *Biblical Hebrew in Transition: The Language of the Book of Ezekiel.* Journal for the Study of the Old Testament Supplement 90. Sheffield: JSOT.

———. 1997. "עזרה." Pages 379–380 in vol. 3 of *New International Dictionary of Old Testament Theology and Exegesis*. Edited by W. A. VanGemeren. Grand Rapids: Zondervan.

———. 2003. "Diachronic Analysis and the Features of Late Biblical Hebrew." Pages 45–57 in *Studies in Hebrew Language, Intertextuality, and Theology*. Edited by M. Rooker. Lewiston, NY: Edwin Mellen.

Rosenthal, D. 1991. "בנימין גנזבייה – מנימין סקסנאה." *Tarbiz* 60: 439–442.

Rosenthal, F. 1939. *Die aramaistiche Forschung seit Th. Nöldeke's Veröffentlichungen.* Leiden: Brill.

———. 1961. *A Grammar of Biblical Aramaic.* Porta Linguarum Orientalium 5. Wiesbaden: Otto Harrassowitz.

Rudman, D. 1999. "A Note on the Dating of Ecclesiastes." *Catholic Biblical Quarterly* 61: 47–52.

Sæbø, M. 1999. "סוֹף." Pages 188–190 in vol. 10 of *Theological Dictionary of the Old Testament*. Edited by G. J. Botterweck, H. Ringgren, and H.-J. Fabry. Grand Rapids: Eerdmans.

Sáenz-Badillos, A. 1993. *A History of the Hebrew Language.* Cambridge: Cambridge University Press.

Sarfatti, G. B. 1969. "אוהל = בית מדרש." *Tarbiz* 38: 87–89.

Sawyer, J. F. A. 1990. "ישע." Pages 441–447 in vol. 6 of *Theological Dictionary of the Old Testament*. Edited by G. J. Botterweck, H. Ringgren, and H.-J. Fabry. Grand Rapids: Eerdmans.

Schattner-Rieser, U. 1994. "L'hébreu postexilique." Pages 189–224 in *La Palestine à l'époque perse*. Edited by E.-M. Laperrousaz and A. Lemaire. Paris: Cerf.

Schiffman, L. H. 1975. *Halakhah at Qumran.* Studies in Late Antiquity 16. Leiden: Brill.

Schoors, A. 1992–2004. *The Preacher Sought to Find Pleasing Words: A Study of the Language of Qoheleth.* 2 vols. Orientalia Lovaniensia Analecta 41, 143. Leuven: Peeters.

Schrader, E. 1885–88. *The Cuneiform Inscriptions and the Old Testament.* 2 vols. London: Williams and Norgate.

Seeligman, I. L. 1980. "Niṣane midraš be-sefer divre ha-yamim." *Tarbiz* 49: 14–32.

Segal, M. H. 1908. "Mišnaic Hebrew and Its Relation to Biblical Hebrew and to Aramaic." *Jewish Quarterly Review* 20: 647–737.

———. 1911–12. "Notes on 'Fragments of a Zadokite Work'." *Jewish Quarterly Review* 2: 133–141.

Seow, C. L. 1996. "Linguistic Evidence and the Dating of Qohelet." *Journal of Biblical Literature* 115: 643–666.

———. 1997. *Ecclesiastes*. Anchor Bible Commentary. New York: Doubleday.

Seybold, K., H. Ringgren, H.-J. Fabry. 1997. "מֶלֶךְ." Pages 346–375 in vol. 8 of *Theological Dictionary of the Old Testament*. Edited by G. J. Botterweck, H. Ringgren, and H.-J. Fabry. Grand Rapids: Eerdmans.

Shaked, S. 1984. "Iranian Influence on Judaism, First Century B.C.E. to Second Century C.E." Pages 308–325 in vol. 1 of *The Cambridge History of Judaism*. Edited by W. D. Davies and L. Finkelstein. Cambridge: Cambridge University Press.

Shin, S.-Y. 2007. "A Lexical Study of the Language of Haggai–Zechariah–Malachi and Its Place in the History of Biblical Hebrew." Ph.D. diss., Hebrew University of Jerusalem.

Sommer, B. D. 1998. *A Prophet Reads Scripture: Allusion in Isaiah 40–66*. Stanford: Stanford University Press.

Stadel, C. 2012. "The 'Remembered for Good' Formula in Samaritan Aramaic and Early Hybrid Samaritan Hebrew." *Journal of Jewish Studies* 63: 285–306.

Strauss, D. 1900. *Sprachliche Studien zu den hebräischen Sirachfragmenten*. Zurich: A. Schaufelberger.

Tal, A. 1975. *The Language of the Targum of the Former Prophets and Its Position within the Aramaic Dialects*. Tel-Aviv: University of Tel-Aviv [Hebrew].

Talmon, S. 1963. "The Gezer Calendar and the Seasonal Cycle of Ancient Canaan." *Journal of the American Oriental Society* 83: 177–187.

Talshir, D. 1987. "The Autonomic Status of Late Biblical Hebrew." *Language Studies* 2–3: 161–172 [Hebrew].

———. 1988. "A Reinvestigation of the Linguistic Relationship between Chronicles and Ezra–Nehemiah." *Vetus Testamentum* 38: 165–193.

———. 1992. "The Significance of Different Orthography in Personal Names." *Language Studies* 5–6 (*Festschrift for Israel Yevin*). Edited by M. Bar-Asher. Jerusalem: Magnes [Hebrew].

———. 1998. "Rabbinic Hebrew as Reflected in Personal Names." *Scripta Hierosolymitana* 37: 365–379.

Talshir, D. and Z. Talshir. 2004. "The Double Month Naming in Late Biblical Books: A New Clue for Dating Esther?" *Vetus Testamentum* 54: 549–555.

Talshir, Z. 1996. "The Three Deaths of Josiah and the Strata of Biblical Historiography (2 Kings XXIII 29–30; 2 Chronicles XXXV 20–5; 1 Esdras I 23–31)." *Vetus Testamentum* 46: 213–236.

Tigay, J. 1996. *The JPS Torah Commentary, Deuteronomy.* Philadelphia and Jerusalem: Jewish Publication Society.

Torczyner, H. (Tur-Sinai, N. H.). 1938. "Milim še'ulot bi-lšonenu." *Lěšonénu* 9: 5–30.

———. 1965. "The Aramaic Influence on Biblical Hebrew." Columns 593–595 in vol. 1 *Encyclopaedia Biblica.* Jerusalem: Bialik Institute [Hebrew].

Tyler, L. R. 1988. "The Language of Ecclesiastes as a Criterion for Dating." Ph.D. diss., University of Texas, Austin.

Vanderkam, J. C. 1992. "Calendars." Pages 810–820 in vol. 1 of *Anchor Bible Dictionary.* Edited by D. N. Freedman. New Haven: Yale University Press.

van Peursen, W. T. 1999. "Negation in the Hebrew of Ben Sira." Pages 223–243 in *Sirach, Scrolls and Sages: Proceedings of a Second International Symposium on the Hebrew of the Dead Sea Scrolls and Ben Sira.* Edited by T. Muraoka and J. F. Elwolde. Studies on the Texts of the Desert of Judah 33. Leiden: Brill.

———. 2004. *The Verbal System in the Hebrew Text of Ben Sira.* Studies in Semitic Languages and Linguistics 41. Leiden: Brill.

von Soden, W. 1966. "Aramäische Wörter im neuassyrischen und neu- und spätbabylonischen Texten. Ein Vorbericht. I." *Orientalia* (NS) 35: 1–20.

———. 1968. "Aramäische Wörter im neuassyrischen und neu- und spätbabylonischen Texten. Ein Vorbericht. II." *Orientalia* (NS) 37: 261–271.

———. 1977. "Aramäische Wörter in neuassyrischen und neu- and spätbabylonischen Texten." Ein Vorbericht. III. *Orientalia* (NS) 46: 183–197.

Wagner, M. 1966. *Die lexikalischen und grammatikalischen Aramaismen im alttestamentlichen Hebräisch.* Beihefte zur Zeitschrift für die alttestamentliche Wissenschaft 96. Berlin: A. Töpelmann.

———. 1974. "אָמַר." Pages 328–345 in vol. 1 of *Theological Dictionary of the Old Testament.* Edited by G. J. Botterweck, H. Ringgren, and H.-J. Fabry. Grand Rapids: Eerdmans.

———. 1978. "דָּרַשׁ." Pages 293–307 in vol. 3 of *Theological Dictionary of the Old Testament.* Edited by G. J. Botterweck, H. Ringgren, and H.-J. Fabry. Grand Rapids: Eerdmans.

———. 1985. "בָּקַשׁ." Pages 229–241 in vol. 2 of *Theological Dictionary of the Old Testament.* Edited by G. Johannes Botterweck, H. Ringgren, and H.-J. Fabry. Grand Rapids: Eerdmans.

Weinfeld, M. 1972. *Deuteronomy and the Deuteronomistic School.* Oxford: Oxford University Press.

Wellhausen, J. 1885. *Prolegomena to the History of Israel.* Edinburgh: Adam & Charles Black.

Whitley, C. F. 1979. *Koheleth: His Language and Thought.* Beihefte zur Zeitschrift für die alttestamentliche Wissenschaft 148. Berlin: de Gruyter.

Williamson, H. G. M. 1977a. *Israel in the Book of Chronicles*. Cambridge: Cambridge University Press.

———. 1977b. "Eschatology in Chronicles." *Tyndale Bulletin* 28: 115–154.

———. 1982. *1 and 2 Chronicles*. New Century Bible. Grand Rapids: Eerdmans.

Wright, C. H. H. 1883. *The Book of Koheleth*. London: Hodder.

Wright, R. M. 2003. "Further Evidence for North Israelite Contributions to Late Biblical Hebrew." Pages 129–148 in *Biblical Hebrew: Studies in Chronology and Typology*. Edited by I. Young. London: T & T Clark.

———. 2005. *Linguistic Evidence for the Pre-Exilic Date of the Yahwistic Source*. London and New York: T & T Clark International.

Yoder, C. R. 2001. *Wisdom as a Woman of Substance: A Socioeconomic Reading of Proverbs 1–9 and 31: 10–31*. Beihefte zur Zeitschrift für die alttestamentliche Wissenschaft 304. Berlin: de Gruyter.

Young, I., R. Rezetko, and M. Ehrensvärd. 2008. *Linguistic Dating of Biblical Texts*. 2 vols. London: Equinox.

Zevit, Z. 1984. "The Khirbet el-Qom Inscription Mentioning a Goddess." *Bulletin of the American Schools of Oriental Research* 255: 38–47.

Zevit, Z. and C. L. Miller-Naudé, eds. 2012. *Diachrony in Biblical Hebrew*. Linguistic Studies in Ancient West Semitic 8. Winona Lake: Eisenbrauns.

Zimmerli, W. 1979–83. *Ezekiel*. Hermeneia. 2 vols. Philadelphia: Fortress.

Zunz, L. 1892. *Die gottesdienstlichen Vorträge der Juden historisch entwickelt: Ein Beitrag zur Alterthumskunde und biblischen Kritik, zur Literatur- und Religionsgeschichte*. Frankfurt: J. Kauffmann.